P9-APL-756

the **UNAUTHORIZED GUIDE** to

the Internet

Shannon R. Turlington

201 West 103rd Street, Indianapolis, Indiana 46290

The Unauthorized Guide to the Internet

Copyright© 1999 by Que Corporation

All rights reserved. No part of this book shall be reproduced, stored in a retrieval system, or transmitted by any means, electronic, mechanical, photocopying, recording, or otherwise, without written permission from the publisher. No patent liability is assumed with respect to the use of the information contained herein. Although every precaution has been taken in the preparation of this book, the publisher and author assume no responsibility for errors or omissions. Neither is any liability assumed for damages resulting from the use of the information contained herein.

International Standard Book Number: 0-7897-1764-6

Library of Congress Catalog Card Number: 98-85924

Printed in the United States of America

First Printing: September 1999

01 00 99   4 3 2 1

Trademarks

All terms mentioned in this book that are known to be trademarks or service marks have been appropriately capitalized. Que cannot attest to the accuracy of this information. Use of a term in this book should not be regarded as affecting the validity of any trademark or service mark.

Warning and Disclaimer

Every effort has been made to make this book as complete and as accurate as possible, but no warranty or fitness is implied. The information provided is on an "as is" basis. The author and the publisher shall have neither liability nor responsibility to any person or entity with respect to any loss or damages arising from the information contained in this book.

Executive Editor
Angie Wethington

Development Editor
Valerie Perry

Managing Editor
Thomas F. Hayes

Project Editor
Karen S. Shields

Copy Editor
Victoria Elzey

Indexer
Greg Pearson

Proofreader
Jeanne Clark

Technical Editor
Doug Klippert

Interior Designer
Kevin Spear

Cover Designer
Karen Ruggles

Copy Writer
Eric Borgert

Layout Technician
Cyndi Davis-Hubler

Contents

Shannon R. Turlington has written several books about the Internet and computing technologies. Her most recent publication is *Sams Teach Yourself Netscape Communicator 4.5 in 24 Hours* (Macmillan Computer Publishing). She also co-authored *On Site Exchange Server 5.5* (The Coriolis Group), and authored *Exploring ActiveX, Walking the World Wide Web,* and *Official Netscape Plug-in Book* (Ventana Press). Shannon lives in Chapel Hill, NC, with her two dogs. In her free time, she publishes various articles and information resources on the World Wide Web at `http://www.arcana.com/shannon/index.html`.

About the Author

xiii

Acknowledgements

Many people put extra time and tons of hard work into this book, and I'd like to take this opportunity to offer them my thanks: Martha Kaufman-Amitay, my agent at Adler & Robin Books; Karen Reinisch at Macmillan, who brought the idea for this book to me; Don Essig and Karen Shields, my editors at Macmillan; Valerie Perry, my development editor, who provided a lot of valuable feedback; and Doug Klippert, my technical editor, who also made many helpful suggestions. I appreciate all their efforts, without which this book would not exist.

Tell Us What You Think!

As the reader of this book, *you* are our most important critic and commentator. We value your opinion and want to know what we're doing right, what we could do better, what areas you'd like to see us publish in, and any other words of wisdom you're willing to pass our way.

As a Publisher for Que, I welcome your comments. You can fax, email, or write me directly to let me know what you did or didn't like about this book—as well as what we can do to make our books stronger.

Please note that I cannot help you with technical problems related to the topic of this book, and that due to the high volume of mail I receive, I might not be able to reply to every message.

When you write, please be sure to include this book's title and author as well as your name and phone or fax number. I will carefully review your comments and share them with the author and editors who worked on the book.

Fax:	317-581-4666
Email:	consumer@mcp.com
Mail:	Greg Wiegand
	Que
	201 West 103rd Street
	Indianapolis, IN 46290 USA

Introduction

Before we get started on our journey across the Internet, I'd like to say a few words about what this book is all about. First and foremost, this book is *unauthorized*. That means that you're going to get the inside scoop, unaffected by marketing hype or brand-name loyalties. I'm here to tell you how use the Internet better, cheaper, and faster—not to sell you a product or a company line.

So, who am I? Like you, I'm not a techie or nerd. I'm just an ordinary person who's been using the Internet every day for the past six years, and I've learned a lot in the process. In this book, I'll pass on what I've learned to you, so you can bypass the trial-and-error and hours of research that I had to go through. You'll just get the best techniques and secrets upfront, ready for you to start using today.

So, who are you? Well, you're not a dummy or an idiot or even a beginner, and you're tired of buying books that treat you like one. You may have been using the Internet for a while—days, months, or years—or you may have just signed up this morning. It doesn't matter. What matters is that you've

1

been online long enough to know that you want to learn the best way to get things done, without spending a long time figuring out how. That's just what this book teaches you.

What's Inside

This book is designed so that you can start at the beginning and work your way through to the end, or turn immediately to the subjects that you're most interested in—it won't make a difference either way. Each chapter is packed with tons of tips, tricks, and secrets, presented in a no-nonsense format. Numbered lists show you how to quickly perform a task, and bulleted lists and tables present chunks of information in an easy-to-read format. Sidebars on almost every page provide even more helpful tips. Every element of every chapter is designed to quickly teach you about some part of the Internet, so you can put what you learn into practice and move right on to something else.

Chapter Topics

This book is divided into 3 parts and 16 chapters, each covering an important aspect of working and playing on the Internet.

Part I: Working the Web

- **Chapter 1: Souping Up Your Access** helps you choose the right ISP and the best Internet connection, and it provides tips on how to improve your computer system for Internet use; even if you've been online for a while, you'll probably find new ways to improve the speed and quality of your Internet access in this chapter.

- **Chapter 2: Choosing the Right Tools** takes you through the steps of putting together a toolkit of Internet software; you'll find overviews of the best tools and learn how to choose software based on how you use the Internet.

- **Chapter 3: Getting More Out of Navigator** teaches Netscape Navigator users how to improve their use of the browser: finding tips and tricks for speeding up Web surfing, managing bookmarks better, and maintaining the cache, among other helpful hints.

- **Chapter 4: Getting More Out of Internet Explorer** covers the same topics for Microsoft Internet Explorer users, including how to become a better Web surfer, manage the cache, and customize the browser to fit your needs.

Part II: Into the Net

- **Chapter 5: Email Magic** provides tips and tricks for improving how you use the number-one Internet function; learn how to manage multiple accounts, get free email, work with mailing lists, and more.

- **Chapter 6: Secure and Spam-Free** tells you the truth about email security issues; find out the best ways to keep others from reading your email and proven methods for fighting unsolicited bulk email.

- **Chapter 7: Getting Personal with Real-Time Chat** shows you how to take advantage of the chatting capabilities of the Internet; learn how to use IRC, virtual-reality chat, voice-conferencing and video-conferencing tools, and Internet pagers.

- **Chapter 8: Neat Net Tools** is a round-up of valuable but underpublicized Internet tools you can get for very little money (or free); discover Internet utilities, email enhancers, browser add-ons, and download helpers, as well as many other useful programs.

- **Chapter 9: Cutting Through the Hype** shares the real facts about recent overhyped Internet technologies and points you to better ways of doing things; you also learn how to recognize Internet hype so that you can avoid all the fads you'll encounter while online.

- **Chapter 10: Internet on the Desktop** helps you discover ways that your other programs, such as Microsoft Word and Excel, can interact with the Internet, saving you time and money; you also learn how to use the Active Desktop, which literally integrates the Windows operating system with the Web.

Part III: Power Surfing

- **Chapter 11: Searching Savvy** teaches you how to search the Web and get the best results from the outset; also discover the best search sites for finding Web pages, people, businesses, and software.

- **Chapter 12: Safe Surfing** lets you know when you might really be at risk online and teaches you how to easily avoid the dangers; also, learn the best ways to protect the kids when they're on the Net.

- **Chapter 13: Secret Sites** is a guide to the best free stuff and services on the Web; you'll also find a rundown of incredibly useful sites, most free and some worth paying for.

- **Chapter 14: Going Shopping** tells you how to shop safely on the Internet, the best way to pay for what you buy, and the locations of the top shopping sites.

- **Chapter 15: Putting Your Web Site to Work** teaches you how to create a Web site that goes to work for you; discover the best tools for designing the site and for getting it on the Web.

- **Chapter 16: Promoting Your Site** is a no-nonsense guide to the most effective ways to publicize your Web site to the Internet community.

Appendixes

Two appendixes provide extra doses of valuable information:

- **Appendix A: Glossary** If you encounter an Internet-related term in the text of the book you don't understand or if you need more information about it, turn to this appendix to find the answers at your fingertips.

- **Appendix B: Unauthorized Resources** In this appendix, you'll find a huge selection of valuable Web sites, mailing lists, and newsgroups covering Internet news, gossip, and other Internet-related topics; there's also an index to the most valuable search sites mentioned in the book.

Sidebars

Each chapter includes a large number of sidebars that give you more valuable information, tips, and tricks. There are six different kinds of sidebars:

Timesaver
These tips tell you a faster way to perform a task or show you a valuable shortcut.

Moneysaver
These tips help you save money on a task or point you toward a free tool that can do an important job.

Bright Idea
These sidebars point out additional techniques or useful tasks that you can perform with the tools that you're learning about.

Watch Out!
Check these sidebars for potential pitfalls associated with a task or an Internet activity and how to avoid them.

Inside Scoop
In these sidebars, find additional information or statistics about the task at hand; occasionally, I share personal anecdotes as well.

Check these sidebars for a quote from a well-known person that relates to the task that you're learning about.

""

A Word About Web Page Addresses

Web page addresses, or URLs, are used throughout this book to point to the locations of the useful resources and software programs mentioned in the text. A URL looks like this: http://www.arcana.com/shannon/index.html (that's the address of my home page). Just type the URL into the address window of your Web browser, press Enter, and you're off.

Unfortunately, Web page addresses tend to change frequently, and often the page's owner doesn't leave a forwarding address. I've tried to choose resources that are relatively stable, but it's very likely that a few URLs may have moved or gone off the air by the time you get your hands on this book. Typically, this results in a "Not Found" or a "404" error message. If you encounter such a URL, here are some suggestions for tracking down the new address:

1. Try lopping off the back end of the URL; for instance, change the http://www.arcana.com/shannon/index.html to http://www.arcana.com/. You may then be able to drill down to the resource's new location from the Web site's main page.

2. Search for the page's new location using one of the Web site search engines listed in Chapter 11, "Searching Savvy."

3. If all else fails, drop me a line and I'll try to locate the new address for you. My email address is shannon@arcana.com. I'd also like to hear your comments about the book or suggestions for improvements in the next edition.

Web page addresses aren't the only Internet resources that change frequently. This book recommends a lot of software programs, and the developers are releasing new versions of these programs all the time. So, expect changes in some features, supported platforms, and especially prices of the programs mentioned in this book. Although I've tried to choose well-established programs that will be supported for a long time to come, it is a fact that certain programs can be discontinued for any number of reasons. So you may find a program or two listed in the book that no longer exists by the time you read this.

Let's Get Started

That's really all you need to know. Enjoy your unauthorized tour of the Internet. I'll be looking for you in cyberspace.

Working the Web

PART I

GET THE SCOOP ON...
Finding an ISP that gives you the best connection
• Deciding whether to sign up with an online service
• Improving the performance of your hardware and
modem setup, and learning what it really costs to
upgrade • Maximizing the equipment you already have,
such as a less powerful computer or a slower modem,
for Internet use

Souping Up Your Access

Chapter 1

I'M SURE THAT YOU'VE already connected to the Internet through an Internet service provider (ISP), online service, or your school's or company's connection, and spent some time on the Net. Whether you've been online for a day or a year, you've probably already discovered one thing—it's too darn slow!

There's not a single Internet user who doesn't wish Web pages would display quicker, software would download faster, and online video and audio would actually look and sound the way it's supposed to. One reason for this is that we're all used to television, and today's computer technology just hasn't caught up. Also, most of us can't afford the fastest connections and most advanced multimedia computers.

But there are ways that even home computer users can get more bang for their buck. This chapter helps you improve your Internet access.

❝
I used to think
that cyberspace
was 50 years
away. What I
thought was 50
years away, was
only 10 years
away. And what I
thought was 10
years away…it
was already
here. I just
wasn't aware of
it yet."—Bruce
Sterling

❞

What to Look for in an ISP

Many people turn to a national ISP or online service when first joining the Internet, because these companies spend the big bucks on advertising. But most often, the small, local ISPs offer the best value for your monthly Internet access fee, in terms of customer service and connection speed. Unless you live way out in the boonies, you should be able to find an ISP in your area.

New ISPs are starting up every day. As in any other business, some are exceptional and some are duds. With very little information about these companies, it might seem like a constant process of trial and error to find one you can live with, and even harder to find one that you really like. But you can narrow your choices and make a reasonably good selection if you follow a few simple guidelines.

When putting together a list of ISP candidates, compile a checklist of necessary qualities that the ISP must have:

Watch Out!
Don't sign up for a
prepaid 6-, 12-, or
24-month deal until
you've given the
ISP a test run. If
the ISP pressures
you to prepay or if
it doesn't have a
monthly billing
plan, move on.
Startup ISPs some-
times go downhill
or even out of busi-
ness in a short
time, so paying for
a year ahead of
time is a risky
investment. But
prepay discounts
are a bargain after
you decide you like
the ISP.

- **Local access:** The ISP must have Points of Presence (PoPs) in your local dialing area, or you'll wind up spending a fortune in long-distance charges.

- **Online time:** Your ISP should offer a reasonable amount of hours for the monthly access fee; unlimited access is best. Avoid ISPs that charge by the hour.

- **Price:** If you're paying more than $30 per month for Internet access, you're paying too much. Again, be sure that you're paying a flat monthly rate and that there are no hidden, startup, or "per hour" charges. Some ISPs even offer a free trial period so you can give them a test run.

- **Connection speed:** Your ISP should support connections of at least 33.6Kbps. Try to find an ISP that supports 56K and ISDN connections, so that you can upgrade.

- **Simple setup:** The installation and configuration process should be fully automated. The best setups build the connection without making you enter a single IP address.

- **Technical support and customer service:** The ISP should offer a toll-free line with a minimal on-hold wait (no more than 5–15 minutes). You'll be lucky to find 24-hour technical support, but look for an ISP that offers help on Saturdays or in the early evenings. (Keep in mind that tech support problems are the number-one complaints about ISPs.)

In addition to these suggestions, you might want to add more requirements to your checklist, based on your Internet needs:

Moneysaver
Check your ISP's connections before signing up. Just dial the local access number at different times and on different days, and see how often you get a busy signal. When you do get through, check whether your modem connects at the expected speed. These tests can help avoid money-wasting accounts with ISPs that have chronic connection problems.

- **Software:** It's standard for ISPs to provide a full suite of Internet tools with your account. You might want to choose an ISP that offers the newest versions of standard software or gives you a choice of browser (although you'll probably end up downloading newer versions of what you need). What is crucial is that the ISP enables you to use any software you want, without locking you into one email program or browser.

- **Email:** Every Internet access account comes with one mailbox, but some offer several for one price. You might want to look for an ISP that enables you to create subordinate mailboxes with their own addresses and passwords, so everyone in your small office or household can have one. If you don't want to download all your mail to your hard drive or if you want to take advantage of the latest email programs, choose an ISP that supports the IMAP standard.

- **Usenet:** Some people spend all their time on Usenet; some don't use it at all. If it's important to you, find out how many newsgroups the ISP supports. If you have a favorite newsgroup, ask whether the ISP provides it.

- **Web server space:** Most ISPs provide a small amount of Web server space as part of the account. If you plan to publish personal home pages, be sure that you get at least 10MB of Web server space. And ask how much it costs to rent additional server space. Also find out whether the ISP supports CGI scripts.

Bright Idea
Some ISPs offer a shell account, which enables your computer to act like a UNIX terminal connected to the ISP's computer. If the shell account comes free with the PPP account, take it— you can do some very cool things with it, and it offers a powerful way to access the Net.

Figure 1.1
An ISP's Web site can give you a good idea of how good the company is; Interpath (http://www. interpath.net/), for instance, provides an easy-to-read table of local access numbers, as well as other valuable information.

Locating an ISP

There are lots of ways to find local ISPs, both online and off. Start by trying the phone book and collecting recommendations from friends and colleagues. Also try comprehensive online lists, such as The List (http://thelist.internet.com/) and ISP Finder (http://www.pcworld.com/top400/isp/), both searchable by area code. These kinds of lists are best for building an initial list of local ISPs, but they don't give you a clue as to the ISP's quality and service.

After you've chosen several local ISPs, you can then eliminate the duds from your list. First, and most obviously, give each ISP a call and be sure that it fulfills all the requirements on your checklist. Also, visit each ISP's Web site and see whether you can easily find basic information, such as how long they've been in business, their rates, features included with an Internet access account, and local access numbers (see Figure 1.1).

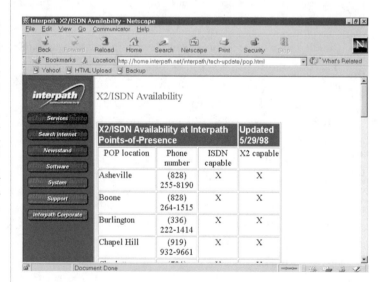

If possible, send email to a few of the ISP's customers and ask whether they're happy with the provider. (Search a few of the major directory services for email addresses that use the ISP's domain name to find people who use the ISP; you'll learn how in Chapter 5, "Email Magic.")

Even after signing up, you might discover that the ISP isn't for you. In that case, you can always switch. Just be sure your initial contract isn't long-term; look for ISPs that offer free trial periods or short-term contracts (month-by-month is best). Later, if you like the ISP, you can sign a longer term contract and perhaps get a rate cut in the bargain.

National ISPs

If you can't find a local ISP or if you're limited in choices and don't like the ones offered by your local providers, then consider a national ISP. National providers are also a good choice if you travel a lot and need Internet access while on the road, or if your operations are located in more than one area, such as branch offices.

All in all, the quality of national ISPs falls somewhere between that of local ISPs and that of online services. Generally, national ISPs' customer service and technical support aren't as good as you're likely to get from a local ISP, because the national provider has more customers and can't spend as much time serving each individual. Establishing a connection and connection speed might be problematic for the same reason. But unlike most online services, national ISPs offer choice—choice of software, choice of Internet activities, and generally fewer restrictions.

Of course, the national ISP that you choose should fulfill all the requirements outlined in the previous section. In addition, look for a national ISP that offers 24-hour customer service, local access numbers across the country so you won't have to pay long-distance charges, and competitive prices or extra services to entice you to sign up.

Table 1.1 describes the major national ISPs, including contact and pricing information and some notes about the special features each provider offers. (All phone numbers and rates were verified at the time of publication, but might have changed by the time you read this.)

Watch Out!
Signs that you should avoid an ISP:
1. It doesn't publish its local access numbers on its site.
2. Its Web site loads slowly.
3. Its Web site hasn't been updated in a while.
4. Technical support and other important information is hidden in a "customers only" area.
5. There's no business address or only a P.O. box listed on the site.

Timesaver

If you're looking for a national ISP, visit Online Connection (http://www.barkers.org/online/index.html), which compares the major national ISPs and online services in terms of pricing and features. Find important details, such as the number of PoPs, supported connections, toll-free number fees, and comparisons of fees for different usage amounts. You can also download the ISP's software and try it out immediately.

TABLE 1.1: NATIONAL INTERNET SERVICE PROVIDERS

ISP	Monthly Access Plan	Hourly Access Plan	Features
AT&T WorldNet 1-800-967-5363 http://www.att.com/worldnet/	$14.95 for 150 hours plus $.99 for each additional hour.	None	Plan includes the largest number of email accounts (6) and the most Web server space (30MB) of any national ISP; you can combine your long-distance and Internet-access services into one bill.
Concentric 1-800-939-4262 http://www.concentric.net/	$19.95 for unlimited access.	$7.95 for 5 hours plus $1.95 for each additional hour.	Free 30-day trial account; 5MB Web server space.
EarthLink Sprint Network 1-800EARTHLINK http://www.earthlink.net/	$19.95 for unlimited access (plus $25 setup fee).	None.	Largest number of local access numbers of any national ISP (1,500).
IBM Internet 1-800-722-1425 http://www.ibm.net/	$19.95–$29.95 for 100 hours (depending on features) plus $1.95 for each additional hour.	$4.95 for 3 hours plus $1.95 for each additional hour.	Very fast, but expensive for heavy users; recommended for travelers, particularly international travelers.
MCI WorldCom Internet 1-800-444-3333 http://www.mci.com/	$19.95 for 150 hours plus $.99 for each additional hour.	None.	Discount for MCI long-distance users.
MindSpring 1-888-MSPRING http://www.mindspring.com/	$26.95–$19.95 for unlimited access, depending on extra features (plus $25 setup fee).	$14.95 for 20 hours plus $1.00 for each additional hour (and $25 setup fee).	Highly recommended for home users; supports more Usenet newgroups (over 20,000) than any other national ISP.

ISP	Monthly Access Plan	Hourly Access Plan	Features
Prodigy Internet 1-800-213-0992 http://www. prodigy.com/	$19.95 for unlimited access.	$9.95 for 10 hours plus $1.50 for each additional hour.	Bilingual service (English and Spanish); several chat options.

Online Services

So, what's the difference between an online service and an Internet service provider? Well, online services hold the user's hand quite a bit more than ISPs. They organize the content found on the service and provide the proprietary software needed to access that content. Access to the Web, Internet email, and Usenet are just a small part of the overall service, which can also include pay-per-view content, chat rooms, games, and the like. ISPs, on the other hand, generally provide full Internet access but no organized content, except what might be found on their Web sites.

Some people like online services because everything is laid out for them neatly, with little fuss and bother. Seasoned Internet users know that you can get everything on the Web that you can get on the online services—and much more—at a cheaper price and a higher speed; you just have to work a little harder. Another advantage of connecting via an ISP is that you can use the Internet software you want; you aren't locked into an online service's proprietary Web browser or email client.

If you're new to the Internet, an online service can help ease the transition into cyberspace. You'll learn how to use Internet tools and functions in a familiar, user-friendly environment. Then, after six months or a year, consider making the switch to a national or local ISP to take advantage of the faster access times, greater software options, and unlimited access to the Web and Usenet that an ISP can offer.

Moneysaver
If you travel frequently and you're looking for a national ISP to give you Internet access while on the road, check whether the ISP offers a local access number in the areas where you'll be connecting from most, such as your home, branch offices, and frequent travel destinations. Without that local number for frequent calls, your Internet access will end up costing you way too much in 800-number surcharges.

Watch Out!
Looking for ISPs to avoid? At http://www. WorldWideWait. com/, readers can post "sober" reviews of ISPs that "done them wrong"—mostly reviews of online services and national ISPs.

Table 1.2 outlines the major online services, their contact information, and their rates for unlimited monthly access. (Note that phone numbers and rates were verified at the time of publication, but may have changed since then. Pricing for online services changes frequently, and trial offers and special deals are offered all the time, so shop around.)

TABLE 1.2: MAJOR ONLINE SERVICES

Online Service	Phone	URL	Rates
America Online	1-800-827-6367	`http://www.aol.com/`	$21.95/month
CompuServe	1-800-369-5544	`http://www.compuserve.com/`	$24.95/month
Microsoft Network	1-800-386-5550	`http://www.msn.com/`	$19.95/month

Bright Idea
Changing your email address each time you change ISPs can be a real pain, particularly if you use email for business. Get a permanent address that remains the same no matter who your ISP is. Free email forwarding services are available (but note that they do tack advertising onto your mail). Check out Bigfoot (`http://www.bigfoot.com/`), Net@ddress (`http://www.netaddress.com/`), and NetForward (`http://www.netforward.com/`).

Upgrading for the Internet

Now that you've found a good ISP, you probably want to improve the speed with which you interact with the Internet. This generally means an upgrade in your computer setup or your Internet connection or both. (You might be able to avoid paying a lot of money by optimizing the hardware and connection you've got for Internet use—more on this in the next section.)

Before upgrading, decide exactly what you want to do on the Internet. Then, you can target your computer system and connection for those activities and avoid buying new components that you don't need. Tables 1.3 and 1.4 describe the optimal configurations for three levels of Internet use:

- **Low-end:** Sending email, reading Usenet, and other text-restricted activities

- **Midrange:** Basic email, chat, and Web browsing, but infrequent multimedia playing, software downloading, and access of high-end technologies

- **High-end:** Full-out, fast Web browsing, including playing streaming video and audio, interacting with the latest technologies, and frequent downloading and uploading of files

TABLE 1.3: COMPUTER CONFIGURATIONS FOR INTERNET USE

Activity Level	Operating System	Processor	Memory
Low-end	Low-end system (68KB Macintosh, DOS, Windows 3.1)	Minimum	Minimum
Midrange	Mac OS 7/8 or Windows 95/NT 4.0	68KB/PowerPC or 133MHz Pentium	16–32MB
High-end	Mac OS 8 or Windows 95/98 /NT 4.0	PowerPC/G3 or Pentium Pro/Pentium II	64MB or more

TABLE 1.4: COMPUTER CONFIGURATIONS FOR INTERNET USE

Activity Level	Hard Drive	Connection	Sound /Video Cards
Low-end	Minimum	Minimum modem and shell account	Minimum
Midrange	1.2GB	28.8- or 33.6Kbps modem and PPP connection	1MB VRAM, sound card optional
High-end	2GB or more	56K modem and PPP connection or ISDN	2MB VRAM, sound card

Note that setting up and using a shell-account connection, specified for the low-end system, is not easy. It requires some knowledge of UNIX and a willingness to tinker around for a while before you figure out what you're doing. Also, it might be nearly impossible to locate an ISP that supports your system. You'll have an easier time going online if you upgrade your entire system first.

If you don't have a computer or you're considering investing in a new system, go ahead and buy a system that meets or exceeds all the specifications for the high-end system. This will give you all the Web-browsing power you need, plus the ability to play the latest multimedia formats, such as RealMedia, Shockwave Flash, and MP3. The cost of such a system runs around $1,000, and prices are dropping every day.

Bright Idea
If you don't have a computer yet, you can still get onto the Internet— through your television. WebTV services enable you to browse the Web and send and receive email without any special equipment other than an Internet Receiver, which runs around $199. You don't even need to install a second phone line. If you're curious about the Internet, WebTV is a good way to get your feet wet. When you're ready, you can upgrade to a computer-based connection. For more information, see http://www. webtv.com/ or call 1-800-GO-WEBTV.

Upgrading Your System

Improving one or two components of your computer system might significantly increase overall performance when browsing the Internet. If you have the money, consider upgrading each component to the levels specified for high-end access in Tables 1.3 and 1.4. If you have the means to upgrade only one or two components, look at your processor and memory first. These two components (other than the modem) play the largest role in Internet performance, because they are most heavily used in displaying Web pages, particularly pages that include multimedia, Java, and the like.

Upgrading the Processor

Upgrading the CPU in your Macintosh computer—moving from a 68KB Macintosh to a PowerPC, for instance—can significantly increase your computer's performance. The newer chip might also offer features that your old chip didn't have; for example, the 68020 doesn't support virtual memory, but the 68030 does. Whenever possible, get the Floating Point Unit (FPU), which makes a big difference in many kinds of activities. Accelerate Your Mac (http://www.xlr8yourmac.com/) has reviews of CPU cards and video cards for upgrades, including price lists.

Moneysaver
An upgrade is a good investment only when the upgrade doubles (at least) the component's performance. The exception is adding memory, which usually significantly increases overall performance.

On the PC, replacing a slower, first-generation Pentium CPU with a faster MMX part is one of the most sensible upgrades you can make. Never attempt a CPU upgrade unless you have the motherboard's original documentation, and select the upgrade processors listed in the documentation. The CPU manufacturer's Web site also generally has documentation, compatibility information, and installation instructions; Intel (http://www.intel.com/), AMD (http://www.amd.com/), and Cyrix (http://www.cyrix.com/) are the major manufacturers. Prices range from 50 dollars for some of the AMD processors to several hundred dollars for Intel CPUs. For most processors, you also need a heatsink and fan, so order one if it isn't already included in the kit.

Upgrading Memory

Increasing memory makes surfing the Web and other computing activities seem faster and smoother, because it lessens dependence on virtual memory. More memory also makes complex operations, such as playing Shockwave movies or running Java applications, run quicker with less tendency to crash. When buying memory, the rule of thumb is to get more than you think you'll need. Memory is not that expensive, it is the easiest upgrade to make, and there is no such thing as extra RAM.

On the Macintosh, a 16MB upgrade costs around $20–$40. Going up to 32MB RAM increases the cost to roughly $45–$60, and a 64MB upgrade runs between $65 and $100. (PowerBook memory tends to be much more expensive.) But how much RAM can your Macintosh really handle? There are some design limitations in older Macs (check your documentation), but most of the later Macs can go to 32MB or more.

Timesaver
RAMSeeker
(http://www.
macseek.com/)
tracks the latest
Macintosh memory
prices from major
outlets. Also find a
RAM upgrade
guide for all Macs
at http://www.
macseek.com/
ramguide.shtml.

On the PC, you must determine how much memory you have and what kind it is before upgrading. Also, you can add memory only in fixed increments, depending on your CPU. To determine what size SIMM you have, either check the original documentation or just look inside the box. All 386s that use SIMMs and older 486s have 30-pin SIMMs, which have 30 contact points. Newer 486s introduced 72-pin SIMMs, which (obviously) have 72 contact points.

After finding out what kind of SIMM your system uses, count the number of SIMMs that are installed; compare the number of SIMMs to the total amount of memory to calculate the size of the SIMMs in megabytes. Also count how many open SIMM sockets are on the motherboard, which is where you will add the new SIMMs.

Finally, count the number of chips in the SIMM (turn the computer off and then remove the SIMM to do this). SIMMs with an odd number of chips are parity SIMMs, and you should buy the same type for your upgrade. While you're holding the SIMM, look on the chips for a number following a dash (–100, –80, –70, or –60), representing the speed of the chips—the lower the number, the faster the chip. Upgraded SIMMs should be the same speed or faster.

Depending on your computer, expect to pay between $25–$75 for a 32MB memory upgrade. SIMM prices vary greatly, so shop around.

Upgrading the Hard Drive

As with RAM, there's no such thing as too much hard drive space. Eventually, you will use it. Where the Internet is concerned, more hard drive space means more room for storing the more advanced programs, such as Web browsers that get bigger with each release.

Most Macintoshes were designed for a single internal drive, so your first decision is whether to replace the internal drive or purchase a second, external drive. Internal drives are less expensive and can be faster than external drives, but they are generally more difficult to install, and you have to figure out how to move your data from your old drive to your new one. With an external drive, you just copy the data from the old drive to the new one. Also, you can reuse an external drive when you buy a new computer. Finally, an external drive adds more capacity to your original drive, instead of just replacing it. You should be able to find a good internal hard drive for under $250. An external drive will cost you $50–$80 more.

If you have room inside your PC, you can add a second hard drive at a cost of $200–$300. Also consider removable hard disk media, such as the JAZ drive; figure on about $300 for the drive and one 1GB cartridge, plus $80 for each additional cartridge.

Upgrading Your Connection

The most reliable way to increase Internet access speed is to upgrade to a faster modem or connection. You have a lot of choices in this area, ranging from moving up to a 33.6Kbps modem to putting in ISDN. Again, base the upgrade on what you want to accomplish online and how much time you intend to spend there; you probably don't need an ISDN connection unless you plan to spend a great deal of time online and frequently download large files.

Moneysaver

When upgrading, compare the cost of new components to the total cost of a new system. Estimate how much you could sell your old computer for and add that to the upgrade cost. You just might find that buying a new computer is cheaper, particularly since you can maximize all the components, rather than just one or two. With the costs of new computers dropping all the time, it's probably not cost-effective to put more than $500 of upgrades into an old machine.

Upgrading Your Modem

When buying a new modem, stay away from those bargain-basement models, no matter how tempting the price. You've already invested a lot of money in your system and you're paying a substantial monthly fee for Internet access, so why scrimp on your primary connection to the Internet? Save yourself a lot of grief—stay with the name-brand models, produced by companies whose primary business is making modems.

You probably already have a 28.8Kbps or 33.6KBps modem, so if you're considering upgrading, you're most likely looking at the 56K modems. The first thing to do is find out whether your ISP supports 56K connections and how many 56K modems your ISP has on its side of the connection. Also find out whether your ISP's 56K access is based on the 3Com x2 or Rockwell/Lucent K56flex standard, and buy a modem that works with your ISP's standard. Be aware that some ISPs add a surcharge for 56K connections. (If you're not getting the answers that you want, this might be a good time to shop around for a new ISP.)

Even with 56K modems on both sides of the connection, you probably won't get on the Internet at that speed. The local telephone network largely determines how well your 56K modem works. Although some of you will see vast improvements, others will get only a slight increase in speed because of noisy phone lines and other factors that are largely beyond your control. (It's a good idea to be sure you can return the modem for a refund if it doesn't work well for you.)

The good news is that 56K technology is improving as it gets cheaper, so a 56K modem is only slightly more expensive than a 33.6Kbps modem. In some cases, you might be able to upgrade your existing modem to 56K by downloading a ROM revision for a minimal fee—check your modem manufacturer's Web site.

Upgrading to ISDN

Like most upgrades, ISDN is faster, better, and more expensive. ISDN can be up to five times faster than a standard PPP connection. It also makes it possible to perform multiple tasks

Bright Idea
When buying a 56K modem, be sure that an upgrade to the final 56K standard is guaranteed. The final V.90 standard, recently approved by the International Standards Organization, might not become widely available for some time, but when it does, you want to be sure that you don't have to pay more to standardize your modem.

on the same phone line. For example, you can fax or talk on the phone while surfing the Internet, using the same phone wire. Or use both channels to surf, with a total bandwidth of up to 128Kbps.

ISDN might not be an option for you, depending on where you live. You must be reasonably close to your telephone company's central office, which must also have the required equipment installed, or you won't be able to get ISDN. Your ISP must also support ISDN connections. Generally, the farther you live from major urban centers, the lower your chances for getting ISDN.

There are two types of ISDN service: Basic Rate Interface (BRI) and Primary Rate Interface (PRI). For individuals and small LANs, BRI is what you want. With BRI, you can simultaneously use up to two devices on the same line. An internal terminal adapter can route calls intelligently with this kind of setup; for instance, if you're surfing the Web on both channels and a fax call comes in, the terminal adapter can route the fax call to the fax machine on one channel, while reserving the other channel for the Internet connection.

Watch Out!
Yes, you can go faster than an ISDN. The next step up is a T1. However, depending on your location, the phone line alone could run you from several hundred to over a thousand dollars a month, and then you have to pay Internet access fees on top of that. A T1 really isn't worth the high costs unless your business plans to host one or more heavily trafficked Web servers or you want to connect a large company LAN to the Internet.

You'll need ISDN wiring, installed by the phone company, as well as an ISDN connection from your ISP. The installation charges generally cost twice as much as that of a standard phone line, and the monthly phone charges will also be about double. Often, a usage charge is associated with ISDN, meaning that the more you use it, the more you pay.

To make the connection through your computer, you'll need a terminal adapter (also called an ISDN modem). Terminal adapters range in price from $300–$1,000. Be certain that you get a terminal adapter supported by both your phone company and your ISP.

You can choose either an internal or external terminal adapter. Internal terminal adapters generally provide better performance than the external ones, because they enable your system to take complete advantage of the ISDN connection. Internal terminal adapters are notoriously difficult to install and configure, though, while external ones set up like a regular external modem and typically don't require special-ized software. The internal terminal adapter also requires an available slot in your computer.

Other Ways to Go

New Internet access technologies are developed all the time, and some of them offer distinct advantages over modems or ISDN—if you can get them. Newer connection types that are now becoming mainstreamed include cable, satellite, and xDSL.

A cable connection is a good choice if you need something faster than 56K but you don't want to spring for ISDN or ISDN isn't available in your area. Cable modems work over your cable line and can enable a connection that is as fast as a T1.

While cable connections are relatively inexpensive (when compared to ISDN), they aren't yet widely available, and cable ISPs usually want to lock you into their television service before giving you Internet access. Many cable ISPs deliver mul-ticasting services and proprietary content over cable's extra bandwidth, including concerts, video broadcasts, and other online events. You can also receive full-motion video and audio over cable, which isn't yet possible on telephone dial-up con-nections. Finally, cable is a 24-hour, dedicated connection.

So, what are the problems? Like any large ISP, cable ISPs reportedly have technical support and customer service prob-lems. And as with your regular ISP, the more people who use the service, the slower it becomes; some customers complain that the speed is inconsistent or less than expected. But down-loading is still a whole lot faster than your phone connection, so you might not care about these hassles.

Uploading, however, does present a major problem. Cable networks were designed to broadcast data downstream, not send it upstream, as with email and file uploads. Only a small percentage of existing cable networks have been upgraded to handle two-way traffic. For most, upstream transmissions are limited to a narrow band and interfering noises can garble the

> 66
> "The Internet is a place you go when you want to turn your brain on, and a television is a place you go when you want to turn your brain off. I'm not at all convinced that the twain shall meet."—Steve Jobs, in an inter-view by *Business Week*
> 99

data you're sending, or else the cable ISP resorts to sending data through your phone line, as with a regular connection.

The installation fee for the cable connection, including the modem, generally runs $100–$200, and the monthly charge for unlimited access costs $30–$50 (in addition to your monthly cable subscription fee). Cable ISPs include Time-Warner Cable's Road Runner (http://www.rr.com/rdrun/) and the @Home Network (http://www.home.com/).

Satellite is becoming a popular way to get a faster Internet connection. DirecPC (http://www.direcpc.com/), for example, enables you to download Internet information from a satellite at speeds of up to 400Kbps. But you still have to connect to an ISP using a standard telephone-based account to send data out. Basic satellite Internet services start at around $30 per month. In addition, you must accurately position a 21-inch satellite dish, which costs you around $100 for professional installation (not to mention the cost of the dish).

xDSL is still in the developmental stages, but it promises to eventually replace ISDN for residential customers. xDSL enables up to 6Mbps of downstream throughput and up to 1.5Mbps upstream. At this time, trials are being conducted in limited areas, and the cost is around $400–$600 per month, which I'm betting is more than you're willing to shell out for Internet access. But keep an eye on this technology; as it becomes more standardized and widespread, prices should drop.

Optimizing Your Setup for the Internet

You might not have the money to upgrade to a new modem, connection, or computer. After all, you've invested heavily in the setup you have—you want to use it to its full potential. Or maybe you're tired of shelling out money for the latest technology only to have something newer and better come out, making your toy obsolete. In that case, you'll want to cheaply maximize the hardware and connection you've already got for best Internet performance.

Optimizing Your System

Before you think about upgrading, try to optimize the memory and hard drive you already have. This ensures that your system is running in its most efficient state. You might be able to squeeze acceptable performance out of your system with just a few tweaks that cost you little or nothing.

Optimizing Macintosh Performance

On the Macintosh, the first step in maximizing performance is to eliminate unnecessary extensions and control panels. You probably have more extensions and control panels than you will ever use, all of them consuming memory and CPU cycles, draining resources and performance with no benefits. Getting rid of these frees up resources and increases performance for Web surfing and other computing activities.

Just use common sense when trimming control panels and extensions. For instance, if your computer isn't connected to a network, you don't need file-sharing and network-related controls. If you don't use speech technology, trash the related control panel, extensions, and libraries. After you've trimmed your system, run it for a while. If you notice a marked performance improvement, you might be able to skip the upgrade.

One way to optimize your Macintosh's use of memory is to use virtual memory, which comes with 68030 and later Macintoshes. Virtual memory steals memory from the hard drive when you're all out of RAM. To compensate, it uses a large amount of hard drive space, and hard drives are much slower than RAM, so you might notice a performance decrease.

Connectix RAM Doubler (`http://www.connectix.com/html/ramdoubler.html`) works with 68030-and-later Macs to emulate virtual memory in RAM when possible (it's also available for Windows 3.x). RAM Doubler thus gives you the best of both worlds—it is cheaper than adding memory ($49.95), but it is faster than virtual memory.

Timesaver
So, you've signed up with a new ISP, and suddenly Web browsing has slowed to a crawl. Before making an angry call to your ISP, find out exactly where the bottleneck is—the remote Web server, the connection to your ISP, the ISP's link to the Internet backbone, or your PC. Net.Medic works with your browser to identify the source of network bottlenecks. Get a free trial for Windows 95/98/NT at `http://www.vitalsigns.com/netmedic/index.html`.

An alternative is Jump Development's RAM Charger
(http://www.jumpdev.com/RAMCharger8.html; $39.95), which
gives each application just enough memory to work as it is
launched, letting you run more programs at one time. When
the application needs more memory, RAM Charger provides
it. It works on all Macs, and it never uses the hard disk for
memory. It is also compatible with virtual memory and RAM
Doubler.

Optimizing Windows 3.x Performance

If you absolutely refuse to upgrade to Windows 95 or 98, you
can still optimize Windows 3.x's use of system resources, such
as RAM and hard disk space, to get better performance.

- Restart Windows every now and then to give it a fresh start.

- If there are any programs in the Startup window that you
  don't need running, delete the icon; this keeps the program from running automatically, but it's still available if
  you need it.

- Close programs when you aren't using them (including
  when you have two instances of the same program open).

- Decrease video settings to 256 colors to keep unnecessary
  colors from hogging system resources.

- Whenever the system locks up because it's running out of
  resources, reboot. Always run ScanDisk after rebooting.

Virtual memory in Windows 3.x can be a real performance
drag. Temporary information is stored in a swap file on the
hard drive, which grows and shrinks as Windows needs it. You
can increase performance by tweaking the swap file settings.
Open the System control panel, select the Performance tab,
and click Virtual Memory (see Figure 1.2). Specify your own
swap file settings, including the file's minimum and maximum
size and its location on the hard drive.

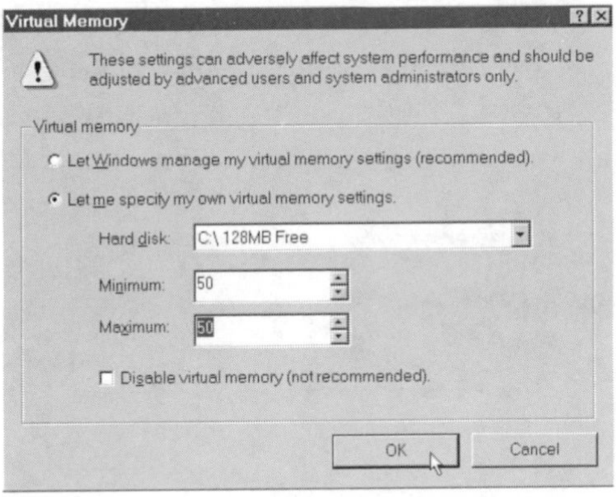

Figure 1.2
Tweaking virtual memory settings can increase system performance.

Windows's automatic resizing of the swap file conserves disk space, but it's hard on performance because the hard drive is continually resizing the file. If you have plenty of disk space, give the swap file a set size (enter the same number in the Minimum and Maximum fields). A typical size is 50MB, but it's a judgment call. Don't set the size too low, though, and definitely don't disable virtual memory. If you run into problems, increase the swap file's size.

You can also optimize performance by placing the swap file near the front of the hard drive, which keeps the read/write heads from traveling as far. Even better, use a second hard drive for the swap file to separate the read/write actions from the operating system and major programs. Even partitioning the swap file can eliminate problems.

66

Want to make your computer go really fast? Throw it out a window.
—Anonymous

99

Optimizing the Hard Drive

As you use files, they fill their space on the hard drive and must be broken into two or more pieces in a process called fragmentation. When the hard drive must go to several places to read a file, performance decreases. Regain that performance by eliminating fragmentation on your hard drive.

You can use several disk optimization tools to defragment your hard drive. Alsoft DiskExpress Pro is available for the Macintosh (http://www.alsoftinc.com/DXPinfo.html). Windows 95/98/NT comes with a defragmenting utility; on the Start menu, select Programs, Accessories, System Tools, Disk

Defragmenter (see Figure 1.3). Defragmenters are also often included in the commercial utilities packages, such as Symantec Norton Utilities (`http://www.symantec.com/nu/index.html`), available for both the Macintosh and Windows.

Figure 1.3
Optimize your hard drive every couple of weeks using the Windows defragmenting utility or a commercial defragmenter.

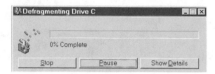

Regardless of the tool you choose, definitely make a backup before defragmenting your hard drive, because there's a small risk when moving data around. Small problems can become very big if you attempt to defragment your drive without fixing the problem first, so run a hard drive diagnostic tool such as Norton Utilities or DiskEssentials before running the defragmenter.

Optimizing Video Cards

Your video settings can affect the entire system's performance. You might be running a video mode that's higher in resolution or color depth than you really need. If a lower color mode looks just as good to you, you don't need to use system resources displaying millions of colors or high color. The same goes for resolution—higher resolution settings than you need places larger loads on video hardware and reduces responsiveness on computers that don't have high-performance video cards.

Be sure that you have the latest video drivers for your video card. Often, the upgraded version increases performance significantly. Video card upgrades are usually provided for free at the manufacturer's Web site.

Maximizing Modems

There are two categories of modem speed. The Data Terminal Equipment (DTE) speed, or port speed, is the data transfer rate between your computer and your modem. The DTE is not nearly as important as the Data Communications Equipment (DCE) speed—also called the line speed—which is the actual data transfer rate between your modem and the remote computer to which you're connected.

You can manually set the port speed to a number of different speeds, including speeds that are faster than the modem speed. Choose the fastest possible speed to ensure that your computer is continuously feeding data to the modem. In Windows, right-click your Internet connection in Dial-Up Networking, select Properties, and click Configure; select the highest port speed in the Maximum Speed list (see Figure 1.4). If nothing happens when you log on, set a lower speed and try again.

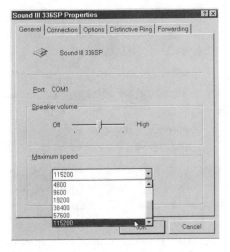

Figure 1.4
Set the fastest speed for your COM port to help maximize modem performance.

Timesaver
Choose modems whose manufacturers have good online support and who make updated drivers readily available on their sites. This saves time when tuning up your modem, and most likely keeps you from having to buy an entirely new modem.

Newer modems can compress data, so the actual line speed might even be higher than your modem's rated speed. Always turn compression on and use error control to take advantage of this. In Windows, open the Modem control panel, click Properties, select the Connection tab, and click Advanced; be sure that Use Error Control and Compress Data are selected (see Figure 1.5).

Figure 1.5
Turning on com-
pression can
increase your
modem's line
speed.

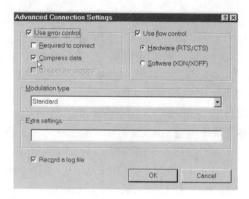

The initialization string is another common cause of line speed problems. Initialization commands are often specific to a particular kind of modem. So, incorrect modem settings can cause slow connections or other problems. Because there are literally hundreds of variations, the best thing to do is to refrain from putting more into the initialization string than specified by the documentation.

The line speed depends on the result of handshaking between your modem and the ISP's modem. A bad quality telephone line always negatively affects handshaking, resulting in much slower connections. If you're still getting slower connections than your modem supports, the problem is most likely with the phone line. You won't be able to do anything about noisy lines outside your house except complain fruitlessly to your phone company, but faulty wiring inside, bad jacks and plugs, cheap or old phones, or too many devices plugged into the line might also cause line noise and can be fixed.

Bright Idea
Test your modem's
speed at http://
members.aol.com/
inventorr/modem/
modem1.html. The
tests calculate the
actual line speed
of your Internet
connection and
compares it to typ-
ical line speeds
for your modem
and type of
Internet connec-
tion.

Clearing Up Connections

Using a variety of software programs, you might be able to boost connection speed. System tweakers like Speedlane Internet Optimizer (http://www.speedlane.com/; Windows 95/98/NT 4.0; $29.95) and CheckIt NetOptimizer (http://www.touchstonesoftware.com/products/fsetnetoptimizer.html; Windows 95/98; $39.95) facilitate communication between your computer and the remote computer you're connected to. These programs automatically tweak several cryptic system settings that prevent you from attaining maximum connection speeds. But you might not get noticeable results as the Internet gets more crowded, particularly if you usually connect during peak times; both products come with a 30-day, money-back guarantee if you don't notice any improvements.

Some programs can improve your PPP connection. PPP Boost (free; Windows 95/98) and iSpeed (free; Windows 95/98/NT) can significantly speed up Internet transfers by changing some network protocol parameters (see Figure 1.6). Windows assumes you are connected to a shared LAN by default, and thus the TCP/IP settings are best suited to a LAN connection. These programs change the TCP/IP settings to those more suited to a PPP connection, thus optimizing the connection. Both programs are available on popular software search engines (see Appendix B, "Unauthorized Resources," for a list).

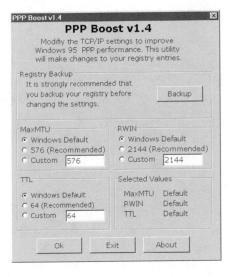

Figure 1.6
Programs like PPP Boost tweak system settings to optimize your PPP connection.

Just the Facts

- Finding the perfect ISP is simply a matter of creating a checklist of services the ISP must provide and then shopping around for a company who's a match.

- Unlike ISPs, online services limit your access to the Internet and your choice in software, and so aren't a good choice for users who want to really work the Net.

- You don't have to buy a completely new system to maximize Internet access; sometimes increased performance is simply a matter of upgrading hardware components or your connection.

- If you don't have the money to upgrade, you can still optimize your system and modem for best Internet performance with system tweaks and inexpensive utilities.

GET THE SCOOP ON...
Putting together a suite of basic tools tailored to
how you use the Net ▪ Selecting the right Web
browser ▪ Finding add-ins that boost your browser's
power

Choosing the Right Tools

Chapter 2

EVERY INTERNET USER NEEDS a suite of basic tools. Most Internet toolkits include a Web browser for surfing the Web, an email program for reading and managing mail, a newsreader for accessing Usenet newsgroups, and an FTP client for transferring files. But you might not need all these programs. For instance, if you never access Usenet, you don't have much use for a newsreader. And if you rarely transfer files, the FTP capabilities of your browser will probably suit you just fine.

Everyone uses the Net differently. For some, email is the primary reason to go online. For others, Web surfing is the most important activity. If you haven't shopped around for the right Internet software—if you're still using the basic tools provided by your ISP, for instance—you might be using ineffi-cient tools or tools that don't fully meet your needs. Some pro-grams can be too large and cumbersome, overwhelming your system resources. Others might not give you the features or power you need.

You should take the time to put together a suite of Internet tools that matches how you use the Internet. This chapter helps you do just that.

Moneysaver
There are free versions of most commercial Internet software programs with scaled-down features or demo versions of the full program. If you're not sure a program is right for you, try out the free version for a while. If you don't find the functionality you need, if you don't use all the features, or if you encounter problems, you can move on to another program before spending any money.

Choosing an Email Program

More people use the Internet to send and receive email than any other online activity. Email is particularly useful for communicating with co-workers, keeping in touch with friends and family, receiving newsletters, and taking part in discussions.

Because everyone uses email in very different ways, everyone has different needs for an email program. Before choosing an email client, observe your email habits. Do you use multiple mailboxes or more than one address book? Do you send and receive a lot of binary attachments? Do you require extensive management features, or need to connect to an IMAP mail server? Do you often filter messages or want an assistant to manage email for you? Make a checklist of features your email program must have—I bet your current program isn't adequately serving your needs.

The following are the best email programs for different kinds of email users: heavy users, average, and light. You should find something to suit you from these selections.

Email Heavyweights

Heavyweight email programs are designed for users who need the most functionality. Heavy users manage hundreds or even thousands of messages a day, requiring extensive organizational features, such as customizable folders, searching, and filters, as well as advanced capabilities, such as security, multiple accounts, and delegate access. If you fit this profile, consider a full-featured program, such as Qualcomm Eudora Pro, Microsoft Outlook 98, or Pegasus Mail.

Qualcomm Eudora Pro

Qualcomm Eudora Pro is one of the most popular and functional email programs around, with a long track record. It is especially tailored for heavy email users. Eudora Pro has all the features of Eudora Light (see the "Middleweight Email

Programs" section following this one), plus message templates, HTML composition, automated replies, and more filter options than practically any other client. It also comes with more useful utilities than any other email program, including McAfee virus protection, Pretty Good Privacy (PGP) encryption, KeyView for viewing attachment files, StuffIt for compressing attachments, and Qualcomm PureVoice for sending and receiving voice-mail attachments.

Eudora Pro is probably too much for all but the most advanced email users who use email heavily and maintain multiple email accounts. If you're thinking about Eudora but aren't sure, download and use Eudora Light for a while. If you need more functionality, go for Eudora Pro. But, if you find yourself struggling to learn the program or you're not taking advantage of all the features, you probably need something more scaled down.

- **System requirements:** Mac OS 7.1 or Windows 95/98/NT 4.0. (Note: Only the Windows version supports IMAP.)

- **Price:** $39 (30-day trial version available)

- **Download:** http://eudora.qualcomm. >com/pro_email/

Microsoft Outlook

Microsoft Outlook is a combination email client and personal information manager. If you purchased Microsoft Office, you already have Outlook, so take advantage of it. If you're purchasing Outlook as a standalone product, though, it does carry a hefty price.

Outlook is a good choice for the heavyweight business email user, due to its wealth of features and its integration with personal information management tools, such as a calendar, contacts list, and task list, as well as with all Office programs

Bright Idea
Before downloading an email program or any other software, open the Download Calculator at http://www.intel.com/home/club/dlc.htm, and enter the file's size to find the download time for different connection speeds. You can then judge whether to download the program immediately, wait until the dinner hour, or let the download run while you sleep. Leave the calculator open while you surf so it's ready whenever you find a new program.

(see Figure 2.1). If you already use Outlook in an Exchange Server environment, you can combine your Internet and Exchange email into one interface. You can also delegate management of your mailbox to an assistant (but only if you're connected to Exchange Server).

Figure 2.1
Outlook's extensive organizational features and its integration with personal information management tools make it a good choice for business users.

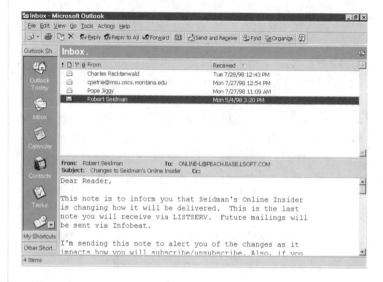

Watch Out!
Don't go crazy with the HTML composition feature of the more advanced email programs and send HTML-format messages to everyone. Many users' email programs can't handle HTML, displaying both the content and the underlying code. Separating the code from the content is annoying and can keep your message from being read. If you must send HTML-format mail, be sure the recipient's email program can handle it first.

If you don't use Exchange Server, Outlook is still a powerful Internet mail client. Its many organizational features include customizable views, automatic archiving, and comprehensive filtering (including a preconfigured junk-mail filter). You can have multiple email accounts and use either the IMAP or POP3 standard. Its searching features are more extensive than Eudora's. It is also easier to configure and use, but there are a lot of features to learn, so it takes some time to get up and running. Outlook is probably too much program for all but the heaviest email users, and it's worth the price and system resources only if you make good use of the personal information management tools.

- **System requirements:** Windows 95/98/NT 4.0; 16MB RAM; between 34MB and 121MB hard disk space, depending on the installation and your software configuration

- **Price:** $249

- **Download:**   `http://www.microsoft.com/office/outlook/`
  `default.htm`

Pegasus Mail

Pegasus Mail is unique among the heavyweight email program—it's free. Pegasus Mail is best suited for email experts
who require advanced features, such as multiple accounts,
message encryption, flexible filters, advanced organizational
features, drag-and-drop attachments, and multiple address
book management. Its customization options give you a lot of
power over how you manage your email. However, Pegasus
Mail has complex configuration options and an obscure interface, so be prepared to spend a lot of time learning the program to take full advantage of its power. (Printed manuals are
available for a fee.) It also works only with POP3 and LAN
email connections.

- **System requirements:** Macintosh, MS-DOS, or Windows
  3.x/95/98/NT 4.0; 4MB RAM; VGA capable of 640×480
  resolution with 16 colors (Windows only)

- **Price:** free

- **Download:** `http://www.pegasus.usa.com/`

Middleweight Email Programs

The average email user needs a middleweight email client.
Average email users send and receive fewer than a hundred
messages a day, belong to a couple of mailing lists, and don't
have a lot of money to spend on Internet software. If you fit the
bill, consider one of these programs: Qualcomm Eudora
Light, ConnectSoft Email Connection, Netscape Messenger, or
Microsoft Outlook Express.

Qualcomm Eudora Light

Eudora Light is probably the best choice for the middleweight
email user—those of you who need a powerful email client but
don't want to spend too much time learning how to use it (see

Bright Idea
If you're wonder-
ing what other
programs you
might need in
your Internet
toolkit, go to
`http://www.`
`matisse.net/files`
`/formats.html,`
where there is a
list of file formats
commonly found
online and direct
links to the soft-
ware needed to
handle each for-
mat for both
Macs and PCs.

Figure 2.2). For a freeware program, Eudora Light has a lot of features: PGP for security, very extensive filters, drag-and-drop attachments, two signature files, support for multiple email accounts, and nested folders, to name some of the more useful ones. Eudora Light doesn't support the IMAP protocol.

Figure 2.2
Eudora Light packs a lot of email management features into a freeware program.

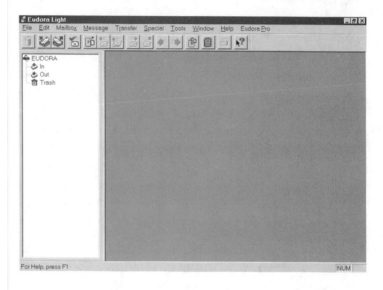

Inside Scoop
According to CNET News, the browser wars are shifting direction. Both Microsoft and Netscape seem to be "going portal," leveraging the browser's start page as an entryway into their Internet gateway sites (Netscape's Netcenter and Microsoft Network). Hoping for new revenue streams from advertising and online shopping, these big companies are also facing hefty competition from established gateways, such as Yahoo!.

- **System requirements:** Mac OS 7.0, Newton 2.0, or Windows 3.x/95/98/NT

- **Price:** free

- **Download:** http://eudora.qualcomm.com/eudoralight/

ConnectSoft Email Connection

Email Connection is probably the most universal email program, supporting more online services, pagers, and fax modems than any other package, which makes it a good choice for frequent business travelers who rely on email from a variety of sources to keep in touch. It is also easy to use, with an integrated address book and a rules-based, point-and-click message interface that handles all the technical stuff for you. But Eudora Light is a better program for users with Internet-only email accounts.

- **System requirements:** Windows 3.x/95/98

- **Price:** $49.95 (free scaled-down version available)

- **Download:** http://www.email-connection.com/

Netscape Messenger and Microsoft Outlook Express

Netscape Messenger is the email (and newsreader) program included with the Netscape Communicator program suite (see Figure 2.3). Likewise, Microsoft Outlook Express is included with the Microsoft Internet Explorer program suite. (See the "Winning the Browser Wars" section later in this chapter for downloading information and system requirements.)

Figure 2.3
Messenger is the email component of Netscape's suite of Internet tools.

Timesaver
What if you want to use Navigator, but have no need for the extras, like Messenger? There's no need to waste time downloading components you won't use or have them taking up space on your hard drive. Just get the stand-alone Web browser—that option is on the Communicator download page.

Both Messenger and Outlook Express are serviceable email programs for the average user, offering similar features. With the release of Communicator 4.5, Messenger's IMAP functionality equals Outlook Express's, and both programs can now handle multiple IMAP accounts. They even look the same, with a three-pane window, HTML composition, and a powerful address book that supports connections to LDAP directories.

These email clients don't offer as many features as stand-alone programs, such as Eudora, but they do integrate well with their respective browsers. For instance, it's easier to send Web pages via email and compose messages in HTML using these email tools. So, if you already heavily use one of the big two Web browsers, an email client that you can operate from the same program suite is probably a good choice—switching back and forth is fast. They are also especially good choices if you like accessing email and Usenet newsgroups from the same window.

However, a dedicated email program offers more features and customization options. For example, both Messenger and Outlook Express lack the extensive filtering and organizational tools of Eudora or Outlook. Choose only one of these email programs if you don't use email heavily and you're planning to make either Navigator or Internet Explorer your main browser.

Lightweight Email Programs

If you receive very little email, or if you don't want to spend a lot of money or system resources for an email client, consider a lightweight email program. Generally, these programs are fully functional in terms of basics, but lack the niftier features, such as filters, organizational capabilities, and searching. They also might not be as user-friendly as their full-featured counterparts. However, loyal users often swear by these "little" programs, and they certainly get the job done.

Download all these freeware programs from any popular software download site (see Appendix B, "Unauthorized Resources," for suggestions):

- **Acorn Email:** A basic email client for Windows 95/98/NT

- **ClickMail:** A very scaled-down client for Windows 95/98/NT

- **MailDrop:** An IMAP client for Mac OS 7

Moneysaver
If you have access to a shell account, Pine might be a more than adequate POP3/IMAP email client for you. Pine's benefits are its low impact on system resources and its price—free. Just type pine at the UNIX prompt to start using it. Learn how to use Pine at http://www.washington.edu/pine/.

Choosing a Newsreader

As with your email client, choose your newsreader based on how you use Usenet. If you monitor several newsgroups, you need a full-featured client that supports extensive searching. A once-in-a-while Usenet reader wants a simple client that won't overwhelm with features or require a lot of learning time. And there's no need to overload your system with a newsreader if you never read news. As with email clients, it's best to start small and upgrade to a more complex program as you outgrow your old newsreader.

Newsreaders for the Mac

On the Macintosh, NewsWatcher is still the standard. The original NewsWatcher is a great basic Usenet client for light-to-medium users and for beginners who want to avoid making "newbie" mistakes. If you're a serious news junkie and need more power, enhanced versions of NewsWatcher are available. MT-NewsWatcher, for example, supports filtering, multi-threading, spell checking, speech recognition, and other cool features that add speed and customization to Usenet browsing. It's also the only version of NewsWatcher that's still being developed.

If you read a lot of news but have limited Internet access—if your ISP allows you only a certain number of online hours per month, for instance—you need an offline newsreader. Offline newsreaders quickly download the newsgroups you want, and then disconnect from the Internet so you can read them. Your posts are saved for batch-sending when you reconnect. I recommend MacSOUP, which enables you to easily select the articles to download so you don't get more than you want. It also supports offline email reading.

Table 2.1 gives an overview of each product.

Timesaver
If you've already chosen Messenger or Outlook Express as your email client, you get a newsreader in the bargain. Both Messenger and Outlook Express let you access news-groups from the same window as your email messages, a handy feature for the casual Usenet reader.

TABLE 2.1: MACINTOSH NEWSREADERS

Newsreader	System Requirements	Price	Download Site
NewsWatcher	Mac OS 7	Free	ftp://ftp .acns.nwu.edu /pub/ newswatcher/
MT-NewsWatcher	Mac OS 7.5.3; 2.5MB RAM	Free	http://www. best.com/ ~smfr/mtnw/
MacSOUP	Mac OS 7	Shareware ($20)	http://www. inx.de/~stk/ macsoup/index .html

Newsreaders for Windows

For Windows users, Free Agent is a full-featured, powerful Usenet client that does practically everything (see Figure 2.4). Free Agent is perfect for users who read newsgroups as much as they do email, and in fact, it includes an email client so you can read mail messages and newsgroup posts in one window. Free Agent's extensive features handle binary attachments, multitasking, multilevel threading, and managing several newsgroups—all necessities for the heavy user. It also supports offline reading of newsgroups and email, a handy feature if you have limited Internet access. With all of these advanced features, Free Agent can be too much for the novice or occasional user.

You want to log on, get your news, and log off—you want News Xpress. This newsreader provides many of the same features as Free Agent and is one of the quickest newsreaders out there. It does lack some niceties, such as offline switching, thread monitoring, and automatic catch-up, but its efficiency, speed, and ease of use make it a good alternative if Free Agent is too much for you.

If you don't need the power of Free Agent or News Xpress, but are just looking for a simple, easy-to-use newsreader, try WinVN Newsreader. This freeware Usenet client provides just the basics for hassle-free newsgroup browsing, although it's not a good choice if you're addicted to Usenet.

Table 2.2 describes the Windows newsreaders.

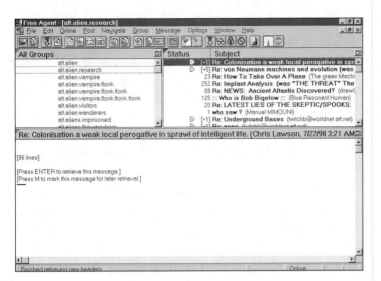

Figure 2.4
Free Agent is a
complete news-
reader for serious
news junkies.

TABLE 2.2: WINDOWS NEWSREADERS

Newsreader	System Requirements	Price	Download Site
Free Agent	Windows 3.x/95/98/NT	Free	http://www.forteinc.com/getfa/download.htm
News Xpress	Windows 95/98/NT	Free	http://www.malch.com/nxfaq.html
WinVN Newsreader	Windows 3.x/95/98/NT	Free	http://www.ksc.nasa.gov/software/winvn/winvn.html

Choosing an FTP Client

Why do you need an FTP client, when all the Web browsers support the FTP protocol? FTP clients generally transfer files more quickly and efficiently than Web browsers do, and they enable you to control files better during transfer. FTP clients also provide timesaving functions, such as pursuing a download at many different sites or searching for a particular file.

If you rarely download software, your Web browser should work just fine. But if you get most of your software from the Internet, maintain a Web site, or use FTP all the time to share files with others, an FTP client should be part of your Internet

Timesaver
The HTTP protocol makes Web pages look good but slows large downloads. FTP bypasses HTTP, transferring files directly from the remote computer to your hard drive. If a program you want is linked to a Web page, don't click the link and make your inefficient browser do the work. Instead, note the FTP address in the URL and retrieve the file with an FTP client. You get your software faster!

toolkit. In fact, you might want to choose two or three clients to employ in different situations. This roundup of FTP clients helps you choose a program that meets your needs and level of expertise.

The Basics

Two FTP clients have proved their worth again and again: Fetch for the Macintosh and WS_FTP for Windows. One of these programs is all you need for the majority of file transfers.

Fetch is a basic FTP client for Mac users that's fast and easy to use. It's a good tool for frequent software and other file transfers and for maintaining an FTP or Web site. You also won't spend a lot of time trying to figure out obscure commands. Most importantly, Fetch supports the essential feature of continuing interrupted downloads right where you left off. Finally, it's compatible with most Macs, including older machines.

- **System requirements:** Mac OS 4.1

- **Price:** $25 (free for educational and nonprofit organizations)

- **Download:** http://www.dartmouth.edu/pages/softdev/fetch.html

WS_FTP is a good, basic client for Windows users (see Figure 2.5). Designed so that even beginners can start using it right away, WS_FTP has enough features to grow as your needs do. For example, you can create profiles for frequently visited sites, resume interrupted transfers, and perform file maintenance. WS_FTP is also a handy tool for maintaining and updating Web sites.

- **System requirements:** Windows 3.x/95/98/NT; 16MB RAM (32MB RAM on Windows NT); 3MB hard disk space

- **Price:** $37.50 (30-day evaluation available)

- **Download:** http://www.ipswitch.com/Products/WS_FTP/index.html

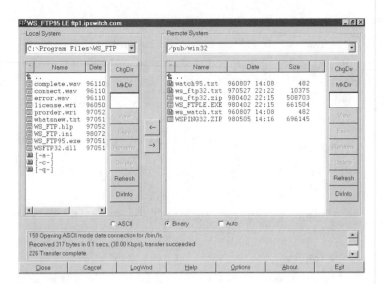

Figure 2.5
WS_FTP fulfills most of your FTP needs.

FTP Extras

Although both Fetch and WS_FTP are solid, basic FTP clients, they might not serve your needs in certain situations. In those cases, turn to an FTP client that offers specialized features. From built-in FTP site searching to integration with the desktop to automation, all these programs offer something extra. Not all of them are suited for every user, but one or two carefully chosen products can save time and energy.

CuteFTP

CuteFTP offers some enhancements over WS_FTP in terms of quickly connecting and navigating favorite FTP sites. Persistent file transfer and auto-reconnect features enable the program to continuously try connecting to a busy site until the transfer is made, freeing you to do other things. CuteFTP also includes many valuable features for Webmasters; for instance, you can automatically send files to selected sites and edit files remotely.

- **System requirements:** Windows 3.x/95/98/NT 4.0

- **Price:** $39.95

- **Download:**   http://www.cuteftp.com/products/cuteftp/
  cuteftp.html

Watch Out!
As you might have discovered already, Windows comes with a basic FTP client (Ftp.exe, located in the main Windows directory). Although it's a functional client, it's clunky, difficult to use, and controlled by UNIX-style command-line operations. You're better off downloading a client that is quicker to learn and easier to use.

Bright Idea
LeapFTP for Windows 95/98/NT is a good choice if you don't have a lot of disk space to spare. Installed, it takes up only 500KB, but its no-frills, austere design is best suited for FTP experts. Get this shareware program from any major software download site (see Appendix B).

File Dog

If automation is what you need, File Dog is the FTP client for you. You set up a schedule for file transfers ahead of time, and File Dog uses its own dialer to make the transfers on schedule. File Dog is a very good choice if you need to frequently mirror a Web or FTP site or automatically update Web pages.

- **System requirements:** Windows 95/98/NT 4.0

- **Price:** $39 (freeware version available with limited features)

- **Download:** http://www.edgepub.com/fd/

FTP Explorer

FTP Explorer is a very fast, easy-to-use client for users who deal with a small number of FTP sites. It's particularly well suited for accessing the same sites on a day-to-day basis. Using FTP Explorer, you can click desktop icons to connect directly to a favorite FTP site and view its directory. You can also choose from several foreign-language add-ons.

- **System requirements:** Windows 95/98/NT 4.0

- **Price:** shareware (free for educational and noncommercial home users)

- **Download:** http://www.ftpx.com/

Go!Zilla

Integrate file transfer with Web surfing using the Go!Zilla client. This program is especially handy for users who frequently download shareware, games, desktop themes, or MP3 files from Web sites. When you find a file you want to download in your Web browser, drag it to Go!Zilla's icon to schedule the download, so you don't have to pause browsing. You can even set up batch-downloading or select multiple FTP locations for a single file and let Go!Zilla select the fastest connection. Go!Zilla also includes an FTP search engine.

- **System requirements:** Windows 95/98/NT

- **Price:** shareware ($24.95)

- **Download:** http://www.gizmo.net/

Anarchie Pro

Anarchie Pro combines an Archie client and an anonymous FTP client in the same interface, enabling you to search for the software you want on public FTP sites and then download it without switching programs. It also has an easy-to-use interface for beginners.

- **System requirements:** Mac OS 7.0 (Mac OS 7.5.5 or later recommended)

- **Price:** shareware ($35)

- **Download:** http://www.stairways.com/anarchie/index.html

NetFinder

NetFinder uses a Finder-like interface to integrate FTPing with the hard drive. You can drag and drop files from the hard drive to an FTP site to upload, move files around on the FTP site, and rename and delete files on the FTP site as easily as on the hard drive—all handy features if you manage a Web site. Try out both NetFinder and Fetch—you might like NetFinder better!

- **System requirements:** Mac OS 7.0 with the Thread Manager 2.1 extension (Mac OS 7.5.5 or later is recommended); 2MB RAM

- **Price:** shareware (30-day trial version available)

- **Download:** http://www.ozemail.com.au/~pli/netfinder/

Internet Neighborhood

Internet Neighborhood integrates with the desktop, this time on Windows. It displays local files and remote FTP sites together in Windows Explorer, so you can perform drag-and-drop transfers. Transferring files can be slow, so if speed is more important to you than integration, skip this product.

- **System requirements:** Windows 95/98/NT; 32MB RAM; 20MB disk space

- **Price:** $29.95 (scaled-down shareware version available)

- **Download:**   `http://www.knowareinc.com/in32docs/index.html`

Choosing a Web Browser

Timesaver
Many new products are available at the company's FTP site before the Web site, so you can be the first on your block to get the latest browser version or the hottest new game.

Other than your email program, I'm betting that your Web browser is the tool that you pull most often out of your Internet toolkit. It can also be the most frustrating component of your Internet suite to decide upon.

At first, it might seem that you're limited to one of the big two—Netscape Navigator or Microsoft Internet Explorer. Actually, things could be worse. Both Navigator and Internet Explorer are robust programs that routinely push the envelope of Internet technology. And there are ways to tailor your browser to fit your specific Web-surfing needs (more on this in Chapters 3, "Getting More Out of Navigator," and 4, "Getting More Out of Internet Explorer").

Whether you choose Netscape or Microsoft, use both for different types of Web surfing, or go with another browser altogether, as long as you are in control, you win the browser wars.

Winning the Browser Wars

Is there really any difference between Navigator and Internet Explorer? Not in the important areas—both are free, and the fundamental browser program is basically the same.

So how do you choose between the two? You could base your decision on whether you like Bill Gates (a lot of people do). If you care about the details, you can decide based on the little differences, such as toolbar configuration or bookmarks and favorites (see Figure 2.6). Or you could follow the lead of a lot of Internet veterans—install both and change browsers from one Web browsing session to another, based on what you're doing at the time.

Internet Explorer

Figure 2.6
Navigator and
Internet Explorer
are basically the
same, but the lit-
tle differences
can help you
choose one for
your main
browser.

Netscape Navigator

Your computer platform and available platform might
limit you to just one browser. Both Navigator and Internet
Explorer have a reputation for consuming a lot of memory
and hard disk space, even more than the minimums listed.
First things first—Table 2.3 describes what each browser
requires and where to get them.

Bright Idea
If your system
doesn't stand up
to the hefty
requirements of
Internet Explorer
5.0 or Navigator
4.x, try an
archived version.
Navigator 2.x–3.x
are still available
on Netscape's
Web Site (http://
home.netscape.
com/download/
archive/index.
html).

TABLE 2.3: NAVIGATOR AND INTERNET EXPLORER SYSTEM REQUIREMENTS

Browser	Supported Operating	Minimum Memory	Minimum Hard Drive Space	Download Site
Netscape Communicator 4.6	Mac OS 7.6.1 (PowerPC only) Windows 95/98/NT 3.51; UNIX (multiple platforms)	32MB (64MB) on UNIX	32MB	http://home.netscape.com/download/
Netscape Navigator 4.0	Mac OS 7.6.1; Windows 95/98/NT; UNIX (multiple platforms)	16MB (64MB on UNIX)	9MB–32MB (depending on the operating system)	http://home.netscape.com/download/

continues

TABLE 2.3: CONTINUED

Browser	Supported Operating	Minimum Memory	Minimum Hard Drive Space	Download Site
Microsoft Internet Explorer 5.0	Windows 95/98/NT 4.0	16MB–32MB (depending on the operating system)	45MB–111MB (depending on instalation)	http://www.microsoft.com/windows/ie/default.htm
Microsoft Internet Explorer 4.5	Mac OS 7.1	12MB	9MB–36MB (depending on the installation)	http://www.microsoft.com/mac/ie/
Microsoft Internet Explorer 4.0	Solaris 2.5	32MB (64MB recommended)	65MB	http://www.microsoft.com/ie/unix/

Watch Out!
When you use two browsers, they are both going to ask to be the default browser—the one registered to handle HTML. If you disable the default browser check in the dialog box that appears when you first start the browser, the other one won't correctly display Web pages. Be careful—on Internet Explorer, be sure the check box in that first dialog box is selected, although the check box must be deselected in Navigator for things to work properly.

So how do the two browsers stack up when you compare them detail for detail? Table 2.4 compares several different features. If you have to choose one or the other, go with the one that better handles the features you use most, the ones that are crucial to an enjoyable Web surfing experience. But if you have the system resources, install both suites and use the one that better suits what you're doing from browsing session to browsing session. You are then able to take advantage of the strengths of both while avoiding their weaknesses.

TABLE 2.4: COMPARING NAVIGATOR AND INTERNET EXPLORER

Feature	Navigator	Internet Explorer
Interface	Simpler and easier to use.	Clunkier interface, not quite as intuitive; more tools accessible via toolbars.
Customization	Add buttons to the personal toolbar; preferences easier to configure; otherwise, customization is limited.	Much more configurable than Navigator; the toolbars and Explorer bars can be customized in many ways.

Feature	Navigator	Internet Explorer
Bookmarks/ Favorites	Strong import/export; must open separate window to edit.	Can view and edit favorites from the main window or from Windows Explorer.
Searching	Limited search from Location window.	Can display search page next to main window.
Caching	More control over cache.	Browsable cache; not as much control; temporary Internet files can consume a lot of hard disk space.
Plug-ins	Supports 200+ plug-ins; basic multimedia plug-ins included.	Supports ActiveX Control versions of some plug-ins; basic multimedia plug-ins included.
ActiveX	Supports ActiveX only with a commercial plug-in.	Native ActiveX support.
Java/ JavaScript	Faster and more stable in version 4.5.	Fast Java support, but not so good with JavaScript.
Security	Supports strong encryption, signed applets and scripts, and security icon.	Supports strong encryption, scripts; doesn't support Netscape Secure Server for online shopping; can set up security "zones."
Cascading Style Sheets	Supports them, but not as well as IE.	IE does a better job than Navigator.
Content filtering	NetWatch must be configfigured online; supports major standards.	Content Advisor can be configured from Options dialog box; supports major standards.

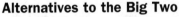

Alternatives to the Big Two

With all the hype about the browser wars, it might seem that the only Web browsers out there are Navigator and Internet Explorer. This can be frustrating if you don't like being limited or if you have a lower-end system that can't handle these resource-hungry monsters. Despite all evidence to the contrary, you still have a lot of choices when it comes to Web browsers, and many of them work just as well (if not better) than the big two. If Navigator and Internet Explorer aren't doing the job for you, consider one of these alternatives.

Inside Scoop
I regularly use both Navigator and Internet Explorer, but Navigator is my main browser. I mostly do research on the Web, using bookmarks to organize my research projects. Navigator's bookmarks are easier to use, with stronger organizational and importing features. I also like Navigator's simpler, cleaner interface, and the options are easier to set. However, I fire up IE when visiting Microsoft's site or downloading Microsoft software, so I can view the Active Server Pages. I also like IE's history list and content filtering better, and its integration with Windows can be very useful.

Timesaver
It can be a hassle
finding out what
browsers are avail-
able for your com-
puter platform,
particularly if
you're not using
Macintosh or
Windows.
BrowserWatch
(http://
browserwatch.
internet.com/
browsers.html)
provides a com-
plete list of avail-
able browsers and
where to get
them, broken
down by platform.
So whether you
use DOS or Amiga,
you can quickly
find a browser
that works on your
system.

Opera

Opera is probably the best alternative to Navigator or Internet
Explorer for users who want a full-featured browser that's still
fast, stable, and doesn't demand too many computer
resources. Opera needs only 3MB hard disk space, and it offers
strong performance without monopolizing memory, even on
slow machines. The main drawback is that you have to pay for
it, but you might find that Opera is worth the money (a trial
version is available for test-driving).

Opera includes all the basics, plus some efficient features
that are missing in the leading browsers. For instance, control
how Web pages look and even zoom in from a toolbar. A toolbar button enables instant toggling between graphics and no
graphics. You can also open multiple viewing windows, each
one capable of loading and displaying different Web pages
(see Figure 2.7); to get the same effect with Navigator or
Internet Explorer, you'd have to open multiple copies of the
browser, which use up much more system resources. It offers
inline multimedia playback, it can run any Netscape-
compatible plug-in, and it supports JavaScript. On the downside, Opera doesn't support Java, ActiveX, or Cascading Style
Sheets at all, but many Web surfers can live without these
extras.

Figure 2.7
Using Opera, you
can open multiple
windows showing
different Web
pages, a feature
that Navigator
and Internet
Explorer lack.

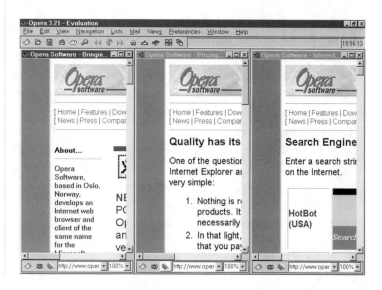

- **System requirements:** Windows 3.x/95/98/NT 4.0; 3MB hard drive space; 8MB RAM (Mac OS and UNIX versions are in development)

- **Price:** $35 (30-day evaluation version available)

- **Download:** http://operasoftware.com/

Arachne

If you're using a DOS machine or don't have the resources to run both Windows and a Web browser, you can still use a graphical browser—Arachne. Arachne includes a graphical browser and even multimedia players in a very small, very fast suite. It can run on as little as an old XT with less than one megabyte of RAM, and it still manages to support most of HTML 4.0. It doesn't even need a mouse. But its toolbar and interface are surprisingly similar to its Windows counterparts. Arachne proves that you don't need a Pentium II processor to browse the Web.

- **System requirements:** MS-DOS 3.3 or later; 3MB hard disk space; 425KB of DOS memory (4MB recommended); EGA or VGA video card

- **Price:** shareware ($30)

- **Download:** http://www.naf.cz/arachne/

Lynx

Lynx is another good browser for low-end systems and Internet connections, such as older PCs, early Macs, and users who get on the Net via shell accounts. Because it is entirely text-based, Lynx is incredibly fast and so is a good alternative to a graphical browser when you want to quickly find something on the Web. It's also ideal for handheld machines that don't have large displays. If you have access to a shell account, you can start using Lynx right away by logging in and typing lynx at the prompt (see Figure 2.8). The disadvantage to Lynx is that you might be left out by Web sites that overly favor graphics, frames, Java, JavaScript, or ActiveX—all the elements that slow Web browsing.

Watch Out!
If you use Windows 95/98, you might think that Internet Explorer is the best choice, due to its integration with the operating system and the fact that it's made by Microsoft. However, many users have experienced serious problems because of that integration. Because Internet Explorer can manipulate the operating system, a small browser crash can lead to a total system failure. Chapter 4 provides tips on how to protect your system from this type of situation.

Figure 2.8
Lynx offers a fast
way to access
the Web if you
don't care about
the graphics.

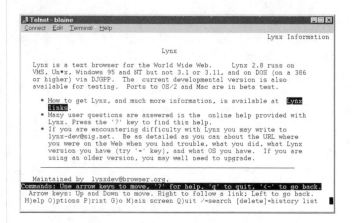

- **System requirements:** MS-DOS, Windows 95/98/NT, or UNIX for basic Lynx (or any computer via a UNIX- or VMS-based shell account); Mac OS for MacLynx

- **Price:** free

- **Download:** http://lynx.browser.org/ for basic Lynx; http://www.lirmm.fr/~gutkneco/maclynx/ for MacLynx

Adding Power to Your Browser

Just like a classic roadster, a Web browser is faster and more fun when it's souped up with add-ons. These low-cost or free utilities beef up performance or add new features, enabling you to get the most out of your browser. There are literally hundreds of add-ons out there, so sorting through them all can be a chore. This section describes add-ons that really do improve browsing power, while avoiding the duds.

This section focuses on three types of add-ons, chosen because they work equally well with Internet Explorer and Navigator and so are ideal if you regularly use both browsers:

- Browser accelerators, for speeding up Web surfing

- Surfing boosts, for enhancing Web-surfing activities

- Bookmarks and favorites utilities, for sharing hotlists when you use both browsers

Browser Accelerators

Browser accelerators are a cheap and easy way to turbo-charge your browser, boosting Web page loading speeds as much as 66%. Most browser accelerators use the cache on the hard drive to speed up Web surfing. While you're reading a Web page, the accelerator predownloads all the links on the page; when you click a link, the page loads instantly from the cache. Look for an accelerator that allows you to prefetch text only, so you have the choice of surfing with images turned off.

The better browser accelerators are history based, rather than link based. These add-ons work on the theory that most of us have a standard surfing regimen, visiting the same sites each time we get on the Web. The accelerator keeps a record of the most frequently visited sites and predownloads those sites into the cache. This avoids wasting bandwidth and hard drive space in downloading links you never look at. But you also won't experience a performance boost when surfing to new sites.

NetSonic

Web3000's NetSonic is probably the best choice. Although it's not the fastest of the accelerators, it's a lot more flexible. By default, NetSonic is a history-based accelerator, but you can switch to link-based caching when you venture into new areas of the Web. Link-based mode predownloads links on the same site only, which is more Internet-friendly than some other accelerators. NetSonic also works with the widest range of browsers. Best of all, it's free.

- **System requirements:** Windows 95/98; 16MB RAM (32MB recommended); 10MB hard disk space (30MB recommended)

- **Supported browsers:** Navigator 3.x–4.x, Internet Explorer 3.x–5.x, AOL for Windows 95 4.x or later, CompuServe 4.0 or later, Opera 3.x, or NeoPlanet

- **Price:** free

- **Download:** http://www.web3000.com/

Watch Out!
Because of the way they work, accelerators present a real problem. Generally, modems remain idle most of the time; however, accelerators force modems to download data all the time. If every user ran an accelerator, every Internet connection would be in constant use, sucking up bandwidth, overwhelming Web servers, and slowing everything. So if you really need the extra speed, use accelerators responsibly—choose a smart, history-based utility.

Moneysaver
Offline browsers enable you to pre-download Web pages and peruse them at your leisure after you disconnect. An offline browser can significantly decrease Internet access fees, particularly if you pay by the hour. Windows users should try Fetch, which can be used by itself or in conjunction with IE or Navigator. Mac users should try Web Devil. Both can be downloaded from any software archive (see Appendix B).

Surf Express

Connectix's Surf Express is a history-based accelerator, making it more Internet-friendly while maintaining a decent speed boost. It uses both a proxy server and cache searching to give the best performance of all the browser accelerators, especially if you frequently visit the same sites. However, if you browse to new sites often, you won't notice any increased speed.

- **System requirements:** Mac OS 7.5.3 (PowerPC only) or Windows 95/98/NT 4.0; 16MB RAM; 12MB hard disk space

- **Supported browsers:** Navigator 3.x or later, Internet Explorer, or AOL

- **Price:** $29.95 (demo available)

- **Download:** `http://www.connectix.com/html/surfexpress .html`

PeakJet 2000

PeakSoft's PeakJet 2000 is a link-based browser accelerator that works particularly well if you frequently surf the Web with images turned off. Although PeakJet 2000 is the fastest option for general, link-based browsing, it's not nearly as bandwidth-friendly as the history-based accelerators. You can set many options to tailor PeakJet 2000 to your regular surfing habits. For instance, you can set it to prefetch only links from the same site you're currently viewing, saving bandwidth and disk space.

- **System requirements:** Windows 95/98/NT 4.0; 32MB RAM; 15MB hard disk space

- **Supported browsers:** Navigator 3.x or Internet Explorer 3.x (or later versions)

- **Price:** $29.95 (demo available)

- **Download:** `http://www.peaksoft.com /peakjet2.html`

Surfing Boosts

Perhaps you'd rather make Web surfing more efficient, rather than just speeding it up. Browser add-ons can help. Take a look at two of the more useful add-ons: Alexa and KatieSoft Scroll.

Alexa

Alexa is a free service that displays detailed information about the site you're visiting, as well as a list of sites with related content (see Figure 2.9). In this way, Alexa emulates Navigator 4.6's What's Related feature and the Show Related Links feature new to Internet Explorer 5.0, but does the job better and more thoroughly. You can also access Alexa's archive of the Web, so you can view pages when the hosting server is offline.

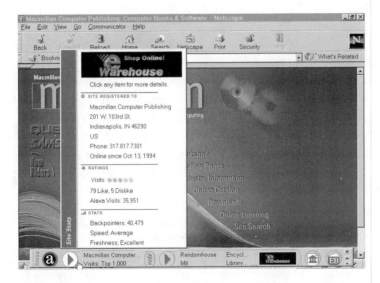

Figure 2.9
Using Alexa, you can find background information and related links for each Web site you visit.

- **System requirements:** Mac OS 7.5 or Windows 95/98/NT 4.0; 24MB–32MB RAM (depending on the operating system)

- **Supported browsers:** Navigator 3.x–4.x or Internet Explorer 3.x–5.x

- **Price:** free

- **Download:** http://www.alexa.com/

KatieSoft Scroll

KatieSoft Scroll gives you a multipaned browser window, so you can surf several sites at once without having to open multiple browser sessions and use more system resources (a feature that Opera supports natively). Use KatieSoft Scroll to explore different areas of one site at the same time, compare information from multiple sources, and otherwise optimize your Web research efforts.

- **System requirements:** Windows 95/98/NT 4.0

- **Supported browsers:** Navigator 4.x or Internet Explorer 4.x–5.x

- **Price:** $19.95

- **Download:** http://www.katiesoft.com/products.html

Sharing Bookmarks and Favorites

One of the most frustrating aspects of using both Navigator and Internet Explorer is the inability to easily share bookmarks/favorites between the two. Many add-ons have been developed to do this job, as outlined in Table 2.5. All these add-ons are shareware or freeware and can be downloaded from any popular software download site (check Appendix B for suggestions).

TABLE 2.5: ADD-ONS FOR SHARING BOOKMARKS AND FAVORITES

Add-on	Operating System	Minimum Browser	Description
Bookmark Converter	Windows 95/98/NT	Any version	Convert bookmarks to favorites and vice versa.
URL Manager Pro	Mac OS 7	Any version	Use the same bookmarks/favorites file in both browsers.

continues

Add-on	Operating System	Minimum Browser	Description
URLMenu	Windows 95/98/NT	Navigator 3.x and Internet Explorer 3.x	Access bookmarks/favorites from the system tray and merge bookmarks and favorites.
Link Sweeper	Windows 95/98/NT 4.0	Any version	Synchronize bookmarks/favorites and clean up old links.

Just the Facts

- Select your Internet tools—email program, newsreader, and FTP client—based on your needs and how you use the Net.

- You have more choice than you think when it comes to Web browsers; you can select one of the big two, use them both in different situations, or go with a lesser-known alternative better suited to your system's resources.

- No browser is perfect by itself; browser add-ons improve Web surfing by speeding things up, making browsing more efficient, and helping you manage bookmarks and favorites.

Getting More Out of Navigator

Chapter 3

Y OU PROBABLY AREN'T GETTING the most out of your Web browser. Netscape Navigator is a huge program with many features hidden away where you aren't likely to discover them if you don't explore beyond the main toolbar buttons. (The same goes for Microsoft Internet Explorer—turn to the next chapter to learn more.)

This chapter helps you use Navigator to its utmost. Learn how to speed up Web browsing, become a more efficient surfer, conserve computer resources, and otherwise tailor Navigator to how you use the Web.

Inside Scoop
Netscape made a comeback in early 1998, when it not only gave away Communicator for free, but also offered the source code up for developers to tinker with and improve. Why is this such a big deal? Because it's a major move back to the nonproprietary software development model that the Internet was built on and that had led to the most innovative developments (such as the World Wide Web). Look for Communicator 5.0—result of that developer input—to be released in the fall of 1999.

Streamlining Communicator

Netscape Navigator comes bundled with a suite of Internet tools in a package called Communicator. However, you might not need or want all these tools. For instance, if you use a standalone email program and newsreader, you won't need Communicator's Messenger component. Getting rid of the Communicator components you won't use frees up system resources that can be put to good use.

Communicator 4.6 (the latest version) comes with the following components:

- **Navigator:** The Web browser

- **Messenger:** An email and Usenet client

- **Composer:** An HTML editor

- **AOL Instant Messenger:** For sending instant messages to Communicator, CompuServe, and America Online users

- **RealPlayer G2:** For playing streaming media in the RealAudio and RealVideo formats

- **Audio/Video Plug-in:** For playing standard audio and video file formats

- **Shockwave Flash Plug-in:** For playing Shockwave-format animations

- **Beatnik Stub Plug-in:** For playing Rich Music Format (RMF) audio files

- **Import Utility:** For importing email messages and address books from Eudora, Outlook Express, and other programs into Messenger

- **PalmPilot Sync Tools:** For synchronizing the Messenger Address Book with the 3Com PalmPilot (Windows only)

- **Calendar:** For personal and group scheduling (you can choose to download Communicator with or without the Calendar component)

You can streamline Communicator and choose just the components you need when you download the program and when you install it. At `http://home.netscape.com/download/`, you can choose one of three options:

- **Communicator 4.6 with Enterprise Calendaring:** This option includes all components. Get it if you have a lot of system resources to spare and want a personal calendar or if you work with Communicator on the company network.

- **Communicator 4.6 Complete Install:** This option includes every component except Calendar. Select it if you want all the Internet tools but don't need the Calendar application.

- **Navigator 4.0:** Download this to get the Web browser only, a good choice if you don't want any extra components at all.

You can also pick and choose the additional components you want during the installation. When the Setup dialog box appears, select Custom instead of Typical. The Typical option installs all the components you downloaded, while Custom enables you to bypass installation of any unnecessary components. Just clear the check boxes beside the components you don't want (see Figure 3.1). You still have to install the base tools—Navigator, Messenger, Composer, and AOL Instant Messenger—and there's no easy way to get rid of them afterwards.

Bright Idea
You might not use AOL Instant Messenger all that much, unless you have a lot of AOL friends to send messages to. To disable the annoying Sign On prompt that appears whenever you reboot Windows, start AIM from the Communicator program group, click Setup, select the General tab, and clear the Start Netscape AIM When Windows Starts check box. On the Macintosh, remove the PromoLauncher alias from your Startup Items folder.

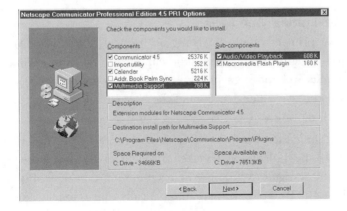

Figure 3.1
Custom installation enables you to control the Communicator components to install.

Inside Scoop
All versions of
Communicator/
Navigator come in
two flavors: stan-
dard encryption
and strong encryp-
tion. You need the
strong encryption
version if you
intend to perform
banking and
investing opera-
tions on the
Internet. (You must
be an American or
Canadian citizen to
download it.) For
normal opera-
tions—online
shopping, for
instance—the
standard encryp-
tion version should
suit you fine.

If you decide later that you want an extra component you didn't install, use Communicator's SmartUpdate feature to get it—select Help, Software Updates. (You have to register to use SmartUpdate, but it's free.) The SmartUpdate page indicates the version of Communicator you're using, whether an upgrade is available, and which components aren't installed. Select the check boxes by the components you want to get and click Begin SmartUpdate to download and install them from inside Navigator. You can also install additional plug-ins and add-ons by using SmartUpdate.

Becoming a Better Surfer

Many of us don't use Navigator very efficiently when surfing the Web, because Navigator's defaults aren't the most efficient settings. With a few tweaks, you can make Navigator a much better information-gathering tool. Here are some things you can do:

- Maximize the page display area to show more of the Web page

- Speed up the downloading and display of Web pages

- Use history lists to get around

- Find searching shortcuts

- Understand and deal with errors when they occur

Maximizing Web Pages

Your primary reason for being on the Web is to look at Web pages, right? So, the Navigator window should show as much of the Web page as possible. You can easily maximize the screen "real estate," or area of the Navigator window devoted to displaying Web pages.

The easiest way to increase screen real estate is by getting rid of the toolbars, which take up quite a lot of space at the top of the Navigator window. When you minimize or turn off tool-bars, the Web page display automatically adjusts to take advantage of the extra space. There are three easy things you can do to get those toolbars out of your way:

- **Minimize toolbars when they are not being used.** Click the small, vertical tab on the left side of each toolbar to tuck it out of sight when it's not needed. If you need the toolbar, just click the tab again to drop it down.

- **Turn off toolbars you never use.** If you do all your navigating via menus or keyboard shortcuts, why even show those bulky toolbars? Turn them off completely by selecting View, Show and removing the check mark beside the toolbars you don't want. With this method, you won't be able to access the toolbars as easily as if you had minimized them.

- **Shrink the navigation toolbar.** By default, the buttons on the navigation toolbar (the top toolbar) show both pictures and text, which is not only redundant but also takes up a lot of space. Significantly shrink this toolbar while still keeping these useful buttons handy by removing either the text or the pictures.

Follow these steps to change the buttons on the navigation toolbar:

1. Select Edit, Preferences.

2. Click the Appearance category.

3. Under Show Toolbars As, select either Pictures Only or Text Only.

4. Click OK.

Minimizing toolbars you don't use and switching to picture-only buttons greatly increase the amount of the Web page that Navigator can display (see Figure 3.2).

Watch Out!
There seem to be a lot of problems with SmartUpdate. For instance, it indicates that components are installed when they're not, and it doesn't always install components correctly, especially with multiple installs. Before using SmartUpdate, ensure that Java, JavaScript, and cookies are enabled in the Advanced panel of Preferences, and in the Advanced, SmartUpdate panel, select Enable SmartUpdate. If you have problems, try this: Select the Advanced, Cache panel in Preferences and click Clear Memory Cache.

Figure 3.2
Maximize the Web page by minimizing Navigator toolbars.

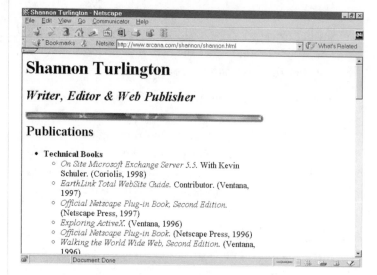

Bright Idea
Sometimes you come across pages made unreadable by clashing colors or illegible fonts. You can force your own preferences at the expense of the page's intended design. To set default colors, select the Appearance, Colors panel in Preferences. Black on white makes for easiest reading. Check Always Use My Colors to bypass the Web page author's choices. Specify fonts by selecting Appearance, Fonts, choosing fonts from the menus, and clicking Use My Default Fonts. Variable-width is the most commonly used font; choose Times New Roman or Arial for best legibility. You also avoid Dynamic Fonts, which can slow Web page loading.

You can also get rid of the status bar at the bottom of the Navigator window by pressing Ctrl+Alt+S on Windows or Cmd+Alt+S on the Macintosh (repeat to turn the status bar back on). Although this shows more of the Web page, it does eliminate your ability to monitor the progress of downloading pages. It also turns off the component bar—that little toolbar in the lower-left corner that enables you to quickly bring up the other Communicator components—but that's easily remedied; select View, Show, Floating Component Bar to pop up the component bar in its own little window.

Finally, try decreasing the font size of the text to show more of the page in the display area. Each time you select View, Decrease Font (Ctrl+[or Cmd+[), the font size decreases by two points. Choosing View, Increase Font (Ctrl+] or Cmd+]) is a handy way to zoom in on very small text in Web pages, as well.

Speeding Up Surfing

If you find yourself reading entire chapters of *Moby Dick* while waiting for a new Web page to display, you are definitely not surfing as efficiently as you could. Let's face it—most of the graphics and Java applets on the Web are just eye candy, serving no more purpose than to look good and considerably slow down surfing. If you won't miss them, you can turn them off and significantly increase your browsing speed. Here's how:

1. Select Edit/Preferences.

2. Select the Advanced category.

3. Clear the Automatically Load Images check box.

4. Clear the Enable Java check box (see Figure 3.3).

5. Click OK.

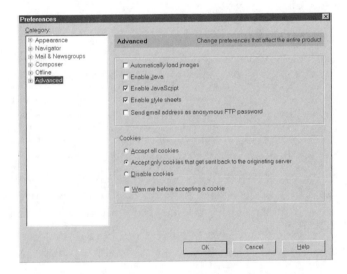

Figure 3.3
Graphics and Java significantly slow the display of Web pages; turn them off to boost surfing speed.

Watch Out!
Sometimes disabling automatic image loading results in graphic placeholders being placed on top of text, obscuring the words below. To bring the text forward, press Cmd+A or Ctrl+A to select all the text, and then click in the browser window to deselect. The obscured words will be revealed.

I recommend that you keep JavaScript and style sheet support turned on. JavaScript doesn't slow Web page loading nearly as much as Java, and often it's necessary for viewing the page properly. You won't encounter style sheets often enough to notice them slowing you down, and they are pretty cool, too.

You might still run into Web pages where you need to see the graphics to navigate properly or to see important information. When you turn off automatic image loading, an Images button appears on the navigation toolbar; click this button to load all the images on the page. If you need to see only one image, right-click over the image placeholder (click and hold on the Mac), and select Show Image from the pop-up menu.

Timesaver
Many people stick
with the default
start page at
http://home.
netscape.com/,
which really slows
you down, because
Netscape's server
gets so much traf-
fic. For faster start-
ing, select a start
page on your local
disk. Your book-
marks are a good
choice because
they link to your
favorite sites.
Select the
Navigator panel in
Preferences, select
the Home Page
button (or Blank
Page for even
faster starting),
click Browse in the
Home Page area,
and find the book-
mark.htm file, usu-
ally located in
Netscape\Users\
your_user_profile\.

(Don't select View Image, though—that loads the image in its own Navigator window.)

Unfortunately, you can't individually load the Java applets you need, and with Java turned off, you can potentially miss out on necessary information or special effects. You probably won't even know that you're missing anything, because there's no applet placeholder icon like there is for images. Perhaps Netscape will implement Java loading on an applet-by-applet basis in a future version of Navigator. Until then, trust me when I say that you're not missing much. But you'll have to decide what's most important—increased downloading speed or the functionality of Java.

Getting Around

Navigator provides several ways to navigate the Web more effectively, especially when revisiting pages. The browser maintains a number of history lists to help you retrace your steps. History lists keep track of pages that you've loaded recently.

Click and hold the Back toolbar button to reveal the series of pages that you traveled to get to the current page (see Figure 3.4). Select any page in the list to jump back to that page. This list is particularly useful if you're trying to retrace your steps along a series of links. (But if you go back and take a new link, the Back button's list records the new series.)

As you go back and forth along a series of pages, you might lose track of where you've been. In that case, click and hold the Forward button to display all the pages that you can travel forward to. The bottom of the Go menu lists the entire series, with a check mark next to the page that's currently displayed. (To get a quick reminder of what the last and next pages are, position the mouse over the Back or Forward button, and the name of the page pops up.)

Click the arrow to the right of the Location window on the middle toolbar to discover another kind of history list. This list displays all the URLs that you've recently typed into the Location window. Select one to connect to a page that you opened directly, rather than by following links.

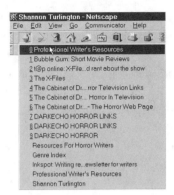

Figure 3.4
The Back button's drop-down menu helps you quickly retrace your steps.

Inside Scoop
For fun, try these unofficial "Easter Egg" URLs (just type them into the Location window and press Enter):
about:mozilla;
about:logo;
about:nihongo;
and about:pics.
Also try pressing Ctrl+Alt+F (Windows) or Cmd+Alt+F (Macintosh) to see where you go.

Select Communicator, Tools, History (press Ctrl+H or Cmd+H) to open the History window, which shows the most complete history list. The History window on Windows is a very useful tool, providing a lot of information about Web pages that you've opened (see Figure 3.5). Besides the title and URL of each page, the History window tells you when you first visited the page, when you last visited, and how many times you've been there. (On the Macintosh, you get only the page's title and URL, and the list is cleared each time you exit Navigator.) Click the column heads to sort the list by any of the criteria. For instance, if you're looking for pages that you visit a lot, click the Visit Count column.

Title	Location	First Visited	Last Visited	Expiration	Visit Count
Shannon Turlington	http://www.arcana.com/sha...	3/13/1998 4:11...	Less than one...	8/11/1998 6:25...	439
Yahoo!	http://www.yahoo.com/	7/11/1998 1:31...	4 hours ago	8/11/1998 2:21...	85
Directory of /export/hom...	ftp://shannon@www.arcana...	6/21/1998 10:5...	5 days ago	8/6/1998 8:51...	50
DOWNLOAD.COM – W...	http://download.com/	7/16/1998 3:36...	1 hours ago	8/11/1998 5:42...	28
Yahoo! Computers and I...	http://www.yahoo.com/Com...	7/24/1998 10:4...	4 days ago	8/7/1998 11:43...	26
bubblegum-template	file:///C|/My Documents/HT...	8 hours ago	4 hours ago	8/11/1998 2:15...	22
Bubble Gum: Title Page	http://www.arcana.com/sha...	5 days ago	4 hours ago	8/11/1998 2:13...	20
Browser Plug-ins	http://home.netscape.com/...	4 days ago	2 days ago	8/9/1998 3:15...	20
DOWNLOAD.COM – List...	http://download.com/PC/R...	7/24/1998 10:5...	4 days ago	8/7/1998 11:32...	19
The hidden features of N...	http://www.cn.cern.ch/~rigau...	2 days ago	2 days ago	8/9/1998 2:32...	18
Bubble Gum: Short Movi...	http://www.arcana.com/sha...	4 hours ago	4 hours ago	8/11/1998 2:07...	17
	http://mott.catalogue.com:86...	4 days ago	4 days ago	8/7/1998 2:55...	17
	http://cosmosoftware.com/g...	2 days ago	2 days ago	8/9/1998 4:32...	16
ZDNet: BrowserUser	http://www.zdnet.com/produ...	7/24/1998 12:5...	4 days ago	8/7/1998 1:44...	15
Hacker's Guide to Navig...	http://www.mods.com/hack...	4 days ago	4 days ago	8/7/1998 2:42...	14
Yahoo! Computers and I...	http://www.yahoo.com/Com...	7/24/1998 10:3...	4 days ago	8/7/1998 11:45...	13
Internet Explorer Product...	http://www.microsoft.com/ie...	6 days ago	5 days ago	8/6/1998 2:36...	13
Tip and Answer Collection	http://search.zdnet.com:80/...	4 days ago	4 days ago	8/7/1998 2:11...	13
Java Technology Home...	http://java.sun.com/	3 days ago	3 days ago	8/8/1998 1:42...	12
DOWNLOAD.COM – Int...	http://download.com/Mac/F...	7/23/1998 2:52...	4 days ago	8/7/1998 11:28...	12
Yahoo! Computers and I...	http://www.yahoo.com/Com...	7/24/1998 10:5...	2 days ago	8/9/1998 1:54...	11
Yahoo! Computers and I...	http://www.yahoo.com/Com...	4 hours ago	4 hours ago	8/11/1998 2:30...	11
Netscape Products	Net...	http://home.netscape.com/...	6 days ago	2 days ago	8/9/1998 11:03...	11
Yahoo! Full Coverage - ...	http://headlines.yahoo.com...	7/24/1998 3:34...	5 days ago	8/6/1998 1:09...	11
Eudora Pro Email v4.0	http://eudora.qualcomm.co...	6 days ago	6 days ago	8/5/1998 11:33...	11
Star Wars: Welcome to t...	http://www.starwars.com/	3 days ago	3 days ago	8/8/1998 3:00...	10
Yahoo! Search Results	http://search.yahoo.com/bi...	4 days ago	2 days ago	8/9/1998 2:01...	10
A Jolt of Efficiency	http://java.sun.com/features...	3 days ago	3 days ago	8/8/1998 1:38...	10
DOWNLOAD.COM – Int...	http://download.com/Fr...	7/23/1998 3:01...	4 days ago	8/7/1998 11:31...	10
ZDNet Products: Web Pl...	http://www.zdnet.com/produ...	4 days ago	4 days ago	8/7/1998 3:53...	9
Search Engine Submissi...	http://www.tiac.net/users/se...	4 hours ago	4 hours ago	8/11/1998 2:38...	9

Figure 3.5
On Windows, the History window shows a lot of information about Web pages that you've visited.

Timesaver
Navigator supports several handy shortcuts when typing URLs. Type Web URLs faster by omitting the **http://** part— Navigator fills it in for you. If the URL is in the www.domain.com form, omit the **www** and **com** parts and just type **domain**. Finally, if you've entered the URL before, Navigator fills it in for you after you type the first few letters.

You can also search the history list by selecting Edit, Search History List; for example, look for URLs containing a specific domain name, or search through page titles for a keyword. Bring up a second search parameter by clicking on the More button. (To search for one parameter or the other, click And and change it to Or.) After you find the page you're looking for, double-click it in the History window to open it in Navigator. The history list is an invaluable tool for tracking down a page you visited long ago and want to get back to, so don't neglect it.

After you start making good use of the history list, you might want to retain pages longer to keep a more complete history. Or you might want to clear the list from time to time— when you start researching a new project, for instance. Follow these steps to do both (Windows only):

1. Select Edit, Preferences.

2. Select the Navigator category.

3. In the text field under History, enter the number of days to retain pages in the history list.

4. Click Clear History to erase the current history list and start over. (You can also clear the menu that appears when you click the arrow beside the Location window by clicking on Clear Location Bar.)

5. Click OK.

Searching Shortcuts

Communicator 4.5 introduced a new feature called Internet Keywords that makes searching the Web easier. If you're using version 4.5 or later, you can type a search phrase directly into the Location window where you'd normally type a URL; Navigator searches Netscape's database of Web sites and displays the results. (This shortcut works in version 4.0, too, except you'll access a random search engine.)

But first, Navigator makes an intelligent guess about what site you're trying to find. For instance, if you type **White House** into the Location window, Navigator assumes you're trying to find the White House's Web site and automatically connects you to http://www.whitehouse.gov/.

The Internet Keywords feature works fairly well for quick searches on one or two broad keywords or to find a specific Web site when you don't know its exact URL. Typing in a company name locates that company's site with a lot of accuracy, even if the domain name doesn't match the company's name (entering **Infiniti** takes you to http://www.infiniti-usa.com/, for instance). But Navigator's built-in searching is limiting for more targeted searches on several keywords. In that case, click the Search toolbar button to open a page where you can search all the major Web page databases.

Another searching feature that's new with version 4.5 is the What's Related button. Click the button to the right of the Location window to retrieve in real time a list of pages that are in some way related to the one that's currently open (see Figure 3.6). This list is based on Netscape's database at its Web site, Netcenter, and works fairly well for major sites. But it's sometimes a mystery exactly how the pages in the list are related to the displayed page, and often no list can be compiled for smaller sites. Nevertheless, the What's Related menu is convenient to check, and the feature is supposed to get more accurate as the Netcenter database grows.

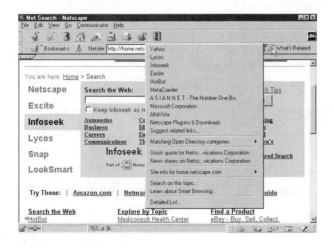

Figure 3.6
Clicking on the What's Related button opens a menu of quasi-related Web sites.

If you hate how the What's Related button reduces the size of the Location window, you can easily remove it:

1. Select Edit, Preferences.

2. Expand the Navigator category.

3. Select Smart Browsing.

4. Clear the Enable What's Related check box. (You can also set preferences for how What's Related works if you leave it turned on.)

5. If you don't like the Location window searching feature and want to turn it off, clear the Enable Internet Keywords check box.

6. Click OK.

Timesaver

If you regularly access a Web site that requires you to log in, Navigator supports a handy shortcut around typing your user-name and pass-word into the pop-up dialog box each time you con-nect. Enter the site's URL into the Location window like this: `http://` `username:` `password@www.` `securesite.com`. If you keep going back, Navigator "remembers" the long URL for you. But be certain that no untrustworthy individuals have access to your computer, because this shortcut shows your pass-word in the Location window until you leave the site.

So what do you do with a Web page after you've found it? Navigator gives you several options, outlined in Table 3.1. Remember that you can access the pop-up menu by right-clicking in Windows or by clicking and holding the mouse but-ton on the Macintosh.

TABLE 3.1: WEB PAGE MANIPULATION FEATURES IN NAVIGATOR

What You Want to Do	How to Do It
Find a keyword in the page.	Edit, Find in Page (Ctrl+F or Cmd+F).
Find the keyword again.	Edit, Find Again (Ctrl+G or Cmd+G).
Copy some of the page's text.	Highlight the text with the mouse and select Edit, Copy (Ctrl+C or Cmd+C).
Copy all of the page's text (does not copy images).	Edit, Select All (Ctrl+A or Cmd+A) and Edit/Copy (Ctrl+C or Cmd+C).
Copy the URL of a link or image in the page.	Position the mouse over the link or image and select Copy Link Location or Copy Image Location from the pop-up menu.
Print the page.	Click the Print toolbar button (change the printing options by selecting File, Page Setup).

What You Want to Do	How to Do It
Save the page (doesn't save the images).	File, Save As (Ctrl+S or Cmd+S); choose File, Save Frame As to save a selected frame. Select HTML to save the page for later viewing in a Web browser, or select Plain Text to save as a formatted text file.
Save an image in the page.	Position the mouse over the image and select Save Image As from the pop-up menu.
Save a page linked to the open page.	Position the mouse over the link and select Save Link As from the pop-up menu.
Edit the page in Composer.	File, Edit Page or File, Edit Frame (this is also the only way to save the page with all its images).
View the HTML source code.	View, Page Source (Ctrl+U or Cmd+U).
Send the page to someone through email (Messenger is required).	Select Send Page from the pop-up menu.

Solving Problems

Many problems that you encounter while surfing the Web are beyond your control—the page might have moved to a new URL, the server might be offline, or there might be a glitch somewhere between your computer and the server. First, try reloading the page a couple of times (click the Reload button or press Ctrl+R or Cmd+R). Reloading works especially well if the page only partly loads. You could also try accessing the page at a later time to see whether the problem has cleared up.

Table 3.2 describes common Navigator error messages and how to fix the problem if these suggestions don't work.

Bright Idea
Want an easy-to-make start page with all your favorite stuff on it? Click the My Netscape button and follow the instructions to set up a start page with your choice of news, weather, horoscopes, search tools, and the like. (You must have Java turned on.) This kind of start page slows you down when you open Navigator, because the browser has to connect to Netscape's busy server to retrieve all that personalized information.

TABLE 3.2: NAVIGATOR ERROR MESSAGES

Error Message	What It Means	What to Try
Unknown File Type, No Viewer Configured for File Type, or Unable to Launch External Viewer	Navigator doesn't know how to handle the file.	Save the file by selecting Save It to Disk and OK; then, you can view it in the correct program.
The Server Does Not Have a DNS Entry	Your Internet connection might have disconnected or is malfunctioning; there can be temporary network problems; the server might have been shut down or might not exist.	If you can reach another remote site, then your Internet connection is up and running properly. Try connecting again later, or Ping the Web server to see whether it exists.
404 Not Found	The URL might not exist.	Search for the page's new location, or email the page's owner.
404 Access Denied	File permissions aren't set correctly; the page can be accessed only by certain people.	If you believe that file permissions are incorrect, email the page's owner.
Connection Reset By Peer	The remote host reset the connection.	Usually, clicking on Reload brings up the page properly.
Connection Timed Out	Network lag or problems.	Ping the Web server to see if it is available.
503 Service Unavailable	Network lag or problems.	Ping the Web server to see whether it is live.
System Call 'Connect' Failed: Connection Refused.	Unable to connect, usually because the server is down or not accepting connections.	Use Ping to see if the Web server is online.
Socket Is Not Connected	Usually a temporary connection problem.	Wait until later. If you keep getting the error on different sites, try reestablishing your Internet connection.
Clicking on Reload doesn't show the latest version of the page.	Navigator is reloading the page from cache.	Force a reload from the server by pressing Shift while clicking on Reload.

Watch Out!
Although the 404 Not Found message usually means that the URL no longer exists or you typed in the wrong address, it can also mean that your cache size is set too low. Change the cache size by selecting Edit, Preferences, expanding the Advanced category, and clicking Cache. Increase the disk and memory caches gradually, by 1000KB each time, until you no longer experience problems.

Building Better Bookmarks

Bookmarks are a great way to keep track of your favorite Web pages—for a while. Then, your bookmarks list grows too large, and it becomes too much of a pain to organize them and weed out old or dead links.

I'm sure that every Navigator user has run into this problem. However, bookmarks are too useful to abandon them altogether. This section helps you create bookmarks faster, manage your bookmarks list better, and discover alternatives to bookmarks that you might not be taking advantage of.

Creating Bookmarks

First, get to know where your bookmarks are. On Windows, the Bookmarks menu is located on the second toolbar to the left of the Location window, labeled—appropriately enough—Bookmarks (see Figure 3.7). On the Macintosh, the Bookmarks menu is on the menu bar, and it looks like a slanted blue line. Opening either of these menus shows all your bookmarks, plus all the bookmarks that Netscape put in there for you. Load any bookmark by selecting it from the list.

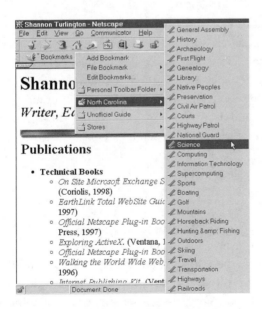

Figure 3.7
Navigator's Bookmarks menu (Windows).

Selecting Add Bookmark from the Bookmarks menu is the quickest way to add a bookmark to the open page (or press

Bright Idea
Hotlists are a wonderful timesaver—someone else has already done the work for you, collecting links related to a subject of interest. You can easily turn someone's hotlist into a folder in your Bookmarks menu. Select File, Save As to save the page with the hotlist; be sure to save it in HTML format, or this won't work. Then, press Ctrl+B or Cmd+B to open the Bookmarks window. Select File, Import, browse to the page you saved, and click Open. All the page's links appear as bookmarks in a new folder called Main Bookmarks (this won't overwrite existing bookmarks); you can then edit the new folder or bookmarks as you normally would. This is also a useful way to save search results for later exploration.

Ctrl+D or Cmd+D). The new bookmark appears at the bottom of your list.

But after you've created some folders and started organizing your bookmarks, it's a lot easier to put the bookmark in the appropriate folder when you create it, rather than creating the bookmark and moving it around later. There's an easy way to do this. Look to the left of the Location window for a small bookmark icon. You can click this icon and drag it to the Bookmarks menu; then, drag it down to File Bookmark and over to the folder or subfolder where you want to put the new bookmark. *Voilà*! our new bookmark is tucked away in just the right place.

Often, you come across links to pages you want to visit, but not now. To quickly create a bookmark to the linked page, drag the link from the Web page to the Bookmarks menu, drag it down to File Bookmark, and select the folder where you want to put it. You can also quickly create and file bookmarks to pages that you've already visited by dragging the page's listing from the History window to File Bookmark on the Bookmarks menu.

Managing Bookmarks

After you have built up a list of bookmarks, it's a good idea to organize them so you can easily find the bookmarks you need. Manage bookmarks from the Bookmarks window—select Edit Bookmarks from the Bookmarks menu or press Ctrl+B/Cmd+B to open it (see Figure 3.8). While in the Bookmarks window, you might want to get rid of those pre-configured bookmarks to keep them from cluttering up your list—just select the folder or bookmark you want to remove and press Del.

Creating New Items

To create a new folder, select New Folder from the pop-up menu, give the folder a name, and click OK. The new folder appears in the Bookmarks window underneath the highlighted bookmark, folder, or separator bar. (If an open folder is highlighted, the new folder appears inside the folder.) Add separator bars and bookmarks in the same way; select New Bookmark or New Separator from the pop-up menu.

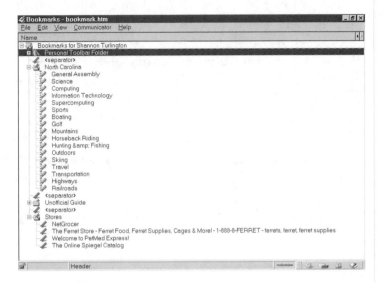

Figure 3.8

Organize your bookmarks in the Bookmarks window.

Timesaver

It's easy to lose track of all the passwords you're asked to remember, but you can use bookmarks to remember them for you. Create a bookmark for the site that requires the password. Then, select the bookmark in the Bookmarks window, choose Bookmark Properties from the pop-up menu, and enter the password in the Description field. Do this only if you're sure no one has access to your bookmarks; you might want to protect your computer with a screensaver password.

You can click-and-drag anything in the Bookmarks window to move it around, so you can change the order of folders, drag bookmarks inside folders, or divide groups of folders with separators. Change the name or description of any item by clicking on the item and selecting Bookmark Properties from the pop-up menu; this dialog box also lists when the bookmark was created and when the page was last visited.

Creating Aliases

You can file the same bookmark in several folders by creating aliases, so that any changes made to the original bookmark are also made to all of its aliases. Select the bookmark you want to copy and choose Make Alias from the pop-up menu. The alias appears in italic under the original, but you can file it wherever you like. The number of aliases a bookmark has is listed at the bottom of the Bookmark Properties dialog box. Click Select Aliases in this dialog box to highlight all of the aliases.

Sorting and Searching

The Bookmarks window, like the History window, has extensive sorting and searching features to make finding items easier. For instance, select View, By Location to sort bookmarks by URL, select View, By Created On to sort them by age, or select View, By Last Visited to sort them by when you last opened them. Choose View, Sort Ascending or View, Sort Descending to change the order of the sort. Note that you can't edit the contents of the Bookmarks window when bookmarks are sorted; you have to select View, By Name to return the bookmarks to their original order and enable editing again.

Bright Idea

Communicator's user profiles organize each user's bookmarks, preferences, email messages, and subscribed newsgroups, so that multiple users don't have to contend with others' bookmarks or email. You can even create multiple profiles for yourself—to make one version for work and one for playtime, for instance. To set up profiles, quit Communicator and select User Profile Manager from the Communicator\ Utilities program group. Click New and follow the instructions.

To search your bookmarks, choose Edit, Find in Bookmarks (press Ctrl+F or Cmd+F). You have a lot of search options. For instance, you can look for a keyword in the bookmark's name, location, or description. Select Edit, Find Again (Ctrl+G or Cmd+G) to look for a second occurrence of the keyword.

Updating Bookmarks

A useful shortcut for managing bookmarks is the update feature, which checks for changes to any of the bookmarked pages. Select View, Update Bookmarks (Windows) or View, What's New? (Macintosh). In the What's New? dialog box, choose whether to check all bookmarks or just the selected ones, and click Start Checking. If you have a large number of bookmarks, this can take a long time because Navigator must contact the Web server of each bookmark, so you might want to check only a chunk of your list at a time. Bookmarks that have changed since you last visited them are marked with a special icon. Bookmarks that couldn't be accessed are marked with a question mark. This helps you figure out the pages you need to revisit and the bookmarks you need to prune because the links have changed or gone defunct.

Other Kinds of Bookmarks

The personal toolbar (the bottom toolbar) is a highly useful but often neglected tool on the Windows version of Communicator. It enables one-click button access to the Web sites you visit most often. Quickly add a new button to the personal toolbar by dragging the bookmark icon, a hyperlink, or an item in the history window to the toolbar.

The items in the Personal Toolbar Folder, located in the Bookmarks menu, determine which buttons display on the personal toolbar. To edit the items in this folder, open the Bookmarks window, and add and delete items as with any other folder. (Just don't go crazy—the personal toolbar can show only a few buttons.) You can drag entire bookmark folders into this folder to create drop-down menu buttons of favorite sites. Or make button links to a favorite newsgroup by creating a new bookmark in the Personal Toolbar Folder with the URL of the newsgroup. If you want to turn any of your other bookmark folders into the Personal Toolbar Folder, just select the folder and choose Set as Toolbar Folder from the pop-up menu.

Internet Shortcuts are another timesaving feature that place bookmarks directly on your desktop. To create an Internet Shortcut, drag the bookmark icon, a hyperlink, an item in your history list, or an item in the Bookmarks window to the desktop. A shortcut icon appears with the name of the page. Just double-click the icon to start Navigator and load the page all in one step. This is a great way to create multiple start pages for Navigator.

Controlling the Cache

Navigator uses a hard disk and memory cache to speed up the display of Web pages that you've recently downloaded. Instead of redownloading the page from the remote server, Navigator just loads the page from the cache, so that it seems to display instantly. The memory cache clears each time you quit Navigator, while the disk cache is maintained from session to session. Although the cache is a useful tool, it can sometimes cause problems by consuming too many of your computer's resources.

The size of the cache should be based on how you use the Web. If you return to the same Web sites every time you go online, your cache should be fairly large; that way, the frequently visited Web sites are retained in the cache and display much faster. On the other hand, if you constantly venture into new areas of the Web, your cache doesn't do much more than take up disk space.

Moneysaver
The cache stores a lot of Web information on your hard drive, which you can access by using a cache browser. These add-ons re-create Web sites from the cache for super-fast offline browsing, saving you from overspending on your Internet connection. They also come in handy if you use a laptop and you're nowhere near your modem—you can still access pre-downloaded sites. I recommend the shareware product CacheX for Windows 95/98/ NT 4.0 and Navigator 2.x–4.6 (http://www.mwso.com/eng/nsce1.htm).

Set your cache's size based on your browsing habits:

1. Select Edit, Preferences.

2. Expand the Advanced category.

3. Select Cache (see Figure 3.9).

Figure 3.9
Adjust your cache settings to match available computer resources and how you browse the Web.

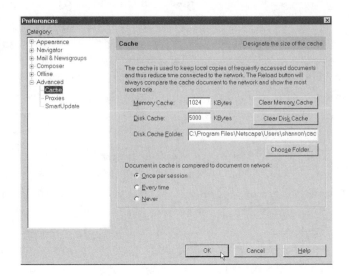

Watch Out!
There's no Memory Cache setting on the Macintosh version of Navigator. To change the amount of RAM that Navigator uses for the cache, do this instead: Quit Navigator and go to the Finder; select the Navigator icon; select File, Get Info; and modify the Preferred Size setting. This number represents the memory allocated to Navigator plus the memory cache, so don't set it lower than the recommended amount.

4. Set the Memory Cache and Disk Cache to 5000KB or more if you frequently visit the same sites; set them a bit lower if you surf to new pages more often, but no less than 1000KB–2000KB. You can also vary the settings depending on how much extra disk space and RAM you have.

5. Select Once per Session or Never under "Document in Cache Is Compared to Document on Network"; this cuts down on the number of times Navigator compares a cached page to the Web server to determine whether the page has been updated, speeding up Web browsing. (Never is the fastest option, but you can miss out on updated content for any cached Web page.)

6. Click OK.

Putting Up with Plug-Ins

Plug-ins are little programs that "plug in" to Navigator, enabling you to view unsupported file formats inside the browser window. Plug-ins open Navigator to audio, video, sophisticated animation, and three-dimensional virtual reality. Navigator pops up a dialog box to let you know whenever you need a plug-in to view an unsupported file embedded in a Web page; just click a link inside the dialog box to get the plug-in.

Several basic plug-ins come with Navigator, so you can access the most common file types (so long as you installed these plug-ins when you installed Navigator). To see the plug-ins that are installed, select About Plug-Ins from the Help menu. These preinstalled plug-ins handle Shockwave Flash animations, Video for Windows, QuickTime video, RealAudio, and RMF, AU, AIFF, WAV, and MIDI audio. After you have the plug-in, it automatically plays any supported files it encounters, so you don't have to think about it. (Although, you can find some plug-ins a bit annoying, such as when you open a page and are unexpectedly greeted by a synthesized version of "Stairway to Heaven.")

As with any nifty technology, everyone has to jump on the bandwagon. Some plug-ins are truly useful, widening Navigator's support for common multimedia formats, such as various video and audio formats. Others seem to have been produced merely to support the developer's proprietary file format, and serve little purpose except to take up space on your computer. This section will help you discern between the plug-ins that you'll actually use and the ones that sound cool but aren't worth the downloading time.

What's Worth Getting

Like any other program, plug-ins take up hard disk space and memory, so you want to be careful which ones you get. Almost 200 plug-ins are currently available for Navigator, and most of them aren't worth your time. (To get an idea of what's out there, visit `http://home.netscape.com/plugins/index.html`.)

A few plug-ins are immediately useful, though, as they support file formats commonly found on the Web and actually serve a purpose. These include the following freeware plug-ins:

- **Adobe Acrobat Reader:** This plug-in displays files in the Portable Document Format (PDF), and it's the most standardized way to view formatted documents on the Web. PDF files are everywhere, from IRS forms to software documentation to college applications, and you need the Adobe Acrobat Reader to see them all. Get it for all platforms at `http://www.adobe.com/prodindex/acrobat/readstep.html`.

Watch Out!
When you use SmartUpdate or set up a personalized start page via My Netscape, you encounter signed Java applets. These request a higher access level than most applets and require your permission to run. A Java Security window describes what the applet wants to do and how much risk it poses, and enables you to grant or deny access. For example, a high-risk rating indicates potentially severe damage to your system or data or a potentially major violation of privacy. You can generally trust signed applets from well-known sources, such as Netscape. But if this level of risk makes you uneasy, avoid SmartUpdate, My Netscape, and any other services that use signed applets.

- **TruDef:** This plug-in extends Navigator's graphics support to include such common file formats as Bitmap, PCX, and a dozen others. It also offers extensive image-manipulation features and is a great way to work with graphics inside the Navigator window. Get it for Windows 95/NT at `http://www.tmmgroup.com/trudef/docs/plugin.html`.

- **Crescendo:** MIDI is probably the most common audio format on the Web, used for background music and samples on all kinds of sites. So, you need a good MIDI plug-in, and Communicator's basic audio plug-in doesn't cut it. Crescendo offers increased speed, more control over playback, and streaming sound, and is therefore a better choice. It supports both Mac OS and Windows 95/98/NT and can be downloaded from `http://www.liveupdate.com/dl.html` or through SmartUpdate.

- **Koan Plug-In:** This plug-in plays the Koan music format and MP3 samples, as well as standard audio formats like WAV and MIDI. If you plan to listen to a lot of new music on the Web, you need this plug-in. The basic version is free for Mac OS (Power Macs only) and Windows 95/98/NT; get it at `http://www.sseyo.com/browser.html`.

- **Shockwave for Director:** Shockwave isn't as hot as it was when it first hit the Web, but enough people use Macromedia Director to design multimedia movies for the Web to make Shockwave a useful plug-in (although you can get along without it if you don't want to spare the RAM). Use it to watch cartoons, play games, and otherwise waste time; you'll even find directories of "Shocked" sites where you can use it. Download Shockwave for all platforms at `http://www.macromedia.com/shockwave/download/alternates/`.

- **ichat Rooms:** This plug-in offers a friendly, fun interface for chatting with others all over the Web. It's used as the basic chat tool at lots of Web sites, so it's an essential tool for anyone who likes to chat. Get it for Mac OS and Windows 3.x/95/98/NT at `http://www.ichat.com/plugin/download/rooms.html`.

Skip It

You won't want to download and install most of the available plug-ins for lots of reasons. Some plug-ins sound cool but are rarely used. Others are only useful to professionals in a narrow field. And because plug-ins are provided by third-party developers, some of them are unstable and cause browser problems or even crashes. I recommend not downloading a plug-in until you encounter a Web page that uses it, and only then if you really want to see what you're missing.

If you don't use a preinstalled plug-in, or if one you downloaded starts causing problems, you can easily get rid of it. First, check whether the plug-in came with an uninstall program (look in the Add/Remove Programs control panel on Windows). If not, delete the plug-in manually. Open the About Plug-Ins page (select Help, About Plug-Ins), and note the plug-in's pathname, listed right under the name of the plug-in. Generally, the plug-in file is located inside the plugins directory, found inside the Netscape Communicator folder on Macintosh and inside Netscape\Communicator\Program on Windows. Just delete the plug-in's file from this directory to get rid of it.

Sometimes two or more plug-ins support the same file format. Navigator recognizes only the plug-in that you installed last, which might not be the one you want to use. Check the About Plug-Ins page to see the file format that each installed plug-in supports and whether the plug-in is enabled for that

Moneysaver
When downloading plug-ins or any other kind of program with Navigator, nothing's more frustrating than having to disconnect right in the middle. Because downloading takes so long, stopping and restarting not only wastes your time, but also your money in the form of Internet access fees. To avoid this, Navigator enables you to cut off a download and resume it later from where you left off—just click Cancel. Then, return to the same link to resume downloading. (This won't work if your modem disconnects on its own, however.)

format. You can temporarily disable any plug-in so that another plug-in is used in its place; quit Navigator, open the plugins directory, and rename the plug-in file (I usually just put an X in front of the plug-in's filename). This is also a good way to temporarily turn off video, audio, VRML, or whatever file the plug-in plays—to keep audio files from playing unexpectedly while you're surreptitiously surfing during work hours, for instance.

The following are some plug-ins that you might have heard about or might be tempted to get but really aren't worth your time:

Inside Scoop
Here's some more unofficial URLs (these are actually useful): `about:global` opens a global history list; `about:plugins` displays a list of installed plug-ins; `about:license` shows the Communicator license agreement; `about:cache` lists the contents of the disk cache; `about:memory-cache` lists the contents of the memory cache; and `about:image-cache` lists all cached image files. (Note: It takes a while to list the cache contents.)

- **Any VRML or virtual world plug-in:** Most VRML files aren't worth the time and trouble it takes to download and view them, and VRML plug-ins are pretty unstable. You can get along without them.

- **CyberCashWallet** (`http://www.cybercash.com/cybercash/wallet/`): The CyberCash Wallet is touted as an essential tool for shopping online, but it isn't; CyberCash has to be supported by the Web store before you can use it, which really limits your choices. Besides, credit card shopping on the Web is no more dangerous than over the telephone and a lot more convenient than CyberCash.

- **NCompass ScriptActive** (`http://www.ncompasslabs.com/`): This plug-in was designed to run ActiveX inside Navigator, but it costs a lot and is pretty unstable. If you want ActiveX, just get Internet Explorer.

Just the Facts

- Decide which Communicator components you need first, so you can download and install as little as possible—you can always upgrade later if you need to.

- Taking advantage of Navigator's well-hidden surfing features makes you a more efficient and faster Web surfer.

- Bookmarks are one of Navigator's most powerful features; use them to their utmost by making the most of Navigator's bookmark creation and management tools, as well as bookmark alternatives.

- You can keep Navigator from taking over your hard disk and available memory by tweaking the cache settings to match your browsing habits.

- Plug-ins are powerful add-ons that extend Navigator's support for different file formats, but you'll keep them in control by downloading the plug-ins only when you need them.

GET THE SCOOP ON...
Adding more components to Internet Explorer ▪ Using
little-known features to improve Web surfing ▪ Finding
better ways to keep track of favorites ▪ Keeping
Internet Explorer from overwhelming the hard drive
▪ Taking advantage of offline browsing

Getting More Out of Internet Explorer

Chapter 4

L IKE NETSCAPE NAVIGATOR, Microsoft Internet Explorer is
a big, complex program. It's easy enough to learn, but
not so simple to master. If you haven't explored beyond
the main toolbars or tweaked the default settings, then you're
missing out on hidden timesavers and customization functions
that can greatly improve your Web-browsing experience. This
chapter shows you ways to improve Internet Explorer to make
you a more efficient surfer, help you take advantage of organizational and personalization features, and save time, money,
and system resources.

Adding More Components

With the release of version 5.0, the Internet Explorer download has been streamlined to include just the Web browser and its companion email program and newsreader, Outlook Express. All of the Internet tools that were installed automatically with Internet Explorer 4.0 are still available, but now you have more control over which tools to install and which ones to skip.

You can install any of the following Internet Explorer components, in addition to the ones installed with the 5.0 download:

- **Microsoft Virtual Machine:** Plays Java applets inside the browser

- **Macromedia Shockwave:** Plays Shockwave for Director multimedia files inside the browser

- **Macromedia Flash Player:** Plays Flash animations inside the browser

- **NetMeeting:** Voice-conferencing and video-conferencing tool

- **Chat:** Easy-to-use Internet Relay Chat (IRC) client

- **Wallet:** Secure shopping tool

- **FrontPage Express:** Web page authoring program

- **Web Publishing Wizard:** Enables you to more easily publish Web pages to a Web server

- **Additional Web Fonts:** Supplmental fonts optimized for Web pages

Getting additional Internet Explorer components is easy, once you've installed Internet Explorer 5.0:

1. Open Settings, Control Panel on the Start menu.

2. Double-click Add/Remove Programs.

3. Scroll down until you see Microsoft Internet Explorer 5 and Internet Tools, and select it.

4. Click Add/Remove.

5. Select Add a Component, and click OK.

6. The Windows Update dialog box opens (see Figure 4.1).

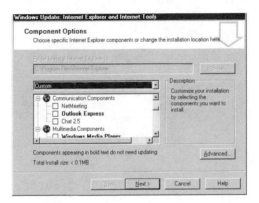

Figure 4.1
Installing additional
Internet Explorer
components.

7. Select the check boxes beside every component you want to install, and click Next.

8. When installation is complete, click Finish and restart your computer.

Becoming a Better Surfer

Internet Explorer is a very full-featured tool, but most users don't take advantage of this. Why? Because you have to dig beyond the toolbars to get to these features. After you learn a few shortcuts, I guarantee that you'll become a more efficient Web surfer by making the most of Internet Explorer's timesaving and customization features. Here are some things that you can do:

- Maximize the Web page display area.

- Set Internet Options to create a personalized, speedy browser.

- Use the history list to get around.

- Find shortcuts for searching the Web.

- Solve problems when you encounter them.

Maximizing Screen Real Estate

Internet Explorer gives you many options for arranging your toolbars, so that the tools you use most frequently are readily available, while the ones that you never use don't take up space on the interface. By judicious arrangement of your toolbars, you can increase the screen "real estate," or amount of space dedicated to displaying Web pages. Try any of the following methods to increase the Web page display (see Figure 4.2).

Figure 4.2
Turning off text labels, rearranging toolbars, removing bars you don't need, and decreasing font size are all easy ways to maximize screen real estate.

Timesaver
You can easily get around a Web page using just the keyboard. Press Tab to jump from link to link (Shift+Tab goes backward). After highlighting a link, press Enter to follow it. This trick also cycles through the links embedded in an image map, making finding hidden links easier. Viewing a page with frames? Press Ctrl+Tab to bounce through each frame or press Ctrl+Shift+Tab to go backward.

- Turn off toolbars you don't use by selecting View, Toolbars and removing the check mark beside Standard Buttons, Address Bar, or Links; you won't have easy access to frequently used tools or personalized buttons, however.

- Reduce the size of the standard toolbar buttons by selecting View, Toolbars, Customize and selecting No Text Labels from the Text Options menu.

- Decrease button sizes even more by selecting View, Toolbars, Customize and selecting Small Icons from the Icon Options menu.

- Put two or more toolbars on the same line or move toolbars up beside the menu bar; rearrange the toolbars by clicking and dragging the gray handle on the left side.

- Temporarily slide a toolbar out of the way when you don't need it by double-clicking on its handle (very helpful if you put two or more toolbars on the same bar).

- Remove the bottom status bar by deselecting Status Bar under the View menu (you are no longer be able to monitor the progress of Web page downloads, however).

- Only open the Explorer Bar when needed.

- Select View, Fullscreen (or press F11) to make the Web page fill your screen and minimize the Internet Explorer interface. Right-click the minimized toolbar and select AutoHide to get it out of the way. To return to a normal view, click Restore in the upper-right corner.

- Decrease the size of Web page text by selecting View, Text Size, and then Smaller or Smallest.

Setting Internet Options

Using the Internet Options dialog box (select Tools, Internet Options), you can tweak settings to speed up the display of Web pages or personalize the browser for how you use it. Let's take a look at some of the more useful settings.

First, set up a start page for Internet Explorer. The default page is http://www.msn.com/, the Microsoft Network portal page, which is heavily trafficked and slow to load, slowing you down when you start Internet Explorer. A speedier option is a start page on the local disk or a blank page. That way, Internet Explorer doesn't have to connect to a remote Web server when you start it.

I suggest a simple HTML file containing links to favorite or frequently visited sites. Or save a useful Web page as a local file in HTML format (select File, Save As or press Ctrl+S). To set a new home page, open Tools, Internet Options and look at the top part of the General tab (see Figure 4.3). You can type the Web address of a new home page in the Address box. If you want to use a HTML file on your hard disk as your start page, which will load more quickly than a page out on the Web, simply drag the file into the Internet Explorer window to open it inside the browser, and then click the Use Current button. If you don't want a start page at all, click Use Blank; this option loads quickest of all. Return to the default setting of http://www.msn.com/ by clicking Use Default.

Bright Idea
Gain control over the way Web pages look by clicking the Accessibility button in the General tab of Internet Options (under the Tools menu). You can tell IE to ignore colors, font styles, and font sizes specified by the Web page's author in favor of your easier-to-read choices (set with the Colors and Fonts buttons). You can also use your own HTML style sheet to display the Web pages you open.

Figure 4.3
Set up a local HTML
file as your start
page for fastest
starting.

Watch Out!
In January 1997,
the Chaos
Computer Club in
Hamburg
announced that
they had created
an ActiveX control
that could modify a
user's Quicken file.
Although to date
no ActiveX viruses
have been encoun-
tered "in the wild,"
I mention this to
illustrate the poten-
tial danger of
ActiveX. Because
ActiveX controls
are programs that
download via IE
and run on your
computer, they can
possibly damage
the hard disk,
access data, and
otherwise do harm
to your computer.
Use IE's built-in
security measures
to filter out con-
trols from unknown
sources. Select the
Security tab in
Internet Options
and choose the
High security level
for the Internet
Zone. As you get to
know different
sites, you can cre-
ate security zones
with lower settings
for trusted sites.

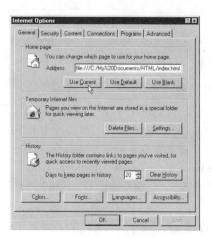

The Advanced tab is most useful for controlling Internet Explorer. You might want to set up the browser to display Web pages more quickly, for instance. Make these changes on the Advanced tab:

- In the Multimedia area, clear one or more of the following check boxes: Show Pictures, Play Animations, Play Videos, or Play Sounds. Doing this, you might miss out on important Web page content, so only turn off elements that you won't miss. (If you turn off pictures, be sure to select the Show Image Download Placeholders check box. You can still load individual graphics by right-clicking on the picture icon and choosing Show Picture or load all graphics by selecting View, Refresh.)

- In the Java VM area, clear the Java JIT Compiler Enabled check box. This turns off Java, so you won't have access to potentially useful applets, but you won't have to wait around for Java to start, either.

Another important tab for personalization is the Programs tab. This is where you can set the Internet programs that are used in conjunction with Internet Explorer. After you set up your email client, newsreader, calendar, and address book to work with Internet Explorer, you can open these programs by selecting them from the Tools, Mail and News menu, clicking on the Mail toolbar button, and following mailto and news links. For instance, if you find a Web page that you want to tell your best friend about, you can click the Mail button and select Send Page to open your email client and compose a message to your friend, even if you don't use Outlook Express for email.

Follow these steps to configure Internet programs:

1. Select Tools, Internet Options.

2. Click the Programs tab (see Figure 4.4).

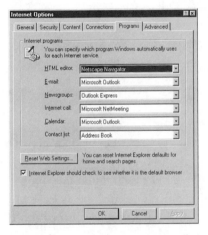

3. In each menu, select the tool that you want to use for that function.

4. If you use more than one Web browser (or think you might), leave the Internet Explorer Should Check... check box selected; only clear this box if IE is definitely your browser of choice.

5. Click OK.

Using History to Get Around

The Explorer Bar provides quick access to some important Internet Explorer tools, including the history list, a search application, and your favorites list. The latter two are covered later in this chapter. For now, let's concentrate on an

Figure 4.4
Set up default Internet tools to use with Internet Explorer on the Programs tab of Internet Options.

Inside Scoop
To really personalize your browser, this trick changes the text on the title bar to whatever you want. Quit IE, run regedit, and go to HKEY_LOCAL_MACHINE\ SOFWARE\ Microsoft\ InternetExplorer\ Main. Select Edit, New, String Value and call it Window Title. Double-click the new entry and insert your pesonal text (I called mine "Shannon's IE"). Then, close the Registry Editor and restart IE to see the new title.

overlooked navigational tool—the history list. Click the History toolbar button to open the History pane of the Explorer Bar (see Figure 4.5).

Figure 4.5
Easily locate pages that you've recently visited using the history list.

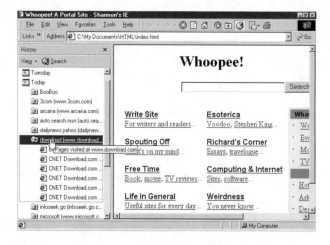

Timesaver
Need a faster way to get around? Click the arrows next to the Back and Forward buttons to drop down a list of pages that you can travel back and forward to. This keeps you from having to click several times on the Back button to get anywhere.

The history list's groupings help you find a page based on when you last visited it and where it's located. The top groups are chronological, showing pages that you visited today and in the past few days. Under each timeframe, individual pages are grouped by domain name, making it easier to find related pages, such as all the pages that you opened on Microsoft's Web site. Click a folder to show all the pages in that domain that you've visited. To return to a particular page, just click it.

Use the View menu to reorder the history list in different ways to help you find specific pages. For instance, select View, By Site to see all the domains that you've visited. Or select View, By Most Visited to find the pages that you open the most, a handy way of locating favorite sites. Finally, you can perform a simple search on your history list by clicking the Search button. Deselect the History button to get rid of the history list when you're finished with it.

By default, the history list retains the last 20 days' worth of Web page information. You can change this to suit your needs. If you rely on the history list, increase the number of days to create a more complete list. But if you're short on disk space, reduce the number of days. Follow these steps:

1. Select Tools, Internet Options.

2. In the History area of the General tab, change the number of days to keep pages in history.

3. Click Clear History to erase your history list and start over—a useful feature if you're starting a new project or if the history list has gotten too unwieldy. Also clear the history list if you experience any problems with history.

4. Click OK.

Internet Explorer also uses the history list to make it quicker to type URLs. When you start entering a URL into the Address window, Internet Explorer tries to find a match from a list of recently visited pages (click the arrow to the right of the Address box to see this list). If the URL that Internet Explorer supplies is correct, press Enter and you're on your way. If not, keep typing to find another match, or press the Up Arrow and Down Arrow keys to cycle through a list of possible matches. You can also press Ctrl+Left Arrow or Ctrl+Right Arrow to jump through the parts of the address, so you can easily edit any part.

Searching the Web

Searching the Web is an often daunting but necessary job. Internet Explorer tries to make this task easier by giving you several ways to search using browser tools.

For quick searches, type a keyword into the Address window instead of a URL. When Internet Explorer guesses that you're trying to search, it opens a window underneath the Address box that says, "search for keyword." Press Enter, and Internet Explorer searches the Microsoft Network database for your keyword. What happens next depends on how you set up the search options:

1. Select Tools, Internet Options.

2. Click the Advanced tab.

3. Scroll down until you see Search from the Address bar, and select one of the following options:

Timesaver
Tired of entering the entire URL in the Address window? You don't have to—just type in the domain name and IE guesses the rest, trying .COM first, and then .EDU and .ORG. (Press Ctrl+Enter to automatically wrap www. and .com around the domain name.) And you can omit the http:// part every time.

Timesaver
After you enter a search keyword in the Address window, Internet Explorer saves it. You can quickly search on the same keyword at a later time by selecting it from the Address window's drop-down menu. Or start typing the keyword, and Internet Explorer automatically completes it for you.

- **Just display the results in the main window:** Opens a list of search results
- **Just go to the most likely site:** Opens the Web site that best matches your search keyword
- **Do not search from the Address bar:** Turns off the quick search feature

4. Click OK.

If your search is more complex or you require more options, click the Search toolbar button to open the Search pane of the Explorer Bar (see Figure 4.6). To search the Web, select Find a Web Page, type the keywords into the box, and click Search. The search results appear in the Explorer Bar, but any links you click open in the main window. After you finish looking over a related page, you can return to the search results list without any back-browsing, which really saves a lot of time. If you turn off the Search pane (deselect the Search button) to get a better look at the found page, and then open the Search pane again, it returns to your last results list, saving you from repeating the search. To start a new search, just click New.

Figure 4.6
The Search pane enables you to search the Web more efficiently by showing the search engine and found Web pages in the same window.

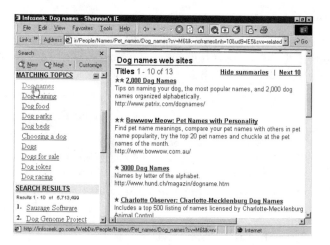

In addition to the Web page search—which you'll probably perform most often—you can run many other kinds of searches from the Search Explorer Bar. Just select the appropriate button to search for a person's address in a white pages directory, search for a business in a yellow pages directory, or find a map to an address. For more options, click More. Then, you can look up a word in an encyclopedia, dictionary, or thesaurus; find a picture related to your keywords; or search Usenet newsgroups. To change the sources for any of these searches, click the Customize button at the top of the Web page. Taking advantage of all these handy features can really save time when you're researching a topic on the Internet.

The Search pane does have some limitations. The Explorer Bar is too narrow to include search result descriptions, for one, so you have to browse results based on their often-cryptic titles. Also, the Search pane uses an application hosted on Microsoft's Web server, so you might not be able to access it due to network problems or too much traffic. In that case, or if you aren't finding what you were looking for, click the Next menu at the top of the Search pane and select an alternative search engine from the drop-down menu.

You have one more searching option. If you find a useful Web page and you'd like to see similar pages, select Tools, Show Related Links. The Search pane opens, displaying a list of Web pages like the one you're currently viewing.

Solving Problems

When you encounter an error message, the first thing to check is that your Internet connection is up and working properly. Try connecting to a site that you know exists, for instance. If your connection is working, follow the suggestions in Table 4.1 to solve the problem. If all else fails or if you get an unusual error message, quit and restart Internet Explorer, or wait and try again later.

Timesaver
Every time you perform a search in Internet Explorer's Search pane, the search is saved. You only have to select Previous Searches to open a list of the last 10 searches you've run—a great timesaver if you frequently search for the same keywords.

TABLE 4.1: INTERNET EXPLORER ERROR MESSAGES

Error Message	What It Means	What to Try
Out of Memory (when launching IE)	Virtual memory could be disabled.	Enable Virtual Memory in the System control panel/Performance tab.
Not Found	The Web page doesn't exist.	Retype the URL—you might have made an error. Email the Web page's owner for the correct URL or search for the page's new address in any search engine.
A Connection with the Server Could Not Be Established	The server doesn't exist or is down; your Internet connection is not working.	Check the connection first; if it's down, log on and try again. Double-check the server's domain name. Ping the server to see if it's live or if it exists.
Cannot Open...	You don't have permission to open the URL.	Email the Web page's author and request access.

Moneysaver
TweakIE is an essential program that optimizes IE's settings to improve performance and otherwise help IE better interact with your system, avoiding potentially costly problems. TweakIE includes a tool for cleaning the cache, history, and cookies, circumventing a bug that consumes way too many system resources. It also has a few other useful IE add-ons. At $15, TweakIE is a real bargain. Get it for Windows 95/98 at http://www.wizsys.com/tweakie.htm.

Taking Care of Favorites

The Favorites menu stores and organizes your most frequently accessed Web pages. You can also access your favorites by clicking the Favorites button to open the Favorites pane of the Explorer Bar, which is useful if you like to keep your favorites handy while you browse (see Figure 4.7). It's very easy to make a page a favorite—just select Favorites, Add to Favorites (or press Ctrl+D).

After using Internet Explorer for a while and adding favorites left and right, your favorites list can grow entirely too large and disorganized to be of much use to you. This section teaches you better ways to manage your favorites and introduces you to other kinds of shortcuts to frequently accessed Web pages that you might not be taking advantage of.

Managing Favorites

The quick way to organize favorites is to open the Favorites pane on the Explorer Bar. Then, you can drag-and-drop favorites and folders to rearrange them. To create a new favorite for the open page, drag that little "e" icon (to the left of the URL in the Address window) to the Favorites pane and drop it in the folder where you want to file it. Select a folder or favorite and choose Delete from the right-click menu to get rid of it, or select Rename to give it a more meaningful title.

For greater management capabilities, click the Organize button. In the Organize Favorites dialog box, you can move, rename, and delete favorites with the click of a button, create new folders for storing related favorites, and even create folders within folders to organize long lists.

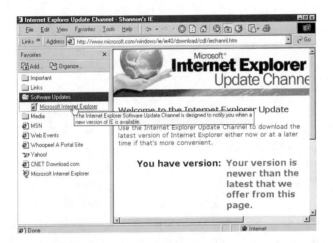

Figure 4.7
The Favorites pane of the Explorer Bar provides easy access to your favorites.

The Favorites folder is just another folder in your Windows directory. (The folder is located in each individual profile directory on Windows NT.) So, you can browse to the folder, open it, and organize its contents as you would in any other folder. Move favorites around, delete items, and create folders and subfolders without even starting Internet Explorer. Or press Shift and select Favorites, Organize Favorites to open the folder while using IE. You can also move shortcuts to other documents and programs on your hard drive into the Favorites folder to make them accessible from within Internet Explorer.

Try to keep up with creating new folders and moving favorites into them as you add the favorites. To file a favorite when you create it, select Create In and choose the folder where you want to put the favorite in the Add Favorites dialog box, or just drag the URL into the correct folder in the

Timesaver
Here's a quick way to get around your Windows hard drive from within IE—type the drive letter and path-name in the Address window to open a directory. You can even quickly open some programs by entering their names in the Address window, such as `Microsoft Word`, or type some folders' names to open them directly, such as `Dial-Up Networking`.

Favorites pane of the Explorer Bar. If you organize as you go, your favorites list won't get out-of-hand. With a little effort and planning, you can keep your favorites list short enough to remain within the confines of the Explorer Bar.

Favorite Shortcuts

The Links toolbar contains button shortcuts to pages that Microsoft thinks are important, but you can easily remove these and create your own buttons to Web pages, folders on the hard drive, Favorites folders, and even programs. To remove a button from the Links toolbar, right-click it and select Delete. Or you can open the Favorites pane of the Explorer Bar, and delete the favorites stored in the Links folder. Now the Links toolbar is ready to become your personal toolbar.

To put a Web page link on the Links toolbar, open the page in Internet Explorer. Notice the little "e" icon that appears to the left of the page's URL in the Address window; just drag that icon to the Links toolbar. Or in the Favorites pane of the Explorer Bar, drag items into the Links folder to make them into buttons; even drag entire favorites folders to create drop-down menus on the Links toolbar. You can't remove the Links folder from your favorites, but you can hide it—right-click it, select Properties, and click the Hidden check box. Use this same technique to hide any Favorites folder that you don't want to remove altogether.

In fact, all hyperlinks in Internet Explorer are eminently draggable. For instance, drag hyperlinks in the open Web page or items in the history list to the Links toolbar to quickly make buttons. Drag a favorite, hyperlink, or the icon in the Address window to an email message or Office document to insert the item's URL. Or drag an item to the desktop to make a short-cut that you can double-click to start Internet Explorer with that page loaded; this is particularly useful if you want to cre-ate multiple start pages for Internet Explorer.

On Windows, dragging works the other way, too. For example, drag a shortcut onto the Links toolbar or into the

Bright Idea
You don't have to live with the default icons on the Favorites pane and Links toolbar. To change any item's icon, right-click it and select Properties. On the Web Document tab, click Change Icon, and select a new icon from the ones shown or from anywhere on your system. (Try Windows\System\shell32.dll or Windows\Moricons.dll to find a bunch of icons.)

Favorites menu to make the shortcut accessible from inside Internet Explorer. Put a button link to your word processor on your Links bar, for instance, or add shortcuts to Office documents and hard drive folders to your favorites list. When adding local drive elements to the favorites list or Links bar, make sure that you create a shortcut to the element first and move that; otherwise, you'll move the actual item from its original location on the hard drive to inside the Favorites folder, which might be confusing when you try to access the item from Windows Explorer.

Controlling the Cache

Internet Explorer maintains a cache for faster browsing. Temporary copies of each page that you open are stored in the cache. This enables Internet Explorer to quickly pull up a page from the cache when you reopen it, rather than taking the time to download it again over the Internet. Web pages that are stored in the cache are called Temporary Internet Files.

The cache can eat up a lot of hard disk space, so you should maintain it regularly and set it up to match your Web-browsing habits. If you load the same Web sites every time you start Internet Explorer, a larger cache (10MB or more) serves you better, because the browser is able to retain more of these frequently accessed sites and display them faster. If you're the explorer type, frequently moving out to new areas of the Web, a large cache only consumes hard disk space, so set it to between 2MB and 5MB.

To change the cache size, follow these steps:

1. Select Tools, Internet Options.

2. Under Temporary Internet Files on the General tab, click Settings (see Figure 4.8).

3. Click and slide the bar under Amount of Disk Space to Use to designate how much of the hard disk is set aside for the cache; select a reasonable amount based on how much space is free and your Web-browsing habits.

Bright Idea
IE has some powerful printing options. To find them, select File, Print or press Ctrl+P (clicking on the Print toolbar button bypasses these options). If printing frames, you can choose whether to print the entire page as laid out on the screen, print the selected frame, or print all frames individually. For all pages, select whether to print every linked-in page to create a comprehensive reference document or to print a table of the links. Select File, Page Setup before printing to set other options, such as headers and footers.

Figure 4.8
Control the cache
size to conserve
hard disk space or
improve Web-surfing
performance.

Watch Out!
Mysterious browser
crashes could
mean that your
Temporary Internet
Files have become
corrupted. (This
problem is also
indicated if you
clear the cache
and history, but
URLs are still auto-
matically com-
pleted in the
Address window.)
To fix the problem,
restart your com-
puter in DOS
mode, and delete
the Windows\
tempor~1 folder.
When you restart
Windows, IE cre-
ates a new, clean
cache folder.

4. If a spare drive is available and you want to have a larger cache, click Move Folder and select a location on the second drive.

5. Under Check for Newer Versions of Stored Pages, select Every Time You Start Internet Explorer; this improves performance by having the browser check for updates to cached pages once per session, rather than every time you open the page. For even faster browsing, select Never, but you might miss out on updated content.

6. Click OK.

7. Click Delete Files under Temporary Internet Files to clear the cache; this is a good troubleshooting measure, especially when experiencing performance problems.

8. Click OK.

Browse the cache by clicking View Files in the Settings dialog box. This is a useful shortcut if you want to load a cached file, but listing all the files can take a long time, particularly if your cache is very large. Clicking on View Objects lists all the ActiveX controls that Internet Explorer has downloaded to your drive. Right-click a control to update the mini-program or delete a control you don't use, freeing up even more hard disk space.

Browsing the Web Offline

You can bring the Web to you through Internet Explorer's offline-browsing feature. This enables you to pre-download subscribed Web content and then disconnect to look at it. If you already know what sites you want to see, offline browsing is a very fast way to browse the Web. And if you pay for Internet access by the hour or have only a limited number of hours per month, offline browsing can save you a significant amount of money. Finally, offline browsing is convenient for when you don't want to tie up a phone line or if you use a laptop and don't have access to your Internet connection.

First, you must select the sites that you want to browse offline. You must add these sites to your favorites list (or as desktop shortcuts). I suggest creating a new Favorites folder called "offline" and putting the sites there. Follow these steps to subscribe to and download a site:

1. When you create the favorite, select the Make Available Offline check box. If you've already created the favorite, right-click it in your favorites list and select Make Available Offline.

2. Click Customize, and click Next to move past the introductory screen.

3. Select whether to download only the page or to get an entire site by downloading the page and all pages linked to it; if it's a big site, the last option might consume too much hard disk space, but you can limit the number of linked pages to download (see Figure 4.9).

4. Click Next.

5. Select when you want to update, or synchronize, the Web page. If you plan to disconnect manually each time you view the page offline, select Only When I Choose Synchronize from the Tools Menu. If you plan to regularly access the page offline, select I Would Like to Create a New Schedule.

6. Click Next.

Bright Idea
Is Internet Explorer's cache slowing performance and consuming system resources? Two freeware tools can help. CacheSentry takes the cache over from IE, increasing your computer's performance and fixing a serious bug. CacheMonitor tracks all changes to the cache, noting when IE improperly removes files, so you know when you're having a problem. Both tools work with IE 3.x or later on Windows 95/98/NT. Get them at http://www.mindspring.com/~dpoch/enigmatic/.

Figure 4.9
Setting up a Web
site for offline
viewing.

Bright Idea
Microsoft's Web
Accessories are a
set of unsup-
ported utilities
that add a lot
more functionality
to Internet
Explorer. You can
install additional
Explorer Bars,
such as a *New
York Times*
Explorer Bar and a
Bloomberg
Explorer Bar. Or
get new IE wallpa-
per and various
useful utilities,
including an
Offline toolbar but-
ton. Get all the
Web Accessories
from http://
www.microsoft.
com/Windows/IE/
WebAccess/
default.asp.

7. If you chose to create a new schedule, choose how often you want to update the page and when to perform the update. You probably want to download pages while you sleep or when you know you're not going to be using the computer, so you don't have to deal with the performance lag. You should also decide whether the computer should connect to the Internet to perform the update, if neces-sary.

8. Click Next.

9. Set up a username and password if the Web site requires it.

10. Click Finish.

11. Click OK.

If you want to update all your subscriptions manually—just before you go offline, for instance—select Tools, Synchronize. After all offline Web sites have downloaded, choose File, Work Offline to disconnect and browse offline Web sites from the hard drive. Now you see the point of that Offline Favorites folder—you can easily select pre-downloaded sites from it. You can also view cached pages while offline; use the Internet Options dialog box to view the files in the cache and find out what's available. When you're ready to get back on the Web, select File, Work Offline again.

Just the Facts

- Decide which Internet Explorer components you need before installation to get the leanest Web browser and conserve system resources.

- Improve your Web surfing by tweaking Internet Explorer settings to maximize the Web page display and increase browsing speed, using the history list to navigate, and taking advantage of built-in searching features.

- By organizing favorites as you create them, adding your own buttons to the Links toolbar, and taking advantage of desktop shortcuts, you can personalize Internet Explorer to more easily get to your favorite places.

- Take control of the cache to reduce Internet Explorer's dominance of the hard drive and tailor IE to your browsing habits.

- You can easily turn Internet Explorer into an offline browser by scheduling automatic updates of favorite Web pages and then browsing them after disconnecting from the Internet, saving Internet access charges.

Moneysaver
Here are some more free and almost-free tools that really beef up Internet Explorer (get them from any major software download site):

- Adobe Acrobat Reader enables you to view PDF-format documents online.
- Cache and Cookie Washer automatically cleans up the cache, history list, and cookies.
- ichat Rooms is a popular chatting tool.

Into the Net

PART II

GET THE SCOOP ON...
Managing multiple email accounts ▪ Becoming a more
efficient emailer ▪ Organizing your mailbox and Address
Book ▪ Finding free stuff that you can get only through
email ▪ Getting the most out of (and getting off)
mailing lists

Email Magic

E MAIL IS PROBABLY THE NUMBER-ONE REASON why people get
online. It's certainly one of the most timesaving and
productive uses of the Internet. You can quickly contact
colleagues, stay in touch with friends and family, get news delivered to your computer, transfer files, and ask questions of
experts—all at a minimal cost and effort. Many of us can't
imagine a day without it.

Because we all rely on email so much, it makes sense that
we should improve our email skills to waste less time, become
more organized, and generally make better use out of our
inboxes. This chapter shows you some techniques for doing
just that. (If you're concerned about spam and email security,
turn to Chapter 6, "Secure and Spam-Free.")

Using Multiple Email Accounts
Although it might seem like too much confusion and work,
maintaining more than one email account holds many advantages. Multiple email accounts are a great way to keep different
kinds of email messages separate, so you can prioritize and
manage all your email more effectively. You can maintain different email addresses for work-related and for personal mail,
for instance. If you manage a Web site or send out a newsletter,
a separate email address can collect email related to those
endeavors.

Multiple email addresses also help out your correspondents. For instance, personal contacts can more easily remember a friendly, casual email address, but a professional email address is better suited for work-related matters. If you run a Web site about your favorite hobby, such as sailing, then a "sailing@domain.com" address is definitely an asset.

With a little planning beforehand and the right email client, it can be just as simple to manage multiple accounts as it is to manage one. In this section, you learn where you can get additional, free email accounts and how to keep track of them after you've got them.

Getting Additional Accounts

Watch Out!
A small number of free email users hide behind false identities to send spam. This has resulted in some ISPs automatically blocking all mail coming from a free email address service, which can mean that some messages you send via a free email address won't ever get to their intended recipients.

You might already have more than one email account. For example, you might have an account at work and one associated with your dial-up account at home. If you want more accounts, talk to your ISP first; you might be able to get a second or third email address added to your Internet access account at little or no charge.

If all else fails, you can always obtain a free email account. Browse the Web for a while, and it'll seem like every other Web site offers free email services. But you should be careful to select a service that fits your needs for an additional email account.

Free email accounts have a lot of advantages. Use them to protect your identity, such as when joining an online support group. Keep your free email address a secret—handing it out only to close friends and family members—to filter out the spam and other junk mail that can accumulate in the inbox of a public address. Use it when signing up for mailing lists to separate nonurgent mass mailings from your personal mail. Or employ it as a "disposable" email address in situations that could generate a lot of unwanted mail, such as posting to Usenet and filling out Web site forms.

As we all know, nothing is really free. All the free email providers support themselves via advertising delivered to your inbox, attached to your email messages, or displayed on the Web site where you read your mail. So, be prepared to endure more ads than you might be used to when reading email.

There are three types of free email services:

- POP mail

- Web-based mail

- Forwarding services

Free POP Mail

POP mail services are the closest match to the type of email account provided by an ISP or company account. As with your regular accounts, you connect to a mail server and download all your messages to your computer.

POP mail accounts have several advantages over the other free email services. You can access the account with your regular email program, so you can manage it along with all your other email. You can also download messages and disconnect to read them offline at your leisure. Because the messages are stored on your computer, you can save what you want and organize your messages however you like. The disadvantage is that you're likely to receive a lot of ads in your inbox, because that's the only way the email service can support itself.

I recommend POP mail as the most flexible and useful kind of free email. The following are the best of the POP mail providers:

- **AmExMail:** http://www.amexmail.com/

- **Crosswinds:** http://home.crosswinds.net/

- **NetTaxi:** http://www.nettaxi.com/

Moneysaver
Juno (http://
www.juno.com/
whatis_basic.html)
offers U.S. residents a free email account that doesn't even require an Internet access account to work. Just install the software and use your modem to dial into the nearest access point. If you live in a large city, you might not even have to pay long-distance charges, so you could get email without paying anything at all!

Watch Out!
A free email address is an easy way to keep your identity a secret—just create an address that's unrelated to your real name. If you intend to use free email in this way, be certain that the service doesn't automatically add your real name to every message you send. Test this by sending a message to yourself. Also be aware that you can't hide behind a free email address to send spam, run a scam, or buy and sell illegal goods—the courts and the email account provider strip your anonymity away if necessary.

Free Web-Based Mail

You access a Web-based email account via the Web—just log in to the Web site you signed up with and read your email inside your browser window. This is the most common kind of free email, because it's easy to implement and guarantees site traffic. It's also the easiest to access, especially if you travel a lot, because you can read your email with any browser. Also, some providers let you choose from a wide selection of domain names to create a more personalized email address.

You won't be able to manage the email you receive via a Web-based account in the same program as your other accounts, a serious disadvantage. (Some Web-based email services offer additional features that you're used to in your email client, such as spelling checkers, Address Books, and personal distribution lists.) You also have to look at a lot of advertising banners with your email that can be distracting and slow things down, and an ad is inserted in every email message that you send using the service.

Web-based email is a good choice if you travel frequently or if you want a more anonymous or disposable address for Usenet postings, Web page forms, and the like. I recommend the following providers:

- **Hotmail:** http://www.hotmail.com/

- **My Own Email:** http://www.myownemail.com/

- **Netscape Webmail:** http://webmail.netscape.com/

- **Yahoo! Mail:** http://mail.yahoo.com/

Free Forwarding Services

Forwarding services don't give you an additional email account, just another email address. You can set up this address to forward messages to any other email address, such as the one provided by your ISP or company.

Forwarding services are a good choice if you don't want several accounts, but you do need additional addresses to handle mail from different sources. For example, set up an alias for your company-based email address to give out to personal contacts. If your email address changes frequently, a forwarding service is a real help, because you always have an address that remains the same—you just change the account that it forwards mail to. It's also advantageous to set up a simple alias if your "real" email address is difficult to remember. However, be prepared for advertisements to appear at the bottom or top of each message the forwarding service sends you.

If free forwarding is what you need, try the following services:

- **Bigfoot:** `http://www.bigfoot.com/`

- **Switchboard:** `http://www.switchboardmail.com/`

- **UserMail:** `http://www.usermail.com/` (charges a fee but doesn't insert ads in your messages)

Managing All Accounts

As long as you choose an email client that can handle multiple email accounts and filters, you can manage mail coming in from all your accounts, including free POP mail and forwarding services. In this chapter, I'll provide instructions for the most popular freeware email clients: Qualcomm Eudora Light, Netscape Messenger, and Microsoft Outlook Express; if you are using another client, consult your documentation for help. (Refer to Chapter 2, "Choosing the Right Tools," for a discussion of email clients.)

The following email clients support multiple mail accounts:

- **Outlook Express (POP3/IMAP):** To set up another account, open Tools, Accounts and click Add, Mail (see Figure 5.1); then, fill out the fields as you did for your primary email account.

Timesaver
If you maintain a Web-based email account, you can find it inconvenient to go to the site and log in each time you check your mail. At `http://www.cyber-info.com/`, download a small utility called Cyber-Info WebMail Notify, which works with HotMail, Yahoo! Mail, and several other free email services. This utility opens a dialog box where you can enter your username and password. The program then tells you whether you have mail, bypassing your browser entirely.

Figure 5.1
Adding email
accounts to
Outlook Express.

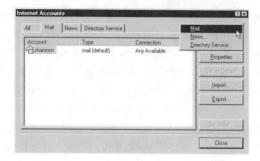

Figure 5.1
Adding email
accounts to
Outlook Express.

- **Netscape Messenger (IMAP only):** To set up another account, open Edit, Preferences, select the Mail & Newsgroups, Mail Servers category, click Add under Incoming Mail Servers, and fill out the fields for the additional IMAP server where you receive mail.

Note: Outlook 98 and Eudora Pro also support multiple email accounts.

Filtering Mail from Multiple Accounts

Bright Idea
Here's another advantage of Web-based free email accounts—they're the perfect way to get around the company firewall that's preventing you from checking your personal email on company time. Just don't tell your MIS manager! (And bear in mind that any email accessed on a company machine can be read by management or subpoenaed for legal action—more on this in Chapter 6.)

After you've up set up two or more accounts in your email program, you need to manage the mail coming into each account. I suggest creating an additional Inbox folder for each account, such as Inbox-work, Inbox-personal, and Inbox-Website. You can then set up a filter that funnels incoming mail into the correct inbox folder based on the email address that the message was sent to. This system helps you prioritize the messages to read first.

Here's how to set up the filter in Outlook Express:

1. Create a new folder by selecting File, Folder, New and naming the folder Inbox-personal, for example.

2. Select Tools, Message Rules, Mail.

3. Under Select the Conditions for Your Rule, select the check box by Where the To Line Contains People.

4. Under Select the Actions for Your Rule, select the check box by Move It to the Specified Folder.

5. Under Rule Description, click the Contains People link.

6. The Select People dialog box opens; type your second email address in the top box, and click Add. Then, click OK.

7. Under Rule Description, click the Specified Folder link.

8. In the window, click the folder you just created; click OK.

9. Under Name of the Rule, type a name, such as Mail Account Filter (see Figure 5.2).

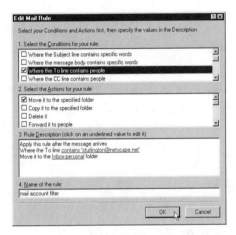

Figure 5.2
Creating a filter to move a second email account's messages into a new inbox folder in Outlook Express.

10. Click OK twice to close both dialog boxes.

Here's how to do the same thing in Messenger:

1. Select File, New, Folder and name the new folder Inbox-personal, for instance.

2. Select Edit, Message Filters and click New.

3. Give the filter a meaningful name, such as Personal Email.

4. Using the drop-down menus in the next five boxes, select The To of the Message Is *your second email address* Then Move to Folder Inbox-personal (see Figure 5.3).

5. Click OK twice to close both dialog boxes.

Figure 5.3
Creating a filter to move a second email account's messages into a new inbox folder in Messenger.

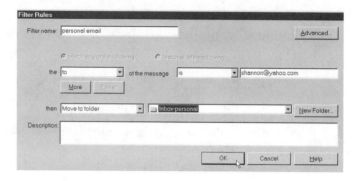

Checking for New Mail

To make things easier on yourself, set up your client to poll all accounts for new messages at the same time. You can also save a step by telling your email client to remember all passwords, although this isn't a good idea if other people have access to your computer. You generally set these options when you create the account, or edit the properties of each account through Edit, Preferences, Mail Servers in Messenger (select the account and click Edit) or Tools, Accounts in Outlook Express (select the mail account and click Properties).

Improving Your Email Skills

You can easily improve your email communication skills if you just remember a few rules and take advantage of your email client's automation features. These tips help you save time and communicate more effectively with your email correspondents.

Getting the Message Across

Email offers many advantages over the phone, snail mail, and fax. It's fast, it (almost) always finds its recipient, and you don't have to answer until it's convenient for you. These are all reasons why email has become a popular communication medium among co-workers, colleagues, and friends.

It's not unusual to receive dozens or even hundreds of email messages a day. Personal and work-related mail, advertisements, newsletters, and mailing lists are all vying for our attention. To be certain that your message doesn't get lost in the crowd, follow the guidelines outlined in this section.

Moneysaver
If you belong to a special group, you might be entitled to a free email account. Here are some examples:
- Broadcasters: http://www.broadcast.net/freemail.html
- College students: http://www.collegeclub.com/
- Kids: http://www.headbone.com/hbzmail/ or http://www.juniormail.com/login/juniormail.asp
- Licensed amateur radio operators: http://www.qsl.net/signup.html or http://www.callsign.net/
- Military personnel: http://www.milmail.com/

Creating Clear Subject Lines

The most important part of your message is the subject. Many people decide which messages to read based entirely on the subject line, so a brief, clear subject ensures that your message gets the attention it deserves. Insert the following shorthand clues into the subject line to help clarify the importance of your letter:

- **Re:** Used in replies to previous messages; many email clients insert this automatically.

- **FW:** Copy of a message that you're forwarding on to a third recipient; again, inserted automatically by most email clients.

- **FYI:** Informational message that doesn't require a response.

- **Urgent:** Time-critical message that requires a quick response.

- **Req:** The message requires an answer but isn't so urgent.

Quoting Messages

If you're responding to someone's message, quoting is a necessary skill. Quoting some of the previous message provides context for your reply and reminds the other person of what you were talking about. Most email programs enable you to include the entire message as a quote in your reply, but this might be too much context. Judicious cutting to include just the relevant text enables the person on the other end to read and understand the reply much more quickly, without having to sift through unnecessary repetition. A good rule of thumb—at least half of the lines in the message should be your own. If you must include the whole message that you're replying to, insert it *after* your response.

Keeping Messages Readable

Be sure that your message is readable. Every email client is different, and so the recipient's client won't necessarily show the message in the same way it looks on your screen. To make your message easier to read, keep paragraphs short. In fact, keep

Inside Scoop
How popular is email? Fifty-seven percent of American business executives say they rely on it (American Management Association). Thirty million people used it in the past 24 hours, including four million who aren't regular Internet users (CommerceNet/ Nielsen Media Research). Eighty-four percent of people say it was what lured them to the Internet in the first place (MarketFact).

your whole message brief to make it easier on those poor souls who contend with hundreds of messages per day. (This also helps people whose email providers charge by the byte or who limit how much disk space email can use.) Another rule of thumb—keep your message to fewer than 25 lines of text.

Most email clients don't automatically wrap long lines, resulting in a strange layout in the recipient's client, so keep each line to under 75 characters. Here's how to make this setting:

Timesaver
Fingering an email address is a quick way to find out whether the address is valid. Fingering returns the person's real name and some-times a "plan" file containing per-sonal data. If you have a shell account, type finger followed by the email address at the prompt. If not, visit the finger gateway at http://www.cs.indiana.edu:800/finger/gateway/. Eudora Light users can finger by selecting Tools, Directory Services and clicking Finger. Some accounts can't be fingered because the host-ing system isn't running a finger server; you should have the most luck with .edu, .net, and .org addresses.

- In Eudora Light, open Tools, Options, select the Sending Mail category, and check the Word Wrap box.

- In Messenger, open Edit, Preferences, select the Mail & Newsgroups, Messages category, select the check box under Message Wrapping, and enter an amount of 75 or less in the text field (see Figure 5.4).

- In Outlook Express, open Tools, Options, select the Send tab, click Plain Text Settings under Mail Sending Format, and select 75 or less from the Automatically Wrap Text menu.

Even though many email programs, such as Outlook Express and Messenger, make it easy to send messages in HTML format, don't be tempted. Many email clients don't support HTML, so your message would contain both the text and the HTML code, making it annoying to read. To turn off HTML formatting in Messenger, open Edit, Preferences, select the Mail & Newsgroups, Formatting category, and click the Use the Plain Text Editor... button. In Outlook Express, open Tools, Options, click the Send tab, and select Plain Text under Mail Sending Format. If you know that the recipient can read HTML-formatted mail, you can configure individual messages in HTML in Outlook Express; choose Rich Text (HTML) from the message's Format menu. Unless there's a good reason to format email messages in HTML, stick to plain text wherever possible.

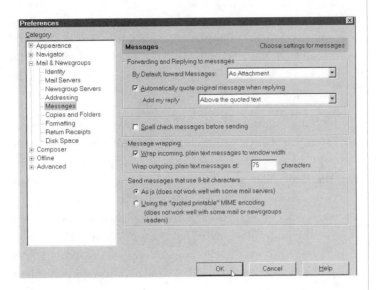

Figure 5.4
Turning on word
wrapping in
Messenger.

Timesaver
If you're sending a
message to a long
list of people,
make use of the
Blind carbon copy
(Bcc) address line
of the message.
This prevents every
recipient's address
from appearing at
the top of the mes-
sage, making the
message substan-
tially shorter.

Bright Idea
Most email pro-
grams let you set
a personal name
that's attached to
your email
address as a text
comment. Always
use this feature—
the personal name
identifies you to
your correspon-
dents much faster
than your email
address alone.
You usually find
the option in an
"identity" or "user
information" sec-
tion of the
account prefer-
ences.

Saving Time

You can take advantage of your email client's functionality to create such shortcuts as template messages, automatic responses, personal distribution lists, and signatures. Spending a little time on these items now can save you quite a lot of time in the long run.

Using Template Messages

If you often have to send out the same message or some version of it, a template message might be just the answer. For example, you might frequently have to answer the same questions from customers or visitors to your Web site. Instead of retyping the message each time, just call up your template, make the appropriate insertions, and send it off.

Here's how to create a template in Messenger (Eudora Light and Outlook Express don't support templates, but Eudora Pro and Outlook 98 do):

1. Create the template as a new message. Be sure to give the message a subject that easily identifies it later on, such as "Customer Response" or "Invoice."

2. When you're done, select File, Save As, Template (or press Ctrl+T or Cmd+T), and close the message.

Watch Out!
Large attachments
can tie up your
modem line and fill
your hard disk.
Avoid them by
telling your email
client to skip down-
loading messages
or attachments
over 100KB (or
whatever setting is
best for your sys-
tem). Most mail
programs let you
easily write a filter
to set the maxi-
mum message
size. Eudora Light:
Open Tools,
Options, and click
Checking Mail;
check the Skip
Messages box;
and set the maxi-
mum size.
Messenger: Open
Edit, Preferences;
select Mail &
Newsgroups, Disk
Space; check the
Do Not Download...
box; and set the
maximum size.
Outlook Express:
Open Tools,
Message Rules,
Mail, and select
the proper condi-
tions and actions
for the filter.

3. When you're ready to send a message based on the template, open the Templates folder under Local Mail and
   double-click the template of your choice. Then, you can
   make any changes, fill in the addresses, and send off the
   message.

Although Outlook Express doesn't have a template feature
like Messenger does, you can easily create boilerplate text and
insert it into new messages. Just save a plain text file containing the boilerplate message (select File, Save As). When you
need to send a boilerplate message, start composing a new
message, select Insert, Text from File, and choose the file containing the boilerplate text. The text is inserted in the body of
the message, where you can edit it. I suggest creating a folder
called "templates" or something similar to store all your boilerplate text in one place.

Setting Up Automatic Responses

Setting up an automatic response can also save you time. If you
get a lot of email and can't respond to it all personally right
away, use an automatic response to tell correspondents that
you will reply as soon as possible. You might also want to send
an automatic response to everybody who sends a message to
one of your email accounts, such as your Web site-related
account.

Follow these steps to set up an automatic response in
Outlook Express (Messenger and Eudora Light don't support
automatic responses, but Eudora Pro does):

1. Compose the message that you want to send out automatically, leaving the To field blank.

2. When you're done, select File, Save As and save the message as the Mail type.

3. Close the message composition window.

4. Select Tools, Message Rules, Mail.

5. Under Conditions, select the For All Messages check box.

6. Under Actions, select the Reply with Message check box.

7. Under Rule Description, click the Message link, select the message that you just composed and saved, and click Open (see Figure 5.5).

8. Click OK twice to close both dialog boxes.

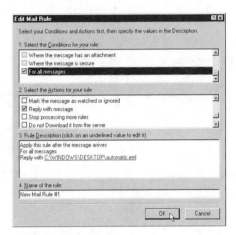

Figure 5.5
Creating an automatic response in Outlook Express.

Creating Personal Distribution Lists

Personal distribution lists collect several email addresses under one nickname, so that you can quickly send messages to a group. Set up distribution lists for your project team, a circle of friends, a club, or any other group. They're a great time-saver when you have to mail notices to the whole group, because you have to compose only one message and address it to one name, the name of the list.

Most email programs let you create personal distribution lists in the Address Book. Here's how to do it in Eudora Light, Outlook Express, and Messenger:

1. Open the Address Book.

2. Eudora Light: Click New. Outlook Express: Click New, New Group. Messenger: Click Create a New List.

3. Give the mailing list a name that's short and easy to remember.

Bright Idea
When setting up an automatic response filter, you might want to limit it to certain From addresses, so that you reply automatically to some people's messages, such as clients, and not to others, such as Mom.

4. Eudora: Click OK and enter the email addresses of every-one on the list in the Address(es) tab (see Figure 5.6). Outlook Express: Click Select Members to choose list members from the Address Book or click New Contact to add new addresses; click OK when you're done. Messenger: Type the addresses into the large window or drag them from the Address Book; click OK when you're done.

Figure 5.6
Creating a per-sonal distribution list in Eudora Light.

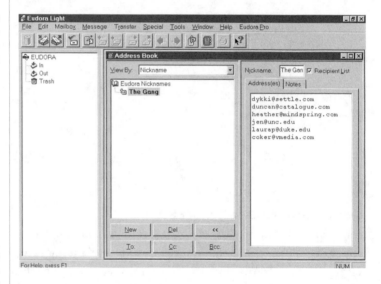

5. Address a message to the mailing list's nickname (or select the list from the Address Book) to send the message out to the entire list.

Using Signatures

Signatures are an easy way to send contact information to all your correspondents by inserting it at the bottom of each mes-sage you send, like a business card that you hand out with every letter. Your signature should be no more than five or six lines, and it should include important contact information, such as your full name, title, organization, email address, Web page address, phone and fax numbers, and street address. Take care with keeping home phone numbers and addresses private; if you can't put work information in your signature, skip it or use a P.O. box instead.

Each email program enables you to create and automatically attach your signature to all outgoing messages:

- Eudora Light supports two signature files, which is helpful if you want to use one signature on business mail and another on personal mail. Open Tools, Signatures, Standard and Tools, Signature, Alternate to edit and save each file; then select the one to use from the signature menu of the message composition area. To set Standard as the default signature for each message, open Tools, Options, click the Sending Mail category, and check the Use Signature box.

- Messenger: First, create and save your signature as a plain text file. Open Edit, Preferences, select the Mail & Newsgroups, Identity category, and click Choose to find the file that you created as the signature.

- Outlook Express: Open Tools, Options, click the Signatures tab, click the New button, and enter the signature in the Edit Signature window (see Figure 5.7). Or select the File button, click Browse, and choose a saved signature file.

Timesaver
In Outlook Express and Messenger, you don't have to open the Address Book every time you want to send a message to one of your contacts. Just start typing the person's nickname in one of the Address fields, and the program fills in the address for you. (In Eudora Light, right-click the address line, select Insert Recipient, and choose the Address Book entry that you want to use.)

Figure 5.7
Creating a signature in Outlook Express.

Finding Email Addresses

Sometimes, you get a bounced email message—one that's returned to you because it can't be delivered to the recipient.

Usually, the problem is temporary, such as server overload, low disk space, or network lag, so you should first try resending the message. If it bounces again, the email address is probably incorrect.

If you can't contact the person through some other means, you can always search for the email address online. Large Web site directories called white pages contain not only email addresses, but sometimes phone numbers and street addresses as well. The following white pages are the most thorough (because no directory is complete, you might have to search several to find the person you're looking for):

Timesaver
To quickly search for an email address, go to MESA, "the largest email address book worldwide," at http:// mesa.rrzn. uni-hannover.de/. There, you can search several major white pages directories at one time.

- **Bigfoot:** http://www.bigfoot.com/

- **InfoSpace:** http://www.infospace.com/

- **Switchboard:** http://www.switchboard.com/

- **WhoWhere:** http://www.whowhere.lycos.com/

- **Yahoo! People Search:** http://people.yahoo.com/

Getting Organized

Organizing your mailbox might be low on your priority list, but with all the messages that you surely get every day, putting some organizational rules into effect can really save time and hassle later on. You've already learned how your email program's filters and folders can be used to sort incoming mail from more than one account. You can also set up filters to process all your incoming mail, and you should set up a system of folders to organize the email messages that you want to save after reading them.

Here are some more ideas of what you can do with filters:

- Move messages from one sender into a folder with that sender's name.

- Funnel messages from subscribed mailing lists and newsletters into one folder for later reading.

- Delete messages from junk mail senders.

- Forward messages with a particular sender or subject to an assistant to answer.

Finding Saved Messages

After you've created several folders and saved a lot of messages, it becomes more difficult to find something specific, such as the phone number that somebody sent you three weeks ago. Fortunately, most email programs include sophisticated searching features that make tracking down specific information or messages a whole lot easier. Here's how to open the search tool in each program:

- Eudora Light: Select Edit, Find, Find or press Ctrl+F or Cmd+F.

- Messenger: Select Edit, Search Messages or press Ctrl+Shift+F or Cmd+Shift+F.

- Outlook Express: Select Edit, Find, Message or press Ctrl+Shift+F or Cmd+Shift+F.

Some of the search tools enable a more precise, and therefore more efficient, search. Eudora Light's is the most basic, allowing you to search only for keywords in the message body. Outlook Express enables you to refine your search to look for keywords in the subject, address, or body of the message, or find messages received within a certain period. Messenger's search is the most precise—you can set a wide range of search criteria, such as a keyword in the body text, the status, or the age of the message (see Figure 5.8).

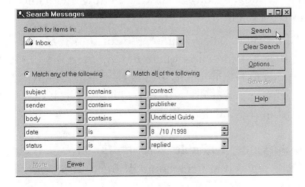

Figure 5.8
Using Messenger's search tool, you can search email messages by a wide range of criteria.

Timesaver
In both Messenger and Outlook Express, you can search the major white pages directories for an email address right from the Address Book window. In Messenger, select the directory that you want to search from the left pane, type the person's name in the text field, and click Search. In Outlook Express, select Edit, Find People, choose the directory service from the Look In menu, and enter the criteria to search for.

Saving Space

To save space—whether on the hard disk with a POP3 account or on the mail server with an IMAP account—delete whatever messages you don't need. (Some commercial programs, such as Outlook 98, enable you to archive old messages to save space without deleting them altogether.) You can set up an automatic deletion schedule for most email clients in the Options or Preferences.

Using the Address Book

You should also take advantage of your email program's Address Book. The Address Book is generally accessible via a toolbar button (look for it on the component bar in Messenger). Play around with the sorting and other organizational features to create a system that works best for you.

Adding contacts to your Address Book when you receive messages from them saves time when looking for hard-to-remember email addresses later. In Outlook Express and Messenger, right-click the sender's address to find an Add to Address Book option; in Eudora Light, you have to copy and paste the sender's address into the Address Book.

Free via Email

Your email inbox is probably your most valuable Internet resource, not only for enabling quick and easy communication with just about anybody, but also for getting useful information delivered straight to you at no cost.

That's right! There's quite a lot of stuff that you can get using email, if you know where to look. And most of it, from daily news to reminders to games, costs you nothing. You can even access most of the Internet, including FTP sites and the Web, from your mailbox.

Free Services Available Through Email

You'll be amazed at the amount of free information and services you can get with nothing but an email address. Of course, some of this stuff is useless or no more than glorified advertisements, but a large percentage of it is actually information you can use or entertainment to lighten your workday. I'm going to tell you about some of the best services and newsletters that I've found, but after you've got an idea of what's out there, go out looking for related services that's of interest to you. (The URLs in the following list point to sites where you can get more information and subscribe to the service.)

- **Get the news.** Many services deliver free headlines straight to your inbox. News Index Delivered (`http://www.newsindex.com/delivered.html`) and Daily Brief (`http://www.incinc.net/db.html`) are some good ones.

- **Sports and weather, too.** InfoBeat (`http://www.infobeat.com/`) offers several specialized news services, including sports, weather, TV listings, and even snow reports. Get personalized business news from NewsPage (`http://www.newspage.com/`), or subscribe to weather forecasts at the Weather by Email Resource Center (`http://www.weatherbyemail.com/`).

- **Find out what's going on in your industry.** Newsletters are an easy way to get news, market leads, and advice related to your profession. I've found the most useful newsletters about the writing industry at my favorite writing-related Web sites, so make sites related to your profession the first places to look. More good places to check are mailing list search engines—the best ones are listed in the next section of this chapter.

- **Get a job.** A new kind of free service scouts job listings posted to a database and sends available positions straight to your mailbox, based on the criteria that you specify. Try out Personal Job Scout (`http://www.nationjob.com/pjscout/`) and CareerBuilder Personal Search Agent (`http://psa.careerbuilder.com/_100_/nspsa02.html`).

- **Get reminded.** Many free services send you notes to remind you of upcoming appointments, birthdays, or special events. The Email Reminder Service (`http://epsilon3.georgetown.edu/~dalec/cgibin/reminder/index1.html`) is good for special events; MemoryMail (`http://www.greatidea.com/memorymail/`) is useful for repetitive

Watch Out!
Deleting unwanted email really saves space, but be careful! Deleting a message might not really remove it; instead, it only moves the message to the Trash or Deleted Items folder where it's still taking up space. To get rid of those messages permanently, you have to empty the trash: In Eudora Light, select Special, Empty Trash; in Messenger, select File, Empty Trash (POP3) or File, Compress Folders (IMAP); and in Outlook Express, right-click the Deleted Items folder and select Empty Folder.

Watch Out!
It's a good idea to subscribe to all newsletters, mailing lists, and other email services using a different address than the one you use for work-related or personal mail. That enables you to easily separate mass mailings from the more important personal messages, as well as helps keep the spam that you can sometimes invite by subscribing to mailing lists from infiltrating your main mailbox.

Bright Idea
You can have Eudora Light remind you of important events and appointments, as well. Insert the reminder message in a new email that you address to yourself, and press Shift when you click Send. Then, specify the time to send the message as the time when you want to get reminded of the event.

reminders; and Candor's Reminder Service (http://www.candor.com/reminder/) helps you remember yearly events, such as birthdays and anniversaries.

- **Expand your knowledge.** You can get almost any kind of useful (and useless) information sent to you via email. For instance, A Word a Day (http://www.wordsmith.org/awad/subscribe.html) sends a new word and its definition every day; and Literary Calendar (http://litcal.yasuda-u.ac.jp/litmailer.shtml) provides the day's literary-related historical events.

- **Get entertained.** You can also get entertainment delivered to your mailbox for your enjoyment. Here are some of my favorites: Internet Horoscopes (http://www.internethoroscopes.com/); Joke of the Day (http://www.joker.org/subscribe.html); and This Is True (http://www.thisistrue.com/subscribe.html) for bizarre but true news stories.

- **Play games.** Playing games by email is free, easy entertainment and a great way to meet people. Your choices range from role-playing to chess to wrestling. Try Richard's PbeM Server (http://eiss.erols.com/~pbmserv/) for a variety of games, or check the PBM List (http://www.pbm.com/~lindahl/pbm_list/) of all known games.

Bringing the Internet to Your Inbox

You can access almost any service on the Internet via email. For instance, you can download files from FTP sites, search the Web and receive HTML documents in return, and read Usenet newsgroups. This section tells you how to access FTP and search the Web.

Accessing FTP Sites via Email

Any file on any public FTP site is available through email via an ftpmail server. Even if you have full Internet access, this can be a handy way to access heavily loaded sites that are difficult to connect to with an FTP client, especially if you aren't in too much of a hurry. Just send messages to one of the following ftpmail servers containing FTP commands, and the results are returned to your mailbox:

- `bitftp@pucc.princeton.edu`

- `ftpmail@ftpmail.ramona.vix.com`

- `ftpmail@btoy1.rochester.ny.us`

- `ftpmail@online.ora.com`

Inside Scoop
The Electronic Messaging Association predicts that by the year 2000, 108 million people will be using email—and each one of us will be receiving 65,000 messages a year.

Your first message might look something like this:

```
open <site>
dir
quit
```

Except you would replace *<site>* with the address of the FTP site, such as wuarchive.wustl.edu. This returns a message containing a list of directories in the site. Then, send the following message:

```
open <site>
chdir pub or cd pub
dir
quit
```

This changes to the pub directory, where publicly available files are generally stored, and returns a list of available directories and files. Continue to browse through the directories until you find what you want, and then get the file delivered to you with a message like this (you need to insert the "binary" line if you're retrieving anything other than plain text files):

```
open <site>
binary
get <name of file>
quit
```

Sure, it might take a while, but if you've got time, it's an efficient way to browse FTP sites. If you get into trouble, try sending the "help" command to the ftpmail server. You usually get instructions for using the server in return.

Timesaver
You can search FTP sites too, using the Archie tool. To find out how to use Archie via email, send a message to archie@archie. bunyip.com or archie@archie. internic.net with the word help in the subject line.

Searching the Web via Email

You can also search the Web via free email search engines such as Iliad. To find out how, send an email message to iliad@algol.jsc.nasa.gov with the subject line start iliad and a blank body. This type of search is best suited for finding pages related to narrow, unique keywords, rather than broad, general searches. In return, you receive either a hyperlinked list of related pages or the pages themselves, based on your specifications.

Finding Other Ways to Access the Internet via Email

If you want to find more ways to access the Internet via email, check out the FAQ at http://www.cis.ohio-state.edu/ hypertext/faq/usenet/internet-services/access-via-email/ faq.html. You can also subscribe to the ACCMAIL list for other cool ways to access the Internet via email; send a message to LISTSERV@LISTSERV.AOL.COM with the message SUBSCRIBE ACCMAIL.

Making the Most of Mailing Lists

Bright Idea
You can use email to find mailing lists. Search a master list by topic by sending an email message to listserv@ listserv.net with a blank subject; in the body, put list global <search-words>, where <searchwords> are the keywords that you want to search for. For instance, send the message list global astronomy to find mailing lists that are related to astronomy.

Quite a lot of subscription-based mass e-mailings fall under the heading of mailing lists, including the newsletters and daily digests mentioned previously in this chapter. This section focuses on discussion-based mailing lists, which invite postings from all subscribers on a topic of interest, ranging from professional networking to gushing over a favorite movie star. Mailing lists often have fewer flames and less off-topic junk than Usenet newsgroups (although not always).

These lists can be founts of valuable nuggets of information, current news, and expert advice, as well as gateways into close-knit communities. They can also, depending on the list, be complete wastes of time and inbox space. The trick lies in finding a list that suits you, dealing with the problems that arise in any online community, and figuring out the commands for subscribing, unsubscribing, and doing various other things on the list.

Finding Mailing Lists

Locating a mailing list to join is not difficult. As you've probably guessed, several specialized search engines have sprung up to help you sort through the tens of thousands of publicly available lists to find something of interest to you. The following are some of the more thorough search engines; all of them make an effort to provide up-to-date subscription information and remove lists that have become defunct:

- **CataList:** `http://www.lsoft.com/lists/listref.html`

- **List of Lists:** `http://catalog.com/vivian/` `interest-group-search.html`

- **Liszt:** `http://www.liszt.com/`

- **Publicly Accessible Mailing Lists:** `http://www.neosoft.com/` `internet/paml/`

- **Tile.net Lists:** `http://tile.net/lists/`

It's been my experience that none of these mailing list search pages is entirely complete. If you're looking for a discussion on a very specific subject, search them all and compare the results. If you're just looking for a new group to join, though, go to Liszt and browse through the categories; you'll probably find discussions that you never dreamed existed (but that you really want to take part in).

Subscribing, Unsubscribing, and Taking Control

Every mailing list has two email addresses: a listname address, where you send any messages to be distributed to the other subscribers of the list; and an administrative address, where you send commands or requests affecting your subscription. Subscribers often send commands to the listname address that should be sent to the administrative address instead, which tends to upset the other list members, so it's important to remember the distinction.

The administrative address generally goes to a computer program, called the mailing list manager. LISTSERV and Majordomo are examples of commonly used mailing list manager programs. Usually, you can find out which program the list runs under by checking the welcome message or

Timesaver
If you live by your email, you might want to sign up with a service that forwards your messages to your pager, regardless of who provides your email account or paging services. Costs are generally based on how many messages you receive and range from $5–$20 per month. Check out Airmail Communications' Email2Pager (`http://www.` `airmailcomm.com/`) and InstantEmail (`http://www.` `instantemail.` `net/index1.htm`).

examining the message headers. Often, the administrative address refers to the mailing list manager as well, such as `majordomo@domain.com` or `listserv@domain.edu`. (By contrast, the listname address takes the form *listname*`@domain.com`.)

When you first subscribe to a list, you usually receive a confirmation message that you must respond to with a specific message or code. The purpose of the confirmation is to prevent people from randomly signing up email addresses to the list and to limit subscriptions only to those people who actually want to join. It's usually a simple matter to confirm your subscription; in most cases, you only have to click reply. After confirming your subscription, you receive a welcome message describing the purpose of the list and how to unsubscribe. Save this letter—I generally keep all mine in a separate mail folder. If you ever want to get off the list, you'll be glad you did.

Mailing list managers can interpret a set of commands to initiate your subscription or end it. They also enable you to access other useful functions. For instance, if the list is generating too much mail, you can switch to digest mode, which combines all the messages sent each day into one long mailing. If you go on vacation and want to suspend the list for a while without actually leaving the list, you can do that, too. That's why it's helpful to be familiar with the mailing list commands and to be aware of everything you can do.

Table 5.1 lists the commands used with the most common mailing list manager programs: LISTSERV, UNIX ListProcessor (Listproc), and Majordomo (just substitute the items enclosed by <> with the appropriate information).

Moneysaver
You say you want to run your own mailing list, but you don't have access to a list server? Arrow Mailing List Manager is a low-cost alternative. This shareware program enables you to set up and manage mailing lists on your Windows 95/98 computer. Get it from any software search engine (check Appendix B, "Unauthorized Resources").

TABLE 5.1: MAILING LIST COMMANDS

Action	LISTSERV	Listproc	Majordomo
Subscribe.	SUBSCRIBE <listname> <yourname>	SUBSCRIBE <listname> <yourname>	SUBSCRIBE <listname>
Unsubscribe.	SIGNOFF <listname>	UNSUBSCRIBE <listname>	UNSUBSCRIBE
Get an informational file about the list.	INFO <listname>	INFO <listname>	INFO <listname>
Digest format (not offered by all lists).	SET <listname> DIGEST	SET <listname> MAIL DIGEST	SUBSCRIBE <listname> -DIGEST
Turn off digest.	SET <listname> MAIL or SET <listname> NODIGEST	SET <listname> MAIL ACK	UNSUBSCRIBE <listname> -DIGEST
Suspend mail temporarily.	SET <listname> NOMAIL	SET <listname> MAIL POSTPONE	Not supported
Resume mail.	SET <listname> MAIL	SET <listname> MAIL ACK or SET <listname> MAIL DIGEST	Not supported
Receive copies of messages you post to the list.	SET <listname> REPRO	SET <listname> MAIL ACK	You always receive your own messages.
Don't receive copies of your posts.	SET <listname> NOREPRO	SET <listname> MAIL NOACK	Not supported
Get a list of subscribers.	REVIEW <listname> F=MAIL	RECIPIENTS <listname>	WHO <listname>
Hide your address from the list of subscribers.	SET <listname> CONCEAL	SET <listname> CONCEAL YES	Not supported
Show your address in the subscriber list.	SET <listname> NOCONCEAL	SET <listname> CONCEAL NO	Not supported
Get a list of archived files.	INDEX <listname>	INDEX <listname>	INDEX <listname>
Retrieve an archived file.	GET <filename> <filetype> <listname> F=MAIL	GET <listname> <filename>	GET <listname> <filename>
Get help.	HELP	HELP	HELP

Watch Out!
When trying to unsubscribe from a mailing list, you might get an error message saying that you're not subscribed, even though you're still receiving mail from the list. This happens when you're subscribed to the list under a different email address than the one you used to send the unsubscribe message. In that case, resend the message in this format: `unsubscribe <listname> <emailaddress>`, where `<emailaddress>` is the address you used to subscribe to the list. If you don't remember the address you subscribed under, request a list of subscribers and look for it.

Whenever you send a message to the administrative address, leave the subject blank, insert the command into the body, and delete any appended signature files. Always refer to the name of the list in the message, because most list servers manage several lists. For instance, to join the NEW-LIST mailing list (which announces new mailing lists), you'd send the following message to the address `listserv@listserv.nodak.edu`:

```
SUBSCRIBE NEW-LIST John Doe
```

Note that the administrative address doesn't always connect to a computer program—sometimes a person manages the list manually. If you're unsure—if the administrative address doesn't include the name of a mailing list manager, for instance—it's best to send two messages, one with the command and one politely requesting assistance. That way, you cover all your bases. If your commands aren't working and nobody's answering, try sending a message with the HELP command; this usually retrieves instructions, no matter what mailing list manager is managing the list.

Last but not least, remember that mailing lists are like any other community, with their own rules and inside jokes. To join in and be accepted, you should lurk for a while after joining the list—read messages without posting anything yourself. Lurking gives you a chance to learn what the tone of the list is, which topics are cheerfully discussed and which ones earn flames, and the overall culture of the list. Many well-established lists also have a home page (check the welcome message) where there are a FAQ, archives, and other useful information.

Just the Facts

- Managing multiple email accounts using free email services and your email program's filters is an efficient way to separate different kinds of email.

- Take advantage of your email client's timesaving features—personal distribution lists, signatures, templates, automatic responses, and directory searches, to name a few—to save time when emailing and communicate more effectively.

- Also get to know your email client's organizational features; by wisely using filters, folders, message searching, and the Address Book, you can effectively manage hundreds or even thousands of mail messages.

- Your email inbox is a valuable resource; use it to receive timely information and take advantage of free services.

- Mailing lists are a fun and effective way to meet others, exchange advice, and otherwise network online; after you master the commands, the biggest problem you'll face is dealing with all the messages they can generate.

Timesaver
A-List is a nifty freeware utility that lists the top 100 mailing lists, sorted by category. After you give A-List some information about your email account, you can subscribe and unsubscribe to any list with the click of a button. You can also add lists and categories to turn A-List into a complete mailing list management tool. Get it at http://www.mmgco.com/alist/.

GET THE SCOOP ON...
Who's reading your email and why ▪ Protecting your
email messages from being read by outsiders
▪ Preventing unsolicited email advertisements and
taking down spammers ▪ Recognizing email hoaxes
and frauds

Secure and Spam-Free

E MAIL HAS PRESENTED NEW PROBLEMS as well as new opportunities. Email's speedy delivery over the Internet backbone and its capability to sit on a central mail server until you're ready to retrieve it make it one of the most convenient forms of communication—and make email vulnerable to being read by outsiders. Plus, the very low expense of sending email messages to millions of recipients has made it a target for mass-mailed, unsolicited advertisements from the scourge of the Net—spammers.

Fortunately, both of these problems are mostly preventable. There are many ways you can keep your email private and your inbox free of spam, ranging from simple preventative measures to all-out warfare. You will never guarantee 100-percent security or eliminate all spam entirely, but you should be able to get to the point where you feel like your mailbox is yours again.

Who's Reading Your Email?

Don't make the mistake of thinking that your email messages are as private as sealing a letter in an envelope and sending it through the post. Actually, sending an email message is more like mailing a postcard; anyone along the route—members of your household, neighbors, post office employees, residents at the recipient's address—can just flip the postcard over and read what you've written on the back.

Each email message travels through many computers to get to its destination, and it is vulnerable at each point along the way. Each stopping point has an administrator who has easy access to every message that passes through, and who knows who else has authorized or unauthorized access? There's just no telling, which is why you should take steps to protect sensitive messages.

Email that you receive via the company network is the most insecure. Not only can your employer legally read your email messages, but many employees of the company can easily get unauthorized access, from the people in the IS department to co-workers who have discovered an unprotected password. My advice: Don't send anything that's not work-related via the company network. Use the email address provided by your ISP for your home connection, or get a free email account for personal mail (turn back to Chapter 5, "Email Magic," to learn more about managing multiple email accounts). Whatever you do, don't compose or receive personal email at the office; it's just not secure there.

Don't think that your home account is totally secure, either. It's just as easy for your ISP to snoop through your messages as the company network administrators, although it's unlikely that your ISP would have a reason to snoop, since your email correspondence is probably of less interest to the ISP, who doesn't know you (after all, your ISP probably isn't interested in juicy gossip about your co-workers).

Remember that all system administrators have an all-powerful root password enabling them to get into any part of the system. This is necessary to effectively manage the system, but it also renders the password protecting your email account meaningless. Just deleting your email messages doesn't protect them, either. Many ISPs and network administrators archive all incoming and outgoing email for six months or more after you think you've deleted it.

So, why would anyone want to read your email? Unless you're Monica Lewinsky, your email is probably not of much interest to anyone besides the sender and the recipient, you

Inside Scoop
In a *MacWorld* survey, 25% of the businesses contacted admitted that they eavesdrop on employee computer files, email, and voice mail. This figure doesn't include unauthorized email monitoring.

think. But that's not necessarily true. I've already mentioned co-workers looking for office gossip to spread around. You should also beware of thieves out to sell company secrets, bosses monitoring your personal habits, outsiders sniffing for credit card numbers and other personal information, and old-fashioned voyeurs.

Securing Your Email

It pays to be paranoid—but not too paranoid. You probably won't care if someone reads messages posted to a mailing list (unless the list is a private support group) or emails about mundane matters, such as "honey, please pick up the dry-cleaning on the way home" or "I need the quarterly budget reports by Friday." But for anything more sensitive, you should take steps to ensure that your messages aren't open to unauthorized eyes.

Watching What You Say

The first and best answer is to just watch what you say in email. Don't write anything that you wouldn't mind seeing on the evening news or being kept "on record" for an indefinite period. Besides the archives of mail on your company network and at your ISP, most mailing lists archive messages indefinitely on the Web, so that anyone on the Internet can read them—including your spouse, neighbor, or boss. (This goes for Usenet posts, too, which are indefinitely archived at sites like www.deja.com and most major Internet search engines.) Also, many recipients save the email they get, so the message you sent six months ago might still be sitting in someone's mail folder. Recipients frequently quote messages to others, forward them on, and print them out, as well. So, be careful what you say and how you say it—it might come back to haunt you!

Finally, take care how and to whom you give personal information via email. For instance, don't send credit card numbers, Social Security numbers, or any other sensitive information in messages that aren't encrypted, and make sure that you're familiar with and trust the company or person on the receiving end. Also, don't send contact information, such

Timesaver
Speaking of passwords, stop using your dog's name or words describing items in your office as your password—they're too easy to guess. The best passwords include a mixture of numbers, upper-case and lower-case letters, and non-alphabetic characters, and aren't found in any dictionary. If you're having trouble coming up with good passwords, get Password Creator, a freeware tool for Windows 95/98 that generates random passwords. Check any software search engine (see Appendix B, "Unauthorized Resources," for some suggestions).

as your home address or phone number, to anyone you don't know. All of this is common sense, I know. But it's incredible how many of us let down our safeguards after we get used to email.

Watch Out!
One improperly sent email could wreck your life. For instance, many email programs automatically fill in the recipient's name for you, based on the first few letters you type. So, you might think you're sending those naughty pictures or that dirty joke to John, when it's really going to Johanna. A little "harmless" fun could lead to getting fired or a sexual harassment suit. It's best to avoid sending these things altogether, especially over the company network.

Encrypting Messages

Encryption is the best way to prevent email messages from being read by outsiders. It encodes the text of the message, and only the writer and the recipient of the message have the keys to decode it.

Most encryption systems provide two keys: a public key and a private key. You give the public key to your correspondents, so that they can encrypt email messages sent to you, turning the messages into indecipherable blocks of text. Only you have access to your private key, and you should protect it well; it's used to decrypt, or decode, the messages.

Unfortunately, there's no industry-wide encryption standard. The two major standards are Pretty Good Privacy (PGP) and Secure/Multipurpose Internet Mail Extension (S/MIME). Both you and your correspondent must use the same protocol for encryption to work properly.

Generally, I recommend PGP—it's the most widely used and supported standard on the Internet, it's free and easy to get, and it works with any email program. In fact, Eudora Light and Eudora Pro come with a free PGP plug-in. Or get PGPfreeware, a free-for-noncommercial-use PGP solution that encrypts email messages and files you send over the network; it works on its own or integrates as a plug-in with Eudora, Outlook, and Outlook Express. Download it for Windows 95/98/NT or Mac OS at http://www.nai.com/products/security/pgpfreeware.asp. (You must be a resident of the United States or Canada to download either PGPfreeware or the PGP plug-in for Eudora; international users should get PGP from http://www.pgpinternational.com/.)

Generating PGP Keys

After installing PGPfreeware, you need to generate your keys. This process should start automatically, or you can do it from within PGPkeys by selecting Keys, New Key (press Ctrl+N or Cmd+N). Follow these steps:

1. Enter a name and email address associated with your keys. It's best to use your full name, including a middle initial, so that your keys won't be confused with anyone else's; also use your primary email address. Click Next.

2. Choose a size for your key pair, from 768–4096 bits (see Figure 6.1). The larger the key size, the more secure the encryption and the slower the encryption process. Generally, 1024-bit keys offer the best balance between performance and security, although you might choose 2048-bit keys for extra security. Click Next.

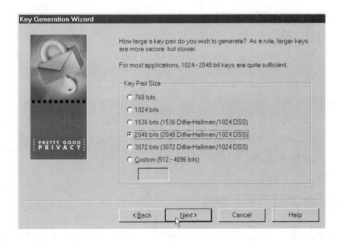

Figure 6.1
Selecting the bit size for your PGP keys.

3. Select whether the keys should expire and the expiration date. In most cases, choose Key Pair Never Expires. However, you can create keys that are only valid for a short time, such as for the duration of a top-secret project. Click Next.

Inside Scoop
Here's an example of just how public email at work can be. This happened at a computer company that shall remain nameless. Too many people knew the root password, which gave them access to all email on the mail server. Almost everyone used the company email network to send personal messages. So, one particularly unscrupulous person read everyone's personal email and spread the news around the office—what the senders thought was private quickly became public knowledge.

4. Select a passphrase of at least eight characters, including a mixture of uppercase letters, lowercase letters, numbers, and punctuation—the more complex the better, but make sure you can remember it! Click Next.

5. Now, PGP must collect random data in order to generate the keys; just move your mouse around the screen until the progress bar fills up.

6. Click Next; your keys are generated.

7. When the process is complete, click Next. If you're connected to the Internet, you can now send your public key to the public key server, so that others can find it and send you encrypted messages; just check the Send My Key to the Default Server Now box. If you're not connected, leave the box unchecked; you can send your key from within PGPkeys. Click Next.

8. Click Finish to add your keys to your keyring, which launches in a new window (see Figure 6.2). Your keyring stores your public keys along with all the public keys belonging to others that you've collected.

9. When you quit PGPkeys, you are prompted to back up your new keys; I suggest you back them up to a removable medium, such as a floppy disk, and put it in a safe place, such as a locked drawer or safety deposit box.

Exchanging PGP Public Keys

Now, you can start exchanging public keys with friends and colleagues. The easiest way to do this is via email. Here's how:

1. Select your public key in the PGPkeys window.

2. Select Edit, Copy (press Ctrl+C or Cmd+C).

3. Go to your email program, open a new message, and paste the contents of the Clipboard into the message (it should look like the message in Figure 6.3).

4. Send the email.

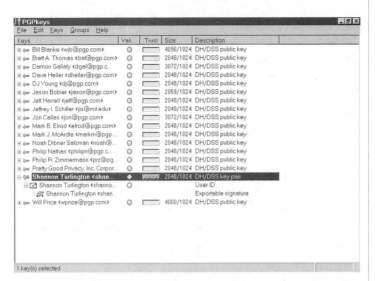

Figure 6.2
Your keyring—the
PGPkeys window—
stores all the
public keys that
you've collected; if
you're using a PGP
plug-in, open the
keyring by clicking
on the Launch
PGPkeys toolbar
button in your
email program.

Figure 6.3
An email message
with a copied pub-
lic key.

Watch Out!
It's a good idea to
change your
passphrase every
six months or so.
To do so, select
your public key in
the PGPkeys win-
dow, open Keys,
Key Properties, and
click Change
Passphrase. If you
forget your
passphrase, you
won't be able to
decrypt any mes-
sages or files
encrypted with your
public key. You
have to generate
new keys and start
all over again.

You might start receiving public keys from others in return.
To save someone else's key, all you have to do is copy the entire
key from the message that contains it, including the "Begin
PGP public key block" and "End PGP public key block" parts.
If you're using a PGP plug-in, just click the Extract PGPkey(s)
from Email Message button to do this. Then, click anywhere in
the PGPkeys window and select Edit, Paste (press Ctrl+V or
Cmd+V). In the Select Keys to Import dialog box, click the
Import button to add the new key to your keyring.

Bright Idea
Some people put
their public key in
their signature to
distribute it to
their correspon-
dents, but this cre-
ates an overlong
sig file. A better
way to distribute
your public key is
to publish it on
your home page
(just copy it from
the PGPkeys win-
dow to the HTML
source of your
home page). Then,
insert the URL to
the page in your
sig, so that your
correspondents
can get the key if
they want. This
method also
enables others to
find your key
before they con-
tact you.

As soon as you receive a new key from a friend or col-
league, check its fingerprint—a unique string of characters
belonging to each key. In PGPkeys, select the new key and
open Keys, Key Properties (see Figure 6.4). The fingerprint
appears at the bottom of the window. Call your friend and read
out the fingerprint to make sure that it matches your friend's
key. (You can also check a fingerprint on the public key server,
but this isn't as trustworthy a method.) Checking the fingerprint guards against using a key that was fraudulently generated by a third party in your friend's name. After you verify the
fingerprint, indicate that you trust the key by signing the key;
with the key selected, choose Keys, Sign. Only sign keys after
you've personally verified the fingerprint.

Encrypting and Decrypting Messages with PGP

Now, you want to use the public key your friend gave you to
send him an encrypted message. If you're using a PGP plug-in,
the toolbar of your message composition window should contain an Encrypt Message button. Just click it. If your email program finds the addressee's public key on your keyring, it
encrypts the message correctly and send it off.

If you aren't using a PGP plug-in, the process is a little
more difficult, because you have to switch between your email
program and PGP.

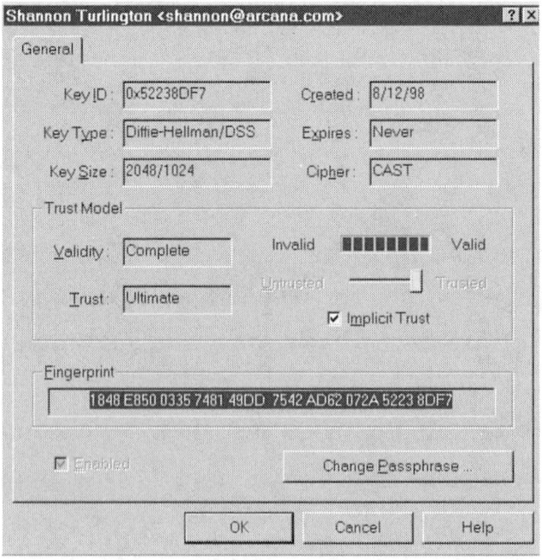

Figure 6.4
The properties of
a public key;
notice the finger-
print at the bot-
tom of the
window.

Shannon Turlington <shannon@arcana.com>	? □ X

General

Key ID: 0x52238DF7   Created: 8/12/98
Key Type: Diffie-Hellman/DSS   Expires: Never
Key Size: 2048/1024   Cipher: CAST

Trust Model
Validity: Complete   Invalid ■■■■■■■ Valid
Trust: Ultimate   Untrusted ──┘ Trusted
                        ☑ Implicit Trust

Fingerprint
1848 E850 0335 7481 49DD 7542 AD62 072A 5223 8DF7

☑ Enabled   Change Passphrase ...

OK   Cancel   Help

1. After typing the email message, select all of the text, and press Ctrl+X or Cmd+X to cut the text to the Clipboard.

2. Click the PGPtray icon in the system tray, and select Encrypt Clipboard from the pop-up menu.

3. In the PGP-Key Selection dialog box, click and drag the public key(s) you want to use to the bottom window.

4. Click OK.

5. Insert the cursor in the message's window, and press Ctrl+V or Cmd+V to paste the encrypted text. Your message should look like the one in Figure 6.5.

6. Send the message.

Decrypting coded messages sent to you is also easier if you have a PGP plug-in. When you receive a message that was encrypted with your public key, your email program prompts you to enter your passphrase. It then decrypts the message with your private key and displays the message. If you don't have a PGP plug-in, you have to copy the entire encrypted message to the Clipboard—including the "Begin PGP message" and "End PGP message" parts—select Decrypt, Verify Clipboard from the PGPtray menu, and enter your passphrase to see the message in PGP's Text Viewer window.

Timesaver
Searching a public key server is a quick way to locate someone's public key. In PGPkeys, open Keys, Search (press Ctrl+F or Cmd+F). Select the server from the top drop-down menu, and enter "User ID contains" and the name of the person you're looking for in the other fields. Then, click the Search button. After you find the key, drag it to the PGPkeys window to add it to your keyring.

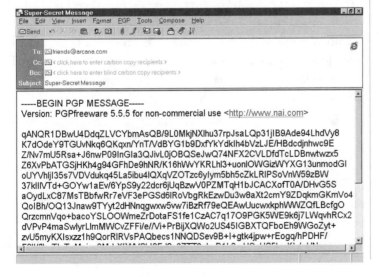

Figure 6.5
An encrypted email message.

Using Digital Signatures

While encryption protects the content of your email messages, digital signatures safeguard your identity. A digital signature is an encrypted data stamp that only you have the key to. When your key matches the digital signature on an email message, it proves that the message came from you, not from someone who forged your email address. It also verifies that the message wasn't altered en route. You can add a digital signature to any message, whether or not you encrypt it. Combining the two makes the message super-secure.

Bright Idea
You can also use PGP to safely store encrypted files on a hard drive, server, or disk. In Windows, right-click any file or folder to open a context menu. The PGP option enables you to encrypt, sign, or decrypt the file or folder. The Wipe option completely deletes the file or folder, so that it can't be recovered. You can also encrypt a file by cutting the text to the Clipboard and using the PGPtray options.

If you use PGP, use your private key to digitally sign messages. Sign any messages that include your public key, so that the recipient can verify that the key really came from you. In email clients that support the PGP plug-in, the Sign Message button appears on the message composition toolbar; just click it to add your digital signature to the message. If you don't have the plug-in, cut the message to the Clipboard as if you were going to encrypt it, but select Sign Clipboard or Encrypt & Sign Clipboard from the PGPtray menu instead. The procedure for verifying signatures in digitally signed messages that you receive is the same as the decryption procedure.

Using S/MIME Encryption

Microsoft Outlook, Outlook Express, and Netscape Messenger natively support S/MIME encryption, which you can use for communicating securely with some people, particularly on company networks. (You can add S/MIME support to Eudora via the Mailsecure plug-in; get more info and download a trial version from `http://www.baltimore.ie/products/mailsecure/index.html`.)

You have to purchase a personal certificate from a certificate authority to encrypt and sign messages with the S/MIME protocol. Instead of a public key, you exchange your certificate with others via digitally signed messages to enable them to send encrypted messages to you; you also need their certificates to encrypt messages to them. Personal certificates can even be required by some secure Web sites to verify your identity through your browser.

Personal certificates have the added benefit of an extra layer of verification via a third-party certificate authority. VeriSign is the most trusted certificate authority, so it's the best one to use; get a free, 60-day trial certificate at `http://www.verisign.com/client/index.html`.

Because S/MIME support is built into Messenger and Outlook Express, the process of encrypting, decrypting, and signing procedures is fairly simple.

In Messenger, click the Security toolbar button to perform all security activities; the Security dialog box also stores all your certificates and the certificates you've received from others. In the Security Info area, you can encrypt or sign an outgoing message (see Figure 6.6). If you want to set defaults for all outgoing email messages, click the Messenger option. To get a personal certificate, select Yours under Certificates, click Get a Certificate, and follow the instructions. If you receive a digitally signed message, Messenger automatically collects and verifies the certificate. Messenger also prompts you to decrypt any encrypted messages you get.

Watch Out!
The legal precedents regarding electronic communications haven't been set. If someone sues you—in a divorce, for example—he or she can subpoena and read your email correspondence. Again, the best course is to watch what you say in email.

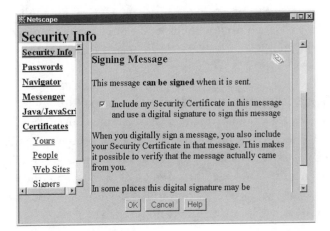

Figure 6.6
Control Messenger's built-in S/MIME security functions from the Security Info window.

Outlook Express (or Outlook) is the ideal client if you need to use both encryption standards, because S/MIME support is built-in and you can add PGP functions via the PGPfreeware plug-in. You can digitally sign and encrypt messages via toolbar buttons in the message composition window (see Figure 6.7).

To get a personal certificate and set security options, open Tools, Options and click the Security tab. As with Messenger, Outlook Express prompts you to decrypt incoming messages and verify incoming certificates.

Figure 6.7
Access both
S/MIME and PGP
encryption func-
tions from the
Outlook Express
toolbar (if you've
installed the
PGPfreeware
plug-in).

Managing a large number of certificates is not easy. You have to periodically check that the certificates are still trustworthy and update expired certificates. You also have to update your own certificate when it expires and distribute a new copy to all your correspondents. On top of all that, you must pay for the privilege of using certificates issued by a certificate authority. PGP, on the other hand, is completely free, already ingrained into the Internet community, and not nearly so much trouble to manage. For all these reasons, you might find PGP to be the better choice for general Internet email security.

Watch Out!
When you send an email message to an anonymous remailer, it is still archived on your ISP's mail server under your name, so it can still be traced to you. Take precautions to protect the message on your end by encrypting it. You could also use a free email account to send the message to the remailer.

Going Incognito with Anonymous Remailers

Free email accounts can provide a sense of anonymity and are often useful for personal mail and for posting in public forums, such as Web page forms, Usenet newsgroups, and mailing lists. However, they aren't truly anonymous; they can ultimately be traced back to you. To effectively hide your identity, you need to use an anonymous remailer.

Anonymous remailers enable you to send an email message without the recipient knowing your email address or name. They strip away the sender's real name and email address, replace it with a dummy address, and forward the message on to the recipient. They also notify the sender that the message was sent under the new identity. If there is a reply, the remailer removes the respondent's name and address and returns the message to the original sender, protecting everyone's privacy.

Anonymous remailers fill an important niche in online communications. They enable you to remain completely anonymous when seeking support, such as in abuse- and alcoholism-related newsgroups and mailing lists. They have been used by whistleblowers to expose company and government wrongdoing. They are also a safe way to post personal ads or newsgroup messages while avoiding harassment or flames (although many newsgroups frown on using an anonymous address just to hide behind your opinions). Of course, there is the potential for abuse, such as for illegal activities like trading child pornography. But in actuality, these abuses are rather infrequent.

With most anonymous remailers, you have to open an account with the remailer's operator in order to pay for the service, so it won't be completely anonymous—the remailer operator knows who you are and might be compelled to reveal your identity, under a court order, for instance. The anonymous remailer should be sufficient for most purposes, unless you're doing something illegal. (Truly anonymous remailers exist, but they're very difficult to use.)

Here are some anonymous remailers to get you started:

- **Mailanon:** `http://www.mailanon.com/`

- **MyEmail.Net:** `http://www.myemail.net/anonymous.html` (This is a free service that sends anonymous email via the Web; it's very easy to use, but not as secure as other anonymous remailers.)

- **nym.alias.net:** `http://www.cs.berkeley.edu/~raph/n.a.n.html`

- **Nymserver:** `http://www.nymserver.com/`

- **Replay Remailer:** `http://www.replay.com/remailer/`

Timesaver
A flame is an angry or hostile email message or Usenet post, designed to provoke an equally acrimonious response. The exchange of several flames is called a flame war. Many flames are the result of a too-hasty response to a misunderstood message, although some are deliberately written to get your goat. Save yourself a lot of time, hassle, and grief—ignore and delete any flame that comes your way.

Bright Idea
For maximum privacy, send your message through two or more anonymous remailers. You send the message to remailer A with instructions to forward it to remailer B, who finds instructions on who the end recipient is. This is much more secure, because remailer A has no idea who the message is going to, and remailer B has no idea who it came from. The more remailers you funnel the message through, the harder it is to trace.

Combating Spam

So, now you know how to protect the email leaving your inbox, but you probably still feel helpless when dealing with what's coming in. Spam—mass mailings of unsolicited ads, generally of a dubious, fraudulent, or pornographic nature—has become an overwhelming problem on the Internet in recent years, one that affects us all.

It costs very little for spammers to send out millions of unsolicited messages, so there is no real incentive for them not to do it. However, Internet providers must deal with all those messages, and that's where it starts to cost all of us. Around 10% of your monthly Internet access fee goes to pay for the extra hardware, staff, and bandwidth that your ISP had to invest in to handle the increased amounts of junk mail. In return, you get a slower Internet connection (processing spam is a significant performance drag), decreased bandwidth due to the bandwidth being consumed by mass mailings, and unwanted mail that you have to take the time to download and deal with.

So, if you've ever wondered why spam makes some people so rabid, it's because spam is the only kind of junk mail that the recipient must pay for, rather than the sender. Imagine if telemarketers were allowed to call your cellular phone—you'd get mad, wouldn't you?

Spam is universally worthless, and an overly large percentage of it is borderline fraudulent or out-and-out illegal. Most of the spam that I've received advertised get-rich-quick schemes, multi-level marketing scams, pirated software, bulk-email software and lists, stock frauds, quack medicines, and pornographic materials. Most legitimate businesses know that spam is an effective way to kill their reputations, so they avoid it.

Preventative Measures

One good way to cut down on the amount of spam you receive is to realize where spammers are getting your email address from and stop them at the source. Spammers harvest email addresses from several major sources, generally using automated robots called spambots:

- Usenet posts

- Mailing list subscriber lists

- Web page forms

- Mailto links in Web pages

Now you know why you started getting so much spam after registering for that "free" software download. You are still in control—you can take steps to stop spammers from obtaining your address at each of these sources. Of course, the best way is to avoid entering your email address in any of these forums, but why let spammers control your online life?

Avoiding Spam on Usenet

One of the most effective ways to keep your email address off spammers' lists is to change the address that appears in the From and Reply-To headers of Usenet posts in a process called munging. Munging foils spambots that harvest anything with an @ sign in these message headers.

Generally, you can change the From and Reply-to email address in the Identity or User Information section of your news account's properties. Before changing your email address, make sure that you aren't violating your ISP's policies. And don't change your address to something that could actually be a real email address or make up domain names, as these might actually be real domains. Your object is to stop the unwanted mail, not send it somewhere else.

Be creative with your mung, and change it often to keep spammers from altering their harvesting programs to accommodate the block. (If you use the same client for mail and news, take care to return your email address to its proper form before sending personal email.) Make your change obvious to humans, so they can easily restore it to the correct address when they reply to your posts. Here are some suggestions:

- yourname(AT)domain(DOT)com

- yournamZ@ZxamplZ.nZt replace Z with E

Inside Scoop
Overwhelming amounts of spam can render your emailbox useless. I had that problem with my old email address after I registered to download a lot of free software on the Web. It got to the point where I was receiving ten spam messages for every one personal email message. The only solution was to discontinue my old address altogether and take care not to reveal my new one to anyone other than legitimate contacts.

- yourname@-REMOVE_THIS-domain.com

- see_my_sig@for.my.real.address

Watch Out!
If you mung your email address, be sure to tell people how to get the correct address somewhere in your message. But don't just put your real email address in your sig—many spambots look for everything in the message with an @ sign. Instead, spell the address out ("my real address is name AT domain DOT com") or just include simple instructions ("to reply via email, remove REMOVE_THIS-from my address").

Many members of the Usenet community frown on munging, because it breaks the automated reply feature of most email clients and newsreaders, forcing readers to manually enter your address in order to reply to your post. It also violates the rules upon which Usenet was built, which call for a valid email address in the From line of every post.

A good alternative is to get a free email account just for posting to Usenet. If you can, set the account to not receive mail, or just never check it for mail. Use your sig to tell people what your real email address is: "DO NOT REPLY TO fake@hotmail.com. It is only used for posting and does not accept any email. To reply by email, use yourname AT domain DOT com."

Avoiding Spam in Mailing Lists

Anyone can send a simple command to a mailing list manager program and get a list of all the list's subscribers in return, complete with email addresses. To hide your name from the subscriber list, send the following message to the administrative address: SET <listname> CONCEAL or SET <listname> CONCEAL YES.

Avoiding Spam on the Web

Avoid entering your email address into Web page forms when you're registering for a product or service, taking a survey, downloading a piece of software, and the like. Only give the address if necessary—if you require feedback or if you're buying something, for instance. Many sites use this information to send unsolicited emails.

But this practice is decreasing, due to self-regulation and the way that spamming seriously hurts a business's reputation. A responsible Web site posts a privacy policy stating exactly what personal information is collected, why, and how it is used. If the site does send out mailings based on addresses entered into a form, there should be an option somewhere on the form enabling you to refuse the mailing. If neither of these elements is present, feel free to fake your address in the form or skip the site altogether. Or get a free, throwaway email address to use in these kinds of situations.

You should also remove your personal information from the white page directories, such as WhoWhere, Four11, and Switchboard. First, search each directory to see if you are listed. (The major directories and their URLs are listed in Chapter 5.) Many of these directories provide a way for you to request removal of your personal information directly from the Web site. If you don't find such an option, send a polite email message to the directory's maintainer requesting that you be removed. Also check your ISP's site, your company's site, and even your alma mater's site to make sure that your email address isn't published in a directory there, as well.

Avoiding Spam from Your Home Pages

Some spambots are programmed to roam the Web, harvesting email addresses from mailto links in Web pages. If you maintain a set of Web pages, removing the mailto link altogether is the best way to prevent spam from this source.

What if you still want to give visitors a convenient way to get in touch with you? Well, you can mung the mailto link so that visitors and Web browsers can still read it, but spambots cannot.

The fastest way to scramble the mailto link is to use the Mailto Encoder at `http://www.siteup.com/encoder.html`, which I used on all of my pages. Just enter your email address in the form—the site promises not to send you any unsolicited email—and you get a mailto code in return, with your email address translated into ASCII code. Visitors can still click the link to send you a message, but spambots can't harvest a readable email address from it. Of course, if the spammers catch on, it is very easy for them to account for the change, so this method probably won't work forever.

If your Web server supports CGI scripts, you can set up a mailer form on your page that allows visitors to send you feedback. Just make sure that your email address isn't included

Watch Out!
Using just your email address, it's possible to find out a lot about you. Try this. Go to `http://in-105.infospace.com/info/reverse.htm`. Enter your email address in the Reverse Email field at the bottom of the page, and click Find—your full name appears. Click that and more information surfaces, most likely your mailing address and phone number. Now, go to `http://maps.yahoo.com/py/maps.py` and enter the mailing address. *Voilà!* Directions to your house. Feeling paranoid yet? If your name doesn't show up, count yourself lucky; if it does, you probably want to click the Remove Your Email Address link to get your personal information out of there.

Timesaver
Microsoft Outlook
is the only email
client I know of
that has a built-in
spam filter, and it's
one of the most
effective spam-
blocking tools I've
used. To turn it on,
click the Organize
toolbar button from
the Inbox, and
select the Junk
E-Mail option.
There are actually
two filters—one for
spam and one for
adult content. You
can change junk
mail into an eye-
catching color,
move it to a junk
mail folder, or
throw it in the
trash. If anything
sneaks through the
filter, automatically
add the address to
the filter list by
right-clicking on the
message and
selecting Junk
E-Mail.

anywhere in the HTML code or text of the page. A free mailer form is available at `http://www.cgi-free.com/`, if you don't want to write your own.

Filtering Out the Junk

Even with all these preventative measures, spam is still going to find its way to you. The best thing to do at this stage is to use your email client's filters to shift unwanted email to your trash folder before you even see it. Or become a part of the fight to stop unwanted email—filter spam to a special junk mail folder, so you can investigate it and send out complaints as you have time.

One option is to set up a filter that deletes all messages that you receive from certain addresses, and add new spammers' addresses to the filter as you continue to receive unwanted mail. But this method is time-consuming and not very effective, because spammers change email addresses so often. A better solution is to create a filter that blocks messages with common spamming terms, such as Make Money Fast, Get Rich, $$$, or XXX. As you receive new spam messages, you can add other common phrases to your lexicon.

Try creating such a filter with Netscape Messenger:

1. Open Edit, Message Filters.

2. Click New (see Figure 6.8).

3. Name the filter Spam.

4. Select Match Any of the Following.

5. Select The Subject of the Message Contains Make Money Fast.

6. Click More and continue to add common spam terms. You can also select specific senders to block.

7. Select Then Delete.

8. Click OK.

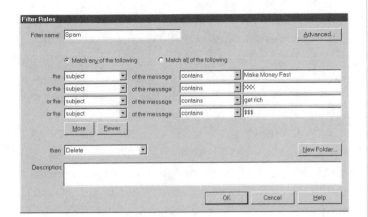

Figure 6.8
Creating a spam
filter in
Messenger.

9. In the Message Filters window, move the Spam filter to the top of the list so it is applied before all other mail filters.

10. Click OK.

The process of creating the spam filter is similar in Outlook Express (open Tools, Message Rules, Mail and click Add) and Eudora Light (open Tools, Filters and click New). Next to Microsoft Outlook, Eudora Light and Eudora Pro have the best spam-fighting filters, allowing you to filter messages based on the body text and headers so that you can better find and delete spam. The important thing, though, is to keep refining your spam filters and making them more effective.

You can also try commercial, shareware, and freeware filtering products that work with your email client to provide more focused spam blocks. They can do a better job than you because they already have built-in anti-spam rules based on message content, known spammers, and the like, and they can adapt to your preferences. The following are some recommended filtering add-ons that you can download from any software archive site (see Appendix B for suggestions).

- **Spam Buster:** Windows 95/98/NT 4.0; requires a POP3 account; shareware

- **SpamKiller:** Windows 95/98/NT 4.0; requires a POP3 or MAPI account; $29.95 (30-day trial version available)

Bright Idea
Your ISP should also institute filters at the mail server level to block the most egregious junk emailers before you have to waste online time downloading and filtering their messages. Ask your ISP what kind of spam filters are in place.

Timesaver

A widely used bulk-email program inserts a defective timestamp into forged Received lines. These lines contain the strings "-0600 (EST)" or "-0700 (EDT)," which aren't the correct time zone offsets. If you can filter based on header content—if you're using Eudora, for instance—set a filter to reject all mail with either of these strings in a Received line. This catches a lot of spam.

Fighting Back

If it's not enough to filter away the spam, or if you want to get back at the spammers whose messages do make it through your filters and into your inbox, take action. Your best course is to attempt to find out who sent the spam and then get the spammer's Internet access account closed by complaining to the service provider.

This process is not as easy as it might seem at first, and it does take some time. But it's worthwhile to learn, because you can use it to trace any email with a forged address—not just mail from spammers, but also from someone who might be harassing or stalking you through email.

You can't assume that the email address listed in the From field is the actual sender of the message. This field, and most of the other fields in the message's headers, can easily be forged. This is a common tactic taken by spammers to prevent revenge replies.

So, the first step is to examine the message headers and try to figure out where the message really came from. Most email clients show an abbreviated form of the message headers by default, but you should easily be able to reveal the full headers while the message is open:

- In Eudora Light, click the Show All Headers (Blah Blah Blah) toolbar button.

- In Messenger, select View, Headers, All.

- In Outlook Express, select File, Properties and click the Details tab.

- In Microsoft Outlook, select View, Options and look in the Internet Headers window.

The message headers for a spam email look like Figure 6.9. The bottom Received line is the best source for learning where the message originated. Received lines document each machine that the message passed through, with the last Received line being the starting point of the message's journey. What you want to look at is the domain name (the last two parts of the address—"domain.com") and the IP address (the number in angle brackets—<xxx.xxx.xxx.xxx>). These two items, particularly the IP address, should reliably indicate the originating system of the message.

First, look at the bottom Received, the From, and the Message-ID lines; if the domain names in these lines don't agree, that's a good sign that the From line (and possibly the other lines as well) has been forged. This is very easy to do and so is almost a characteristic of spam messages, which is why you can't count on the From line to reveal the sender's identity. (However, if the sender has a private domain name on a commercial ISP, the Message-ID and Received lines indicate the ISP's domain name while the From line shows the sender's private domain name.)

The bottom Received line contains the most useful information, but it and any number of Received lines above it can also be forged. It's very common for this line to be located beneath the Message-ID line in forged headers. Forged headers often show discrepancies that you can easily look for. If any number in the IP address is greater than 255, it's definitely a fake. Also look for discrepancies in the time the message was received; spammers often make obvious mistakes here. If you determine that the bottom Received line is forged, move up to the next-highest Received line, and check it for forgeries.

Bright Idea
Another good spam filter is one that moves all messages that aren't addressed directly to you (in either the To or CC lines) to a junk mail folder or deletes them. Of course, if you belong to any mailing lists, you have to create filters that move these messages to a designated folder before checking for spam. Your email program's filter manager should enable you to set up the order in which filters are processed.

```
Internet headers:   Received: from mail2.catalogue.com (mail2.catalogue.com [199.72.20.4]) by
                    arcana.catalogue.com (8.8.8/8.7.2) with ESMTP id SAA04749 for
                    <shannon@arcana.com>; Sat, 15 Aug 1998 18:45:22 -0400 (EDT)
                    From: robertw610@linkonline.net
                    Received: from girl@linkonline.net (207.77.216.99) by mail2.catalogue.com with
                    SMTP (Eudora Internet Mail Server 2.1); Sat, 15 Aug 1998 18:42:35 +0100
                    To: <shannon@arcana.com>
                    Subject: New Kit - Send Your Own Mass E-mail
                    Date: Sat, 15 Aug 1998 12:10:49
                    Message-ID: <1308915937-89728077@mail2.catalogue.com>
                    Content-Type: text
                    Content-Length: 3174
```

Figure 6.9
Message headers for a spam email.

After you locate the correct originating domain name, send an email address to the system's administrator to report the spam. The address postmaster@domain.com always works, but a good address to try first is abuse@domain.com as this goes straight to someone whose job is to deal with spam; not all ISPs support the abuse address, though.

Bright Idea
Abuse.net
(http://www.abuse
.net/) makes sure
your complaints
about spam make
it to the person at
the offending sys-
tem who can do
something about
it. Just send your
complaint to
domain@abuse.net
and the service
forwards the mes-
sage to the cor-
rect abuse
address at that
domain name. You
have to register to
use the service,
which prevents
spammers from
abusing
Abuse.net.

It is very important that you insert all of the message headers for the spam in your complaint exactly as they appear in
your email client. Without this information, the system administrator cannot track down the spammer.

You might also want to CC the letter to the postmasters or
abuse addresses of the domains indicated in the Received lines
between the originating system and your own computer, in
case the bottom Received lines are forged. This also lets the
other system administrators know that spam is traveling
through their servers, especially if the spam seems to advocate
illegal activities.

You can use Whois to find some more people to complain
to, if you're so inclined. If you have a shell account, type whois
at the prompt, followed by the domain name. On the Web, go
to the Whois gateway at http://www.allwhois.com/, which performs an international domain name search. The results provide the administrative, technical, and billing contacts for the
domain name, complete with email addresses.

Finally, check the body of the unsolicited message. Often,
the message includes a Web site or email address that you can
contact for more information, which has to be legitimate if the
spammer wants to make any sales. Try sending your complaint
to the postmaster or abuse address at this address's domain
name.

If your first complaints don't get satisfactory results or even
elicit threats, find the spammer's upstream provider by entering the domain name or IP address from the header into
Traceroute (http://net.yahoo.com/cgi-bin/trace.sh is a
Traceroute gateway on the Web). Complaining to the postmaster or abuse address at this provider could get the spammer's Internet access revoked, particularly if the spammer
owns his or her own domain name.

If you want to be a really responsible netizen, track down
the source and complain about every spam message you
receive. Be polite in your message, and be sure to include the
entire spam message, plus message headers. Most ISPs have a
zero-tolerance spam policy and will remove the offending

account. Some states, such as Washington, have even instituted anti-spam laws.

You might want to create a form letter that goes something like this:

> Subject: Junk Email From Your Site: (Subject: {insert the original subject of the spam letter})
>
> Dear Postmaster,
>
> A user on your system has sent me (and apparently many others) the UNSOLICITED COMMERCIAL EMAIL at the end of this message. You are being contacted either because the message originated at your site, used your SMTP mailer, has replies directed to your site, or solicited visits to a Web page hosted by your site.
>
> As I'm sure you're aware, unsolicited bulk email is a misuse of Internet resources. It also wastes the time, money, and resources of any person it's sent to and the systems it passes through. Please take whatever steps are necessary to cut off the offender's Internet access and stop unsolicited bulk email.
>
> Thank you.
>
> ----Begin Spam----
>
> {insert the spam message with all message headers here}
>
> ----End Spam----

Moneysaver
You can easily find free DNS lookup and Traceroute tools, so you don't have to go through the Web. Windows users should download WSPING32 from any major FTP software archive; Mac users should get Mac TCP Watcher. Search FTP sites for these programs via the Archie gateway at `http://archie.rutgers.edu/archie.html`.

What Not to Do

Many mass mailings include specific instructions for unsubscribing from the list, usually by sending a "remove" message to an email address. **Don't ever do this!** You won't get removed from any lists—you will just verify that your email address is valid and end up receiving even more spam.

Several opt-out lists were established after spam became so prevalent, but you should avoid these, as well. In theory, you put your name on an opt-out list to get yourself removed from all mass-mailing lists. For opt-out lists to work, the spammer

Timesaver

Spam Hater is a freeware utility that works with your email client to automate the complaint process. It analyzes message headers, offers four editable complaint messages, and enables you to send the complaint with just a click to the originating domain, any supporting domains, and several email abuse organizations. It can even funnel your complaint through an anonymous remailer or send it under a fake email address (which I don't recommend to get your complaint taken seriously). Download it from http://www.cix.co.uk/~netservices/spam/spam_hater.htm.

must comply with removing your address; because spammers are so unscrupulous, why would they go along with these lists? Also, some opt-out lists are actually attempts by spammers to garner more legitimate email addresses, resulting in even more spam for you!

Don't get really nasty or give the spammer an excuse for retaliation, no matter how angry unsolicited email makes you. For instance, don't mailbomb the spammer (mailbombing is the process of sending a huge attachment or large quantities of email messages to someone in an effort to fill up their inbox and render it useless). There's a real possibility that your mailbomb will get bounced back to you (whoops!) or go to the mailbox of some poor soul whose address was forged. Also, mailbombs affect the entire mail system, including all the innocent users of the system. Finally, mailbombing is technically a Denial of Service attack, which is illegal in the United States. It's much more effective to complain (nicely!) to the spammer's Internet service provider.

Some spams include toll-free phone and fax numbers, which you might be tempted to abuse. After all, now you're costing the spammer money, right? Wrong. If the spam includes a toll-free number, that indicates that the business doing the advertising really doesn't have a clue and was taken advantage of by some unscrupulous bulk-email company. Phone harassment is a crime, and the phone numbers of all callers to 800-numbers are recorded. You could try calling once to complain or sending a polite fax; this might do some good if the business owner honestly didn't realize that spamming is an unacceptable way to advertise online.

Guarding Against Email Hoaxes and Frauds

Anyone with an email address is a prime target for hoaxes and frauds. As I mentioned before, a lot of spam mail is fraudulent. You could also be personally targeted for more sophisticated scams. In addition that that, well-meaning netizens often forward hoaxes to anyone they can, thinking they are doing a good deed when in actuality they're only consuming bandwidth with needless mass-mailings. Your best defense is to recognize a scam or fraud when it finds its way into your mailbox and then report it to the appropriate agencies.

Good Times, the Internet Tax, and Other Email Hoaxes

How does a hoax get started? Some unknown prankster crafts a fake email and sends it to Usenet or to several email addresses, usually with a forged address. People who believe the hoax's often outrageous claims forward it on to everyone they know, who in turn forward it to everyone they know. Before long, it becomes an unstoppable chain. While these hoaxes might seem harmless on the surface, they actually cause a serious problem. The constant forwarding of these messages clogs mail servers and consumes bandwidth needlessly. Some hoaxes of this type have been circulating for years.

The most common type of hoax is the email virus; one of the first of these hoaxes was the Good Times Virus email, which is why email viruses are often referred to as "Good Times" viruses. Email viruses generally warn you against reading email messages with a particular subject line, such as "Good Times," "AOL4FREE," "Penpal Greetings," or "Letter from a Friend"; they claim that just opening these messages transmits a virus to your computer, wrecking your system, trashing your hard disk, and basically bringing about the end of the world.

The important thing to remember when you come across a message like this is that it's impossible to transmit computer viruses via email. Viruses must be contained in executable code to cause any damage, and you have to run the code to infect your system with the virus. Because email messages are plain text files, they can't contain viruses.

Email attachments can carry viruses, though, if the attachment is executable code. You should never open an attachment if you don't know the sender, particularly attachments

Watch Out!
Spammers are now using the return receipt feature of some email clients to verify live email addresses. What generally happens is you receive a message that appears to be addressed to someone else. You open the message to find that it is encrypted, and of course, you don't have the password, so you delete it. A return receipt then appears in your outbox, verifying that you opened the message. Lists of valid email addresses are a valuable commodity for spammers and can be sold for a high price.

that you receive via spam mail. Delete all unknown attachments without opening them, and run attachments from known sources through an antivirus scanner, just to be on the safe side. (Learn more about computer viruses and antivirus scanners in Chapter 12, "Safe Surfing.")

Here are some other famous hoaxes. Be on the lookout for these or anything like them:

- The FCC is planning to charge an Internet or modem tax.

- The Internet is shutting down for cleaning.

- Microsoft is buying the Catholic Church.

- Bill Gates is testing some new email-tracking software—just forward the message to 1,000 people and he'll send you $1,000 and a free copy of Windows 98.

- You must forward the message to a certain number of people, or a virus will be let loose on your computer.

- Send postcards to the little boy dying of cancer. (Note: He's no longer a little boy or dying.)

- Send your old shoes to Nike, and they'll send you a new pair in return.

- The Neiman-Marcus or $250 cookie recipe (based on a classic urban legend).

- Your kidney could be stolen (another urban legend classic—to read it and more like it, go to http:// urbanlegends.com.

- Anything that plays on your fears, spouts a lot of technical gobbledy-gook, and requests you to forward the message to everyone you know.

More serious hoaxes request personal information for nefarious purposes. Consider the following, which was an actual mailing:

Bright Idea
The proliferation of email virus hoaxes has rendered real virus notices via email ineffective. The Department of Energy Computer Incident Advisory Capability maintains an alert page of virus hoaxes, plus information on how to tell a genuine warning from a hoax, at http:// ciac.llnl.gov/ ciac/CIACHoaxes. html. There's also some good info on recognizing email-based chain letters.

IMPORTANT INFORMATION FOR PARENTS OF CHILDREN BORN BETWEEN 1985 and 1997 INCLUSIVE: GERBER BABY FOOD company lost a class action. Gerber has been marketing their baby food as "all natural." The baby food was found to contain preservatives. Under this settlement, Gerber is now responsible for giving every child born between 1985 and 1997 a $500 savings bond. However, Gerber is not responsible for advertising this settlement in any way. To obtain the bond, send a copy of your child's birth certificate and Social Security card to: **GERBER FOOD** Settlement Administration Infant Litigation, PO Box xxxx, Minneapolis, MN 55480

Examine this letter closely—it asks you to send a birth certificate and Social Security number to an unknown post office box. This is all the ammo someone needs to obtain bank accounts, credit cards, and other identifying documents in your child's name. Although this particular mailing wasn't a scam, just a misunderstanding, the lesson here is guard your personal information zealously. In the information age, personal information is a very powerful tool for scam artists and criminals.

Another, more common version of this scam comes from someone claiming to be your ISP. For some reason or another—failed equipment, security measures, and so on—the ISP needs you to confirm your email account username, password, billing address, and/or credit card number. No ISP would ever request this kind of sensitive information, especially a password, through email (if at all). If you receive a message like this, report it to your ISP immediately—whatever that person plans to do with your password, you can be sure that he or she is up to no good.

Watch Out!
Be especially wary of suspicious or unusual emails around April Fool's Day—it seems to be the sanctioned day for email and Usenet pranks. In fact, April Fool's, 1994, is when the infamous "Microsoft to buy the Catholic Church" hoax got started. Visit http://www.2meta.com/april-fools/ for a collection of past April Fool's hoaxes. They're a lot of fun to read—if you don't fall for them!

Losing Money Fast!

Probably the most common kind of email scam is of the Make Money Fast variety. Generally, these are just garden-variety chain letters or pyramid schemes. Just because they're sent via email doesn't make them any less illegal.

Bright Idea
To prevent prankster co-workers from sending hoax emails using your email address while you're away from your desk, protect your computer with a screensaver password. Most preinstalled and commercial screensavers support passwords. On Windows, right-click over the desktop, select Properties, and click the Screen Saver tab; check the Password Protected box and click Change to set your password.

Here are some common varieties of the Make Money Fast scam:

- **Multi-level marketing scams:** Most often, these messages promise you lots of money for very little investment and work. These scams are illegal and a great way to lose money, as well.

- **Make $$$ working at home:** You just end up spending $$$ to find out that you can't make it working at home. Multi-level marketing scams often travel under this guise, as well.

- **Make money by sending bulk emailings:** These scams want to sell you lists of email addresses or mass-emailing software—spam, in other words. You already know how the Internet community feels about that.

Besides the Make Money Fast scams, be on the lookout for other scam artists trying to bilk you out of your money in creative ways. The following are the more common scams to watch out for:

- **Health and diet scams:** Typically offering miracle cures, scientific breakthroughs, secret formulas, or ancient ingredients, these are just electronic snake oil. If it sounds too good to be true...

- **Investment opportunities:** You're promised an outrageously high rate of return with little or no risk from people you've never heard of who claim to have high-level financial connections. Don't you believe it.

- **Credit repair schemes:** No one can legally remove accurate, non-obsolete, negative information from your credit report.

- **Cable descramblers:** Get cable for free—by purchasing a cable descrambler. These devices often don't work, and they're illegal.

- **Free vacations:** You've just won a vacation to an exotic locale, or you've been selected to receive a luxury vacation at a bargain-basement price. After you get there, you find that you're staying in the basement, and you have to pay a hefty fee just to get out.

If any of these scams sound familiar, that's because they aren't new. In some form or another, they've been around forever. It's just that now the scam artists use cheap, easy email to troll for victims.

Doing Something About It

The first thing you should do—and do it right now—is get skeptical. Don't trust anything unless you can personally verify it, and the more urgent it sounds, the less you should trust it. If an email message isn't a scam or a hoax, you should be able to easily contact the message's originator and verify the originator's identity through some other means. If you don't want to bother checking the message's validity, then don't bother forwarding it, either.

Whenever you receive a message that you suspect is a fraud or hoax, do the exact opposite of what the message wants you to do. If it asks you to forward the message to all your friends, don't. If it wants you to send money, don't. Never, never send your Internet access account password or other personal information to someone who requests them via email, even if the message purports to be from your ISP.

If you suspect that the hoax was passed on to you by an innocent but well-meaning third party, reply to the sender and explain to him or her that it was a hoax. Stress that he or she shouldn't send the hoax out to anyone else.

Watch Out!
Top 10 signs that
an email offer is a
scam:
1. Forged return
   address.
2. Lots of capital
   letters and
   exclamation
   points.
3. Unsolicited
   offers.
4. Unverifiable
   references.
5. Claims a
   secret method
   available to a
   limited num-
   ber of people.
6. Too much
   about money,
   not enough
   about the
   deal.
7. Pay first, learn
   the details
   later.
8. Requires
   sending a
   chain letter.
9. States that it
   is not a scam.
10. Sounds too
    good to be
    true.

Also report the mailing to the appropriate agencies to help stop the hoax or fraud from spreading, particularly if it appears to be illegal. Table 6.1 lists the appropriate places to report different kinds of frauds, scams, and hoaxes. Many of the Web sites listed also maintain alert lists of recently reported frauds and hoaxes.

TABLE 6.1: PLACES TO REPORT EMAIL FRAUDS, HOAXES, AND SCAMS

Agency	Email Address	Phone Number	Web Site	Purpose
Federal Trade Commission	UCE@FTC.GOV (spam complaints); pyramid@ftc.gov (pyramid schemes)	(202) 382-4357	http://www.ftc.gov/bcp/conline/fraud.htm	Consumer fraud and spam.
Internal Revenue Service	net-abuse@nocs.insp.irs.gov	None	http://www.irs.gov/	Get-rich-quick schemes.
National Consumer Complaint Center	access@alexander-law.com	(408) 289-1776	http://www.alexanderlaw.com/nccc/cbintro.html	Consumer fraud; forwards complaints to investigative agencies.
National Fraud Information Center	Use the form at the Web site.	1-800-876-7060	http://www.fraud.org/	Consumer fraud.
ScamBusters	SBinfo@netrageous.com	1-800-780-0090	http://www.scambusters.org/	Any Internet hoaxes or scams.
Securities and Exchange Commission	enforcement@sec.gov	1-800-SEC-0330	http://www.sec.gov/enforce.htm	Unsolicited stock tips and offers.
Software and Information Industry Association	netpiracy@spa.org	1-800 388-7478	http://www.spa.org/piracy/default.htm	Pirated software offers.

Agency	Email Address	Phone Number	Web Site	Purpose
U.S. Postal Service	consumer @email. usps.gov	Your nearest postal inspection office.	http://www. usps.gov/ websites/ depart/ inspect/	Anything involving postal mail, particularly chain letters and child pornography.
Web Police	Use the form at the Web site.	(317) 823-0377	http://www. web-police. org/	Any Internet crime or fraud.

Just the Facts

- Contrary to most people's assumptions, your email messages are not private; they can be archived on your mail system, snooped into while sitting on the mail server, intercepted during transit, or forwarded all over the Internet.

- PGP and S/MIME encryption are easy, effective ways to keep your email messages private, while anonymous remailers offer a convenient method for protecting your identity when sending email.

- Unsolicited bulk email has become a prevalent, costly annoyance, but by protecting your email address, taking advantage of spam filters, and lodging complaints with the right people, you can greatly cut down the amount of unsolicited mail you receive.

- Email has become the perfect medium for transmitting hoaxes, false or misunderstood rumors, frauds, and scams; don't believe everything you read.

Inside Scoop
What's even scarier than email snooping at work or chain letter frauds are the occasional cases of harassment and stalking that some people experience via email and spam. Take the case of Jayne Hitchcock, who was the target of several revenge spams forged in her name, some of them publishing her home address and phone number (read the whole story at http:// members.tripod. com/ ~cyberstalked/). This is pretty scary stuff, but fortunately cases like Jayne's are putting cyber-stalking laws on the books.

GET THE SCOOP ON...
Finding and using the best chat tools ▪ Understanding the
culture of chat worlds ▪ Keeping safe in chat rooms
▪ Conferencing over the Internet ▪ Sending instant messages
over the Internet

Getting Personal with Real-Time Chat

C HATTING IS A HUGELY POPULAR activity on the Internet, probably because it's an easy (and free) way to waste lots and lots of time. Real-time chat can be an avenue to building lifelong friendships with people you never meet face-to-face, starting romances with people whose genders you can't be sure of, or having disease-free, commitment-free "cybersex" with total strangers. But chat is not all illicit fun and games. It can also be an effective means for conferencing with several people at once, networking with people around the world who share your interests or profession, or attending virtual lectures given by experts or celebrities.

When it comes to chat, there is a dizzying array of choices— the type of chat, the tool to use, the places to go. And there are many ways beyond old-fashioned chat to use the Internet for quick and easy communication, including voiceconferencing, videoconferencing, and instant messaging. Even if you know your way around the rest of the Net, the endless choices in this particular area might be a real turn-off. This chapter will help you sort through it all and find the real-time communication methods that suit your needs.

Choosing Your Chat

Timesaver
IRCFerret is a nifty program that searches IRC networks for your friends, so you don't have to waste time connecting to and disconnecting from a bunch of different servers. A freeware version is available for Windows 95/98 at http:// www.ferretsoft. com/netferret/ products.htm.

Chat is so fun and addictive because the conversations take place in real time. Unlike email and Usenet, chat conversations occur while you're sitting there typing, enabling a much more dynamic communication. It's like getting on a big party line, except with chat you don't have to pay toll charges.

Chatting is not as simple as other Internet activities, such as sending email or reading Usenet news, however. You can't just get one software program, fire it up, learn a few addresses, and be on your way. Your chat options are numerous, and each requires a different software program and connection procedure. After some experimentation, you might find that only one is right for you, that you like them all, or that all chat stinks.

This section covers the three major categories of chat—the best tools to use, how to start chatting, and places to talk. You'll learn about the following:

- Internet Relay Chat (IRC)

- Non-IRC text-based chat

- Non-IRC virtual world–based chat

IRC—The Original Chat

The first chat network—and still the most popular, with hundreds of thousands of users—is Internet Relay Chat. If you're looking for a plethora of choices, in terms of what to talk about and who to talk with, IRC is the place for you. It's an especially effective way to meet people from around the world, which you might like if you're from out of town or out of the country and feeling homesick.

Like Usenet and other long-established Internet communities, IRC has its own rules, ways of behaving, and language, which you have to learn. Because IRC is so open, it's also most vulnerable to such distasteful activities as pornography, cybersex, and stalking (learn ways to protect yourself later in this chapter).

Because IRC is the most popular chat system, you have the largest choice here when it comes to clients. Searching for an IRC client easily finds more than a dozen. But only a few clients stand out, combining ease-of-use with the broadest functionality.

Microsoft Chat

If you're a beginner and just want to test IRC to see if it's right for you, then Microsoft Chat is a good choice. This chat client is very easy to use. It automatically connects to an IRC server at the Microsoft Network and provides buttons for listing, joining, and leaving channels.

Microsoft Chat starts out in comic mode, which shows everybody as a cartoon figure and is fun for about five minutes (see Figure 7.1). After the novelty wears off, and it does quickly after you realize that the small number of cartoons makes it difficult to tell anybody apart, click the Plain Text View button to switch to a text chat, which is much easier to understand.

- **System Requirements:** Windows 95/98/NT 4.0

- **Price:** free

- **Download:** `http://www.microsoft.com/msdownload/iebuild/ chat25_win32/EN/chat25_win32.htm`

If you do get addicted to IRC, you may soon find that Microsoft Chat doesn't have enough power. Microsoft Chat doesn't support the multiple windows, file transfer, secure chat, and other capabilities that you might want, and it limits you to Microsoft Network IRC servers. In that case, you're ready to graduate to a full-featured IRC client.

Bright Idea
There are actually quite a few IRC networks. The major ones are best for finding lots of people to talk to, but by joining a local or special interest network, you might discover a more thoughtful or interesting discussion. Smaller networks that limit the number of users can provide a more tightly knit community and friendly atmosphere, while avoiding the problems of bigger networks, such as lagging conversations and netsplits (discussed later in this chapter). Try them out sometime! You'll find a list of all the IRC networks and their servers at `http://www.irchelp.org/irchelp/networks/`.

Figure 7.1
Microsoft Chat
eases newcomers
into IRC with cute,
cartoon chatting.

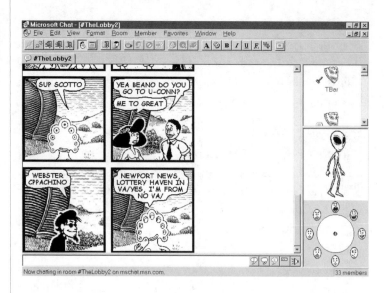

Now chatting in room #TheLobby2 on mschat.msn.com.   33 members

mIRC

Timesaver
If you have already
installed Internet
Explorer 5.0, you
can quickly get
Microsoft Chat.
Open the Control
Panels and
Add/Remove
Programs. Scroll
down until you see
Internet Explorer
5.0 and Internet
Tools, select it,
and click on
Add/Remove.
Then, select Add a
Component and
click OK. Scroll
down until you see
the Chat option,
select that check
box, and click on
Next to install it.

mIRC is the best all-around IRC client you can get, and it certainly should have everything that the average IRC user needs. Its interface is simple and easy to use (see Figure 7.2), and the help files are very complete, so you can quickly get up to speed on how to use IRC. mIRC makes the connection process easy, giving you the choice of connecting to a random IRC server on any of the major IRC networks or selecting from a preconfigured list of servers, and it provides a folder of popular channels that you can join. Once you get the hang of IRC, mIRC is very configurable, supporting macros and scripts.

- **System Requirements:** Windows 3.x/95/98/NT

- **Price:** shareware ($20)

- **Download:** http://www.mirc.co.uk/index.html

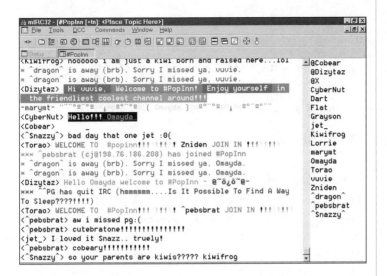

Figure 7.2
For heavy-duty IRC users, mIRC is the best client—it's easy to use but has a lot of powerful features.

PIRCH

PIRCH specializes in multimedia IRC, if you like snazzy effects. Using it, you can send and receive video, sound effects, MIDI music, and synthesized speech files. It is very customizable and includes a powerful Friends/Enemies feature, which enables you to make the program do anything upon the appearance of certain other users. PIRCH is probably too much for most casual IRC users, but if you become an IRC fanatic, you should try it.

- **System Requirements:** Windows 95/98/NT 4.0

- **Price:** shareware ($20)

- **Download:** check your favorite software download site (see Appendix B, "Unauthorized Resources," for some suggestions)

Ircle

On the Mac, Ircle is the long-established IRC client of choice. It supports all the basic IRC functions, plus file transfer, private messages, sound, and video (multimedia requires QuickTime 2.x and SoundApp). You can even identify yourself with a little face drawing or photo. It will take you a little while to learn

Watch Out!
You might not be able to connect to the IRC server of your choice. Sometimes there are network problems. Some servers are restricted to local access. Bad behavior by you, your friends, your ISP's customers, or even your entire country can result in you being banned by the server. The best thing to do when you can't connect for any reason is to try another server.

Timesaver
If you have access to a shell account, you might already have an IRC client—just log in and type `irc` at the prompt. Connect to an IRC server by typing `/server domain`. You'll have to learn the IRC commands (covered later in this chapter), and you won't have a user-friendly interface, but this is a quick way to get onto IRC.

how to use Ircle, but after you do, it should give you all the IRC functionality that you could want.

- **System Requirements:** Mac OS 7.0 (Mac OS 8.0 is recommended); MacTCP 2.0.x or OpenTransport 1.1 required

- **Price:** shareware ($15)

- **Download:** `http://www.ircle.com/`

Getting Connected to IRC

There are actually several IRC Networks, each made up of many IRC servers connected together. To get on IRC, you must connect to an IRC server. Then, you can chat with anyone else who is on that network, regardless of which server they're connected to. The most popular IRC Networks are DALnet, Undernet, IRCnet, and EFnet, so choose a server on one of those networks if you're looking for a lot of channels and people.

Here's how to connect to a server using mIRC (the process is similar in any IRC client):

1. Start mIRC (or your IRC client of choice).

2. Select an IRC server on the network that you want to join (see Figure 7.3). It's best to choose a server that's geographically close to you, because they are usually faster and give unrestricted access. If the server you want isn't listed, just click the Add button to put it in the list; find a list of servers for all the major networks at `http://www.irchelp.org/irchelp/networks/servers/`.

3. Don't enter your actual name in the Full Name field; instead, put an alias or a witty saying. Ditto your email address—don't put anything or use a fake address. (IRC is way too public to reveal anything personal about yourself.)

4. Enter a nickname (your "nick") of up to nine characters in the Nickname field; this is the handle that others see when you chat. Because there are so many IRC users, your first choice might be taken, so enter an alternative, as well. If both of those are in use, you are prompted to change your nickname after you connect.

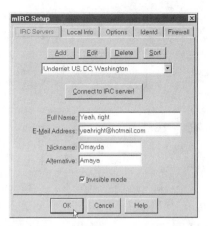

Figure 7.3
Connecting to an
IRC server with
mIRC.

5. Select the Invisible Mode check box if you don't want other users to be able to find you; I recommend this to cut down on harassment.

6. Click on the Connect to IRC Server! button. You might have to choose another server if your first choice isn't accepting connections for some reason. After you connect, the Message Of The Day (MOTD) appears, which provides information about the server's rules and policies, the server's administrators, and places to go for help. (Redisplay this message at any time by typing /MOTD.)

Once you get onto a server, you have to join a channel to start chatting. All channels have a number sign (#) in front of their names, so to join one, type /join #channelname. Channel names beginning with an ampersand (&) are local only to the server you're connected to, so other users on the IRC Network can't join them.

Each channel is controlled by a channel operator (or Op), who decides who can join the channel and has the power to kick people out; the operator has an at sign (@) in front of his or her nick in the list of people in the channel. If you join a channel that doesn't exist—create a new channel, in other words—you become the operator of that channel. By the same token, when the last person in a channel leaves, the channel disappears. Therefore, IRC is very dynamic, with channels appearing and disappearing all the time.

Bright Idea
When you join a channel, you don't leave any channels that you're already in. Only parting the channel does that. So, you can monitor several channels at once and turn to another channel if the conversation grows stale. Most IRC clients support multiple channels by opening a separate window for each channel; however, opening too many channels at once can overwhelm your connection or may not be allowed by the IRC server.

Watch Out!
Occasionally, you see the words PING? PONG! in the status window of your IRC client. This is the IRC server checking to see if you're still on the system. You don't need to do anything in response. But if you see this a lot, that means there's a lot of lag or a bad server connection, so you should try connecting to a different server.

Many IRC clients give shortcuts to finding channels. For instance, click the Channels Folder button in mIRC to open a list of popular channels (see Figure 7.4). Select one and click the Join button to go to it, or click the Names button to see who's in the channel before you join. For the best chats, look for a channel with a small number of users, but not too small—between 5 and 10. That way, you can more easily keep up with the conversation; it doesn't move too quickly or get too disjointed to follow.

When you join the channel, you'll see the channel's topic (often something silly) and a list of the people inside. Just type into the text entry area to start talking. When you first join a channel, it's a good idea to listen for a while before joining in. Often, the channel's name has nothing to do with what's being talked about, so lurking is the best way to pick up on the conversation's focus. Table 7.1 lists some good channels to start with.

Figure 7.4
mIRC's list of popular channels.

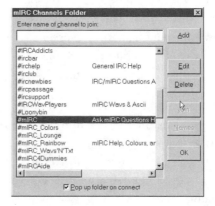

TABLE 7.1: POPULAR IRC CHANNELS

Channel(s)	Description
#new2irc, #newbies	For beginners
#chat, #hottub, #ircbar	Popular, busy destinations
#riskybus	Nonstop game
#winsock, #windows95	Help with Windows
#irchelp, #ircnewbies	Help with IRC
#mirc, #mirchelp, #new2mirc	Help with mIRC

Once you're inside IRC, you can do a lot by giving commands. As you might have noticed, all IRC commands start with a forward slash (/). mIRC and many other clients enable you to access the most frequently used commands through toolbar buttons or menu options, but I still find it easier to just type the command into the text entry area.

Table 7.2 is a reference to the most useful IRC commands (most of these commands can be accessed from the Commands menu on mIRC).

TABLE 7.2: USEFUL IRC COMMANDS

Command	What It Does
/join #channel	Joins a channel.
/part #channel	Leaves a channel.
/list -min # -max #	Lists channels that contain the number of people between the minimum and maximum numbers.
/list *keyword*	Lists all channels that contain the keyword.
/list #channel	Displays information about the channel.
/me message	Tells the channel what you're doing.
/topic #channel new_topic	Changes the topic for the channel.
/nick nickname	Changes your nick to the new nickname.
/whois nickname	Shows information about the person behind the nickname.
/invite nickname #channel	Invites the user to the channel.
/msg nickname message	Sends a private message.
/query nickname message	Starts a private chat.
/dcc chat nickname	Requests or answers a request for a private chat connection; DCC chat is faster and more secure than /query.
/kick #channel nickname	If you have Op status in the channel, kicks the user off the channel.
/mode #channel +o nickname	If you have Op status, gives the user Op status as well.

Watch Out!
On IRC, channels are owned by channel operators, who have total power, including the ability to make other users operators as well. If you're an Op, don't give operator status to just anyone, because that person can turn around and kick you out of the channel. Too many Ops quickly lead to mass-kicking. But you should make enough Ops so that the channel isn't left without an operator.

continues

Timesaver
At Liszt's IRC Chat Directory (http://www.liszt.com/chat/), you can search all IRC networks for a particular channel. If you configure your browser to recognize "chat" links, you can click a channel in the search results to open your IRC client and join that channel. Here's how to do this with Navigator: open Edit, Preferences; select the Navigator, Applications category; click New Type; type CHA, CHAT in the File Extension field and type application/x-chat in the MIME Type field; browse to your IRC client and select it for the Application to Use; and click OK.

TABLE 7.2: CONTINUED

Command	What It Does
/mode #channel +b nickname	If you have Op status, bans the user from the channel.
/mode #channel +i	If you have Op status, makes the channel by invitation only.
/motd	Displays the message of the day for the IRC server you're connected to.
/away message	Leaves a message that you're away from your computer.
/away	Turns off the away message.
/quit message	Exits IRC and displays your parting message.

Alternatives to IRC

IRC is a chatting free-for-all. It's also not very elegant and can take some time to master. For these reasons, you might prefer one of the smaller chat networks that are springing up everywhere these days. Each of these networks can be accessed via a different client. Some clients are standalone and offer a lot of additional features, such as voice chat and collaboration tools; others are Web browser plug-ins that enable you to easily access chat rooms through the Web.

Like IRC, most of these alternative chat clients support simple text chatting. But the more interesting clients have applied a graphical metaphor to chat. Chat sessions are organized into rooms that you can walk through. You can display graphical icons to indicate emotions and activities. You might even be able to create an avatar—an image that represents you in the chat world.

Also look for a client that's widely used. You're limited to the chat rooms that your client supports—it won't be much fun if you connect and there's no one to talk to.

Because these smaller chat networks are under tighter control and are often associated with a particular Web site, they can provide a more focused chat than IRC. For instance, many chat networks hold moderated sessions at pre-scheduled times on specific topics. You might attend a virtual talk given by someone in your industry or meet with colleagues once a week to discuss business technology news. It's not all work, either. These chat sessions are perfect vehicles for celebrity Q&A sessions, reading groups, support groups, and other social and entertainment activities. But these chat networks also have a large number of unmoderated chats that can be every bit as chaotic (and offensive) as the ones you find on IRC.

The following sections discuss some alternatives to IRC.

LOL Chat

If you're looking for a chat community that's less frenetic and doesn't have as much offensive content as IRC, consider the LOL (Laughing Out Loud) Chat client and community, a much smaller chat network than IRC. LOL Chat is a standalone client with a lot of features, such as file exchange, sounds, macros, and custom colors and font styles. On top of that, you can maintain an Address Book of friends, leave messages for people when they're offline, surf the Web as a group, search for someone across all LOL servers, and perform other community-friendly functions. LOL Chat does ban users who engage in lewd or offensive behavior. And it is supported by advertising, so be prepared for some intrusiveness.

- **System Requirements:** Windows 95/98/NT

- **Price:** free

- **Download:** `http://www.lolchat.com/`

PowWow Online Communities

Another alternative chat network is PowWow Online Communities, a large network of friendly, subject-oriented chat rooms that features a more toned-down chat than IRC, with a lot less cybersex. PowWow also manages to avoid the advertising and monitoring of LOL Chat. The client, PowWow, is a lot of fun—it has unique voice chat and text-to-speech features (see Figure 7.5). Besides voice-chatting, you can use PowWow for text chatting, bulletin board messaging, online

Watch Out!
Typing /list lists all the existing channels. Avoid doing this, though, because often thousands of channels are available and listing them all can cause you to disconnect from the server. Instead, refine the /list command with search keywords.

gaming, a collaborative whiteboard, group Web browsing, and voice mail. I've found that PowWow has the nicest interface and the most interesting chat rooms of all the chats I've played around in.

Figure 7.5
PowWow supports a lot of fun functions, including voice chat.

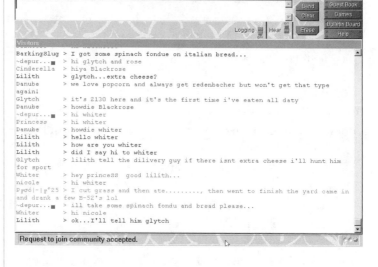

Timesaver
Almost all chat clients have a list of supported chat rooms that you can open either by clicking on a button or opening a menu. These are not only good places to start chatting if you're new to the program or the network, but they're often the busiest and most popular rooms.

- **System Requirements:** Windows 95/98/NT

- **Price:** free

- **Download:** http://www.tribal.com/products/whats_powwow.cfm

Chatting Through the Web

The ichat Rooms plug-in is the best of the Web-based chat clients: It works as a plug-in to your Web browser; it supports a lot of fun chat features; and it's in wide use on an extensive network of Web sites, including Parent Soup, Town Hall.com, Sporting News, and CollegeBeat (see Figure 7.6). ichat is the client of choice for many of those scheduled talks I mentioned earlier; in one day, for example, you can get financial advice, meet with single moms, play a trivia game, talk about what you're watching on TV, and meet the members of an up-and-coming band. You can also engage in open chat at ichat's Open24 network of rooms, although the rooms there aren't as full as on IRC, LOL Chat, or PowWow Online Communities. Finally, ichat provides lots of graphics and sounds, including simple avatars, to make chatting more fun.

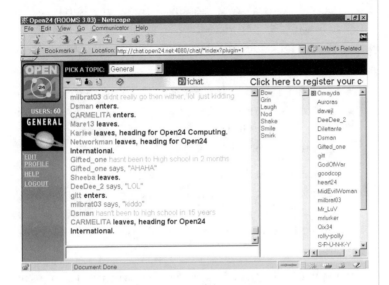

Figure 7.6
The ichat plug-in supports friendly, graphical chatting from within your Web browser.

- **System Requirements:** Windows 3.x/95/98/NT or Mac OS; Netscape Navigator 3.x or Internet Explorer 3.x (or later versions)

- **Price:** Free

- **Download:** http://www.ichat.com/

ichat is just one way to chat through your Web browser. With HTML-based chat and Java chat applets, you don't even need to download and install a software program—you just go to the site and start chatting. Hundreds of these Web-based chats are available, with more coming online all the time.

But these sites seem to lack the sense of community and loyal participants that you find on IRC or in the LOL Chat and PowWow networks. They also lack the chatting features that you might be used to, and the conversation can be frustratingly slow or choppy. Still, if you enter a Web site and feel inspired to start chatting right away, these sites are just the ticket. You'll get the best experience if you use the latest version of Navigator or Internet Explorer.

Here are some of the better HTML- and Java-based chats:

Timesaver
If you're looking for
scheduled chats,
check Yahoo! Net
Events (http://
events.yahoo.
com/). You'll find a
schedule for the
upcoming week,
today's recom-
mended chats, a
list of ongoing
chats, and chats
sorted by category.
This chat calendar
is a real timesaver
when you're in the
mood for a virtual
lecture or celebrity
talk.

- Chathouse (http://www.chathouse.com/) has three levels—public access for unregistered guests, members only for registered users (registration is free), and subscription access for $25 per year, which buys the right to create your own rooms, among other features; over 100 rooms and several hundred users are inside when you visit.

- ChatPlanet (http://www.chatplanet.com/) is a huge Java chat network with hundreds of rooms on many different topics and thousands of users; you need a browser with fast Java support for this chat.

- Chatropolis (http://www.chatropolis.com/) has more than 100 rooms, and usually there are several hundred people inside. If you want to avoid the heavy adult content, you can confine your chatting activities to a General Topics area.

- Ultimate Chat List (http://www.chatlist.com/) is a great site to search for more specialized chats.

Going 3D

When chat meets virtual worlds, the results can be awe-inspiring—or mind-numbing. By combining a chat tool with a VRML world, you create a fully immersive world, where your three-dimensional avatar walks around talking with whoever you meet. The visual aspects can really enhance the chat, if you have the high-end computer system to display them. Virtual reality–based chat requires a super-fast processor, a speedy Internet connection, a high-resolution monitor, and a lot of system resources, or you are left yawning. But this is the fastest-growing chat area, so you've got the most choices.

All 3D chat clients are basically the same, although The Palace is by far the most popular. After you install the client, it connects you to the chat server. You can then enter and explore a 3D world and even build onto the world. A 3D, ani-mated avatar represents you, and when you meet others, you can start talking. There might also be games, puzzles, and mazes to keep you amused. If you pay for the service, you get more privileges, such as the ability to make your own personalized avatar and create rooms. This is the most recreational chat of all, with less of the community flavor of IRC, PowWow, or LOL Chat and less of the scheduled, topic-oriented chat of ichat. It's basically just high-end fun, but if you have the system resources, give it a whirl.

Table 7.3 lists the most popular 3D chat clients and where you can get them.

TABLE 7.3: 3D CHAT CLIENTS

Client	Download Site	System Requirements	Price
Active Worlds	http://www. activeworlds. com/	Windows 95/98/NT; Pentium processor; 50MB hard disk space; 32MB RAM; 16-bit color	Free
Microsoft V-Chat	http://www. microsoft. com/ie/ chat/ vchatmain. htm	Windows 95/ 98/NT 4.0; 100MHz Pentium processor; 11MB hard disk space; 16MB RAM; Super VGA videocard; DirectX 5.0 driver	Free
The Palace	http://www. thepalace. com/	Windows 95/98/NT or Mac OS; Navigator 3.x or Internet Explorer 3.x	Free
Worlds Chat	http://www. worlds.net/ 3dcd/index. html	Windows 3.x/95/98; Pentium 133MHz processor; 30MB hard disk space; 48MB RAM	$9.95 (free demo available)

Bright Idea
You're likely to meet so many people on chat that you might have a hard time keeping up with them. Of course, there are software programs to help. For example, ChatStats is a freeware program for Windows 95/98/NT that stores info about your online friends, including a photo album. Download it from any software search engine (see Appendix B for suggestions).

Understanding Chat Culture

Chat—IRC in particular—is a world all its own. Over time, IRC has developed its own culture and way of doing things. You'll fit in and better understand what's going on if you enter chat rooms and channels armed with an understanding of this culture.

Because chat is so text-based, its culture revolves around writing. What started out as a shorthand way to type has evolved into a language peculiar to chat. For instance, chatters

Watch Out!
Sometimes the people you're chatting with might seem to all leave the channel or disappear at once. This happens because of netsplits, a routine part of life on IRC. Netsplits occur when the servers on the IRC Network split apart, and you can't do much about them—eventually, they'll come back together. Don't change your server, though, because your old nick will most likely collide with your new nick, which causes trouble.

rarely use punctuation or capital letters, and typos are common and ignored. Often, letters are replaced by shorter substitutions, such as putting in 'x' for 'cks.' Other times, words are misspelled just to be kewl (I mean, cool). Smilies and other means of expressing emotion through ASCII text have evolved into an art form on chat; you'll see lots of people giving each other {{{{{hugs}}}}} and ***kisses***, for instance.

A huge number of acronyms and abbreviations have been developed by the chat community, which can make the conversations look like nonsense to newcomers. Table 7.4 lists some of the more common shortcuts.

TABLE 7.4: CHAT ACRONYMS AND ABBREVIATIONS

Acronym	Meaning
AFK	Away From Keyboard
BBL	Be Back Later
BRB	Be Right Back
BTW	By The Way
CWYL	Chat With You Later
FWIW	For What It's Worth
GIWIST	Gee I Wish I'd Said That
HHOK	Ha Ha Only Kidding
HTH	Hope This Helps
HTHBE	Hope This Has Been Enlightening
IMHO	In My Humble Opinion
IMNSHO	In My Not-So-Humble Opinion
IOW	In Other Words
IRL	In Real Life
ITRW	In The Real World
K	Okay
L8R	Later
LMAO	Laughing My Ass Off
LO	Hello
LOL	Laughing Out Loud
NE1	Anyone
NP	No Problem
OIC	Oh, I See
OTOH	On The Other Hand

Acronym	Meaning
PPL	People
RE	Re-hello (hello again)
RL	Real Life
ROTFL	Rolling On The Floor Laughing
SS	Smiles
TTFN	Ta-Ta For Now
TTYL	Talk To You Later
TY	Thank You
U	You
WB	Welcome Back
Y	Why
<g>	Grin
<bg>	Big Grin
<vbg>	Very Big Grin

Inside Scoop
You might some-
times see chan-
nels or
conversations in
IRC about "warez."
This term refers to
the illegal distribu-
tion of pirated soft-
ware over the
Internet. You'll
probably want to
steer clear of this
kind of activity.

Keeping Safe While Chatting

IRC and all chat worlds present a serious risk, if you don't approach them with common sense and caution. There's something about real-time chat with strangers that's addictive, and once a while, we all tend to let our guards down, forgetting that we don't really know the people on the other end of the line. That's why chat has attracted some of the Internet's creepier types—harassers, stalkers, and pedophiles, to name a few.

But you don't have to worry, as long as you maintain your privacy and remember to get out if things get uncomfortable. Here are some rules that you should always follow to keep safe while chatting:

- Configure your chat client to maintain your anonymity; don't use your real name, username, or email address.

- Don't select a nickname that identifies your gender— particularly if you're female—or otherwise invites harass- ment.

- Never give out personal information of any kind on chat, including your real name, phone number, address, the

Watch Out!
All IRC clients can run scripts, or sets of commands. Many scripts have been hacked so that they will seriously compromise your security or endanger your computer if you run them. Never accept a script from anyone, whether you know the person or not (your well-meaning friends might not be able to detect the hack). Don't run any scripts that you didn't write yourself. Remember that other IRC users can send you files, including scripts, through DCC, so check the DCC options to make sure that your client isn't set to automatically get all files.

place where you work, the town where you live, your email address, picture, and so on.

- On IRC, you can set personal mode to invisible to make it more difficult for others to find you using the /who or /names commands—type /mode yournickname +i.

- If someone is harassing or bothering you, change your nickname frequently.

- Every chat should have an ignore command that will hide messages from bothersome users; on IRC, type /ignore nickname.

- Don't accept a private chat or file transfer from someone you don't know; in the DCC options section of most IRC clients, you can set DCC Chat and Send to Ignore All to avoid problems from this direction.

- Don't do anything that anyone asks you to if it sounds fishy or if you don't know what the results will be. For instance, on IRC, don't type anything that someone else asks you to; this might be a trick to gain control of your system.

- Don't let kids chat. Whenever you hear those horror stories about grown men starting relationships online with young girls and boys, 10 times out of 10 it started in chat. Chat just isn't safe for the kids, so keep them off.

- Always remember that you don't know who you're talking to. Just because they say they are female, 16, blond, and a cheerleader (or whatever) doesn't make it so.

Chat's anonymity can be a lot of fun, as well as a way for creeps to hide behind offensive behavior. Besides using anonymity as a way to protect yourself, try letting go and being someone else for a night. You might find it exhilarating! But never use your anonymity as an excuse to be rude or crude, just as a way to have fun.

Turning Your Computer into a Telephone

Imagine calling a friend across the country or halfway around the world and chatting for an hour or more, without paying any long-distance charges. Using real-time voice-conferencing software, you can do just that. You can even add video, send files, collaboratively edit documents, and send voice mail through your computer.

Of course, you don't want to throw away your telephone. Until everyone adopts a voice-conferencing standard, you won't be able to talk to anyone who doesn't have software that's compatible with yours. And the voice quality leaves a lot to be desired, due to network traffic, the way data is transmitted over the Internet, and the speed of your computer and Internet connection. Every voice-conferencing product suffers from choppiness. In fact, the quality can vary throughout your call from excellent to unusable and back again. If you add video, that too will be choppy and slow.

Because of the audio quality problems, I wouldn't recommend using the Internet to make most of your long-distance calls. But it can be satisfactory for casual chatting with a friend or family member. It's also very effective when you need to work with someone who's far away; most voice-conferencing software includes shared whiteboard, file exchange, and other collaborative tools. And the savings on international calls can't be beat.

What You Need

To use voice-conferencing software, you need a minimum 16-bit soundcard and drivers, speakers, and a microphone, as well as the software (I'll get to that in the next section). Headphones are a good investment, as well. The best audio quality requires a Pentium, PowerPC, or G3 processor, a lot of available memory, and a fast, stable Internet connection. If you want to send and receive video, you need a video camera and a video capture card; check the conferencing software's documentation to find out what video hardware it works with.

Bright Idea
Some kids' sites host kid-safe, Web-based chat. These sites use registration to keep out adults and employ full-time monitors to keep the conversation clean. If you decide to let your kids chat, use one of these services; read the site's policies first and supervise for a while to make sure that the chat is appropriate for your kids. The best of these are Headbone Zone at http://www.headbone.com/ (no software needed) and FreeZone Chat at http://chat.freezone.com/ (requires ichat).

Watch Out!
Just because you
go by a nickname
and guard your per-
sonal information
on IRC and other
chat networks, you
still aren't truly
anonymous. Chat
servers capture
your computer's IP
address and log
visitors to a file.
Chat conversations
can also be cap-
tured and
recorded. For the
most part, your
anonymity is pre-
served, but still
take care what you
say and do,
because it is possi-
ble to find out who
you are.

For best audio quality, turn the volume on both the speakers and microphone all the way up. If your microphone supports Automatic Gain Control, turn it on. You should be able
to make all these changes in the Multimedia control panel on
Windows or in the appropriate hardware control panels on the
Mac.

Voice conferencing comes in two modes: half duplex,
which is analogous to a CB radio; and full duplex, which is
analogous to a telephone. The mode you can use depends on
your soundcard. Most soundcards support full duplex,
although you might have to install an additional driver
(check the soundcard manufacturer's Web site). Most
voice-conferencing software supports both modes.

Although full-duplex mode is more convenient and more
like talking on the phone, it can pick up a lot of background
noise, destroying audio quality. For that reason, you might
want to use half-duplex mode, which mutes one party when
the other is talking, eliminating the background noise from
the other end. You probably have to click a button when you
want to speak, as you would with a CB radio, although some
software supports voice-activated switching; this technology
doesn't work perfectly yet, but it's getting better.

Choosing the Software

You have a lot of choices when it comes to conferencing software, if you're running a high-end system. Select a product
based on what your resources are and what the people you
want to talk to are using. You might have to make a trade-off,
depending on your needs; for instance, you might have to
dump the highest quality audio in order to reach the most
people.

VDOPhone

For person-to-person voice conferencing with the best
audio quality, the best choice is VDOPhone. VDOPhone
does require a powerful high-end computer, so it won't suit
everybody. VDOPhone has the best audio quality of all the
voice-conferencing products, even on slower Internet connections.

It's easy to configure, a must for voice-conferencing products that often require precise settings to get the best quality. You can also add video conferencing, if you like, but it's not required.

- **System Requirements**: Windows 95/98; 133MHz Pentium processor; 16MB RAM; 6MB hard disk space, 16-bit sound-card

- **Price**: not available at publication (free trial available)

- **Download**: `http://www.clubvdo.net/store/products/` `vdophone35/home.asp`

NetMeeting

If you don't have the resources to support VDOPhone, consider Microsoft NetMeeting (see Figure 7.7). A major advantage of NetMeeting is that it's widely used, so there's a better chance that the person you want to call already has it and uses it. Many companies have established NetMeeting servers and networks, for instance. Since NetMeeting supports the H.323 conferencing standard, you can call other standardized Internet phones with it, such as the Intel Internet Phone. NetMeeting also has the advantage of being free. The audio and video quality of NetMeeting aren't nearly as good as VDOPhone's, though. Finally, NetMeeting has the widest selection of collaboration tools of all the voiceconferencing products, including a shared whiteboard that can show Windows applications (invaluable for tech support), group Web browsing, and file transfer.

- **System Requirements:** Windows 95/98/NT 4.0; 133MHz Pentium processor; 16–32MB RAM; 4MB hard disk space; Internet Explorer 4.0 or later; soundcard; video capture card or camera that supports Video for Windows (optional); for videoconferncing, a 56K, ISDN, or LAN connection is recommended

- **Price:** free

- **Download:** `http://www.microsoft.com/windows/netmeeting/`

Bright Idea
For the most secure phone calls, encrypt them! Of course, this only works if you make your phone calls over the Internet or via a modem-to-modem connection and if you have PGPfone. Get this free Internet phone for Windows 95/98/NT or Mac OS 7.1 at `http://web.mit.edu/network/pgpfone/`.

Figure 7.7
NetMeeting pro-
vides a low-end
solution for voice
conferencing

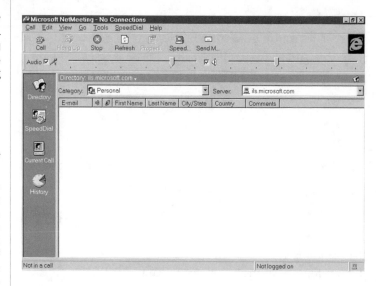

Moneysaver
What if you need
to call someone
who doesn't have
a computer and
you're too much of
a cheapskate to
pay the high long-
distance charges?
Get Net2Phone
(http://www.
net2phone.com/),
which makes the
connection from
your computer to
their phone. You'll
still have to pay for
the call, but the
rates are cheaper
than the phone
company's, espe-
cially if you're call-
ing overseas (rates
are posted on the
Web site). Expect
much poorer sound
quality from
Net2Phone than
from your tele-
phone, though. But
act quickly,
because the phone
companies are tak-
ing steps to raise
the rates of
Net2Phone and
similar services to
the same amount
as if you were
making a regular
phone call.

CU-SeeMe

On the Mac, CU-SeeMe is the voice-conferencing and video-
conferencing product of choice. CU-SeeMe has been around
for a long time and an extensive Internet community has built
up around it, so you should be able to reach a lot of people.
For instance, CU-SeeMe has been widely adopted by K–12
schools and NASA, and you can always find ongoing public
conferences and scheduled cybercasts. You can use it for voice
conferencing even if you don't have the third-party video hardware, although video conferencing is definitely CU-SeeMe's
strength; you can even run group video conferences. The system requirements are hefty, and I would only recommend it
for the fastest computers.

- **System Requirements:** Mac OS 7.6 with a 100MHz
  PowerPC processor and OpenTransport 1.1.2; 32MB
  RAM; 10MB hard disk space; video camera and video capture card (optional); for video conferencing, a LAN, cable
  modem, or ISDN connection is recommended

- **Price:** $69 (evaluation version available)

- **Download:** http://www.wpine.com/products/CU-SeeMe/
  index.html

Sending Instant Messages

Internet pagers—also called instant messengers—are the latest craze in real-time, person-to-person communication over the Internet. They enable you to send a short message instantly to anyone else connected to the Internet, and most of them then let you start up a one-on-one chat session with that person (see Figure 7.8).

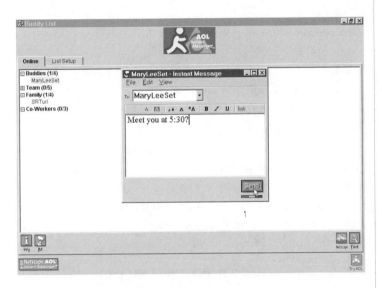

Figure 7.8
AOL Instant Messenger is a typical Internet pager; send instant messages to other AIM users and start one-on-one chats.

Timesaver
If you have already installed Internet Explorer 5.0, you can quickly get NetMeeting. Open the Control Panels and Add/Remove Programs. Scroll down until you see Internet Explorer 5.0 and Internet Tools, select it, and click on Add/Remove. Then, select Add a Component and click OK. Scroll down until you see the NetMeeting option, select that check box, and click on Next to install it.

Internet pagers can be very handy for quickly getting in touch with someone, but they do have a major drawback—both users must have the same software *and* be connected to the Internet *and* be running the software for the pager to be really useful. I've found that the best way to make use of Internet pagers is to make sure that everyone in your group of friends or co-workers has a copy and leaves it running all the time. Then, it comes in real handy for conversations like this:

John: Let's get together to discuss our latest team assignment.

Jane: Okay, why don't we have lunch today?

John: Sounds good. Want to meet at O'Malley's around noon?

Bright Idea
UNIX users have been chatting one-on-one since the early days of the Internet, using a little program called Talk. If you have a shell account, try it out by typing `talk` at the prompt, followed by the email address of the person you want to talk to. You can also get Talk for Mac OS 7 and WinTalk for Windows 3.x/95/98/NT from any software search engine. Because these programs implement the Talk protocol, you can use them to chat with any UNIX user and with other Macintosh Talk and WinTalk users.

Jane: I've got another meeting, but I'll see you there at 12:30.

John: Okay, I'll just send a message to my assistant and tell him when to meet us.

Internet pagers are a free and easy way to trade messages with people you know, without the hassle of making a phone call or composing an email message. All Internet pagers offer similar features, including a list of buddies or people that you send messages to frequently, a way to block harassing messages, and an "away" message that you can turn on while you're not at your computer. Buddy lists also notify you when your friends come online and when they leave. Finally, the pagers give you a way to locate people, usually by searching a Web site for an email address.

Table 7.5 describes the most popular of these Internet pagers. They're all free, so price won't be an issue. You'll probably want to choose the one that all your friends are using, or you won't be able to send messages to them. If you're the trailblazer, look for a pager that has a large user base, so you have a better chance of finding people who use it.

TABLE 7.5: INTERNET PAGERS

Pager	Download URL	Supported Platforms
AOL Instant Messenger (included as part of the Communicator 4.x suite)	`http://www.aol.com/aim/`	Windows 3.x/95/98 and Mac OS 7.1
ichat Pager	`http://www.ichat.com/plugin/download/pager.html`	Windows 95/98/NT 4.0 or PowerPC
ICQ	`http://www.mirabilis.com/`	Windows 95/98/NT and Mac OS 7.5

Just the Facts

- There are so many chat options that you're bound to find one (or many) that suits you, whether it's the raucous IRC network, a community-oriented private network, a topic-oriented prescheduled Web chat, or a high-end virtual world.

- Chat has developed a culture and a language all its own; understand it going in, and no one will think you're a newbie.

- Chat is also one of the most dangerous places on the Internet, but if you take care to protect your anonymity, you can stay safe and have fun in the bargain.

- Using Internet voice-conferencing and video-conferencing tools, you can save on long-distance charges and find a high-tech way to talk, as long as your computer system is up to the challenge.

- Internet pagers are the latest craze in real-time online communication; they enable you to send short messages to your friends more quickly than email and with less trouble than a phone call, but they're only really useful if everyone's got the same program and keeps it turned on.

GET THE SCOOP ON...
Tools for maintaining your Internet connection ▪ Tools
for performing basic activities on the Internet ▪ Tools
for staying in touch with others ▪ Tools for becoming a
better Net researcher ▪ Downloading even more tools

Neat Net Tools

A S YOU'VE NO DOUBT DISCOVERED by now, the Internet is a terrific place for finding software, particularly free and almost-free programs. The problem is that there's too much out there, so it's difficult to locate what you might find useful. You might not even realize that you need a particularly nifty program until you stumble across it. And often you don't find out if the program is any good until after you take the time to download and install it.

This chapter helps you sort through all the dreck and find just the best, most useful tools that enhance how you use the Internet, so you won't waste your time downloading programs that don't work well or don't do what you thought they did. And as always, you'll discover the system requirements and price before you download, so there won't be any surprises. A URL where you can get more info and download the latest version is provided where available, but you should be able to pick up most of these tools, including those without URLs, at a software search engine (Chapter 11, "Searching Savvy," discusses these software search engines and how to use them in more detail.)

Managing Your Internet Connection

So you finally got Dial-Up Networking or Mac TCP working properly and you think you're done. You're not. Several little utilities can help you get connected, stay connected, and close your connection when you're finished. Any of these nifty tools saves you a lot of time. Put a few of them together and you've got an Internet connection toolkit that streamlines the entire process of getting on and off of the Net.

Launching Internet Programs

Bright Idea
I download a lot of software, so I find it easier to keep track of all those compressed files by saving them to a download folder, such as C:\Download. That separates unin- stalled software from everything else on my hard drive until I can scan it for viruses, decompress it, and run the installer.

When you connect to the Internet, there are probably certain things you do right away—check your email, look in on your favorite newsgroups, visit regular Web sites. The following tools launch the Internet programs that you need automati- cally, as soon as you connect (see Figure 8.1). They also per- form other housekeeping duties, such as retrying failed connections, hiding the Connected dialog box, and closing Internet programs when you disconnect. These tools only work with dial-up accounts:

- **Advanced Dialer:** Windows 95/98; requires Dial-Up Networking; shareware

- **NetLaunch:** Windows 95/98/NT 4.0; requires Dial-Up Networking; free

Monitoring Online Time

Once you're connected, it's all too easy to let the time slip away from you, which can be a bummer if you pay for Internet access by the hour or have a limited number of online hours each month. The following timers simply remind you how long you've been online, so your bills won't get too big:

- **Online Meter:** Windows 95/98/NT; shareware ($15); http://www.webutils.com/en/om/index.html

- **PPPop:** Mac OS 7.1 (PowerPC only); requires 400KB RAM, a PPP client and Open Transport; shareware

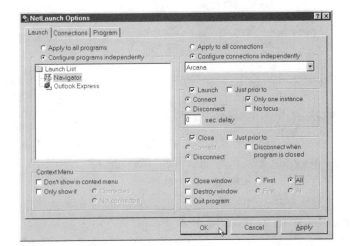

Figure 8.1
NetLaunch can open any Internet applications you choose as soon as you connect to your ISP.

Maintaining Your Connection

Don't you hate it when you step away from your computer to take a phone call or eat dinner, and your ISP disconnects you for being idle? Then, when you return to your computer, it takes forever to get reconnected because of busy signals or traffic. These tools keep your dial-up connection active while you're away from your computer by tricking your ISP into thinking that you're still doing stuff online:

- **Internet Loafer:** Windows 95/98/NT; shareware

- **StayOn Pro:** Windows 95/98/NT 4.0; supports all major online services; shareware ($19.95); `http://209.132.85.42/`

Connecting Multiple Computers

What if you have two home computers—how do you hook them both up to one Internet connection at the same time? The following tools connect two or more networked computers (up to an entire LAN) through one Internet connection:

- **RideWay:** Windows 95/98/NT; requires 16MB RAM; compatible with any type of connection; $50–$350 (depending on the number of users); `http://www.itserv.com/`

Watch Out!
Once you start downloading, installing, and uninstalling software, your computer acquires a lot of flotsam that just takes up space, such as unnecessary backup, temporary, help index, duplicate, and orphaned files. If this is happening to you, Space Hound is the solution. It sniffs out the useless files, zaps them, and recovers valuable hard disk space. Windows 3.x/95/98; $40 (trial version available); `http://ssl3.pair.com/fineware/`.

- **SoftRouter Plus:** Mac OS 7.5.x and Windows 95/98/NT 4.0; $155–$395 (trial version available); `http://www.vicomtech.com/softrouter/sfr.main.html`

- **SurfDoubler:** Mac OS 7.5.x or Windows 95/98/NT 4.0; for two computers only; $54 (demo available); `http://www.vicomtech.com/surfdoubler/surf.main.html`

- **WinGate Home:** Windows 95/98/NT 3.5.1; $39.95–$69.95 (depending on the number of users); `http://www.wingate.net/features/wingatehome.htm`

Bright Idea

Is your computer drab, but you don't want to waste time changing the wallpaper to gussy things up a bit? NetWallpainter to the rescue! This program downloads the Web graphics you want and rotates them as wallpaper at the interval you choose. Wait, this can actually be useful. Set it to download a weather map, stock quote, live Web cam, or daily cartoon, and the changing images are delivered whenever you want them. Windows 95/98/NT; shareware; `http://www.engr.orst.edu/~schonfal/`.

Basic Internet Utilities

There are quite a few things that you might need to do on the Internet, but you don't have the right utilities. If you had access to a UNIX shell account, you could perform all of these activities by typing a command at the prompt (as I've indicated at several points throughout this book), but shell accounts are becoming less common. Don't worry—these same useful software tools can be installed and run from your Windows or Mac OS computer.

Internet Utility Packages

So, what do you do when you need to ping a server to see if it's live, finger someone's email address, look up a domain name or IP address, or trace the route from one computer to another? You get one of the Internet utility packages listed in Table 8.1. You won't believe how many tiny but necessary functions these utilities fulfill, such as synchronizing your computer's clock to the Internet time server or displaying useful information about your network connection.

TABLE 8.1: INTERNET UTILITY PACKAGES

Package	What You Get	System Requirements	Cost	Download URL
CyberKit	Check for New Mail, DBScanner, DNS Lookup, Finger, Keep Alive, Quote, Ping, Time Sync, Traceroute, Whois	Windows 95/98/NT	Free	http://www.ping.be/cyberkit/
IPNetMonitor	Address Scan, Connection List, DNS Lookup, Finger, Monitor, Ping, Subnet Calculator, TCP Info, Traceroute, Whois	Mac OS 7.5.3 with Open Transport 1.1.1	$20 (21-day trial version available)	http://www.sustworks.com/products/ipnm/demo/readme.html
NetScan Tools	Chargen, Daytime, DNS Lookup, Echo, Finger, Ident Server, NetScanner, Ping, Port Scanner, Quote, TCP Terminal, Time Sync, Traceroute, URL Grabber, Whois, Winsock Info	Windows 95/98/NT 3.51	$25 (30-day trial available)	http://www.nwpsw.com/nstmain.html
Network Toolbox	DNS Lookup, Finger, Internet Speedometer, IP Address Search, Mail Tracer, Network Info, Ping, Port Scanner, Quote, Time Sync, Traceroute, Whois	Windows 95/98/NT 4.0 or UNIX	$29.95 (free trial available)	http://www.jriver.com/products/network-toolbox.html
WS_Ping ProPack	DNS Lookup, Finger, HTML, Info, LDAP, Ping, Quote, Scan, SNMP, Throughput, Time Sync, Traceroute, URL Query, Whois, WinNet	Windows 95/98/NT	$37.50 (evaluation available)	http://www.ipswitch.com/products/ws_ping/

Moneysaver
If you administer a company Web or FTP server, you know that a few minutes of downtime can cost a lot of money. That's where Ping comes in handy—it checks on the server to make sure it's still functioning. But you don't want to sit around pinging the server all day, so you need something like PingIt 95, which automatically sends pings to the server of your choice at a preset interval. It's a simple, quick way to keep tabs on your server, and it's a lot cheaper than most other solutions. Windows 95/98/NT; shareware; check your favorite software search engine for a download link.

Telnet Clients

Another necessary Internet tool is Telnet. Telnet enables you to log on to a computer on the Internet and access the files there, as if your computer was a terminal to that remote computer (see Figure 8.2). You might not use it too often, unless you have a UNIX shell account, but you need it from time to time. For instance, some information resources and games are only available via Telnet. You might even run into Telnet links on the Web, in which case your browser launches your Telnet client when you click on the link.

A basic Telnet client comes with Windows (it's located in the Windows directory), but you might want the additional features of these free programs:

- **BetterTelnet:** Mac OS; free; http://www.cstone.net/~rbraun/mac/telnet/

- **EasyTerm:** Windows 95/98/NT; free; http://www.arachnoid.com/easyterm/

Assorted Internet Utilities

The following are some more Internet utilities that defy categorization but really come in handy when performing common tasks online:

- **InterBack:** Backs up directories or files from your hard drive to a remote server. The whole process is automated, including zipping the files, encrypting them, cataloguing them, and transferring them. For someone like me, who uses my FTP site as my backup medium, this tool is invaluable. You can even locate a backup host through InterBack's Web site. Windows 95/98; $24 (30-day evaluation available); http://www.edgepub.com/iback/.

- **Internet Config:** Consolidates all your Internet settings in one place for your Internet tools to access, so you don't have to set up accounts in multiple applications. Use it for your email client, newsreader, Web browser, and more. Mac OS 7; free; http://www.stairways.com/ic/index.html.

Figure 8.2
Use a Telnet client
such as EasyTerm
to log on to
remote comput-
ers, as with a
UNIX shell
account.

- **NetBots:** Are automated programs that perform little tasks at scheduled intervals. You can do a lot with them, such as get them to tell you if a Web site goes down, if you have new email, or if a friend has logged on. They can also check favorite Web pages for changes or look for unauthorized users on your UNIX shell account. Mac OS 7; shareware ($15); http://www.printerport.com/klephacks/netbots.html.

Staying in Touch

The Internet offers so many ways to communicate quickly and easily with others. You've got your email program, newsreader, chat clients, video-conferencing tool, and Internet pager—what more do you need? Well, you might find that a group collaboration or remote control program is an invaluable part of your communications arsenal. You might need better ways to find other people so you can make use of all of those real-time communication tools. Or perhaps you just want to jazz up your email with some easily implemented effects. I've got all of these for you right here, and maybe a bonus or two.

Watch Out!
Once you install a
software program,
you no longer need
the compressed
file that you down-
loaded—it's only
taking up valuable
disk space. If you
think you need to
run setup again or
if you want to pass
the file on to
friends, move it to
a floppy.
Otherwise, just
delete it. If you
save all your soft-
ware downloads to
one directory,
those compressed
files and unneces-
sary setup files
should be easy to
find.

Working Together

In Chapter 7, "Getting Personal with Real-Time Chat," you learned about voice-conferencing and video-conferencing software, which help you collaborate with someone far away using the Internet. Several tools take this real-time communication a step further, enabling you to look at or even control the remote computer. The applications for these collaboration tools are endless. Get together with someone and edit a presentation, report, or other project, even if your partner is a continent away. Provide or receive on-target tech support. Do your part for the environment and become a telecommuter.

The following is a selection of the best remote control tool:

- **ControlIT:** Enables you to dial into and work remotely on the desktop of any PC. It's perfect for telecommuters; if you leave an important file on your computer at work, you can still access and edit it from home. Windows 95/98/NT 3.51; prices vary (30-day trial available); `http://www.cai.com/products/controlit.htm`.

- **Look@Me:** Enables you to peek at someone else's desktop (see Figure 8.3). It works especially well for reviewing projects or giving tech support. Choose the standalone application, the Navigator plug-in, or the Internet Explorer ActiveX control (Windows 95/98 only). Windows 3.x/95/98 or Mac OS; free; `http://www.netopia.com/software/lookatme/`.

- **Timbuktu Pro:** Adds more remote control capabilities. Look@Me just enables you to view the other desktop, while Timbuktu Pro enables control over that desktop, file exchange, and flash notes. Windows 95/98/NT and Mac OS 8.1; $69.95–$89.95 (depending on your OS); `http://www.netopia.com/software/tb2/`.

Timesaver
Email notification utilities relieve you of the need to keep your email client running all the time just so you'll know when a new message comes in. Instead, they sit in the system tray and quietly check for new messages while you do other things. Cyber-Info Email Notify is one of the best email checkers out there. Use it to monitor multiple POP3 and Hotmail accounts with your choice of alerts. It also has built-in spam filters and previews message headers. Windows 95/98/NT 4.0; shareware ($20); `http://www.cyber-info.com/`.

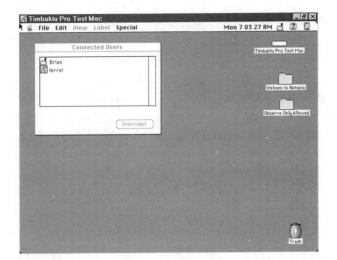

Figure 8.3
Use Timbuktu Pro
to peek at the
desktop of
another computer
over the Internet.

Making Time to Play

Don't worry—I know that work isn't your whole life. You've got to make time to play, too, especially during office hours. So I've rounded up a set of cool timewasters. Full versions—not limited demos of expensive commercial games—of all these games can be downloaded online, so you can start playing right away, and keep playing. And because it's much more fun to play with a friend, all of these games can accommodate two or more players, either over a local network or the Internet. The Web sites listed should get you started in finding ongoing Internet games:

- **Avara:** 3D combat simulation; Mac OS; shareware ($20); http://www.Avara.com/

- **Greebles:** Action game involving bulldozers, cockroaches, and fish (you've got to play it to understand); Mac OS 7.0; requires OpenTransport 1.1; shareware ($15); http://www.stairways.com/greebles/index.html

- **iMagic Online Games:** Warbirds, Dawn of Aces, and Raider Wars on a community gaming network; Windows 95/98 and Mac OS; software is free, membership packages start at $9.95 per month; http://www.imagiconline.com/home.shtml

Watch Out!
Many popular multimedia games, from Quake II to Orbsters, won't run on Windows 95/98 without the Microsoft DirectX drivers. If you install a new game and get a cryptic message, such as "DINPUT.DLL Not Found," then you're missing these drivers. You can get them from any software search engine (they're free).

Moneysaver
Can't find somebody to play with? Join a multi-player game network. Mplayer (`http://www.mplayer.com/`), for instance, has over one million members and enables you to play more than 60 games—everything from Quake to Risk to Hearts. Best of all, everything is free—even the games. Mplayer requires Windows 95/98, a Pentium processor, and 16MB RAM.

- **PBTerm:** Enables you to join in on the fun at Paintball NET; Windows 95/98/NT 3.51; free; `http://paintballnet.com/`

Keeping Track of Dynamic IP Addresses

So you've lined up CU-SeeMe, NetMeeting, and all your other conferencing tools, not to mention your multi-player games, but you've found it almost impossible to find anyone. Why? Because nearly everyone with a dial-up connection is assigned a dynamic IP address that changes every time they reconnect to the Net. That IP address is the magic number that enables you to connect to and start communicating with the other computer, but it's impossible to keep track of. You could try calling up your friend and arranging a conference, but that kind of defeats the whole purpose of using the Internet. Some other clever solutions to this problem have been developed, including the following:

- **DynIP Client:** Registers a personalized subdomain name that constantly refers to your IP address and can be used in place of your IP address in any Internet application. Even use this service to run a Web, FTP, mail, or chat server. This seems to be the most elegant solution, as well as the most costly. Windows 95/98/NT 4.0, UNIX, and Linux; $39.95 per year (30-day evaluation available); `http://www.dynip.com/`.

- **IPView:** Displays your IP address in your taskbar at all times, so it's right there when you need to give it out to your contacts. Windows 95/98/NT; requires Visual Basic 5.0 Runtime Module; free.

- **MyIPAddress:** Copies your IP address to the Clipboard each time you connect; whenever you need to give it to someone, just select MyIPAddress from the Apple menu and copy it to an email message, chat session, or whatever. Mac OS 7.0; shareware.

Dressing Up Your Email

There's only so much that you can do with plain old email, and it can get boring after awhile. For a special occasion or for a special person, you might want to jazz things up a bit. The tools in this section bring out your creative side, while still doing most of the work for you. Granted, you shouldn't incorporate these nifty effects into every little email message you send, but it's nice to have them on hand for birthdays and when you're trying to impress the boss.

- **Barking Cards:** Helps you create and send animated, multimedia greeting cards and invitations for almost any occasion or reason (see Figure 8.4). You can even download extra editions for special holidays. They sure are a lot cooler (although more expensive) than Hallmark. The recipient must be running Windows. Windows 3.x/95/98; prices range from $1.99 for individual cards to $19.95 for value packs (free samples available); http://www. barkingcard.com/.

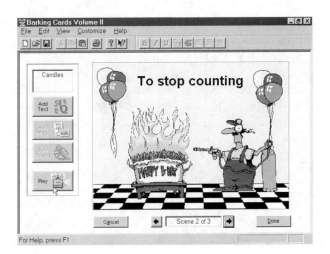

Figure 8.4
Barking Cards makes it easy to create email greeting cards.

- **CoolCards Light:** An email greeting card creation tool that enables you to embed graphics and styled text in the electronic cards and then send them with any email program. Windows 3.x/95/98/NT and Mac OS 7.0; free (you can purchase additional content); http://www.coolcards.com/ download.html.

- **PureVoice:** I really don't see much point to voice email messages. I hate my answering machine enough already. But PureVoice plugs right into Eudora or works on its own, it compresses voice files so they're real small and don't take too long to transfer, and the audio files it produces run on just about anything (you do need PureVoice to play the messages, though). Sometimes, only voice will do, and we're just too lazy to go find the cordless phone. Windows 95/98/NT 3.51 or Mac OS 7.5 PowerPC; requires Eudora 3.0.1 or a MIME-supported email program, 8MB RAM, 16-bit soundcard or Sound Manager 3.2.1, and a microphone; free; `http://www.eudora.com/purevoice/plugin.html`.

Doing More with Signatures

Watch Out!
Many Windows shareware and freeware programs are written in Visual Basic. That means you'll need the Visual Basic Runtime Module to obtain all the necessary files for running the program (the latest version at the time of this writing was 6.0). You can get the Runtime Module for Windows 95/98/NT at any software search engine (it's free).

Once upon a time, the signature file was an art form—line after line of nifty cartoons, big words, and other artwork, all rendered in ASCII text. That was back before companies actually wanted to hire us Internet geeks and we all had a lot of time on our hands, enough time to spend hours painstakingly rendering those sigs that have since been relegated to the Hall of Fame. But with these nifty tools, sig art might make a comeback, because they do all the hard work for you:

- **Email Effects:** Just for creating tables and drawings with ASCII text. Use it to effortlessly make one of those impressive text pictures that adorn the more interesting sigs. You can also create special effects, such as flipped and exploded text, or get clip art. Windows 95/98/NT or Mac OS; shareware ($15); `http://www.sigsoftware.com/emaileffects/index.html`.

- **Quotes:** A nifty tool that generates random quotations for your signatures. It also manages multiple signature files. Windows 95/98/NT; shareware ($5); `http://www.xs4all.nl/~ed/`.

- **SchizoSigz!:** For those people who like nicely formatted sigs, with a witty quote of the day (see Figure 8.5). Using the wizard, you can can create headers, footers, and banners, and add quotes and taglines to your sig. You might just get inspired to make 20 or 30 sigs; this program randomizes them for you, putting a different one into each email message. Windows 95/98/NT; free.

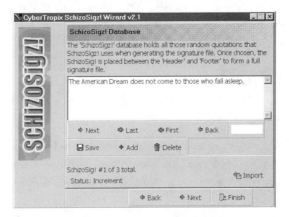

Figure 8.5
Use SchizoSigz! to generate interesting email signatures.

Timesaver
If you need to quickly convert a PICT graphic to ASCII text to jazz up your signature or send the picture through email, get pict2ascii for Mac OS 7.0 from your favorite software search engine. It's free and fun.

Becoming a Better Researcher

The Internet has quickly become the world's largest information repository. There's a lot of knowledge out there, and some of it is actually useful. Precisely because there is so much, it's difficult to find what you need and use it efficiently. The tools in this section help you become a better information seeker and manager in the Internet's two best places to research—the Web and Usenet. You'll also learn about tools that bring the data you need to your computer, rather than making you go out and get it.

Improving Web Researching

Improving your Web researching skills starts with becoming a better surfer. You've already learned how to speed up Web surfing and make better use of your browser, but you don't have to stop there. Several utilities enable you to refine your Web-browsing habits so you can surf faster and better. These tools

Watch Out!
Despite our best intentions, we often download software that we just don't want. All too often, the application's uninstall program leaves orphaned files and empty folders behind, cluttering up your hard drive. That's what makes Norton CleanSweep 95 so useful. It removes applications you don't want and finds the leftover pieces that should have been deleted, getting rid of them, too. It also removes cached and history files, cookies, ActiveX controls, and plug-ins. Windows 95/98/NT; requires 17MB hard drive space and 16MB RAM; $29.95; http://www.symantec.com/sabu/qdeck/cleansweep/fs_cs45.html.

range from ways to cut down on your typing to all-out customized browsers. Grab a few of them and you'll be surfing like a pro:

- **Dropit:** Just when you come to what promises to be a really useful site, you run into yet another registration form that keeps you from entering. There it is again, before you can download that promising software program or subscribe to a free email newsletter. This utility saves you from wearing out your typing fingers. You create a file that contains the information these forms usually ask for; then, when you come across a form, just drag and drop the file on top of it and it's all filled out. It even encrypts passwords for you. Windows 3.x/95/98; requires Internet Explorer 4.x; shareware ($10); http://spinnerbaker.com/dropit.htm.

- **NetJumper:** The basic back and forth navigation tools on your browser are often too limiting. NetJumper enhances your browser's navigation in a number of ways, enabling you to pre-cache links, run automated Web slide shows, surf hands-free, manage bookmarks, and more. It works with Internet Explorer 3.x and later and Navigator 2.x and later. Windows 95/98/NT or Mac OS; $19.95 (30-day trial available); http://www.netjumper.com/netindex2.htm.

- **RealNames:** Here's a better way to bookmark. Instead of typing in a long, cryptic URL or searching through all your bookmarks for the one you need, just type a short nickname that you've assigned to the frequently accessed URL into the location window and you're off. It works with all major Web browsers (if you use it with Navigator 4.5, though, it overrides the Internet Shortcuts feature). Mac OS 8.5 or Windows 95/98/NT; free; http://company.realnames.com/download.asp.

- **URLMenu 98:** There are quite a few URL managers, but most of them are just extensions of your browser's bookmarks tools or way too complicated to use regularly. This utility is the only truly useful URL manager I've found. It sits in the system tray, out of the way when you don't need it, easy to get to when you do. It also acts as a URL launcher for any program, not just your browser. You're not limited to using it with just one browser either, so it's perfect for those of you who switch between Internet Explorer and Navigator. Finally, it can resurrect lost links, check for dead URLs, and launch URLs from other sources, such as email or text files. Windows 95/98/NT; free; http://www.elphin.com/products/urlmenu/.

- **Web Stalker:** This browser offers an alternative way of getting into the Web, one that's focused on textual information delivery—just what the Web researcher needs. Web Stalker gathers data about the structure and layout of a site, creating a site-wide map that makes it much easier to navigate and find needed information. While moving through the site, you can grab the text of any page, peek into the HTTP datastream, or save a document for later perusal. Web Stalker doesn't work like any browser you're familiar with, so you might hate it. But you won't know until you try it. Mac OS and Windows 95/98; free; http://www.backspace.org/iod/index.html.

- **Web Squirrel:** For Mac users, Web Squirrel offers a more visual way to organize bookmarks. You group URLs into neighborhoods, and then use Web Squirrel's agents to keep track of updated pages and dead links. Mac OS; $49.95 (free demo available); http://www.eastgate.com/squirrel/.

Taking Notes from the Web

Searching the Web is a chapter all by itself (see Chapter 11), but it can be just as perplexing to figure out what to do with the information you do find. Just saving or printing the page brings too much extraneous stuff, such as decorative graphics and unwanted content. There's no efficient way to take notes from a Web page—copy and paste also copies weird formatting and retyping is too time-consuming. The following tools offer better ways to make notes about Web page information:

Bright Idea
Ads, especially the pop-up kind, can really get in your way when you're power-surfing. So a number of tools have come out to block what you don't want. The best of these are WebFree, which screens unwanted ads inside Web pages (Mac OS 7.0; shareware), and OnTrack, which prevents pop-up windows (Windows 95/98; free). Get either from your favorite software search engine.

Timesaver
If you're downloading software with Navigator or Internet Explorer, you can start the download and then keep on surfing while the Saving Location dialog box works in the background. This won't cause any problems with your download, although Web page loading might slow significantly.

- **Hot Off the Web:** Enables you to save pieces of Web pages in a scrapbook. Then, mark up what you've saved with annotation tools such as notes, markers, highlighters, and stickers (see Figure 8.6). It's perfect for a research project. You can even email your scrapbook pages, complete with markups, to other people on your project team. It works by itself or in conjunction with your browser. Windows 95/98/NT 4.0; $29.95; http://www.hotofftheweb.com/.

Figure 8.6
Hot Off the Web is the ultimate tool for Internet researchers, because you can mark up any Web page with your own notes and annotations.

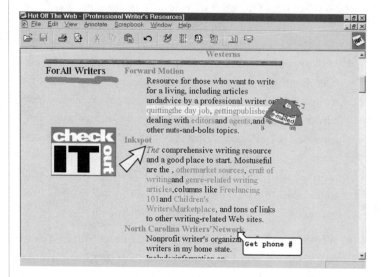

- **NetPad:** A freeform note-taking program that helps you track ideas and projects. A window to the Web enables you to easily take notes as you search, as well as copy and paste from Web pages, so it's perfect for merging text and links from the Web with your own notes. You can also hyperlink notes together or link to Web pages to make cross-references. Windows 95/98/NT; $19.95 (90-day evaluation available); http://www.netpadsoft.com/netpad_intro.htm.

- **Surfer Central:** Keeps track of all your Internet addresses. Organize URLs, email addresses, FTP sites, and newsgroups in one place. It also imports your Navigator bookmarks to organize along with everything else. Windows 3.x/95/98/NT; $22 (30-day trial version available);

`http://www.npsnet.com/waletzky/scinfo.html.`

- **SurfSaver:** A small, easy-to-use program enabling you to save Web pages, including graphics, into folders, as if in a filing cabinet. All the pages are indexed as you save them, so you can easily search through collected information later. Windows 95/98/NT; requires Internet Explorer 4.x or Navigator 4.x; $29.95 (30-day trial version available); `http://www.SurfSaver.com/`.

- **Web Buddy:** Floats over your browser while you surf. If you like a page and want to download it regularly, just click on a button and set the download schedule. Web Buddy then downloads and displays the page on cue, so you can keep up with changes or news. Web Buddy also manages bookmarks and supports offline browsing. Windows 95/98 and Mac OS; $39.95 (free trial available); `http://www.dataviz.com/Products/WebBuddy/WB_Home.html`.

Researching on Usenet

The Usenet network is like a huge bulletin board, containing nuggets of valuable information hidden among the thousands of posts that you don't care about. Because it's so vast and populated, it's almost impossible to find just what you're looking for. Even searching Deja.Com (`http://www.deja.com/`) only turns up archived information, not breaking news as it's posted (see Chapter 11 for more information).

That's where the software tools in this section come in. They can be programmed to scan newsgroups for the information you specify. Some are even tailor-made for certain searches. Any one of the following would be a good addition to the Internet researcher's toolkit:

- **Job Watcher:** Searches the jobs newsgroups for postings that conform to your preferences. It's not limited to watching for jobs, but can also search for any keyword. Windows 95/98; free; `http://rjsoft.com/jobwatcher.htm`.

- **NewsMonger:** Monitors any newsgroups for postings on a specific subject. NewsMonger even includes a host of fil-

Moneysaver
Use Pagoo to save your friends some money—instead of calling you or your machine and paying long-distance charges, they can call a toll-free number, key in your ID number, and leave you a short message. The message is then sent to your desktop, so you can play it with Pagoo's audio console. It's also useful if your modem and telephone share the same line. The service costs just $3.95 a month (try to get a pager or second phone line for that price). Get Pagoo for Windows 95/98/NT at `http://www.pagoo.com/`.

ters to weed out unwanted messages and spam. You can schedule automated searches and read and reply to posts from within NewsMonger. Windows 95/98/NT; $39.95 (evaluation available); `http://www.techsmith.com/products/nmonger/overview.htm`.

- **News Robot:** One of the best automated grabbers for posted binaries. It grabs meaningful posts from the binary newsgroups of your choice, while eliminating the trash, such as spam and cross-posts. Use it to grab pictures, sounds, and executables. Windows 3.x/95/98/NT; shareware ($19.95); `http://smbaker.simplenet.com/sbnews/`.

- **Picture Sucker:** Searches Usenet for all UUE-, MIME-, and Base64-encoded binary files in any newsgroups you specify. You can also fine-tune the settings to ignore certain kinds of articles. It's perfect if you monitor any of the binaries newsgroups, such as `alt.binaries.clip-art` or `alt.binaries.pictures.astro` or (ahem) whatever else. Windows 95/98/NT; free; `http://jfm.bc.ca/psp.html`.

Bringing Information to You

Having the information you need delivered right to you is certainly a lot better than going out and looking for it yourself. You've already seen how utilities like Web Buddy can download favorite Web pages and show you changes, but you still have to find the pages. The programs in this section are different because they bring what you want to your desktop without you having to look for it first. And unlike the much-hyped push technology, these programs don't overwhelm your

Internet connection or computer resources, or fill your hard drive with unwanted advertisements and multimedia enhancements. Of course, they aren't very useful for specialized research and most of them require some kind of 24-hour Internet connection, but when keeping up with changing news, they're just the right tools.

The following are the best of the programs that deliver the news to your desktop:

- **MSNBC News Alert:** This program informs you of breaking news in the areas of your choice, such as world and national headlines, technology news, sports scores, and stock alerts. When news breaks, an alert icon flashes in the taskbar; click it to see the headlines. So when nothing's happening, there's no constantly running news ticker to distract you from your work. Windows 95/98/NT 4.0; free; `http://www.msnbc.com/tools/alert/alermain.asp.`

- **Wall Street Explorer:** Unlike other stock tickers, this one actually has a brain. You can program it with the stock you want and the price you're looking for, and Wall Street Explorer notifies you when the stock hits that price. So, you can log on to your trader's site and buy or sell at just the right time. Stock quotes are delivered in real-time, and you get only the information that you're interested in. You can also use it to manage your portfolio, export quote data to Quicken, and get reports, charts, and graphs. Windows 95/98; requires Internet Explorer 3.x (although you don't need to run the browser to use Wall Street Explorer);

Bright Idea
Want to tune in radio Brazil or Australian TV? Then you need EarthTuner, a database of over 1,400 TV and radio stations that are broadcasting over the Internet using RealMedia technology. It's great for expanding your horizons or catching up with what's going on in your hometown, even if you live thousands of miles away. Windows 95/98/NT; shareware ($22.95); `http://www.earthtuner.com/.`

Watch Out!
Real-time news
delivery services
can be discontin-
ued abruptly, leav-
ing you without
your news. For
instance, both of
the popular pro-
grams After Dark
Online and IBM
NewsTicker were
discontinued with-
out warning. Don't
lay down money for
these kinds of ser-
vices unless you
get a guarantee
that they're going
to be around for a
while.

shareware ($30); http://www.latte.com/wsx/.

Download Helpers

In this chapter and others, you've downloaded a lot of software from the Internet, so you've probably already discovered how tedious and frustrating the process can be. The tools in this section make it a lot easier for you to continue getting neat Net tools.

Download Utilities

From scheduling downloads to watching out for updates and new versions, these utilities are essentials for the software junkie:

- **Download Butler:** A complete download manager (see Figure 8.7). While you're zipping around the Web, downloading software left and right, it automatically extracts a description of each file, enables you to organize downloaded files into tabbed folders, remembers where you put them, and saves each file's URL. So you don't come back two days later, look at a bunch of cryptic filenames, and wonder what in the world you put on your hard drive. It

Figure 8.7
Download Butler
is a complete
download-
management tool.

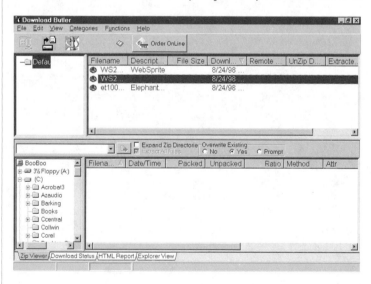

also has built-in zip-file extraction. Windows 95/98/NT; $29.95; `http://www.lincolnbeach.com/butler.asp`.

- **Download Deputy:** A must-have utility for any Mac-based software junkie. All you have to do is tell it the URLs of the files you want to download, and Download Deputy batch-downloads them using your FTP client or Web browser, even if they're on different sites. You can also schedule downloads, so you don't even have to be there to get software. Mac OS; shareware ($21); `http://www.ilesa.com/software/deputy.html`.

- **GetRight:** Helps you recover from any of the errors that can occur while you're downloading. For instance, if you lose the connection, GetRight resumes downloading from where it left off. You can also schedule files for later downloading, and GetRight dials up, gets the file, hangs up, and even shuts down your computer for you. Finally, it can transparently switch between FTP sites to ensure that you find the fastest place to download from. Windows 3.x/95/98/NT; shareware; `http://www.headlightsw.com/get.html`.

- **WebWolf:** A search tool that automates the process of finding software. It roams the Web looking for the types of files that you specify and provides a Web-based report of what it finds and their locations. Windows 3.x/95/98/NT; shareware ($25); `http://www.msw.com.au/webwolf/index`.

Timesaver
Many of the Windows software programs that you download over the Internet are zipped, which means that you must first extract all the files using a utility such as WinZip, and then run the installation. If WinZip detects an Install or Setup file in the archive, it creates an Install button at the right end of the WinZip toolbar. So, you can click this button to go straight to the installation program, saving yourself a step. (WinZip is available for Windows 3.x/95/98/NT for $29 at `http://www.winzip.com/`.)

Watch Out!
Most software
won't install prop-
erly if other pro-
grams are running,
because the instal-
lation might need
system files that
are in use. So you
should quit any
running programs
before starting the
installation. If the
installation has
already started,
press Alt+Tab (on
Windows) to toggle
between programs
and quit everything
without canceling
the installation.

html.

Version Managers

It's all too easy to get download-happy and grab every piece of software that you think you might need. What's a lot more difficult is keeping up with the software after you do have it. New versions of Web browsers, FTP programs, email clients, news-readers, and everything else come out all the time, and unless you happen to visit the developer's site, you might not know anything about it. You might also miss important updates, patches, and enhancements, which can fix bugs and add more needed features.

If you're running Internet software, you need a version manager. These utilities keep track of your software versions and notify you where there are updates (see Figure 8.8). Some of them even download and install the updates for you, although choosing a product that just notifies you of updates enables you to control what is put on your computer. Also, they only monitor what's in the developer's database—often the most popular freeware, shareware, and commercial applica-tions; hardware drivers; and system utilities—so they won't check everything on your system. But they do go a long way

Figure 8.8
Oil Change keeps
track of the soft-
ware updates you
need and down-
loads them for
you.

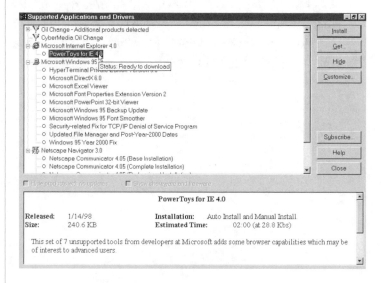

toward helping you keep your system bug-free and keep everything working well, so they make a good investment.

See Table 8.2 for the best of these version managers.

TABLE 8.2: SOFTWARE UPDATE MANAGERS

Program	Download URL	System Requirements	Price	Notes
Catch-UP	http://www.manageable.com/catchup.html	Windows 3.x/95/98/NT	Free	Doesn't automatically install updates.
Oil Change	http://www.cybermedia.com/support/faq/ocsupp.html	Windows 95/98	$39.95 per year (free trial available)	Automatically backs up old software and installs updates.
Update-Agent	http://www.theInside.com/iutop.html	Mac OS 7.0	$49.95 per year (free demo available)	Automatically downloads but doesn't install updates.
Version Master	http://www.versionmaster.com/	Mac OS	$19.95 per year	Doesn't automatically update software, but does support email notification.

Bright Idea
Several nifty Internet tools are available for the 3Com PalmPilot, but it might not be obvious how to get the downloaded files from your desktop to your PalmPilot. Actually, the desktop software includes an install application for just this purpose. It's located in the PalmPilot directory, and it's called Instapp.exe on Windows and InstallApp on the Mac. Just run this and browse to the downloaded program. Your add-on is transferred during your next HotSync. To find PalmPilot programs, go to http://download.com/ and click on the PalmPilot category.

Just the Facts

- A whole lot of software is out there ready to be downloaded, most of it free or very cheap, and some of it fulfills needs you never knew you had; for example, a wide range of utilities have been developed to help you manage your Internet connection.

- Basic Internet utilities such as Ping, Whois, Finger, DNS Lookup, and Telnet belong in every Internet user's toolkit—you never know when they might come in handy.

- There are a lot more ways to keep in touch on the Internet besides email, Usenet, chat, and video conferencing; for instance, you can share computers or play games with your friends.

- The Internet is a researcher's boon, but sorting through all that information on the Web and Usenet can be a nightmare unless you choose some tools to help you out.

- Downloading software over the Internet has become so commonplace that many tools designed only to help you do just that have been developed; these download managers are also must-haves for every Net user.

GET THE SCOOP ON...
Why push technology doesn't work ▪ The latest thing
in Web sites—portals ▪ Where the Web has been and
where it's heading ▪ Cookies and why they're not as
dangerous as you might have heard

Cutting Through the Hype

A S YOU'RE WELL AWARE, THE INTERNET has been big news for the past few years. Those of us who were online in the early days remember the Internet as a low-tech, non-commercial place. But with the advent of the Web, businesses began to take notice of the Internet and the growing market base there, and that changed everything.

Businesses coming online have been both good and bad for you and me, the average Internet users. For one thing, it's become a lot easier to research products we want to buy and the companies that make them, and to keep up with developments and updates. Plus, the convenience of shopping and conducting other business online, such as paying bills, is unparalleled. Furthermore, businesses have provided professional content and news on the Web, often for free.

But the tradeoffs can be severe. Now you can't go to a Web site without running into a banner ad, and you can't get through the day without hearing about the latest technology that you simply must have right now. Many of these much-hyped Internet developments are simply attempts by online businesses to grab your attention away from all the competitors. But a handful of them really do change the Internet and take it a step further into its evolution. So, how do you distinguish the hip from the hype?

This chapter helps you by discussing some recent hypes, why they don't deliver what's promised, and how you can still work with them. Of course, by the time you read this, the "next big thing" might already be here. I hope that by learning about these over-hyped technologies, you become better equipped to figure out what new Internet technologies you can safely live without.

Avoiding the Push

Push technology is a textbook case of the failure of business-fueled and media-hyped technology. "Push" essentially refers to subscribed, updated information that is delivered to your desktop, rather than you having to go out and find it. This obviously covers a lot of ground, but what most people mean by push is something like a Web site that is broadcast to your computer, but with more multimedia, nifty effects, and advertising than the average site. (This is also referred to as Webcasting.)

In this form, push failed because the push content developers have misjudged how users want content to be presented and the computer setup of the average user. Most of the early services, such as PointCast (http://www.pointcast.com/), require major downloads and eat up a lot of processing power just to get the pretty presentation (see Figure 9.1). PointCast, for instance, requires 25MB hard disk space and 16MB RAM (although 32MB RAM is recommended). It also needs a speedy processor and fast, dedicated Internet connection to work correctly.

Push content is so resource-intensive because push content vendors assume that users want as many whizbang effects as they can get. While that's all very well for TV and movies, it's a lot for your computer to handle. And most people use push to get information, rather than entertainment. For this purpose, it's much more efficient to receive streamlined, simple content that we can digest quickly.

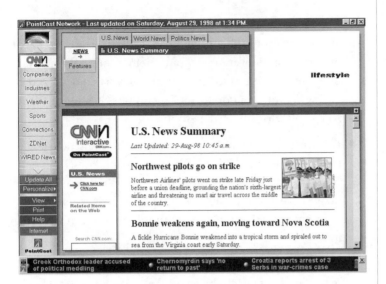

Figure 9.1
PointCast pushes news, ads, and other multimedia content to your desktop.

Another mistake of push content vendors is assuming that we want to know the second anything is delivered. Many push clients set off alerts, pop-up windows, animations, and the like when new information comes in. Most of us don't need any more distractions. We'd rather read our news when we make time for it.

Finally, push wasn't developed to make life easier for you and me. It was developed to make life easier for the companies who were pushing content to you. Instead of hoping that you'd visit the Web site on a more-or-less regular basis, push guaranteed a captive audience by delivering the Web site, and all of its advertising, to you everyday. It took control out of the hands of the Web surfer and put it in the hands of the Web content publishers. Naturally enough, Web surfers didn't go for it. When we feel like being a captive audience, we go watch TV.

The case of push technology illustrates that every new technological advance might not necessarily be an improvement over what you've already got. Just because the media and businesses are hyping it doesn't mean that you've got to use it. So, I advise skipping the massive PointCast download and avoiding similar push services. If you want information pushed to your computer, here are some simpler solutions that are a lot easier on both you and your computer:

Watch Out!
The constant drain that push places on bandwidth can become a serious problem when you're dealing with a network of computers, all of them busily pulling in content, as with a company network. The best solution is to ban resource-draining push clients entirely at work or on any network.

- **Use smaller, targeted push clients.** News tickers, news alerts, and other small programs are effective ways to have information delivered without them monopolizing too much bandwidth or too many resources. Turn back to the "Bringing Information to You" section in Chapter 8, "Neat Net Tools," for some suggestions.

- **Use email.** Many Web sites publish an email newsletter that informs you of developments and updates. This is a very effective way to get pure information delivered to you on just what you're interested in. Email newsletters are also very small files that sit in your inbox until you're ready to read them.

- **Use your bookmarks.** Netscape Navigator and most bookmark managers enable you to automatically check whether bookmarked Web sites have been updated, so you can revisit and see the new information. While this isn't the most elegant solution—all that might have changed was a graphic, for instance—it is easy and you are still in control.

Bright Idea
Once you subscribe to a few email newsletters, set up a rule that filters them into their own mail folder. (I find that it's easiest to do this when I receive the first issue of each newsletter; I use a filter that funnels all messages from the newsletter's return address into a folder called "Newsletters.") This keeps your inbox from getting cluttered and organizes all the unread newsletters in one place until you have time to look at them.

Checking for Updated Bookmarks in Navigator

You might need a refresher course in how to check bookmarked Web sites for updates. With Navigator, you check all bookmarks at one time. Here's how:

1. Press Ctrl+B (Windows) or Cmd+B (Mac) to open the Bookmarks window.

2. Select the bookmarks that you want to check. The fewer bookmarks you select, the less time updating takes. It's a good idea to group bookmarks for changing Web sites into one folder so that you can easily select them.

3. Open View, Update Bookmarks (see Figure 9.2).

4. Click Selected Bookmarks.

5. Click Start Checking.

6. Changed pages are marked with a different icon than normal bookmarks. Visit these sites to check the updated content.

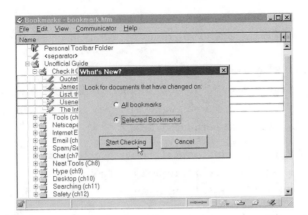

Figure 9.2
Updating book-
marks in
Navigator.

Going Portal

The latest thing in Web sites is the portal site, which promises to be all things to all Web surfers. The idea behind portals is simple—become the most popular entry point for the Web, build up huge amounts of site traffic, and sell lots of advertising and products. Most of the major Internet companies have jumped on the portal bandwagon. To get you to make them your browser start page, portals offer a lot of content and free services. Each one has pretty much the same thing, including

Timesaver
Create special
bookmarks folders
for favorite Web
sites that change
daily or weekly,
and call them
"Daily Routine" or
"Weekly Visits" or
something similar.
This reminds you
to visit these sites
on a regular basis,
as you have time,
and it groups the
sites' URLs
together so you
don't have to go
hunting through
your bookmarks
for them.

- Web search

- Categorized directory of Web sites

- Free email services

- Chat rooms and/or bulletin boards

- Updated content, such as weather reports, news headlines, and sports scores

- Shopping

- Software downloads

- A way to create your own personalized start page

That doesn't sound so bad, you say. And it's not. Many of these offerings are valuable services. I can't get through a day without searching Yahoo!, and as you've already learned, a free email account is a must-have in many situations. You can pick

Moneysaver
The idea of combining the Internet and TV continues to receive a lot of hype without delivering. There are just too many problems, such as poor viewing quality and a technology that's still in the developmental stages. Right now, your TV can't display Web pages much better than your computer can play video. Internet TV might have a future, if it integrates Web content with television shows or taps into multiplayer online gaming. Until then, avoid investing in any hardware that promises it delivers the Web to your television.

and choose what you want from these sites and benefit from all the freebies, as long as you don't mind the advertising.

The Best of the Portals

You can get free email, news headlines, white and yellow pages, maps, and a basic search engine at any portal. But here is my take on what each portal does best:

- **AltaVista** (http://www.altavista.digital.com/): Specialized channels help you look for a job, take care of your health, take care of your money, and plan a vacation.

- **Excite** (http://www.excite.com/): Heavy on the personalization, enabling you to track the news topics, weather, stock quotes, sports scores, horoscopes, chat rooms, shopping sites, and cartoons that you choose (see Figure 9.3).

- **Lycos** (http://www.lycos.com/): Gives you space to build your own home page and calendars you can share with other users.

- **Microsoft Network** (http://home.microsoft.com/): Offers a free, popular, multi-player gaming network; Hotmail is a good choice for free email because you can get a lot of add-ons for it.

- **Netscape Netcenter** (http://www.netcenter.com/): Netscape has teamed with Excite to provide a lot of original content on general subjects; for instance, there's a small business center (see Figure 9.4), information for the college-bound, and (of course) lots of cool software.

- **Yahoo!** (http://www.yahoo.com/): The largest Web site directory, the most extensive chat network, and lots of specialized Web guides, such as one for kids and one for seniors.

The Future of Portals

I mention portal sites in this chapter because they are simply the latest thing in the search to create the ultimate, advertising-driven, traffic-laden Web site. You should see this trend continue as the big Internet sites jump on one bandwagon after another to try to attract your attention.

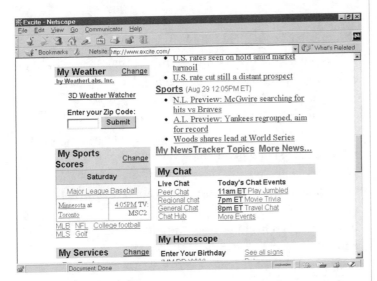

Figure 9.3
Of all the portal sites, Excite offers the best personalization.

Figure 9.4
Netscape's Netcenter offers more original content than the other portal sites, such as the Small Business Source.

Notice that one portal site is not all that different from the next. Portals are great for offering general content to a mass audience, but they are not so great for targeting your particular interests. You might need to keep up with what's happening in K–12 education, you might collect glass insulators and want to meet others who share your passion, or you might be fascinated by NASA space missions. You'll find plenty of sites to match your interests on the Web, and the portal sites might

Inside Scoop
Yahoo! is currently leading the portal horserace, with more than 30 million users per month according to a Relevant Knowledge poll.

Watch Out!
Don't get too comfortable with your favorite portal. Due to the competitive nature of these sites, they change frequently, so that they seem to metamorphose into an entirely different service from day to day. Features are showcased prominently when they're hot and shoved into a back corner or removed entirely when they're no longer hip. The rapidly changing nature of portals defeats the whole idea behind them—to help you find a home base on the Web that feels comfortable and familiar.

help you locate them, but they won't give you this specialized content that really makes the Web interesting.

So, what's the next best thing in Web sites? I think you will start to see portals evolve from general-interest mega-sites to more specialized hubs—Web sites that provide services and information aimed at a specific group of people, such as those who share a hobby or a profession. These hubs will publish a lot of original content and links out to more stuff on the Web, and they will create a community through chat, bulletin boards, free email, and shared applications. For instance, hubs might focus on computers and Internet technology, small businesses, family, personal finance, health and fitness, education—almost anything that would attract a large number of interested users. Some portals are already heading in this direction, as evidenced by AltaVista's channels and Yahoo!'s specialized content areas.

Another important kind of hub is the local hub, and ISPs are best poised to take over this area (see Figure 9.5). Would you rather spend time at a place that has general content aimed at the widest audience or a place that concentrates on your community, with local news, weather, sports, events, chat, bulletin boards, and shopping—an online extension of where you live? Your ISP might have already started moving in this direction—check its home page.

The Future of the Web

In its inception, the Web was built on standards in terms of how Web page information is formatted and presented. Standards are what make the Internet work so well. The TCP/IP protocol makes it possible for computers connected to the Internet to communicate with each other, for instance. Without standards, you wouldn't be able to send email to anyone, regardless of the email client the sender or recipient uses. The same is true of posting messages to Usenet newsgroups, downloading software from FTP sites, and viewing Web pages.

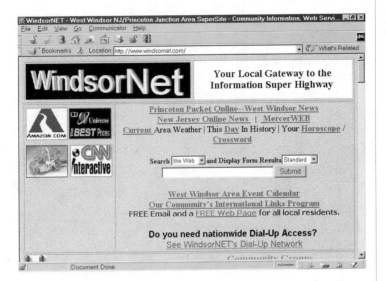

Figure 9.5
WindsorNet is a
New Jersey ISP
that offers local
information and
services so that
it functions as
a more
specialized—
and more useful—
portal site.

The trouble with the Web is that its growth has outpaced the slow process of developing, approving, and implementing standards. Businesses were demanding more eyeball-grabbing ways to present information in Web sites, and Netscape and Microsoft were competing for top place in the browser wars. So, the two big browser companies developed extensions to HTML that were not standardized. Some of these extensions were worthwhile developments, such as tables. But for the most part, they created problems for you and me, such as

- **Big downloads:** Such as Java applets, gigantic backgrounds, huge multimedia files, and VRML worlds that don't really enhance Web page content.

- **Distractions from content:** Such as blinking text and animated GIFs.

- **Unreadable sites:** Brought about by an overabundance of frames and busy backgrounds.

- **Incompatibility between browsers:** As with Microsoft's proprietary ActiveX, two different versions of Dynamic HTML, and two implementations of JavaScript/JScript.

Bright Idea
Using an HTML editor and a little creativity, you can make your own portal site. This has two advantages: generally, your home pages are stored on your local drive or your ISP's server, making them faster for you to access; and you can customize your own portal site six ways from Sunday, with just the information you're interested in and none of the excess baggage. You'll find tips for creating a personal portal in Chapter 15, "Putting Your Web Site to Work."

I'm not saying that all of these new Web technologies should never have existed. When implemented properly, they really do enhance Web page content. For instance, I've seen Java applets that enable you to set the options, color, and style of a car you're thinking about buying, a really useful application that just isn't possible with HTML alone (see Figure 9.6). And I've visited sites that use frames correctly, as a consistent index that helps you navigate deep into the site's content without getting lost.

The problem is that when each of these technologies comes out, it is immediately hyped as the best thing since inline images—it becomes the technology that revolutionizes the Web. And so every Web site must implement the technology immediately just to have the latest thing, without a clue as to how to use it properly to actually enhance the site, and without regard for the user's available bandwidth and computer resources. So, we're stuck trying to find our way around sites that have eight frames or downloading huge Java applets just to find out that they are yet more useless animations or tickers.

What can you do about this? Not much, except get out quick when you encounter a Web site that an overabundance of overhyped Web technologies has rendered unusable. I like to cruise the Web in fast mode, with Java disabled and only loading images when I absolutely have to. If I come across a site that I can't navigate easily, that insists I use a particular browser, or that wants to send me all sorts of huge files, I leave. I don't need whatever that site has to offer that badly—there are millions of other sites out there.

XML: The Next Real Thing?

The real future of the Web is a move away from the hype of the latest thing—whether that is Dynamic HTML, ActiveX, or JavaScript—and a move back toward universality. The World Wide Web Consortium (http://www.w3.org/), the organization that determines Web standards, is hoping that eXtensible Markup Language (XML) is the solution. XML might also bring about an end to the browser wars by taking Web page rendering away from the browsers and putting it in the hands of the Web content publishers.

Watch Out!
The most annoying thing about frames is how you sometimes get trapped inside them, even when you've jumped via a hyperlink to an external Web site. That's why "break out of frames" links have begun to appear on many Web sites. Here's another way to get out if you're using Navigator: right-click (Windows) or click and hold (Mac) inside the frame, and select Open Frame in New Window from the pop-up menu. This opens the page inside the frame in its own Navigator window. You can then close the original window and keep surfing, frame-free.

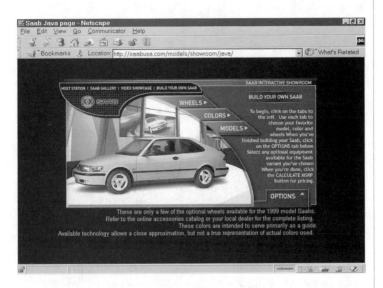

Figure 9.6
Go to Saab
(http://saabusa
.com/) to build
your own car with
Java.

The power of XML is that it gives Web page developers the tools to design their own document standards, enabling consistent Web site designs. Developers can use any number of methods, such as Cascading Style Sheets, scripting, and custom-built applications, to define Web content. The developer designs the rules and the tags for marking up his or her own pages. Any XML-compliant browser renders these tags correctly, eliminating incompatibility issues while retaining the coolness of the Web. (In case you're curious, Internet Explorer 5.0 is already XML-compliant, but because nobody is using XML yet, compatibility doesn't really matter at this point.)

Timesaver
If an animated GIF is annoying you, don't get mad—just stop it from playing. In Navigator, the process is quick and painless: Select Stop Animations from the View menu.

Implementation of XML requires a massive overhaul of existing Web sites and Web page authoring tools, however. It also means Web page developers have to adopt an entirely new way to code Web pages, which is pretty daunting. But XML is not hype, which is probably why it hasn't already been implemented in every Internet application you own and on every Web site you visit. It is the true direction in which the Web is heading.

In the meantime, the easiest way to keep up with Web developments—both hyped and otherwise—is to keep up with your Web browser. Check in with your browser's Web site regularly and get the latest *final release* version when it becomes

Inside Scoop
Speaking of standards, the World Wide Web Consortium is drafting the Synchronized Multimedia Integration Language (SMIL) standard, which promises to bring television-like content to the Web. (I don't know why everyone keeps trying to merge the Web and TV; personally, I like them separate.) Maybe this will provide a low-bandwidth way to deliver streaming cybercasts. Or maybe you just get a plethora of personal TV shows like there are personal home pages today. Either way, you'll soon be hearing a lot of hype about it.

available. But avoid betas—they are too unstable and crash way too often.

Your Privacy and You

It never fails to amaze me how a problem can get blown all out of proportion just by adding the words "on the Internet." First, it was sex on the Internet. Our kids were doomed to irreparable harm by all the sex-related Web pages. Never mind that you could turn on the TV and watch soap operas or *Jerry Springer* in the middle of the afternoon. The Internet was where the real danger lay.

Now, privacy on the Internet has become the big bugaboo. As soon as you go online, Big Brother is watching you, or so the hype goes. The Internet is not the only threat to privacy; how do you think all those telemarketers who call you during the dinner hour or while you're trying to sleep late got your number? It's not even the worst threat. Did you know that some government agencies, such as the Department of Motor Vehicles, can sell your personal information? Think about what they've got on file about you.

If you use a little common sense, you can protect your privacy when you go online without a lot of effort. For instance, be careful about what you say in email, and take steps to protect sensitive messages. Keep yourself anonymous in chat. Watch what you put in Web page forms; just because a site asks for your home address or phone number doesn't mean that you have to give it.

Nothing has been more demonized in the privacy wars than the cookie. A cookie is a text file that a Web server puts on your hard disk and that it can later access. Cookie files are extremely small, comprising no more than 255 characters and taking up less than 4KB of disk space.

Generally, cookies identify you each time you return to the Web server that set the cookie. They're very useful for many kinds of activities, while posing very little risk. For instance, when you go shopping at a Web storefront, putting items in your virtual shopping cart and then placing the order, a cookie is at work. If you register to use a Web site's services, a cookie remembers your user ID, password, and registration information, so you don't have to reenter it when you return to the site. Some cookies detect your preferences and display the best page when you return to the site; for example, a software download site can record whether you visit the PC or Mac section when you first visit and automatically display that section when you return. Cookies also enable all those portal sites to personalize the information they display.

Cookie Facts

There's a lot of misinformation floating around about cookies. Here are some facts you should know:

- **Cookies can't modify or read data off your hard drive.** They are just plain text files—they can't run programs, inject viruses into your system, or anything like that.

- **Cookies only contain the information that you give them.** For instance, when you fill out a Web page form, that information is recorded in a cookie. Cookies can't know anything that you don't want them to know.

- **Cookies can only be accessed by the Web server that created them.** Just because a cookie contains personal information doesn't mean that any Web server you connect to can grab that information. Only the Web server that set the cookie can access it, and you already gave the information to that site.

- **Cookies are limited to a small size (4KB) and each Web server can only set a limited number of cookies.** This prevents cookies from getting out of hand or filling your hard drive.

- **Many cookies are temporary and aren't written to your hard drive at all.** Cookies are only written when you exit your browser. Many cookies, such as shopping cart cookies, are erased when you quit. However, cookies that record customized settings or registration information must be retained permanently.

Inside Scoop
Internet pagers (refer to Chapter 7, "Getting Personal with Real-Time Chat") are already being hyped to death. Since they're free, handy, and low-load, I see no reason not to get one. But Internet pagers do have one serious problem, and again it all comes back to standards. Since there is no standard for instant messaging, you can't use one pager to talk to another; you can't use ICQ to page someone with AOL Instant Messenger, for instance. Until a standard is reached, look for 2 or 3 pagers to compete for the most market share—the pager wars.

Moneysaver
All the hypesters
have been
promising that
e-commerce would
finally take off in
1999. I think
e-commerce has
already taken off.
Every time I need
to buy something,
I can find it on the
Web—laundry
detergent, ferret
toys, personalized
CDs, anything.
Along with all this
buying and selling
has come the
usual dire warn-
ings about how
dangerous it is to
use your credit
card on the Web.
Trust me—using
your credit card
on the Web is a
whole lot safer
than giving it to a
waiter in a restau-
rant who then
takes it into the
back for 10 min-
utes. Just make
sure that you
order from a
secure server that
uses encryption to
protect the order
during transit, and
that you trust the
companies you
buy from. (Turn to
Chapter 14,
"Going Shopping,"
for more informa-
tion.)

Taking Care of Cookies

People get upset about cookies because a file is written to and accessed from their hard drive without their knowledge. You do have a choice, however. You can tell your browser what to do with any cookies it encounters. And you can look at the cookie files whenever you like. So you are still in control and able to decide what makes you feel most secure.

Another concern is the possibility that cookies might be used to build a personal profile of you based on the Web sites that you visit. This profile would then be resold to businesses hoping to target advertisements to your particular interests. This doesn't strike me as a practical way to advertise. Take the example of a 16-year-old boy who browses Web sites of high-priced sports cars—targeting this interest just wouldn't work, because the kid doesn't have the money to buy his fantasy car (or even a fantasy car's accessory). Meanwhile, the same adver-tiser can purchase a mailing list from the DMV that specifies exactly what kind of car you own—that's much more targeted. I think most advertisers realize that targeted ads based on the Web sites you visit isn't practical, and those that don't are just throwing their money away.

Checking for Cookies

Let's check to see what cookies are actually on your system:

1. If your browser is running, quit it.

2. Use your computer's Find function to locate the cookie file. If you use Navigator, look for cookies.txt (Windows) or MagicCookie (Macintosh). If you use Internet Explorer, look for a folder called Cookies.

3. Use a text editor to open the cookie file(s) and see what's inside. If you use Navigator, you should see a file such as the one in Figure 9.7. For Internet Explorer users, each cookie is a separate short text file maintained inside the Cookies folder. You should recognize all the domain names listed; these are Web servers that you've visited that have set cookies. Most cookies are very short, consisting

mainly of an ID number that identifies you to the server when you return.

```
cookies.txt - Notepad                                                    _ B X
File  Edit  Search  Help
# Netscape HTTP Cookie File
# http://www.netscape.com/newsref/std/cookie_spec.html
# This is a generated file!  Do not edit.

e12.zdnet.com:8080      FALSE   /clear  FALSE   946684716       cguersion
.yahoo.com      TRUE    /       FALSE   915145117       GET_LOCAL       last=u
www.chefolder.com       FALSE   /       FALSE   1293735553      EGSOFT_ID
www.thirdage.com        FALSE   /       FALSE   942171423       NGUserID
www.bhome.com   FALSE   /       FALSE   1293735521      EGSOFT_ID       199.72
www.webcrawler.com      FALSE   /       FALSE   1042510282      AnonTrack
goodhousekeeping.com    FALSE   /       FALSE   942201485       NGUserID
.washingtonpost.com     TRUE    /       FALSE   946666733       RMID    c74814
fantasy.miningco.com    FALSE   /       FALSE   942170373       NGUserID
marktwain.miningco.com  FALSE   /       FALSE   942170210       NGUserID
www.ericajong.com       FALSE   /       FALSE   1293735537      EGSOFT_ID
www.magick.net  FALSE   /       FALSE   946580515       MAGICK_ID       199.72
scholastic.com  FALSE   /       FALSE   942189160       INTERSE 19916388524785
authors.miningco.com    FALSE   /       FALSE   942170372       NGUserID
www.accd.edu    FALSE   /       FALSE   1293735498      EGSOFT_ID       199.72
www.pathway.net FALSE   /       FALSE   1293735558      EGSOFT_ID       199.72
library.law.duke.edu    FALSE   /       FALSE   1293735648      EGSOFT_ID
www.law.duke.edu        FALSE   /       FALSE   1293735648      EGSOFT_ID
www.netscapeworld.com   FALSE   /       FALSE   1011315493      WPI     885563
www.gateway.com FALSE   /       FALSE   942170945       INTERSE 19914188556860
www.zott.com    FALSE   /       FALSE   1293753600      EGSOFT_ID       199.72
```

Figure 9.7
The cookie file set by Navigator is a small text file that you can open in any text editor.

4. See a domain name that you don't recognize or that you're unlikely to visit again? You can delete the cookie without dire consequences. If you use Navigator, just cut the line containing the cookie from the cookies.txt or MagicCookie file. If you use Internet Explorer, just trash the individual cookie files that you don't want.

Setting Cookie Preferences in Navigator

Now, set your browser to deal with cookies the way you like. If you use Navigator, here's what you do:

1. Select Edit, Preferences.

2. Select the Advanced category.

3. Choose an option in the Cookies section. I recommend selecting the Accept Only Cookies That Get Sent Back to the Originating Server radio button (see Figure 9.8). This accepts all "safe" cookies—cookies that are set by a form you fill out or a site you visit; it avoids cookies set by banner ads and the like—sites that you haven't yet visited.

Watch Out!
If you edit the cookies.txt file, be sure to save it in DOS text format, or it won't be able to accept any more cookies. Using Notepad is the safest way to edit this file, because saving in Notepad defaults to the DOS text format.

Note that if you choose to disable cookies, you won't be able to access many personalization features and shopping sites.

Figure 9.8
Setting cookie
preferences in
Navigator.

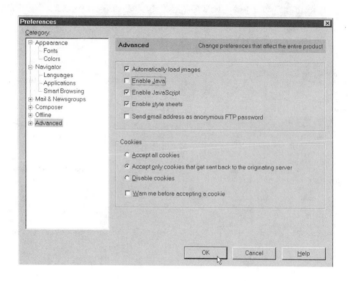

Watch Out!
In both Navigator
and Internet
Explorer, you can
set the browser to
pop up an alert
before accepting
any cookies. While
this can be tempt-
ing because it
makes you more
aware of who is
giving you cook-
ies, it quickly
becomes frustrat-
ing. If you visit a
site that uses
cookies, you are
interrupted by a
string of pop-up
windows that
really hamper your
surfing speed.

4. Click OK.

Setting Cookie Preferences in Internet Explorer

Internet Explorer users, here's how to set your cookie preferences:

1. Select Tools, Internet Options.

2. Click the Security tab.

3. Select the Internet zone.

4. Click the Custom Level button.

5. Scroll down until you see Cookies in the Settings window
   (see Figure 9.9).

6. You can choose to disable or enable per-session cookies
   (which are erased when you quit the browser) and permanent cookies (which are stored on your computer).
   Remember, if you disable cookie support, you won't be
   able to access personalization features and shopping carts

on many sites. Also, Active Server Pages rely heavily on cookies to operate properly.

7. Click OK.

Figure 9.9
Setting cookie preferences in Internet Explorer.

Cookie-Filtering Programs

If you're really concerned about cookies, a cookie-filtering software program might give you some peace of mind. These programs enable you to block or allow cookies based on where they come from, without all those annoying dialog boxes popping up. They can also clean cookies off your hard drive. The following are good products to try (look for these at your favorite software search engine, listed in Appendix B, "Unauthorized Resources").

- **Cookie Monster:** Mac OS 7.0; works with Navigator and Internet Explorer; free

- **Cookie Pal:** Windows 95/98/NT 4.0; works with Navigator 3.x, Internet Explorer 3.x, and AOL 3.x (and later versions); shareware

The Platform for Privacy Preferences

The cookie problem might soon disappear, though. The World Wide Web Consortium, Netscape, Microsoft, and several other companies have proposed a new system for collecting user information on a voluntary basis. This standard, called the Platform for Privacy Preferences (P3P), would allow you to create a personal profile containing any information that you want Web sites to have. This gives you the ability to control what personal information is revealed on a site-by-site basis. When a site requests information from your personal profile, you can verify the site owner's identity via a digital certificate and then pass on only the parts of your profile that you want the site owner to have. P3P is still in the implementation phase, and whether it raises a whole new level of privacy invasion hype remains to be seen.

By the way, Internet Explorer has already implemented a version of P3P, called the Microsoft Profile Assistant. To set up your profile, select Tools, Internet Options, click the Content tab, and click the My Profile button (see Figure 9.10). Select the Create a New Entry button and click OK. You can fill out any of the tabs with personal and professional information that you might like to share. To turn on the profile, you have to select the Advanced tab, scroll down to the Security section, and click the Enable Profile Assistant check box.

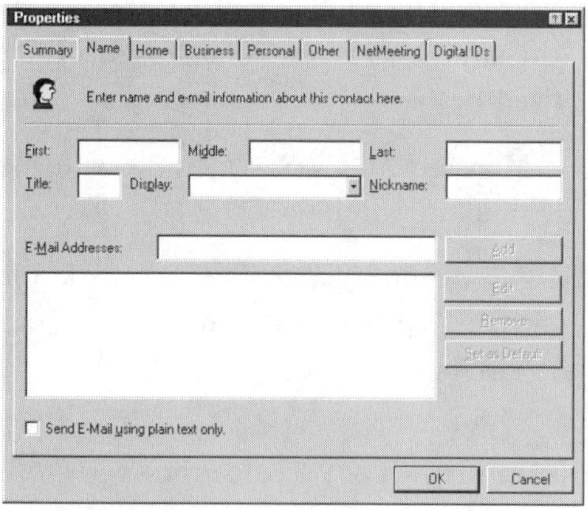

Figure 9.10
Setting up a personal profile in Internet Explorer.

After you turn on Profile Assistant, a pop-up alert appears whenever a Web server requests your profile. You can then check the identity of the server's owner via a digital certificate and specify the parts of your personal profile to share. It's up to you how much personal information you give. Since this technology is still in the developmental phase, take care when using it, and don't reveal too much about yourself when you don't have to.

Just the Facts

- Beware of new technologies that consume too many of your computer's resources, are advertising-heavy, or aren't designed to help you work more efficiently, such as push technology; more often than not, you can find a better way to get the same results.

- Web sites are always going to be coming up with new concepts to bring in traffic and sell more advertising, such as the portal craze; take what suits you and leave the rest, but be prepared for the site to abandon your favorite services when the next fad comes along.

- The Internet was built on standards, but lately, Web development has sprinted past the slow pace of standard implementation in favor of newer, more hyped technologies; only with a return to standards can problems such as incompatibilities among Web browsers be solved.

- The Internet's phenomenal growth has spurred many dire, exaggerated warnings, such as the threats posed to your privacy; if you ignore the hype and just learn the facts behind technologies like cookies, you'll know how to protect yourself while taking full advantage of the technologies.

GET THE SCOOP ON...
Using Microsoft Office's FTP, Web, and email
functionality ▪ Using the Internet features of other
popular applications ▪ Integrating the Web with
Windows using the Active Desktop

Internet on the Desktop

M ANY OF OUR DAILY WORK and home activities make use of the Internet. We communicate with colleagues and exchange files via email. We go shopping, buy and sell stocks, pay bills, and otherwise manage our personal finances online. We use the Web and company intranets to share documents in HTML format.

As the Internet becomes integrated into almost everything we do, it also becomes a part of the software programs that we use everyday, from your word processor to your personal finance manager to the operating system itself. Internet functionality, such as integration with email and the Web, make these familiar applications even more powerful tools. This chapter examines the Internet functionality of many widely used applications and explains how you can make the best use of these features.

Microsoft Office and the Internet

Microsoft Office is one of the most Internet-aware program suites available. Office helps you share and publish documents more easily by incorporating email, FTP, and HTML functions directly into the programs. But they're well hidden, so you might not even be aware that these features exist. This section helps you find them and use them efficiently. (You might also want to visit the Office Web site at http://www.microsoft.com/office/default.htm for more information about Office in general.)

239

Moneysaver
Don't forget to
check Help,
Microsoft on the
Web on all your
Office programs.
You'll find links to
online support,
free updates and
add-ins, and news
about the pro-
gram.

Using FTP in Office Programs

Office incorporates FTP functionality directly into each application, making it possible to save and retrieve files on the
Internet from inside the Office program that you're working
in. If you back up important files on an FTP server, as I do, this
comes in handy for creating backups and retrieving saved files
without leaving the program that you're working in. Many
companies share documents via FTP, so you can take advantage of Office's built-in FTP functionality to publish Word
reports, Excel spreadsheets, and PowerPoint presentations to
the company FTP site. And if you convert your Office documents to HTML format as described in the "Office and the
Web" section following this one, you can use the built-in FTP
functionality to publish the documents to a Web server.

Identifying an FTP Server in Office

First, you need to identify the FTP server to the Office pro-
gram(s) that you want to use to FTP documents:

1. Open Word, Excel, Access, or PowerPoint—whichever
   program that you want to use to access the FTP site. You
   have to repeat these steps for each program.

2. Click the Open button.

3. Click the down arrow to the right of the Look In drop-
   down list box, and select Add/Modify FTP Locations from
   the drop-down menu; the Add/Modify FTP Locations dialog box opens (see Figure 10.1).

4. In the Name of FTP Site text box, enter the domain name
   of the FTP server that you want to access.

5. Under Log On As, select the User button and enter your
   username if you have an account on the FTP server. If
   you're accessing a public FTP server, select the
   Anonymous button; you are able to retrieve Office documents from the FTP site, but you won't be able to upload
   them or edit them on the site.

6. If you have an FTP account, enter your password in the
   Password field; if you're accessing a public FTP site, enter
   your email address.

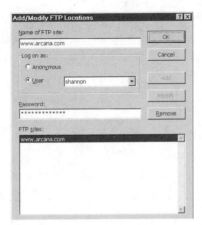

Figure 10.1
Identifying an FTP site to Office.

7. Click the Add button; the FTP server appears in the FTP Sites window.

8. Add any more FTP sites that you want to access, or click OK to close the dialog box.

Connecting to the FTP Server

You should see the Open dialog box, with Internet Locations (FTP) displayed in the Look In menu and the FTP site(s) you added in the large window (see Figure 10.2). You can now open the FTP server at any time by selecting it from the Look In menu in the Open dialog box. After you're connected, the FTP server's directories display in the Open dialog box.

Browse through the directories to find the file that you want to retrieve. When you select a file and click Open, a temporary copy of the file downloads to your hard drive and displays in the open Office program (this process can take a little while if you're retrieving a large file). If you have an account on the FTP server, you can edit the file and save changes directly to the copy of the file stored on the FTP site. If you're accessing a public FTP site, the file is read-only. You have to save the file locally to make any changes (use Save As), and you won't be able to return the edited file to the FTP site.

Watch Out!
Office's FTP feature is meant only for accessing files of the same type as the open Office program—Excel to transfer Excel spreadsheets, Word to transfer Word documents, and so on. If you try to use it as a standard FTP client—to transfer a WAV file in Word, for instance—you end up with a Word document containing several pages of code instead of an audio file.

Figure 10.2
Opening an FTP
server from an
Office program.

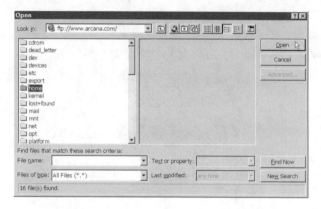

Saving Files to the FTP Server

Now, let's say that you created a file on your computer but you want to save it to the FTP server where you have a user account. The process for saving to the remote FTP server is just as easy as the one for opening files on it. Follow these steps:

1. Select File, Save As.

2. Click the down arrow to the right of the Save In drop-down list box and select the FTP server where you want to save the file (see Figure 10.3); if the server isn't listed, select Add/Modify FTP Locations and create it.

3. Browse through the FTP directories until you find the location where you want to save the document.

4. Click Save.

Office and the Web

Office integrates with the Web in three ways:

- Using the Web toolbar, search the Web or access favorites from within an Office program.

- Insert clickable hyperlinks to Web pages in your documents; clicking on the link launches the default Web browser and displays the referenced page.

- Convert any Office document into HTML format for publication on your Web server space or on the company intranet.

Timesaver
You can quickly pull data from the Internet into your Excel spreadsheet to update it with stock prices, exchange rates, or any other data found on the Web. Select Data, Get External Data, Create New Query and set up a Web query (you must have selected the Microsoft Query option when you installed Excel for this to work). To pull in data, open Data, Get External Data, Run Web Query and select the query in the dialog box that opens; some sample queries are already there so you can see how this feature works.

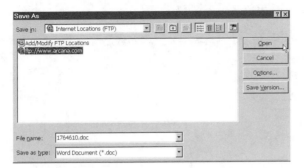

Figure 10.3
Saving an Office
file to an FTP
server.

Using the Web Toolbar

The Web toolbar is available from any Office program—just select View, Toolbars, Web (see Figure 10.4), or click the Web Toolbar button, located on the Standard toolbar. The Web toolbar looks a lot like the Internet Explorer toolbar, and it connects directly to the options set in Internet Explorer. (If Internet Explorer isn't your default Web browser, these functions won't work.) For instance, click the Home button to load your default start page in Internet Explorer, or select any of your favorite pages from the Favorites drop-down menu. Click the Search the Web button to load the default search page in Internet Explorer, so you can quickly find a Web site that's related to your data or search for a fact that you're missing. Finally, enter a Web-page address into the Address box to open the page directly in Internet Explorer.

You can even turn an Office document into your start page by selecting Go, Set Start Page. This changes the Internet Explorer start page to the document that's currently open in the Office program. For instance, if you created a local HTML-format document in Word that you want to use as your entry-way into the Web, select Go, Set Start Page while the document is open in Word. When you open Internet Explorer, it automatically shows that page. You can also select Favorites, Add to Favorites to add the document that you're working on to your favorites list; then, it is just a click away from inside Internet Explorer or from the Web toolbar of any Office program.

Bright Idea
Web-style hyper-links are a simple way to connect an Office docu-ment to other files on your com-puter or on the network. Follow the steps for inserting a hyper-link, but click the Browse button and locate the document that you want to link to on your hard drive instead of typing in a Web-page URL; make sure that the Use Relative Path For Hyperlink box is checked. You can then use the Back and Forward buttons on the Web toolbar to navigate among linked files.

┌─Web toolbar

Figure 10.4
The Web toolbar
looks the same in
each Office pro-
gram; here it is in
Excel, showing the
Address box's
drop-down menu of
recently accessed
URLs.

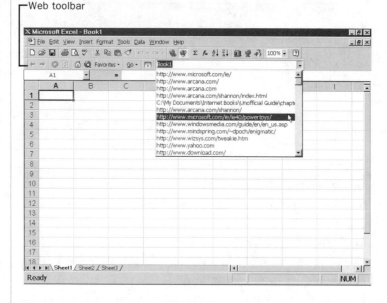

Watch Out!
If you edit the text
of a hyperlink, the
link might display
the correct
address but still
link to the old
URL. This happens
because the link is
made up of two
parts: the link ref-
erence, and the
link label. You're
editing the label
but not the actual
link. To edit the
link reference,
right-click the link
and select
Hyperlink, Edit
Hyperlink. Enter
the correct URL
into the Link to
File or URL field.

Creating Hyperlinks in Office Documents

You can easily create a hyperlink in any Office document. Like in a Web page, hyperlinks in Office are clickable—the reader can click the link to launch the page in the default Web browser (or in the appropriate program, if it's a link to a non-HTML document). Use hyperlinks to reference related Web documents in a Word report, to link companies listed in an Excel spreadsheet to their Web sites, or to create your own searchable Access database of favorite Web sites.

To create a hyperlink, select Insert, Hyperlink (press Ctrl+K on Windows or Cmd+K on the Mac). In the Link to File or URL field, type the URL (see Figure 10.5). Click the down arrow to the right of this field to open a list of shortcuts, including common URL protocols and recently entered links. Click OK and the linked URL shows up in the document. If you want to link a URL to some text, select the text before choosing Insert, Hyperlink. To remove the link, carefully select it (so you won't launch your browser), open Insert, Hyperlink, and click the Remove Link button.

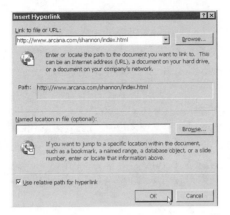

Figure 10.5
Creating a hyper-
link in an Office
document.

If you start typing an email, FTP, or HTTP address into your Word document, Word automatically converts it into a hyperlink. Automatic hyperlinking can be very useful when creating some documents, like HTML-formatted pages, but it can frequently get in the way. Also, hyperlinked text is hard to edit; when you click it, you launch your browser instead of selecting the text. And it doesn't look right when printed. Follow these steps to turn off automatic hyperlinking:

1. Select Tools, AutoCorrect.

2. Click the AutoFormat As You Type tab.

3. Deselect the Internet and Network Paths with Hyperlinks check box.

4. Click OK.

Now, any URLs that you enter remain in the normal text style. If after finishing your document, you want to convert all URLs into hyperlinks, select Format, AutoFormat, make sure that AutoFormat Now is selected, and click OK. This formats the document according to the selections on the AutoFormat tab of the Tools, AutoCorrect dialog box, so check that the Internet and Network Paths with Hyperlinks check box is selected on that tab.

Converting Office Documents to HTML Format

Each Office program has a Save As HTML option on the File menu. Selecting this option converts your document into HTML format for publication on a Web server or company intranet. The Web Publishing Wizard guides you step-by-step through creating a Web page based on your Office document. Each Office program works best for creating a different kind of Web page or Web site. In this section, I describe what you can do with the Web Publishing Wizard in each program, but if you need more detailed instructions, consult the program's Help.

Moneysaver
The Web Documents Toolkit for Word update turns Word into a more powerful HTML editor, and it's free. Use the update to publish HTML documents to a Web server, look for broken links, edit inline images, and use templates, styles, and backgrounds to enhance Web pages. Download the update from `http://officeupdate.microsoft.com/downloadCatalog/dldWord.htm` (scroll down the page until you find it).

Word's HTML editor is best used for editing Web-page files that are mostly text and don't have a lot of fancy formatting. (For more complex pages, you need a dedicated HTML editor, like Netscape Composer or Microsoft FrontPage Express; turn to Chapter 15, "Putting Your Web Site to Work," for suggestions.) It's easiest to convert existing documents, such as reports and articles, into HTML format for Web publication; just open the document and select File, Save As HTML. Most Word elements translate automatically into their HTML equivalents, including bulleted lists, numbered lists, centering, headers, bold, italics, underlining, and text color, so your document looks approximately the same in HTML format as it does in Word format.

You can also use Word's HTML template to create HTML files from scratch. To open the HTML template, select File, New, click the Web Pages tab, and choose Blank Web Page from the list of templates (or choose Web Page Wizard if you need extra guidance). If the HTML template isn't installed, you can fake it: Use Word to save a blank file in HTML format, close the file, and then reopen it. Now, your menus are modified with HTML elements. Check the Style menu, for instance—you should see a long list of HTML styles you can use to modify your document.

If you don't see Save As HTML on the File menu or if you can't find the HTML templates, you need to install the Web Page Authoring Tools. Follow these steps:

1. Quit Word.

2. Insert the Microsoft Office or Microsoft Word CD-ROM into the CD-ROM drive.

3. Run Add/Remove Programs (select Start, Settings, Control Panel to find it).

4. Select Microsoft Office or Microsoft Word.

5. Click the Add/Remove button.

6. Rerun Setup.

7. When you get to it, select the Web Page Authoring (HTML) check box.

Converting a PowerPoint presentation into HTML creates more attractive Web sites than Word's HTML editor. You can also use the AutoContent Wizard to set up a basic Web site from scratch and then just fill in the information that the wizard asks for. Follow these steps:

1. Start PowerPoint.

2. Select the AutoContent Wizard button and click OK.

3. Under Presentation Type, select Personal Home Page.

4. Under Output Options, select the Internet/Kiosk button.

5. Fill out the fields on Presentation Options as you like.

6. Click Finish and start making your home pages (see Figure 10.6).

Watch Out!
Word's HTML files contain extraneous code, making the final Web pages larger than necessary. To optimize the size of Web pages that you create with Word, choose Times New Roman font with a size of 12 points, single-spaced, and left-justified. Remove any special characters, such as copyright symbols and font formatting.

Figure 10.6
Using the
AutoContent
Wizard to create
a personal home
page in
PowerPoint.

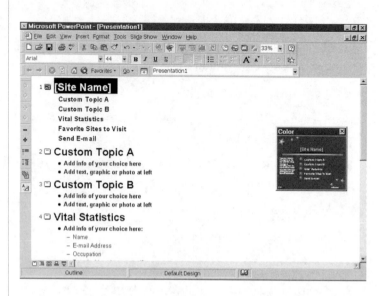

Figure 10.6
Using the
AutoContent
Wizard to create
a personal home
page in
PowerPoint.

Timesaver
Here's a fast way
to save data from
a Web page and
incorporate it into
an Office docu-
ment or manipu-
late it in an Office
program. Click the
Open toolbar but-
ton, and type the
Web page's URL
directly into the
File Name box.
Save the page
locally, convert it
into Office format,
or do whatever
you like with it.

Access offers many options for HTML conversion. For instance, you can output a long report to static HTML using the File, Save As HTML command; this breaks the report into multiple linked documents for easier reading. You can also use the Web Publishing Wizard to export datasheets and forms to Dynamic HTML format. Dynamic HTML enables Web sites to store and retrieve live data from your Access database, so that information can be updated dynamically; you must publish the output pages on Microsoft Internet Information Server, though; get more information at http://www.microsoft.com/iis/default.asp. If your copy of Access doesn't have the Save As HTML option or the Web Publishing Wizard, you can easily install them:

1. Quit Access.

2. Insert the Microsoft Office or Microsoft Access CD into the CD-ROM drive.

3. Browse to and open the WebPost subfolder.

4. Double-click WebPost.exe to install the Web Publishing Wizard.

You can insert data from an Excel spreadsheet into a Web page to add a table to that page containing the Excel data, or you can create an entire Web page based on the spreadsheet data. You can also use Excel's Web Form Wizard to create forms for publication on your Web site. First, though, you have to install Excel's Internet Assistant:

1. Quit Excel.

2. Run Add/Remove Programs.

3. Select Microsoft Office or Microsoft Excel and click Add/Remove.

4. Insert the correct CD and run Setup.

5. Select the Web Page Authoring (HTML) check box.

6. After Setup has finished, restart Excel.

7. Select Tools, Add-Ins.

8. In the Add-Ins Available box, select the Internet Assistant check box and click OK.

Office and Email

If you have the Office suite, you might already use Outlook as your personal information manager. As I described in Chapter 2, "Choosing the Right Tools," Outlook makes a good Internet email client, because its email functions integrate with the personal information management functions. For instance, you can quickly address email messages to anyone in your contacts list or turn an email message into a task or appointment by dragging it to the appropriate module. Outlook's filters, organizational folders, and archiving functions make it ideal for dealing with large amounts of email.

Because Outlook is an Office program, it works well with other programs in the suite. This means that you can use Word functions for email. For instance, you can use Word to compose and format email, or you can take advantage of Word's Mail Merge feature to batch-email a large number of personalized messages.

Watch Out!
When you start Excel's Internet Assistant, it asks you for the cell range to convert to HTML. You must enter this in a cryptic format, like $B$34:$G$95. You don't have to figure out how to enter the cell range, though. Just select the range of cells that you want to convert before starting Internet Assistant, so that Excel enters the correct range for you.

Making Word Your Email Editor

If Outlook is your Internet email client, you can use Word as your email editor. This gives you all the functionality of Word when writing email, like AutoCorrect, AutoFormat, and spell-checking as you type. You can also create tables, add high-lighting, and insert other Word-specific formatting, although this converts to plain text if the recipient doesn't have Word; for instance, tables convert to tab-delimited text. Follow these steps to set up Word as your email editor:

1. In Outlook, select Tools, Options.

2. Click the Mail Format tab.

3. Under Message Format, select Microsoft Word from the drop-down menu (see Figure 10.7).

Figure 10.7
Making Word your email editor in Outlook.

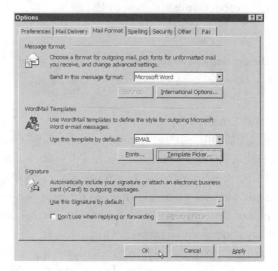

4. Under WordMail Templates, select the email template that you want to use from the drop-down menu.

5. Click OK.

Using Mail Merge for Email

If Outlook is your email program, you can use Word's Mail Merge feature to send a batch of personalized email messages.

For instance, you can mail out a form letter to clients or customer contacts but personalize each message with names, company names, addresses, and anything else that you like. Follow these steps (if you need more help with Mail Merge, consult Word's documentation):

1. In Word, select Tools, Mail Merge.

2. Create the form letter and data source; be sure to include an email address field in the data source.

3. When you're done, click the Mail Merge Helper toolbar button.

4. Click Merge.

5. In the Merge To menu, select Electronic Mail.

6. Click the Setup button.

7. In the Data Field with Mail/Fax Address menu, select the field containing the email addresses.

8. Enter the message's subject in the Mail Message Subject Line field.

9. Click OK and Merge. Your messages are sent straight to Outlook's Outbox.

10. In Outlook, click the Send and Receive toolbar button to send off your messages.

Internet Access from Other Programs

Many other applications besides the Office suite include Internet functionality. This can be useful for automating a wide range of online activities, including sharing documents through email, publishing documents to a Web site, and retrieving online information from inside the program.

This section describes the Internet features of some popular applications, but check the help file of any programs that aren't mentioned to find out if they, too, can be used online. And save yourself some time when shopping for software from

Timesaver
Want to email a copy of an Office document? If Outlook is your default email program, select File, Send To, Mail Recipient. The email message opens with the document attached, ready for you to address and send off. You can also do this with Outlook Express, but first you have to make Outlook Express your default email program: In Outlook Express, open Tools, Options; on the General tab, click the Make Default button to make Outlook Express the default mail handler; click OK; and restart Windows. After you make this change, however, you won't be able to use Outlook's PIM features.

now on. For instance, if you buy a new word-processing or desktop-publishing package, be sure that it supports HTML conversion in case you have to publish documents to the Web. If you buy an image editor, check that it can convert graphics to GIF and JPEG formats for inclusion in Web pages.

Gathering Information from the Internet

The following programs help you gather information from the Internet with built-in tools:

- **AskSam:** Database enables you to turn old email messages into a searchable archive of contacts. Just create a new file using the Email template and select File, Import to bring in the data. AskSam includes a Eudora filter, but messages from other email clients can be imported using the standard Text filter. (Get more information at http://www.askSam.com/.)

- **GoldMine:** A contact manager, enables you to set up a Web-page form that retrieves user data and automatically creates a GoldMine contact from that data. Use it for tracking existing and potential customers who visit your Web site. GoldMine also includes a full-fledged email client that integrates with your contacts. (Get more information at http://www.goldminesw.com/.)

- **Intuit Quicken:** Money management software, has several online functions, including paying bills electronically, reviewing bills over the Internet, updating account information, tracking investments, and transferring money electronically. This ensures that you've got the latest information, saves money and time, and automates monthly tasks. To get started, select Online, Online Financial Services Setup (see Figure 10.8). (Get more information at http://www.quicken.com/.)

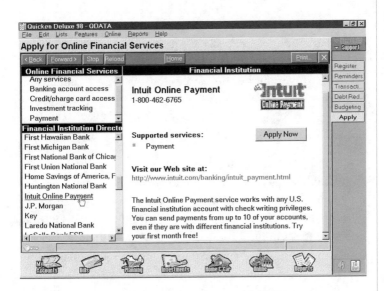

Figure 10.8
Quicken offers a
wide range of
online services to
help with manag-
ing personal
finances.

Moneysaver
If you plan to pub-
lish Excel spread-
sheet data on the
Web, you need the
free Web
Connectivity Kit. It
contains tutorials
and working exam-
ples to make the
job a lot easier.
Get it from the
Office Update
site at http://
officeupdate.
microsoft.com/,
where you also
find a lot more
freebies for all
your Office pro-
grams. You have
to register as an
Office Update
member, but regis-
tration is free as
long as you own
an Office product.

- **Lotus Organizer 97:** The Notepad section can be used to create a list of bookmarked Web sites. Just copy the URLs onto a Notepad page; when you double-click the URL, Organizer launches your Web browser. You can organize bookmarks into categories that Notepad displays automatically in its table of contents. The Web Calendar application can also publish Organizer information dynamically to the Web. (Get more information at http://www.lotus.com/home.nsf/tabs/organizer/.)

Sharing Files Through Email

The following applications simplify the process of sharing files via email:

- **AccuVAR BusinessWorks:** Accounting software that enables you to quickly send reports with their original fonts, styles, and colors by clicking the Send Email button. The program prompts you for the email address and how much of the report to send. (Get more information at http://www.accuvar.com/bw/bw_index.htm.)

- **Adobe PhotoDeluxe:** A photo editor and card maker that enables you to easily share your creations with family and friends: Click the Send button; select the Internet tab; click the Email button; and follow the steps to email your project to others. You can also post your creations on the Web. (Get more information at `http://www.adobe.com/prodindex/photodeluxe/main.html.`)

- **Corel WordPerfect:** It's easy to send a document by email—just choose File, Send. It also automatically formats URLs as hyperlinks; you can even define automatic conversion of normal words into hyperlinks—select Tools, Web Links to find this feature (see Figure 10.9). For example, you can link your company name to its Web site or link your email address in your document's header. Finally, use the Internet Publisher (located under the File menu) to format documents for the Web. (Get more information at `http://www.corel.com/products/wordperfect/`

Hypertext toolbar

Figure 10.9
Use WordPerfect's Hypertext toolbar to create Internet links in your document.

`cwps8/index.htm.`)

- **Presto! PageManager:** Image scanner software that enables you to quickly send images via email. Just drag and drop the images that you want to send onto the Email icon, and the Presto! Wrapper application (included) packages the image with a viewer and compresses it into an executable file. So the recipient is able to view the image without having compatible software already installed. You can also share images over the Internet by connecting to the PhotoNet. (Get more information at `http://www.newsoftinc.com/nsiweb/products/windows/pmag/ppm98-info.html.`)

- **WinZip:** Enables you to send ZIP files via email in one step by selecting File, Mail Archive. (Get more information at `http://www.winzip.com/`.)

Publishing Files on the Web

The following programs include HTML conversion and publishing features:

- **Corel Presentations:** Part of the WordPerfect Office suite that enables you to create slideshows that can be viewed on the Internet, preserving animation, sound, movies, and transitions, via the Publish To Internet feature, located under the File menu (see Figure 10.10). You can also insert hyperlinks into your presentations or build in Java applets. (Get more information at `http://www.corel.com/Office2000/index.htm`.)

- **Corel VENTURA:** A desktop publisher that automatically maps VENTURA tags to HTML for instant Web publishing. You can also use the Publish As HTML function to control conversion of text, layout, and graphics. You can even create Java applets or Cascading Style Sheets. (Get more information at `http://www.corel.com/products/graphicsandpublishing/ventura8/index.htm`.)

- **FileMaker Pro:** The database has a built-in Web Companion (located on the File, Sharing menu), which makes it easy to translate your database into a format for Web or intranet publishing. Users can access and modify the database over the Internet, using just a Web browser and with no need for a specialized server. FileMaker Pro even includes Shopping Cart, Guest Book, and Employee Database templates. (Get more information at `http://www.filemaker.com/products/filemakerpro/filemakerpro.html`.)

- **Lotus Word Pro:** The word processor has a Web toolbar that enables you to quickly save pages to HTML, preserving all document settings. All graphics are automatically converted to JPEG format, as well. To find Word Pro's Web

Timesaver

If you use Windows, you can quickly connect to a URL without first having to launch your browser. Select Start, Run and enter the URL into the Open field. Clicking OK starts the default browser and opens the URL. If you use Dial-Up Networking, this also opens your default connection. As a bonus, the URL is kept in the Open drop-down menu for fast access later.

Timesaver

Here's how to include an image of a Gantt Chart created in Microsoft Project in an HTML file: Click the Copy Picture toolbar button and select the To GIF Image File option. Project automatically assigns a path and filename to the new GIF file, which you can reference in the HTML document.

authoring tools, right-click a toolbar and select Internet Tools. (Get more information at http://www.lotus.com/.)

Figure 10.10
Corel Presentations' Publish To Internet feature makes it easy to turn a slideshow into a Web site.

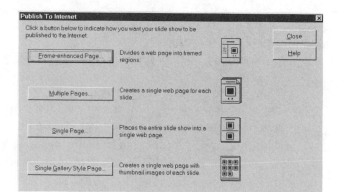

- **MGI PhotoSuite:** The photo editor has a unique feature that enables you to collect and publish your PhotoSuite images in an HTML-format photo album that anyone with a Web browser can look at. Select New, Album under the File menu to create the album, and select Album, Create HTML Album to convert it to HTML format. (Get more information at http://www.mgisoft.com/ Products/ProductShowcase/Product09/.)

- **Scitor Project Scheduler:** A project-management tool to enable one-click HTML conversion of any report—just click the Output To Web Page toolbar button. You can also define customized HTML templates. (Get more information at http://www.scitor.com/ps7/Index.asp.)

Using the Active Desktop

The ultimate integration of the Internet and the desktop is the Windows Active Desktop, which Windows 98 and NT 5.0 users get with their operating system. Windows 95 and NT 4.0 users can also access the Active Desktop, by installing the Windows Desktop Update with Internet Explorer 4.0.

Some people love this integration, and some hate it. You probably love it if you really like the Web metaphor for navigation, if you're a push content junkie, or if customization of

Moneysaver
If you use Lotus Word Pro for Windows 95 to import, edit, and export HTML documents, Lotus's HTML filter makes the job a lot easier. The HTML filter includes support for tables and better matching to Navigator defaults. It's free but not easy to find. Go to http:// www2.support. lotus.com/ftp/ pub/desktop/ WordPro/win95/ updates/ and click the html32.zip file to download the filter.

your desktop, taskbar, Start menu, and folders is a priority. However, you might find that the new features are not enough compensation for the Active Desktop's slowness, instability, and tendency to do weird things to your programs. (When I installed the Windows Desktop Update, it totally wiped out the data I had stored in Outlook, including my entire Address Book; fortunately, I was able to restore from backup, but only after removing the Windows Desktop Update and reinstalling Outlook.)

The Active Desktop integrates Windows with the Web in many ways:

- The desktop can display HTML pages and Active Channel content.

- Internet Explorer replaces the Windows Explorer for navigating files and folders.

- Your computer behaves more like the Web; files and folders turn into single-click hyperlinks, for instance.

Installing the Windows Desktop Update

If you're a Windows 95 or Windows NT 4.0 user, you may have already installed the Desktop Update when you installed Internet Explorer 4.0, if you chose the Standard Install option. To turn on the Active Desktop, right-click the desktop and select Active Desktop—make sure that View As Web Page is selected.

If you didn't install the Desktop Update, you're going to have to jump through some hoops to get it—first, you have to restore Internet Explorer 4.0; then get the Desktop Update, and then reinstall Internet Explorer 5.0. Here's what you need to do:

1. Run a full backup—don't take any chances!

2. Open the Start menu, and select Settings, Control Panel.

3. Double-click Add/Remove Programs.

Timesaver
You don't need the Windows Desktop Update to take advantage of one timesaving integration of Windows 95 and the Internet. Select Start, Find—you should see On The Internet and People listed. Selecting On The Internet launches the default search page in your browser, so that you can quickly search the Web. Selecting People opens a Find People dialog box, which enables you to search any of the major white-pages sites. Choose the directory that you want to search from the Look In menu, and fill out the fields with the search criteria.

Bright Idea
You're familiar
with Internet
Shortcuts by
now—they're
desktop shortcuts
that link directly
to Web sites.
Actually, these
shortcuts are sim-
ple text files that
you can create
anytime, even
from outside your
browser. Right-
click the desktop
and select New,
Shortcut. In the
command line,
type http://www.
arcana.com/
shannon/index.
html. Click Next
and type
Shannon's Home
Page in the Name
field. Click Finish,
and you have a
new Internet
Shortcut to my
home page. You
can attach the
shortcut to an
email message
and send it to any
Windows user—
they'll be able to
click the shortcut
to connect to the
Web page. (This
trick doesn't
require the
Windows Desktop
Update.)

4. Select Internet Explorer 5 and Internet Tools, and click Add/Remove.

5. Click Restore the Previous Version of Internet Explorer, and click OK.

6. Restart your computer.

7. Select Settings, Control Panel from the Start menu, and double-click Add/Remove Programs again.

8. Click Microsoft Internet Explorer 4.0, and click Add/Remove.

9. Click Add Windows Desktop Update from the Web Site.

10. When the Desktop Update has downloaded and installed, restart Windows. Windows comes back up with the Active Desktop enabled.

At this point, you can reinstall Internet Explorer 5.0. If you later decide that you don't like the Active Desktop and you want to remove the Desktop Update, simply follow these steps again to uninstall it.

Customizing the Active Desktop

The Active Desktop integrates your desktop with the Web (see Figure 10.11). You can put parts of Web pages on your desktop, like a stock ticker or weather report, and they'll update automatically. Or make an entire HTML file your wallpaper—all the links remain active. For instance, you might want to turn your start page into desktop wallpaper, so that it's always easily accessible. If you're a Windows 98 user, or if you upgraded from Internet Explorer 4.0, the Channel Bar also appears on the desktop, giving you easy access to your Active Channels (the Channel Bar feature was discontinued with Internet Explorer 5.0).

Figure 10.11
Customize the
Active Desktop
with the Channel
bar, ticker-like
Web content, and
taskbar toolbars.

Customizing the Active Desktop

To customize your Active Desktop, right-click the desktop and select Properties. On the Background tab, select a wallpaper. You can choose a standard Bitmap graphic, select wallpaper (the standard Active Desktop wallpaper), browse to a locally saved HTML file, or set the background to None.

The Web tab determines what Web elements are displayed on the Active Desktop. For instance, deselect the Internet Explorer Channel Bar check box if you want to remove it from the desktop. To find additional Active Desktop components, click the New button on the Web tab. This launches Internet Explorer and connects to the Desktop Gallery, where you find a list of Active Desktop items. After you subscribe to an Active Desktop item, just click the Add To Desktop button inside it to put a new item on your desktop.

Unfortunately, the Active Desktop uses a lot of memory and processing power, so turning it on can slow your computer to an unbearable level. The more stuff you put on your desktop, the slower your computer is going to be. Each component that you add can be turned on and off on the Web tab of the Display Properties dialog box. If you want to turn off the Active Desktop altogether, returning to the more familiar desktop

Timesaver
Windows retains everything that's typed into the Address toolbar, so it's particularly useful for remembering long pathnames of folders and programs that you access infrequently. Just type the pathname once. When you go back and start retyping the pathname, the complete name is filled in. If it's not correct, keep typing or press the up and down arrow keys to cycle through a list of possible matches.

view, right-click the desktop, select Active Desktop, and uncheck View As Web Page.

Customizing the Taskbar

You can also customize what appears on the taskbar. Shortcuts to Internet Explorer, Outlook Express, and Active Channels appear next to the Start button by default. You can add shortcuts to other favorite programs, files, folders, and Web pages, giving one-click access to them from the taskbar. Here's how

1. Right-click a blank part of the taskbar.

2. Select Toolbars.

3. Select the toolbars that you want to appear on the taskbar (you can add as many toolbars as you like):

   • **Address:** Adds an Address window where you can enter URLs and pathnames to quickly find files, connect to Web sites, or launch programs. All of the shortcuts of the Internet Explorer Address window apply here.

   • **Links:** Displays the Links toolbar from Internet Explorer on the taskbar.

   • **Desktop:** Turns all the shortcuts currently on the desktop into toolbar buttons.

   • **Quick Launch:** Provides shortcuts to Internet Explorer, Outlook Express, and Active Channels; it's displayed by default. To quickly hide all your open windows and peek at what's happening on the desktop, click the Show Desktop button.

As with Internet Explorer's toolbars, these taskbar toolbars are very customizable. For instance, you can add more programs to the Quick Launch toolbar by dragging and dropping a shortcut onto the toolbar, or get rid of existing icons by dragging them to the Recycle Bin. You can also place any of these toolbars anywhere on the desktop by dragging around the gray handle to the left of the toolbar.

Turning Your Computer into a Web Site

Turning on the Active Desktop enables you to navigate through directories on the hard drive using an Internet Explorer-like interface. Certain browser functions, like Back and Forward buttons and an Address box where you can enter pathnames or Internet URLs, appear at the top of each folder window. Notice that Internet Explorer's Favorites menu is available as well. Go into the View menu, and you can turn on and off toolbars (including the Links toolbar), access the Explorer bar, and organize items in the folder by their properties. The standard toolbar also provides easy access to familiar features, like the Properties dialog box, a Delete button, and a menu for changing folder views.

You can make your view of folders and drives even more like the Web. On the Start menu, select Settings, Folder Options and click the Web Style button under Windows Desktop Update. Now, directory views are presented as Web pages rendered in Dynamic HTML, and all programs, files, and folders inside the open folder are changed into single-click hyperlinks (see Figure 10.12). Position the mouse over a file, folder, or hardware device to dynamically display its properties in this Web page.

You can write your own Dynamic HTML code to customize any folder, determining what information is displayed. Open the folder, right-click its background, and select Customize This Folder. You get three choices:

- **Create or edit an HTML document.** This loads the folder's Dynamic HTML document into your default HTML editor, enabling you to fully customize the folder's appearance and behavior. I don't recommend this unless you're already familiar with Dynamic HTML, but it can be a powerful way to customize the look and information presented in your folders.

- **Choose a background picture.** This just puts wallpaper in the background of the folder. It's a very easy way to dress up your folders.

Bright Idea
You can create your own taskbar toolbars using the contents of any folder. First, create a folder containing favorite shortcuts, frequently opened documents, or anything you like. You might want to create a system toolbar containing Dial-Up Networking, Printers, My Computer, and Control Panels, for instance. Right-click the taskbar, select Toolbars, New Toolbar, and type the pathname of the folder that you want to turn into a toolbar.

Figure 10.12
The Active
Desktop turns
Windows into an
Internet Explorer-
like interface and
transforms your
folders into Web
pages.

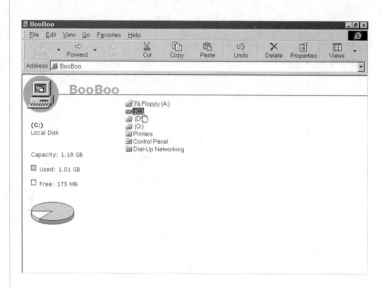

Timesaver
While browsing
through folders in
Web view, select
any HTML file to
display a thumb-
nail icon of the file
directly in the
folder view. You
can also highlight
any GIF or JPEG
graphic and view a
thumbnail of it.
This feature saves
a lot of time when
looking through a
bunch of crypti-
cally named files
for one particular
HTML document
or image, saving
you from having to
launch Internet
Explorer or an
image viewer to
view them.

- **Remove customization.** This returns the folder to its original state.

Of course, you might hate this Web integration. You can
return to what you're used to by selecting Settings, Folder
Options from the Start menu and clicking on the Classic Style
button. Or select Custom and click Settings to pick and choose
from the various Webified behaviors; for instance, you can
turn off Web content in your folders while retaining single-
click program launching and file navigation.

While the Start menu is open, notice the new addition—
your Favorites folder. This gives quick access to your favorite
Web sites via Internet Explorer. You can also drag items
around on the Start menu—you can put your most-accessed
programs at the top of the Programs menu, for instance. Even
drag items from Windows Explorer to the Start menu to
dynamically add them to the Start menu.

Just the Facts

- Take advantage of Internet features in your favorite applications to quickly access data online and share files more easily; for instance, FTP access, Web browsing, extensive HTML authoring and conversion, and email integration are all incorporated into the Microsoft Office program suite.

- Many other applications besides Office feature Internet integration; when shopping for software, look for Internet features that can make your job easier, such as integration with online information, simplified email access, and full-featured HTML conversion.

- The Active Desktop offers the ultimate integration of the Internet and the operating system; although it's not for everybody, it does enable you to fully customize your computer, display updated Web content on the desktop, and navigate your computer as if it were a Web site.

Bright Idea
A Messaging toolbar on the taskbar makes sending email messages a snap. First, create a new folder called Messaging. Right-click inside the folder and add a shortcut with the following command line: `mailto:`. Call this shortcut "New Message" or something similar. You can also create mailto shortcuts that are pre-addressed to frequent correspondents (`mailto:dad@ family.net`, for instance). Turn the Messaging folder into a Messaging toolbar. You now have a desktop toolbar that enables you to send email messages with a single click.

Power Surfing

PART III

GET THE SCOOP ON...
Finding the most effective search engines ▪ Getting
the search results you want the first time ▪ Using
software tools to help you search ▪ Performing
specialized searches

Searching Savvy

Chapter 11

T HE INTERNET IS A TREASURE trove of information on practically any subject, and thus it makes a wonderful
research tool. But the Internet is not like the local
library with its helpful card catalog. The Web is so big, and
growing bigger every day, that no one could completely catalog
it or organize what's available into helpful categories.

That's why it's so important to develop online searching
skills. Search sites are plentiful, but none of them is much good
unless you put a little effort into your searches. Unless you
learn how to search effectively, your searches are likely to
return a list of several thousand Web sites, many of them having nothing whatsoever to do with what you're looking for.

At this point, you might be tempted to get the car keys and
drive down to the local library. But if you develop your searching skills, you'll find just what you're looking for, the first time
you look. This chapter teaches you how.

Watch Out!
The Internet, and consequently search engines, are busiest from 3–5PM and 7–11PM EST. During these times, search engines can slow so much as to become unusable. You can perform speedier searches at low traffic times, such as during the early morning. If you use AltaVista to search, take advantage of low traffic times in other parts of the world, even when it's busiest at home, by searching with one of these mirror sites: http://altavista. skali.com.my/ (Asia) and http:// www.altavista. yellowpages.com. au/ (Australia).

Choosing a Search Site

Before you even start to search, you must pick the right tool for the job. Each search tool is different and so returns vastly different results. There are four basic kinds of search sites:

- General search engines

- Searchable Web-site directories

- Specialized search engines

- Meta-search pages

Each one of these kinds of search sites has its good points and its drawbacks. In this section, you'll learn about these different kinds of search tools, so you can choose the one that best meets your needs. If you start with the right kind of search site, you're much more likely to find what you're searching for.

Using Search Engines

Software programs called worms or spiders compile the databases that search engines search. These robots, or bots for short, crawl through the Web along hyperlinks, indexing each page they come across for the search engine's database. You can then search the database for all of the indexed Web sites that contain your search keywords.

Each search engine uses a different kind of bot to perform the indexing and a different mathematical algorithm to determine the ranking of the search results, so you're likely to get very different results for the same keywords from different search engines. And none of the search results is comprehensive—way too many pages are published on the Web everyday for indexing bots to keep up with them. At best, each search engine has indexed about a third of available Web sites. Still, any search you perform might turn up too many sites for you to ever look at.

Search engine databases are made up of millions of uncataloged Web pages. So, if you search for a general subject, such as dogs, you're likely to find several hundred-thousand matching pages, some of them only marginally related to dogs.

Search engines are most useful for performing very specific, refined searches. If you're looking for information about a certain breed of dog, such as the Nova Scotia duck-tolling retriever, a search engine is the best choice.

The search engine ranks the results of your search, with the best matches appearing at the top of the list, so you shouldn't have to look beyond the first 10 or 20 listings to find some good matches. But because these rankings are based on mathematical formulas, they can be hit or miss. Generally, the highest-ranked Web pages contain multiple instances of your search keywords, or the search keywords appear in the page's title or in the description and keyword META tags. A short excerpt of the page appears in the search results list, generally the first 200 characters or at best a description culled from the page's heading. Sometimes, this excerpt gives you a good idea of what the page is about, and sometimes it just looks like nonsense.

This section describes the best search engines, including a brief rundown on what's good and bad about each. I've listed the URL of the search engine's main page and the location of its advanced search form, which helps you create more focused search queries (see the "Refining Your Search" section later in this chapter for tips on how to perform advanced searches).

Try several search engines, pick the one that feels most comfortable to you, and get to know its advanced search functions very well. As you keep working with the same search engine, you'll get increasingly better results.

AltaVista

AltaVista is a very accurate search engine, but learning how to use the advanced search functions is not easy. It's worth it, though, because the advanced search really makes AltaVista perform. This search engine is the best choice when posing detailed queries and looking for very specific search terms.

If your search term is too general, AltaVista displays several related searches that may help you zero in on exactly what you're looking for. You can also confine search results to the language of your choice or translate any page you find to a language other than English, a nice feature for international users. The search results aren't very customizable, though. For instance, you can't sort them, turn off the page excerpts, or show more detailed descriptions.

- **URL:** `http://altavista.digital.com/.`

- **Advanced Search:** Click the Advanced link.

Excite

Excite is a user-friendly choice for the less experienced searcher and for simple searches. (After you get into more complicated searches, you might want to turn to another tool.) Excite suggests keywords that you can add to the search to refine the results—a helpful feature for beginners. The Search for More Documents Like This One link that appears beneath each search result is very helpful if you find a good match and want to look for similar pages. And the search results are very customizable—you can organize them by Web site, look for news articles only, and turn summaries off and on.

- **URL:** `http://www.excite.com/.`

- **Advanced Search:** `http://www.excite.com/search_forms/ advanced/` and click Advanced Web Search.

HotBot

HotBot is my favorite search engine—it's easy to use, it's very accurate, it's fast, and it has powerful advanced search options that are easy to configure, so you can really refine your search (see Figure 11.1). You can filter the search results by date, media type, domain name, the page's geographical location, and the page's depth in its site; for more general searches, you can look for top-level pages, for instance. HotBot is also very diligent about weeding out those useless dead links. Another nice feature is a link to the most popular sites on the same search term, which generally takes you straight to the best sites.

Timesaver
If you decide to make AltaVista your primary search tool, you need to go to `http:// discovery. altavista. digital.com/` and download AltaVista Discovery. This free software program for Windows 95/98/NT 4.0 puts a search toolbar on top of Navigator 3.x or Internet Explorer 3.x (and later versions), so that you can search AltaVista from any location on the Web. And it gives you more power by highlighting relevant text, instantly finding similar pages, and enabling backward searching. It also enables you to search your email messages and hard drive.

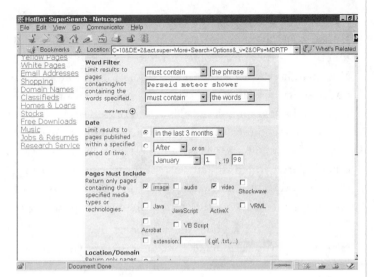

Figure 11.1
HotBot's advanced search form enables you to create more focused searches.

- **URL:** http://www.hotbot.com/.

- **Advanced Search:** Click the Advanced Search button.

Infoseek

Infoseek is a good choice for simple, fast searches of keywords and short phrases. It's very accurate, and it weeds out duplicates, so you won't find the same pages repeatedly in the same search. Infoseek is also a powerful tool for searching current news stories, looking for a company, or searching Usenet; the drop-down menu next to the search box enables you to choose the kind of search you want to perform.

Infoseek displays results in a unique way—grouped by domain name; this helps you quickly find the main page in a site on the topic. Infoseek also allows you to search again within your first set of search results, so that you can refine the list. Or you can refine your search by choosing from suggested topics. On the downside, Infoseek's advanced searching is limited, especially when compared to AltaVista and HotBot.

- **URL:** http://www.infoseek.com/.

- **Advanced Search:** Click the Search Options link.

Timesaver
Infoseek offers a free, timesaving tool to complement its search engine—Express Search. Installing Express Search puts a search taskbar on your desktop so you can search the Internet without even opening your browser (Windows 95/98/NT 4.0 only). To get it, go to http://express .infoseek.com/ subdocuments/ expressdetails. html.

Using Web Site Directories

Unlike a search engine's database, a Web site directory is put together by people. Some directories, such as Yahoo!, Magellan, and About.Com, have editors who select and categorize sites; these directories contain fewer sites, but often the sites listed are good quality, stable, and on topic. Other directories, such as the Galaxy, rely on contributions by their visitors, so they tend to be larger but don't have the same level of quality as the edited directories. (You can visit the Galaxy at http://galaxy.einet.net/galaxy.html, but I find it too chaotic and disorganized for anything more than casual browsing.)

Directories are a good starting point if you're not sure exactly what you're looking for. For instance, you might be researching camping, but you don't really know if you need information on equipment, good places to camp, or tips for camping with the family. And you didn't even realize that there were sites about camping in the winter or good camping recipes. Directories give you a good idea of the scope of what's available on a general subject and help you find mega-sites, which eventually lead you to more specialized sites. However, they're not much good for finding very specialized information, such as information about camping in the winter in the Catskills.

This section lists the best of the directory sites, with a brief rundown of what they do well, what they do badly, and how they compile search results. Again, you should choose one as your main Web-site directory source and get to know it very well, so that you can find relevant information easier each time you return.

Magellan

Magellan is very selective about which sites are included in the directory, and each listing comes with a pithy review and a rating. The reviews provide a lot more information about the site than Yahoo!'s bare listings, so you can better decide what to visit.

However, Magellan's search leaves something to be desired, especially when compared to Yahoo! Although supposedly ranked by relevance, the order of the search results seems rather haphazard. And searching doesn't find categories or even reveal in which categories Web sites are located, greatly reducing your ability to discover sites under one general heading. You can click a Find Similar link to look for related pages, but this doesn't always work very well. It's a lot easier to drill down through the categories to locate the general subject area that contains the information you're looking for.

- **URL:** `http://www.mckinley.com/`.

- **Advanced Search:** None, but you can choose between a search of reviewed sites (called *green light* sites) or a database of robot-indexed Web sites (similar to Excite).

About.Com

What I really like about About.Com is that each of its 500-plus subject guides is edited by a separate person, called a guide. This person decides which sites go into the guide, annotates each listing, organizes the sites into subcategories, and writes weekly features. Think of About.Com as a collection of well-compiled hotlists. It's an excellent resource for finding information on a very broad subject, although it's not as comprehensive as either Yahoo! or Magellan.

What I don't like about About.Com is that it's really slow, which makes it a chore for quick searches and extensive browsing alike. And some guides are better than others, which means that some of the subject areas contain tons of links and articles, while others are pretty scanty—it's a hit-or-miss proposition. But if you're looking for lot of truly useful information about a broad subject, About.Com should be your first stop.

- **URL:** `http://www.about.com/`.

- **Advanced Search:** None

Yahoo!

Yahoo! is probably the most comprehensive of the Web site directories, and it's the one I use most often. When you search

Bright Idea
If you don't have time to page through search results right away, or if you want to browse them offline and then reconnect to try out the best matches, just save the search results as HTML files on your local disk (select File, Save As in your browser).

Yahoo!, it lists matching categories first, and then matching Web sites (see Figure 11.2). This is helpful for finding a group of sites related to the topic that you're looking for, even if the title or description of some of the sites don't match your search term, and it saves you from having to browse through the extensive categories to find the one you want. Yahoo! groups the most complete reference sites at the top of a category, so you should connect to them first.

Figure 11.2
When searching for a general term such as "astronomy," Yahoo! lists the most comprehensive categories first.

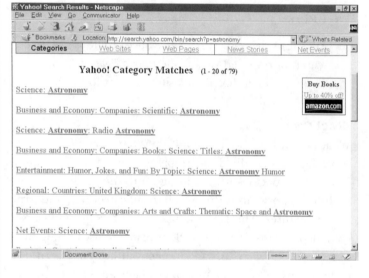

Timesaver
If you find a broad Yahoo! category that you're pretty sure contains what you're looking for, don't waste time searching the whole index—you can limit your search to that category by selecting Just This Category from the drop-down menu underneath the search form. (You have to be inside the category first.)

Yahoo! also performs a full Web search using the Inktomi search engine (the same one that HotBot uses), and appends the results to the end of the list of matching Yahoo! categories and listings. This feature makes Yahoo! particularly useful—if the directory turns up nothing useful, you can connect directly to a more general Web search.

Yahoo! also provides many valuable specialized searches. The most useful are the Yahoo! Get Local directories; just type a zip code into the text field at the bottom of the main Yahoo! page and click Enter Zip Code to turn up events, weather, news, yellow pages, and a specialized Web directory for that town. Another great feature is the kids' directory, Yahooligans! (http://www.yahooligans.com/), a Yahoo! clone with sites chosen just for kids.

Yahoo! does have some limitations, though. Lately, it's turned away from building the Web-site directory, which is really its core service, and has focused a lot of attention on developing portal services, such as chat and free email. So, it seems that the main directory isn't growing as fast or is as complete as it used to be. And you're going to run into a lot of dead links—Yahoo! never does any housekeeping.

- **URL:** http://www.yahoo.com/.

- **Advanced   Search:**   http://search.yahoo.com/search/ options/.

Using Specialized Search Engines

Search engines or Web-site directories are sometimes too generalized. By trying to include everything, they might leave out valuable resources or return so many results that they're unusable.

That's where specialized search engines come in. Like Web-site directories, these are compiled by human beings, so they're only as good as the people that make them. But if you're looking for something specific, such as a computing- or business-related site or a site about a specific country, these specialized tools often turn up a more complete list and more valuable resources than a search engine or general directory can. The best of them index the entire Web page content of selected sites, so you can search for specific data just as with a general search engine. And all the searching tricks that you'll learn later in this chapter apply to these specialized search sites as well. I'd recommend a specialized search engine over the general search sites every time, if one's available for the subject that you're interested in.

Watch Out!
You have to watch out for editorial bias in some search sites, including Yahoo!, which has partnered with several content providers, such as Ziff-Davis and ESPN. Links to these partner sites often turn up at the top of a category listing, enticing you to visit them first, even if they're not exactly what you're looking for.

Timesaver
It can be difficult tracking down the really useful specialized search engines. Here are some that I've found:
- http://www.brint.com/ —business, management, and technology search.
- http://www.sbfocus.com/— findsinformation of interest to small businesses and entrepreneurs.
- http://www.moneysearch.com/ — finance and investment search.
- http://www.netpartners.com/resources/search.html—finds all the Web and FTP servers owned by a particular company.

The best place to start looking for a specialized search is Search.Com (http://www.search.com/), which is a directory of most of the specialized search sites out there, so you can find everything from concert tickets to jobs to restaurants to sports scores to air fares. Just click the Find a Search link to start, or browse through the categories.

Performing Meta-Searches

If one search engine is good, ten are better—at least, that's the theory behind meta-search pages. These search pages query multiple search engines with one form and display the results in a unified list. The best meta-searchers turn up closer matches to your search keywords and filter out duplicates. However, you might not get a big enough results list with these. The different search and indexing methods required by the various search engines can lead to some unexpected results, so meta-searches tend to come up with more inaccuracies. Also, you can't make use of the full power of the individual search engines. Finally, these meta-searchers tend to be very slow, because they must access and search each popular search engine.

If you're performing a quick, specific, one-word search, the meta-searchers are convenient tools. Otherwise, go right to the source. Here are the best meta-searchers:

- **Ask Jeeves** (http://www.askjeeves.com/): My favorite. You ask questions, rather than putting together search queries; Ask Jeeves returns less than ten matches from the major search engines, including Excite, InfoSeek, AltaVista, Lycos, and WebCrawler, and its accuracy is very high (see Figure 11.3).

- **DogPile** (http://www.dogpile.com/): Searches the most places. Select from Web, Usenet, FTP, and other focused searches. You can also set a time limit for the search, but this can truncate your results list.

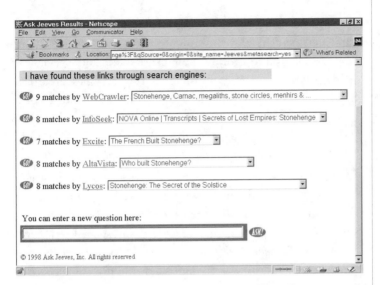

© 1998 Ask Jeeves, Inc. All rights reserved.

Figure 11.3
Ask Jeeves returns accurate, focused search results based on questions that you ask, such as these answers to my question, "Who built Stonehenge?"

- **The Internet Sleuth (http://www.isleuth.com/):** Enables you to pick and choose which search engines to search by selecting them on a simple form. You can also set how long the search should take.

- **MetaCrawler (http://www.metacrawler.com/):** Offers the most searching choices, including a customized search, a power search, a fast search for low-bandwidth users, and the free MiniCrawler, which enables you to search from the desktop (go to http://www.go2net.com/tools/minicrawler/ to get it).

- **SavvySearch (http://www.savvysearch.com/):** Offers several meta-specialized searches in addition to a general search. For instance, you can search multiple sites for jobs, kid sites, or movie information.

Finally, you might like to try out the mega-search pages. Unlike meta-searchers, these pages just put the interfaces for several search pages on one Web page, making it more convenient to search them from a central spot. They also connect to specialized searches, such as Usenet, white pages, yellow pages, software searches, and the like.

Watch Out!
Don't trust your search site to be objective. All of them make money from advertising, and companies pay a lot of money to have their ads featured on targeted or popular searches. Some of them even sell preferred listings that appear at the top of the results.

Mega-search pages are all right for quick searches, but you can't perform the really useful advanced searches with them. They're also handy for finding overlooked and specialized search tools. (You can easily build your own mega-search page by grabbing the code for the search forms from your favorite search engines and Web site directories and pasting them into your own Web page—more on this in Chapter 15, "Putting Your Web Site to Work.")

The All-In-One Search Page (http://www.allonesearch.com/) is probably the most comprehensive of the mega-search sites. There's almost too much here, with direct searches for virtually every search engine, directory, and specialized search engine on the Web. Use this page to find specialized searches and less well-known search engines, or when you have to perform a really comprehensive search.

Timesaver
After coming up with the perfect search query, bookmark it! This is a great time-saver if you have to perform an identical search on a regular basis. Just turn the search results page into a book-mark or favorite. When you want to rerun the search, open the book-mark—the search results are updated. Look for links that you haven't yet accessed—that haven't turned purple—to find new listings.

Refining Your Search

It doesn't matter how many results a search engine returns—you're probably only going to take the time to look at the first 20 or so. If you don't find what you need in the first few listings, your search wasn't precise enough. After you learn a few searching tricks, you can pose effective queries the first time out and eliminate a lot of wasted time sifting through documents that don't match what you're looking for.

Choosing Keywords

Most searchers tend to use only one or two keywords in a query. This is the biggest mistake you can make. Even a search for one very specific keyword can come up with several hundred or several thousand matches—not a long list comparatively, but still a lot more than you're probably willing to sort through. Refining your query with additional keywords greatly narrows this list.

Web site owners have come up with ways to trick you into visiting their sites by ensuring that their pages show up in your search results, even if their pages have nothing to do with what you're looking for. For instance, they stuff titles and META tags with commonly searched keywords, such as sex, shopping,

Internet, and free. Targeting your search with several keywords should avoid this kind of spam.

Keep the following rules in mind when choosing keywords:

- **Select more than two but less than six keywords.** Unless the word you're looking for is very specific, if you use fewer than two keywords, your search results are too broad. However, if you use too many keywords, your search results are too narrow, potentially omitting the information that you need or not returning anything at all.

- **Use nouns as query keywords.** Other words, such as verbs, adjectives, adverbs, and conjunctions, are either discarded by the search engine or too variable to be useful in your search.

- **Make each keyword as specific as possible.** If you're searching for falcons, for instance, don't use the keyword, "bird." More specific keywords zero in on the information you need.

- **Look for phrases rather than specific words.** A phrase is often much more specific than a single word can be; for instance, the phrase, "peregrine falcon," is better than "falcon" alone. Using full names when looking for people also results in a more targeted search.

- **Search for synonyms.** For instance, the search term, "four-wheel drive," might not turn up everything. Using an equivalent term, such as "sports utility vehicle," nets a more comprehensive results list.

- **Use common abbreviations.** Your search results are based on the actual contents of Web pages, so a search for a long term, such as "sports utility vehicle," might not net as many good matches as a more commonly used abbreviation, such as "SUV."

- **Avoid the tendency to search for plural words.** When entering keywords, we tend to use the plural form of the word—"birds" instead of "bird," for instance. Using the

Timesaver
If you use Internet Explorer, you can perform a quick search by typing ? followed by the search term into the Address window.

Timesaver
Sometimes after following a link to a page found by a search engine, it's not immediately apparent why the page turned up in the search results. To quickly find the relevant section of the page, press Ctrl+F (Windows) or Cmd+F (Macintosh), and type your query keyword into the Find dialog box. Your browser high-lights the first occurrence of the keyword in the page. Press Ctrl+G (Windows) or Cmd+G (Mac) to find the next occurrence.

simplest form of the word turns up more matches. Some search tools match parts of words, so searching for "bird" finds pages that contain the words birds, birding, and bird-brain. Others require you to use wildcards (more on this in the next section).

- **Take advantage of case-sensitive search engines.** If you're looking for a proper name, capitalize it—some search engines only look for exact matches to capital letters. This is particularly helpful if the proper name is also a common word—Prince as opposed to prince, for instance.

Also watch out for stop words, such as "a," "and," "the," "of," and other short, common words. Most search engines just ignore them. So if you search for a title, such as *The Graduate*, the search engine finds all pages containing the word, "graduate," most of which probably have nothing to do with the movie.

Searching the Boolean Way

Stringing together a bunch of keywords still isn't the most effective way to search. Most search engines find all pages containing just one of your search words, resulting in a long list of worthless pages, none of them focused on your query. Some search engines find pages containing all your keywords, but you can't count on it. You have to make sure that the search engine understands exactly what you're looking for.

Using a system called Boolean logic, you can structure your query and use logical operators to target the results that you want. Boolean logic isn't that difficult to learn. If you have trouble, many search engines provide forms that insert the most common Boolean terms for you, but this limits how advanced your searches can get.

Table 11.1 describes all the Boolean expressions, with the most commonly supported and useful expressions listed first. (Always put Boolean expressions into all capital letters, so the search engine interprets them properly.)

TABLE 11.1: BOOLEAN OPERATORS

Operator	Use	Example
AND or plus sign	Finds pages that include both of the keywords.	horror AND movie; +horror +movie
OR	Finds pages containing one keyword or the other, which works best when searching for synonyms.	porpoise OR dolphin
Enclose two or more keywords in quotation marks.	Finds exact phrase matches; you can also include stop words within quotes to search for them as part of the phrase.	"federal deficit"; "The Graduate"
AND NOT or minus sign	Finds pages containing the first keyword but not the second one.	beehive AND NOT hairdo; beehive –hairdo
* or ? (wildcard)	Finds pages containing words in which the beginning characters match the keyword; you should still include as much of the word root as possible to avoid turning up unrelated words.	terrori* or terrori? (finds pages containing terrorism, terrorist, and terrorize)
Enclose two or more Boolean expressions in parentheses.	Nests expressions so that they are evaluated left-to-right and inside-out.	processor AND NOT (Intel AND Cyrix); (oil OR petroleum) AND (environment AND disaster)
NEAR	Finds pages in which both words are within ten words of each other.	Mary NEAR lamb

Not every search engine supports Boolean logic fully or in the same way. Of all the search engines, AltaVista allows the most complex Boolean expressions. Whenever you encounter a search engine—whether it's a site-only search, a specialized search, a Web directory search, a meta-search, or anything else, it's a good bet that at least simple Boolean expressions work. Try it and see!

Table 11.2 provides a rundown on the Boolean support provided by each of the major search engines.

Bright Idea
After performing a search, consolidate the data all in one place. First, create a search-results folder on your hard drive. While examining the search results, right-click any links that look promising (hold and click on the Mac). Choose Save Link As or Save Target As from the pop-up menu to save the destination page to the local folder, and give each file a meaningful name. Now you can browse the results offline, or use Windows Find or any other search tool to look through all the pages in your folder.

TABLE 11.2: BOOLEAN LOGIC SUPPORT IN THE MAJOR SEARCH ENGINES AND WEB SITE DIRECTORIES

Search Engine/ Web Site Directory	Boolean Expressions Supported
AltaVista	Everything (enter a simple Boolean expression into the search field using plus and minus signs and asterisk wildcards, or consult Help to find out how to use the Advanced search form for more complex queries).
Excite	Everything but NEAR and wildcards (enter the expression directly into the search form or go to the advanced search form and choose from the drop-down menus; to add more expressions, click the Add More Constraints button).
HotBot	Everything except NEAR and wildcards (select Boolean Phrase from the Look For drop-down menu and type the expression into the search field).
InfoSeek	Everything except NEAR and wildcards (click Search Options and select from the drop-down menus, or type the expression directly into the search field, using plus and minus signs).
Magellan	Everything except NEAR and wildcards (type the expression directly into the search field).
Yahoo!	Everything except NEAR (type the expression directly into the search field using plus or minus signs and asterisk wildcards, or click Advanced Search and select the appropriate buttons).

Filtering Your Search

Most search engines provide some kind of filtering system so that you can confine the search results to a particular type of file, geographical region, or part of the Web page. How you set up filters varies widely from search engine to search engine; for example, some provide a handy menu where you can check off filter options, while others require that you type the filter into the search query itself.

After you pick your main search engine, find out what filters it supports so that you can better control the search. In fact, you might want to choose a search engine based on its filters, depending on the kinds of searches you run most frequently. Tables 11.3 and 11.4 describe the filters supported by the major search engines, how to set them up, and what they're good for.

TABLE 11.3: SEARCH ENGINE FILTERS

Use	AltaVista Support	Excite Support	HotBot Support
Restrict the search to Web page titles.	Type `title:` keyword.	Not supported	Select The Page Title from the Look For drop-down menu.
Restrict the search to Web page URLs.	Type `url:` keyword.	Not supported	Not supported
Restrict the search to a person's name.	Not supported	Not supported	Select The Person from the Look For drop-down menu.
Restrict the search to page text, omitting links and images.	Type `text:` keyword.	Not supported	Not supported
Restrict the search to image filenames; useful for finding pages that contain specific pictures.	Type `image:` keyword.	Not supported	Not supported
Restrict the search to a specific domain; useful for searching a large company's or organization's documents.	Type `host:` domain.	Not supported	Click Advanced Search and enter the domain name in the Location/ Domain section.
Restrict the search to a type of site (.com, .edu, .mil) or country (.ca, uk, .jp).	Type `domain:` suffix.	On the advanced search form, click Country or Type of Domain, and set options in the drop-down menu.	Click Advanced Search and enter the domain suffix in the Domain/ Location section.

continues

TABLE 11.3: CONTINUED

Use	AltaVista Support	Excite Support	HotBot Support
Restrict the search to a site depth; for more comprehensive documents, keep to the top levels.	Not supported	Not supported	Click Advanced Search and select the depth in the Page Depth section.
Restrict the search to a range of dates.	Click Advanced and enter the date range in the From and To boxes.	Not supported	Click Advanced Search and make your selection from the Date section of the form.
Find recent pages (within a certain time period).	Not supported	Not supported	Select an option from the Anytime drop-down menu.
Find pages that contain a link to a link to a specific URL; useful for finding pages that link to your site.	Type link:url.	Not supported	Select Links To This URL from the Look For drop-down menu.
Find pages that contain a specific media file type or scripting language.	Type applet: keyword to find Java applets.	Not supported	Click Advanced Search and select the file types from the Pages Must Include section.

TABLE 11.4: SEARCH ENGINE FILTERS

Use	Infoseek Support	Yahoo! Support
Restrict the search to Web page titles.	Click Search Options and select Title from the first drop-down menu.	Type title: keyword or t:keyword.
Restrict the search to Web page URLs.	Click Search Options and select URL from the first drop-down menu.	Type u:keyword.
Restrict the search to a person's name.	Click Search Options and select Name from the third drop-down menu.	Click Options and select A Person's Name.

Use	Infoseek Support	Yahoo! Support
Restrict the search to page text, omitting links and images.	Not supported	Not supported
Restrict the search to image filenames; useful for finding pages that contain specific pictures.	Not supported	Not supported
Restrict the search to a specific domain; useful for searching a large company's or organization's documents.	Click Search Options; on the fourth line, select Show Only and type the domain name into the text field.	Not supported
Restrict the search to a type of site (.com, .edu, .mil) or. country (.ca, uk, .jp).	Click Search Options and select a location or suffix from the Search By Location drop-down menu.	Not supported
Restrict the search to a site depth; for more comprehensive documents, keep to the top levels.	Not supported	Not supported
Restrict the search to a range of dates.	Not supported	Not supported
Find recent pages (within a certain time period).	Not supported	Click Options and select an option from the Find Only New Listings Added During The Past drop-down menu.
Find pages that contain a link to a specific URL; useful for finding pages that link to your site.	Click Search Options and select Hyperlink from the first drop-down menu.	Not supported
Find pages that contain a specific media file type or scripting language.	Not supported	Not supported

Timesaver
Limiting the age of Web pages searched not only speeds up your search but also ensures that the information returned is more timely. This is particularly helpful when searching for current events or recurring events. For instance, you might only want information about this year's World Series, not World Series from last year or last decade.

A Sample Search

To get an idea of how to craft an effective search query, follow along with a sample search. You can use AltaVista, Excite,

HotBot, or Infoseek for this exercise, although I'm using HotBot. (If the search doesn't seem to be working, replace AND with a plus sign and replace AND NOT with a minus sign, leaving no space between the plus or minus sign and the word following it.)

Let's say we're seeking information about the John F. Kennedy assassination, specifically any evidence that a conspiracy was involved. Follow along with the steps to learn how to get from a bad search to a good one:

1. Connect to the search engine of your choice.

2. Start with the first thing that comes to mind—enter John Kennedy into the search field and press Enter.

3. For me, this returned a whopping 123,000 Web pages, and looking at the top ten results, I couldn't find anything about the assassination; in fact, some sites don't seem to have anything to do with John F. Kennedy (see Figure 11.5). Let's make sure that the results include information about the former president—type "John F. Kennedy" to find an exact phrase match, and press Enter.

Figure 11.4
HotBot returns way too many unrelated pages when we search for the keywords, "John" and "Kennedy."

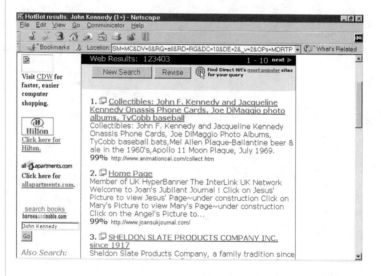

4. That reduced the number of pages quite a bit, down to 31,000, and we can be fairly certain that most of them are related to President Kennedy. But not many of the top ten have anything to do with the assassination. Try focusing the search—type "John F. Kennedy" AND assassination into the search field at the top of the page, and press Enter.

5. That cut the number of search results to 3,000. Now, the top-ten list is very focused, all of the listings having some-thing to do with the Kennedy assassination. But not many of them (if any) seem to have any evidence about a poten-tial conspiracy. Add another keyword—type "John F. Kennedy" AND assassination AND conspiracy into the search field at the top of the page, and press Enter.

6. That reduced the number of results to 900. Even more importantly, every one of the top-ten listings is definitely related to conspiracy theories about the Kennedy assassi-nation. But now we've decided that we're not interested in any sites that discuss Jack Ruby's role in the assassination. Type "John F. Kennedy" AND assassination AND conspiracy AND NOT Ruby, and press Enter.

7. We're down to 200 sites, and we can be sure that all of the results are focused on the Kennedy assassination conspir-acy without discussing Jack Ruby's part in it. However, I'm concerned that we might have eliminated some sites that use JFK to refer to Kennedy. This requires use of the OR expression and nesting. Enter ("John F. Kennedy" OR JFK) AND assassination AND conspiracy AND NOT Ruby into the search field, and press Enter.

8. Now, we can be certain that our search results are com-plete and on-target (see Figure 11.5). So we can start visit-ing Web sites.

Figure 11.5
By focusing the
search, we get
just the informa-
tion we need.

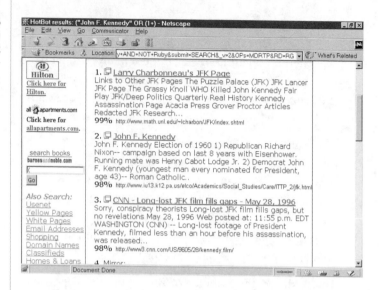

Watch Out!
This detailed
search query
works great in
search engines
that look through
millions of Web
pages. But when
searching a single
site or a Web site
directory—even
Yahoo!—you don't
need to make
things this compli-
cated. You might
not turn up any-
thing! So, the
smaller the data-
base being
searched, the sim-
pler your query
should be.

If we'd just begun the search with the query in step 7, we'd
have gotten to the relevant Web pages a whole lot faster. To get
the best search results the first time, begin your search by coming up with several specific phrases and keywords that the
search results must contain, decide if there are any related topics that you don't want to know about, and construct a query
based on the keywords and phrases that you come up with.

Using Search Software

A number of software tools have been developed to make
searching easier, faster, and more comprehensive. If you're a
serious Web researcher, investing in one of these shareware
utilities can save you a lot of time in the long run.

Most search tools enable you to perform a search on several different search engines at one time. These are preferable
to meta-search Web sites because they work on the desktop,
performing searches faster and in the background. Therefore,
you can do other work while the program is busily searching.
These software tools also search more sources than the meta-
search Web pages do. Finally, they offer more advanced management of search results than any Web site can—you can sort
the results on several criteria, organize them, and browse them
offline.

- **Copernic:** Searches up to 30 sources at one time—not only search engines, but also newsgroups and email directories. It filters out duplicates and dead links, a valuable timesaver. You can browse the results offline and organize them several different ways (see Figure 11.6). Even save frequent searches. Copernic is a great tool for serious and casual researchers alike. Windows 95/98/NT 4.0; requires Internet Explorer 3.x or Navigator 3.x (or later versions), 8MB RAM, and 5MB hard disk space; free; download from `http://www.copernic.com/`.

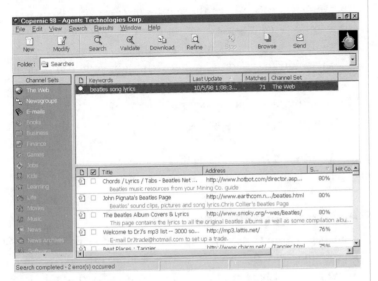

Figure 11.6
Copernic enables you to customize search results culled from over thirty sources.

- **NetFerret Suite:** Comprises several valuable search tools, including WebFerret, which searches 10 popular search engines. The real value comes with the entire toolkit, which expands your searching capabilities to Web-based databases, telephone white pages, email address databases, FTP sites, Usenet newsgroups, and IRC servers. All searches are very customizable and very fast. Windows 95/98/NT 4.0; $49.95 (scaled-down freeware versions are available); download from `http://www.ferretsoft.com/netferret/`.

Bright Idea
When beginning a research project, it's a good idea to break it up into small steps to keep track of where you are in the process. Idea Keeper is a shareware tool for Mac OS 7.5 that can help. Jot down notes, link ideas to files (such as saved search results), add check boxes, and otherwise organize your researching. Get it from any Macintosh software search engine.

- **Web Archer:** Unfortunately, Mac users have fewer choices when it comes to meta-search software tools, but there is Web Archer. Web Archer's nicest feature is its capability to confine your search to special categories, such as news, stocks, phone numbers, Macintosh products, and software downloads, and its searches are both fast and accurate. Mac OS 7.5 and Windows 95/98/NT; $29.95 (free demo available); requires Navigator 2.x or Internet Explorer 4.x (or later versions); download from `http://www.clearway.com/WebArcher/`.

- **WebSeeker:** Searches the most sources, over 100 search engines, including a large number of specialized search tools. As a result, it's very slow, but fortunately it gives you the ability to schedule your searches for when you're away from your computer. Like Copernic, WebSeeker eliminates duplicates and dead links, and you can organize the search results. WebSeeker is the best tool for the power searcher who requires completely comprehensive results. Windows 95/98/NT; $49.95 (evaluation available); download from `http://www.bluesquirrel.com/seeker/`.

Performing Other Searches

Web pages aren't the only type of information you need to search for, and the Web isn't the whole Internet, either. Sometimes you have to turn to other sources to find the data that you're missing. In this section, learn how to quickly track down all of the following:

- Usenet posts

- Mailing list messages

- People

- Businesses

- Software

This section doesn't cover more specialized searches, such as song lyrics, recipes, facts about a movie, news stories, online books, and things of that nature. If you're trying to track down anything this specific, turn to the Web first. Perform a general search for a front end to an applicable database, such as the Internet Movie Database for movie information (`http://www.imdb.com/`) or the Online Books Page for electronic publications (`http://www.cs.cmu.edu/books.html`). A specialized search engine can help with this kind of research, as well.

Searching Usenet

You might wonder what value searching the messages posted to Usenet could have. After all, Usenet messages are temporary, and the information is not necessarily accurate or written by an expert. For certain kinds of research, however, Usenet posts are the best source of information:

- Track what people are saying about your company or product.

- Find recent rumors, gossip, and news, particularly about celebrities, television shows, and movies.

- Locate discussion about and help with solving specific problems, particularly with computing- and technology-related problems.

- Discover discussion and debate about a specific subject that adds to your background research.

- Quickly get answers to very detailed questions or locate someone who might provide the answers; Usenet FAQs are good resources for this kind of information.

- Find knowledgeable sources of advice on almost anything.

You can search Usenet postings from almost any search engine, but Deja.Com (`http://www.deja.com/`) is the best way. Deja.Com is completely dedicated to archiving and providing a search interface to Usenet postings, so it's a more comprehensive source. Also, it has lots of features to make finding relevant newsgroup posts easier, including a category structure for aiding with general searches, and a Power Search that

Timesaver
If you often find yourself searching for a particular topic and you want to keep up with new sites as they're added to search engine databases, the TracerLock service at `http://peacefire.org/tracerlock/` is a handy timesaver. You have to register to use it, but it's free. TracerLock monitors search engines for whatever you like and sends you an email message when something new and interesting appears.

enables you to filter your search by newsgroup, language, author, subject, or date range and organize the results (see Figure 11.7). For instance, you can search for posts that contain the word FAQ in the subject list to restrict your findings to newsgroup FAQs. Deja.Com's Usenet search also supports all Boolean expressions. After you locate a relevant post, you can follow its entire thread to see the scope of the discussion.

Figure 11.7
Deja.Com's Power Search form gives you several filter and organizational options to help you search Usenet postings better.

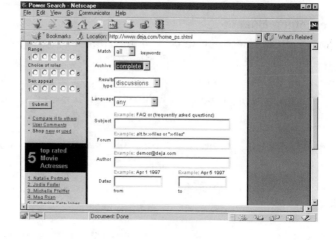

Watch Out!
To speed things up, Deja.Com searches only recent Usenet postings—the last few weeks' worth. If you want to find older articles, you have to go to Power Search and select a range of dates in the search form.

Even if you don't find the answer to your question in an archived newsgroup message, you might find a relevant newsgroup or the email address of a person who appears knowledgeable on the subject. A politely worded message to either generally nets an answer to your question. Be sure to read the FAQ before posting to any newsgroup. Request responses via email so you don't have to monitor the newsgroup for replies and so the newsgroup doesn't haven't to read the same answer to your question over and over. It's generally considered polite to offer to summarize the responses you receive for the group, in case other readers are interested.

Searching Mailing List Archives

Mailing list archives can provide all of the benefits of Usenet newsgroups. But because mailing lists are limited to interested subscribers, the discussions are often more focused and expert than those found on Usenet. However, it's not so easy to find and search these archives. Also, it can be more difficult to locate a mailing list that's relevant to your question, as opposed to finding a relevant newsgroup.

The best source for searching mailing list archives is Reference.Com (`http://www.reference.com/`). This site archives over 150,000 mailing lists, as well as Usenet newsgroups—you can select a comprehensive Usenet and Mailing List Archive search or Mailing List Archive alone from the drop-down menu above the search field. Go to the Advanced Search form to filter your search by author, subject, date, groups, or organization. The search form also supports full Boolean expressions. After you find a good match, you can follow an entire conversation thread or email the message's author with a question.

If Reference.Com doesn't archive the relevant mailing list, another Web site—typically the mailing list's home page—might. This usually applies only to well-established mailing lists, which are also the best sources of information.

First, you need to locate a relevant mailing list by searching a directory of mailing lists, such as Liszt at `http://www.liszt.com/` (return to Chapter 5, "Email Magic," for more suggestions). Go to your favorite search engine and look for pages about that mailing list. If you find any, chances are it contains an archive of posts to the list.

Searching options and accuracy vary from archive to archive, however. Some of the archives might even be on FTP sites or might not be searchable at all. You could also join the relevant list, read the FAQs that you get upon subscribing to discover the answers to frequently asked questions, and pose your question directly to the group.

Tracking Down People

As you learned in Chapter 5, you can use Web-based white-page directories to locate a person's email address. White pages are also the best sources for finding a person's home phone number or address, although your search can easily

Timesaver
Sometimes you don't want to search all Usenet posts, but you do want to find a group related to a general subject and see what's being talked about. And you don't want to take the time to fire up your newsreader, or you don't ever use a newsreader, or you don't have access to a news server. RemarQ (`http://www.remarq.com/home.asp`) is the site for you. Search for newsgroups on a topic or drill through the categories, and then read current messages right in your Web browser.

come up blank if that person removed his or her listing. (You could always obtain the email address and then write the person for more information.)

Table 11.5 points to the best general people finders. All of these services provide home phone numbers and addresses, and some offer extras such as driving directions and street maps. You might have to search two or three to find the person that you're looking for.

TABLE 11.5: WHITE-PAGE DIRECTORIES

Directory	URL
Switchboard	`http://www.switchboard.com/` (click People Search)
WhoWhere?	`http://www.whowhere.lycos.com/ wwphone/phone.html`
Yahoo! People Search	`http://people.yahoo.com/`

When searching for someone, think beyond the obvious. The following resources might be of more help to you:

- **College directories:** If you know where the person went to school, locate the college's Web site—a URL such as `http://www.collegename.edu/` or `http://www. collegeinitials.edu/` is often a good guess, or search Yahoo! for the college. Most college Web sites include directories of current students, faculty, and alumni.

- **Employee directories:** If you know where the person works, find that business's Web site and see if an online employee directory is provided—try forming a URL such as `http://www.businessname.com/`, or search the Company Locator at `http://www.netpartners.com/resources/ search.html` for the business's name. At the very least, you might find an active email address.

- **Professional directories:** Some professions, particularly scientific and academic professions, have published directories on the Web. You might also find online directories for professional associations, such as the AMA or the Bar Association. If you know the person's profession, try looking for a directory like this with your favorite search engine.

As with searching the Web, there are ways to speed your search and get better results when trying to find a person. Keep the following tips in mind:

- Narrow your search by confining it to the city where the person lives. If you're not sure of the city, you can still confine the search to a state, cutting down the results list to something manageable.

- Remember that people often go by nicknames, middle names, or initials. If you're not sure of the first name, search by last name only. If you want to find possible initials, full names, and nicknames that all start with the same letter, use a wildcard; to find S. Smith, Sam Smith, Sammy Smith, or Samuel Smith, you'd search for "S* Smith," for instance.

- Keep in mind that women might be listed by maiden name, last name, or a hyphenated combination of the two.

Tracking Down Businesses

If you're looking for a company, particularly for a phone number or street address, a search engine isn't much use. (Search engines can help you find business URLs, although often it's quicker to guess the URL from the name of the company—www.ford.com or www.sony.com, for instance.) Online, you should turn to the same source that you would check offline—the yellow pages.

You probably only have your local yellow pages lying around the house. On the Web, you can access yellow pages for the entire country and even the world. So, if you need to find the phone number for a computer parts maker in California or the mailing address for an investment firm in London, online yellow pages are a handy resource. They can even provide extra information that your phone book doesn't contain, such as driving directions, maps, and reviews.

The following are the most comprehensive online yellow pages:

Timesaver
A quick way to find a business's Web site if you use Navigator 4.x is to enter the company or product name in the Location window. Navigator tries to find the best-fit Web site. This is also a quick way to perform a simple search, although it works best for general searches on one or two broad keywords.

- **GTE SuperPages** (`http://superpages.gte.net/`): The best general yellow pages for finding U.S. businesses. Search by business name, category, city, state, phone number, zip code, or street name, or find a business within a certain distance from your house (see Figure 11.8). GTE SuperPages is particularly useful if you're looking for a particular kind of business, but don't know the company's exact name.

Figure 11.8
Use GTE
SuperPages to
find contact infor-
mation and direc-
tions to a
business near
you.

- **Maps On Us** (`http://www.mapsonus.com/`): The best resource if you need to find a business and find out how to get there. Click Yellow Pages to search for a business within a certain distance of where you live. You can have the results display as a map or as driving directions that tell you exactly how to get there.

- **AnyWho** (`http://www.anywho.com/tf.html`): A great resource for finding toll-free numbers. Search by category, business name, city, or state.

- **WorldPages** (`http://www.worldpages.com/global/wpglobal.html`): The quickest way to find businesses outside the U.S. Just select a country from the drop-down list, and

WorldPages connects you to yellow pages listings available for that country. There's also a convenient link to a list of international calling codes.

Finding Software

There are just as many software search engines on the Web as there are Web-page search engines, if not more. I've mentioned them several times throughout this book because a software search engine is the fastest way to locate and download freeware, shareware, and commercial demos. Generally, you can search for a title, software developer, or keyword, and you can narrow your search to a particular category, such as Internet software, games, or utilities. You can usually get detailed information about the software programs that you find, including a description, ratings, system requirements, license, download statistics, and a direct download link. Some search engines focus on one platform, while others are more comprehensive.

In my experience, no one software search engine is that much more complete or easier to use than any other. As with the search engines I listed earlier, I suggest that you try a few, pick the one that you like the best, and get to know it really well. Some of you might prefer Download.Com (my personal favorite) because it covers both Windows and the Mac, and the site makes it easy to find new, popular, or top-rated software in specific categories. Others like ZDNet's Software Library because of the more detailed reviews and rating system. No matter which one is your favorite, none of them is going to have everything. So, choose a backup or two to help you find rare pieces of software.

Table 11.6 lists the major software search engines, including their URLs, special features, and platforms covered.

TABLE 11.6: SOFTWARE SEARCH ENGINES

Search Engine/ URL	Platforms	Special Features
Download.Com http://www.download.com/	Windows, Mac OS	Quickly get a list of the most popular, newest, or top-rated software in any category.
Filez http://www.filez.com/	Windows, Mac OS, UNIX, DOS, OS/2, Novell NetWare, Newton, Acorn, Amiga, and Atari	Find not just software, but also multimedia files: RealAudio, MP3, graphics, movies, and sounds.
Freehound http://www.freehound.com/	Windows	Freeware only.
MacUpdate http://www.macupdate.com/	Mac OS	Specializes in Mac OS software.
Shareware.Com http://www.shareware.com/	Windows, Mac OS, UNIX, DOS, OS/2, Novell NetWare, Amiga, and Atari	Shareware only.
WinFiles http://www.winfiles.com/	Windows	Specializes in Windows 95/98/NT/CE software.
ZDNet Software Library http://www.hotfiles.com/	Windows, DOS, OS/2, and Novell NetWare	Most software reviewed and rated; an entire section is devoted to commercial demos.

All the software found at any of these search engines can be downloaded via FTP sites. So if you want to bypass the Web altogether, you can search through FTP servers to find the software (and other files) that you need using a search tool called Archie.

This kind of search is not as user friendly, though. Instead of searching for keywords, you have to look for actual filenames or directory names, which can be almost anything, so Archie is only really helpful if you already know the program's filename. You can also use Archie to search for particular file types; a search for "bmp" finds all bitmap files, as well as all files with "bmp" in their names (like bitmap conversion programs) and all bmp directories, or collections of bitmaps.

There's an Archie gateway on the Web at `http://archie.rutgers.edu/archie.html`; just go there to search FTP sites using a friendly form. Some FTP clients have Archie built in, such as Anarchie for the Mac OS (`http://www.stairways.com/anarchie/`) and fpArchie for Windows (`http://www.fpware.demon.nl/downloads/index.htm`), which works with an external FTP program, such as WS_FTP or FTP Explorer.

Just the Facts

- Select a search site based on the type of search that you want to perform: a search engine for finding specific information; a Web-site directory for finding information about a broad subject; specialized search sites for finding a specific type of site; and meta-search pages for getting the most comprehensive search results.

- No matter what search tool you choose, you'll never get good search results unless you learn how to construct precise queries using multiple keywords, Boolean expressions, and filters.

- Software search tools can help build more accurate and more comprehensive search results that you can organize, sort, and browse offline.

- Web sites are not always the best sources of information; searching Usenet posts, mailing-list archives, white and yellow pages, or software archives can sometimes yield better results.

Timesaver
Most software search engines have an advanced or power search (look for a link next to the search form on the front page). Take advantage of the advanced search form's filters to greatly speed up searching and to reduce the number of returned search results. Typically, you should confine the search to your computer platform and to the category of interest—if you're looking for Windows 95 games, you don't want your search to turn up Macintosh utilities, for instance.

GET THE SCOOP ON...
Browsing the Web safely and privately ▪ The truth
about computer viruses and how to protect your
computer ▪ Keeping the kids safe—really

Safe Surfing

Chapter 12

I F YOU BELIEVE THE NEWS REPORTS, the Web is a place fraught with danger, where shady characters try to steal your privacy, destroy your computer with viruses, and show dirty pictures to your children. But the truth is that the Web is no more dangerous than anywhere else you might go in your day-to-day activities. If you ignore the hype and learn where the risks really lie, you can protect yourself without a lot of effort.

This chapter tells you the truth about privacy risks and computer viruses on the Internet, and it gives you simple solutions to protecting your privacy, your computer, and your kids. After employing the strategies outlined in this chapter, you can surf the Web without fear.

Staying Safe on the Web

Most of the time, browsing the Web is perfectly safe. The only activities that might pose a risk are giving out information about yourself via a Web page form and downloading executable code to your computer. One might compromise your privacy, and the other might harm your computer or allow access to your data. (Shopping online requires additional precautions, which you'll learn about in Chapter 14, "Going Shopping.") But protecting yourself is no big deal—it just takes common sense and simple precautions.

Keeping Private Information Private

In Chapter 6, "Secure and Spam-Free," I told you that one of the best ways to protect your privacy when using email is to watch what you say in email messages. The same rule applies to Web page forms. Often, *you* are the biggest threat to your own personal privacy, when you give away information to marketers and others who ask for it. The Web sites that you visit are frequently going to ask you for personal information—when you purchase something, when you download free software, when you sign up for a newsletter, when you sign a guestbook, or even just to access the site. But it's your choice what information you give them or whether you give them any information at all.

Keep two simple rules in mind when asked to fill out a Web page form:

- Don't give any more information than is necessary for the activity that you want to perform.

- Don't give personal information to people or companies you don't trust.

Often, Web page forms request a lot more information than is necessary to do what you want to do. For example, only your name and email address is needed for subscribing to an email newsletter; this activity doesn't require a home address, phone number, or average household salary. But if you purchase something, you have to give away a lot more information—an address where the purchase can be shipped, a phone number to call if there are problems with the order, and a credit card number so you can pay.

Web page forms request so much personal information so that online companies can more effectively market to you. It's the same principle behind warranty cards. Why does the maker of your stereo need to know if you like windsurfing? So they can sell your name and personal information to windsurfing-related companies, who then send you junk mail and call you during the dinner hour with special offers.

So, the key is, if they don't need to know, don't tell them. You get to decide what the site needs—if you don't think that downloading free software requires a phone number, don't give them one! Even if the form indicates that certain fields are required, you don't have to fill them out truthfully. (For software downloads, my default phone number is 000-000-0000.)

But if the activity does require some personal information, how do you know if you can trust the company asking for it? You should find a privacy policy on every site that requests information from you. This policy indicates why information is needed and what the site owners intend to do with it (such as sell it). If you don't agree with the privacy policy or don't find one, move on. Even if you do find a privacy policy, limit what you tell the site. If you give your email address but not your phone number, the worst result might be some spam (and you already know how to deal with that), but at least you have foiled the telemarketers.

Both Navigator and Internet Explorer have built-in safety measures to help you recognize when you might be submitting personal information insecurely and to give you a chance to change your mind. They also both support encryption—any information you submit via a secure Web page form is scrambled during transit, so that it can't be intercepted along the way. Encryption can even scramble the Web pages you look at, so they are decrypted in your browser window, but kept in a protected state in the cache.

But these encryption features only work if you're interacting with a secure Web server. Check the status bar to find out if a Web site is secure. Navigator displays a locked-padlock icon in the lower-left corner on secure sites and displays an open-padlock icon on insecure sites. Internet Explorer displays a lock icon in the middle of the status bar at the bottom of the window on secure sites. Only submit personal information via forms to secure Web sites.

Watch Out!
As you surf through a site, the site owner can determine your IP address, which browser you use, and the link you last clicked. While some see this as a privacy threat, I don't think it's a big deal. Most sites use this information to determine advertising revenues or which pages are most popular. If you're really concerned, though, you can subscribe to a service such as Anonymizer (`http://www.anonymizer.com/`), which keeps your surfing patterns secret. But the service itself gets a complete record of everywhere you go on the Web—not just on one site—and they can tie it to your name and address. It seems to me that the solution is riskier than the problem.

Setting Security Options in Navigator

Navigator can warn you when you're about to send information insecurely or when you're entering or leaving a secure site. Follow these steps to set Navigator's security warnings:

1. Click the Security toolbar button; the Security Info window opens.

2. Click the Navigator category (see Figure 12.1).

Figure 12.1
Setting Navigator's
security options.

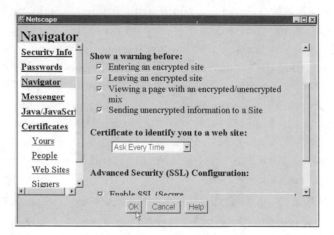

3. Under Show a Warning Before, select any or all of the following options:

   • **Entering an Encrypted Site.** This setting alerts you whenever you connect to a secure server, so you don't have to check for the locked-padlock icon.

   • **Leaving an Encrypted Site.** This setting alerts you when you leave the secure server.

   • **Viewing a Page with an Encrypted/Unencrypted Mix.** This setting identifies Web pages that are made up of both encrypted and unencrypted information; click the Security toolbar button to find out which parts of the page are encrypted.

   • **Sending Unencrypted Information to a Site.** This setting warns you when you submit information via an unencrypted Web-page form, and it gives you a chance to cancel the transmission (see Figure 12.2).

Selecting it is a good way to add an extra layer of security, but the constant warnings can get annoying, especially when you're only trying to use the form as a search engine.

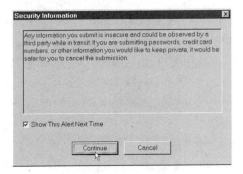

Figure 12.2
Navigator displays a warning when you submit information insecurely via a Web-page form if you select the Sending Unencrypted Information to a Site setting.

4. Under Certificate To Identify You To A Web Site, select whether Navigator should send your personal certificate (if you have one) to Web sites that request it automatically or whether it should ask you first; I recommend that you choose Ask Every Time.

5. Under Advanced Security (SSL) Configuration, select both check boxes to ensure that your browser fully supports Secure Sockets Layer (SSL), a technology used to submit encrypted information to secure sites.

6. Click OK.

Setting Security Options in Internet Explorer

Internet Explorer has a variety of security settings that protect you against submitting information insecurely, dealing with untrustworthy and secure sites, and more. Here's how to set them up:

1. Select Tools, Internet Options.

2. Click the Advanced tab.

3. Scroll down to the Security section (see Figure 12.3), and select any or all of the following options:

Timesaver
Quickly check the security status of any Web page by clicking the Security button. The Security Info window indicates whether the page is encrypted. If it is, click View Certificate to establish the site owner's identity. If the page isn't encrypted, you can learn what domain it came from and determine who published the page. Checking a page's security status is a good first step before submitting personal information via a Web-page form or accepting program code.

- **Check for Publisher's and Server Certificate Revocation:** These two settings check that personal certificates belonging to software publishers and Web-server hosts haven't been revoked before accepting them as valid. You might receive certificates from downloaded programs, signed Java applets, signed Web pages, and ActiveX controls.

- **Do Not Save Encrypted Pages to Disk:** Selecting this check box prevents you from saving any encrypted Web pages that you open, keeping them from being accessible to any other users of your computer.

- **Empty Temporary Internet Files Folder When Browser Is Closed:** Selecting this check box deletes cached Web pages when you close your browser, preventing any other users of your computer from determining which Web pages you've been viewing.

- **Enable Profile Assistant:** Internet Explorer enables you to set up a personal profile on the Content tab of the Internet Options dialog box; when a Web site requests personal information about you, you can decide which parts of your profile to send to the site. Deselect this check box if you haven't set up a profile or if you don't want to let any Web servers access your profile.

- **Use Fortezza, PCT 1.0, SSL 2.0, SSL 3.0, and TLS 1.0:** Select all of these check boxes to ensure that your browser fully supports all encryption standards.

- **Warn About Invalid Site Certificates:** This setting alerts you if the Web site URL in a personal certificate isn't valid, indicating that the certificate is untrustworthy.

- **Warn if Changing Between Secure and Not Secure Mode:** This setting alerts you when moving between secure and insecure Web sites.

- **Warn if Forms Submittal Is Being Redirected:** This setting alerts you if you submit information via a Web-page form to a different Web server than the one hosting the form, keeping you from submitting personal information to unknown sites.

4. When you're done setting the security options, click OK.

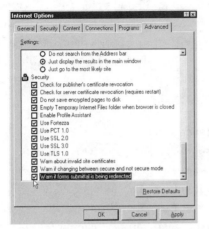

Figure 12.3
Internet Explorer's security settings.

Protecting Your Computer Against Security Holes

Both Navigator and Internet Explorer have been subjected to numerous security holes. In theory, these holes, which are just flaws in the program's code, could allow a malicious hacker to put a virus on your computer or access the files on your hard drive without your knowledge. With continuous browser upgrades and releases, it's virtually impossible to work out all the design flaws. It's important to remember that all security holes have been discovered under laboratory conditions, and that none of them has led to an actual attack on someone's computer. So, the risks are there, but they're relatively minor.

The best way to protect yourself against security holes is to keep up with the latest releases of your preferred Web browser. When a hole is discovered, Microsoft and Netscape release a patch or a browser upgrade right away, usually within hours. Regularly check your browser's Web site for these new releases, and when you find them, install them.

Developing technologies might also present security holes. For instance, ActiveX controls and some Java applets download and run on your computer, posing a security risk. They

Bright Idea
Unlike in stores, software on the Internet isn't labeled and shrink-wrapped. Internet Explorer natively supports Authenticode technology, which acts as a virtual shrink-wrap, using personal certificates to tell you who created the software and whether anyone has altered the code since. When you download software with a digital certificate, IE verifies the certificate, giving you the chance to cancel the download if you don't trust the publisher. If the code has been tampered with, a warning appears. Use Authenticode as an extra layer of security when downloading software. To edit the list of software publishers that you have deemed trustworthy, select Tools, Internet Options, click the Content tab, and click the Publishers button.

could carry a virus, or security loopholes could give outsiders access to your computer files. Again, no one has reported problems in the real world due to malicious ActiveX controls or Java applets; but you never know.

All ActiveX controls and Java applets that execute on your computer are digitally signed and come with a personal certificate, revealing the identity of the company or person who issued the applet or control. You then decide whether to let the applet or control run based on whether you trust the issuer of the component's certificate.

Navigator and Signed Applets

You don't have to worry about ActiveX controls if you use Netscape Navigator—it doesn't natively support them. However, Navigator version 4.5 and later does support signed Java applets. Because they download and run on your computer, these signed applets can perform more powerful functions than regular Java applets, such as install software programs. But they also get access to your computer and the files on your hard drive, which can pose a security risk. (Unsigned Java applets run in a buffered area called the sandbox, which prevents harm to your system from dangerous code, but also limits what the applet can do.)

When an applet requests access to your computer, Navigator opens a Java Security dialog box to tell you what level of access the applet is requesting and to give you a chance to grant or deny access. Navigator assigns the applet low, medium, or high risk to give you an idea of the degree of risk involved in granting access:

- **High:** Indicates the possibility of a major security attack that could cause severe damage to your system or data; the possibility of a major violation of privacy, such as reading information from your hard drive; or a request of very significant services, such as establishing a connection to a remote computer.

- **Medium:** Indicates the possibility of a major violation of privacy, such as reading information from your hard drive, or a request of a significant service, such as writing files to your hard drive or sending email on your behalf.

- **Low:** Indicates the possibility of a minor violation of privacy, such as reading your user ID, or a request of a relatively minor service, such as writing a file to a non-critical directory.

Navigator's risk assignments are just guidelines. You might have a different opinion about the degree of risk involved with running a particular signed applet. Click Details to see exactly what kind of access the applet is requesting, and make up your own mind whether to give the applet access to your computer. If you trust the applet's issuer, click Grant to let the applet do its thing. If you don't trust the issuer, click Deny and go on your way.

Configuring Internet Explorer's Security Zones

Internet Explorer natively supports both ActiveX controls and signed Java applets. Its security settings work a bit differently than Navigator's. Instead of warning you whenever you encounter a signed Java applet or ActiveX control, which can result in quite a few warnings on pages that heavily use ActiveX, you can set up security zones that group Web sites depending on how much you trust them. There are four security zones:

- **Local Intranet Zone:** This zone encompasses all Web sites on your local network. Generally, these are very trustworthy sites and should receive the Low security setting, which runs all components, including ActiveX controls and signed Java applets, without warning you first.

- **Trusted Sites Zone:** These are Web sites that you're familiar with and trust not to download components that could damage your computer. Generally, this zone should receive the Low or Medium-Low security setting, but you should be very careful about what sites you add to this zone.

Watch Out!
You might face a greater threat to your privacy from those who have access to your computer— co-workers, family members, or roommates—than from outside parties. Anyone who can get onto your computer can check your browser's history list and cache to see what Web sites you've been looking at. If this is a concern, clear both the cache and history before exiting your browser.

Bright Idea
If others have
access to your
computer, you can
set a password to
keep them from
misusing your
copy of Navigator.
This is especially
important if you
have purchased a
personal certifi-
cate to prevent
others from imper-
sonating you. To
set a password,
click the Security
toolbar button,
select the
Passwords cate-
gory, and click the
Set Password but-
ton. Once you've
set the password,
select one of the
options to deter-
mine when
Navigator asks for
your password;
Every Time Your
Certificate Is
Needed is the
most secure
choice.

- **Internet Zone:** These are Web sites that you're not familiar with. Any Web site that you haven't assigned to a zone
is automatically placed in this zone. Generally, sites in this
zone should receive a Medium security setting, which
warns you before running potentially damaging content
and gives you a chance to cancel the operation. (If you're
really concerned about security, you could designate the
High setting for this zone, but this will disabled many Web
site features, including cookies.)

- **Restricted Sites Zone:** Web sites that you have decided are
untrustworthy go in this zone. This zone should receive
the High security setting, which automatically excludes all
potentially damaging content.

As you get to know different Web sites, you can add them
to the appropriate zones. Here's how you add sites and change
security levels:

1. Select Tools, Internet Options.

2. Click the Security tab (see Figure 12.4).

3. To assign a basic security level to a zone, select the zone
   from the top window and drag the slider under Security
   Level For This Zone to the appropriate setting.

4. To customize a zone's security level, click the Custom
   Level button (see Figure 12.5). You can then make your
   own decisions about which risky activities are allowed in
   each zone, which ones aren't allowed, and which ones
   prompt a warning. For example, in the trusted sites zone,
   you might want to run ActiveX controls without prompting but receive a warning whenever you encounter a
   signed Java applet. Click OK when you're done.

5. To add a Web site to a zone, select the zone in the top window and click the Sites button. Enter the domain name of
   the site that you want to add and click OK.

6. When you're done setting up security zones, click OK.

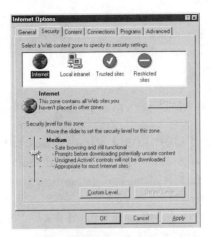

Figure 12.4
Setting up Internet Explorer's security zones.

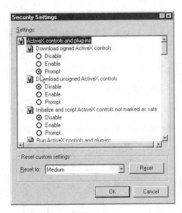

Figure 12.5
Customizing the security levels in Internet Explorer.

Watch Out!
If you've connected a private network to the Internet, you need a firewall. Firewalls prevent unauthorized access to the private network from the Internet by blocking all data that doesn't meet specified security criteria. For more information, check out Rotherwick Firewall Resources at http://www. zeuros.co.uk/ generic/resource/ firewall/.

Getting Personal Security

If you don't trust the safeguards of your browser, you can go a step further and get a personal security suite. These suites try to protect you from all potential risks, including computer viruses, ActiveX controls, and signed Java applets. Some also include personal firewalls, encryption tools, and backup utilities. I think these tools are way too much security for the average Internet user, and I personally don't use one. But if your computer contains sensitive business or financial information, a security suite could be a worthwhile investment. For most home users, eSafe Protect Desktop provides adequate protection. This suite uses the sandbox security model to run downloaded programs, controls, and applets in a safe area—the

Bright Idea

A proxy server sits between your computer and the Internet, keeping your IP address, computer type, location, and other personal information private. Many businesses use a proxy server to protect the company network and improve Internet performance. If you're connecting from home, you might want to consider getting a personal proxy server. I like the Internet Junkbuster Proxy, which is free, supports Windows 95/98/NT and UNIX, and blocks Web ads and cookies while protecting your privacy; get it at http://internet. junkbuster.com/.

sandbox—without giving them access to the rest of your system. It provides protection against Java applets, ActiveX controls, plug-ins, modem dialers, and computer viruses. eSafe Protect is a good choice for individual users. eSafe Protect Desktop is available for Windows 3.x/95/98/NT from http://www. esafe.com/. It costs $39 (a free 30-day evaluation is available).

Preventing Computer Virus Infections

A computer virus is malignant, manmade computer code that is secretly attached to an executable program file. When the program is run, the virus wreaks havoc on your computer. It might spread throughout your hard drive, delete files, or display stupid messages on your screen, and it can always replicate itself. On an individual computer, a virus can range from an annoyance to a major problem, destroying data or even forcing you to reformat the hard disk. Many viruses can spread throughout a local network, causing enormous problems for businesses and organizations.

Computer viruses are much rarer than the hype suggests, and they're almost never found in the shrink-wrapped software you buy in the store. Whenever you download software from the Internet, however, it pays to be safe rather than sorry. Keep the following tips in mind to keep your computer safe:

- Keep backups of all important data and programs on a removable drive, tape, or floppy disk, so you can easily recover from an attack (or any other kind of system failure, including those not caused by viruses).

- Only download what you really need; don't just snag whatever looks good, but learn as much as you can about the program, including who its developer is, and make sure that you're actually going to use the program before you install it.

- Don't download or run anything unless you trust the source. Software programs on commercial sites and the major shareware and freeware archives are generally kept virus-free. Certainly don't install anything found on a suspicious Web site or sent to you through email by someone you don't know.

- Don't download programs directly to the network at work. Install the program on a standalone computer and test it before putting the entire network at risk.

- Use an antivirus scanning program. Scan any executable file before you run it, and delete any files that contain viruses. You should also periodically scan all the files on your hard drive.

If you think a computer virus has already infected your system, an antivirus program detects it and can generally repair the file. When it can't, you can always delete the file, which removes the virus from your computer. Signs that you've been infected include the following:

- Unusual messages or displays appear on the screen.

- Unusual sounds or music play randomly.

- There is less available memory than there should be.

- A disk or volume name has been changed.

- Programs or files are suddenly missing.

- Some files have become corrupted or no longer work properly.

Choosing an Antivirus Program

While many shareware and freeware antivirus programs are available, in this case, I recommend a commercial program. Your antivirus program is only as good as its updates. With as many as three new viruses appearing each day, keeping up with new viruses is hard work, and companies dedicated to the job have the time and resources to find new viruses and issue updates quickly. (Updates are generally free the first year and require a fee—between $5 and $30 per year—afterward.) Also crucial is the ability to manually scan files, folders, and drives, repair viruses that are found, and automatically monitor new

Watch Out!
Generally, only executable files can contain computer viruses, and they can only infect your system when the executable is run. But that's not always the case. Macros can carry viruses inside Microsoft Word template documents. There are currently over 2,000 known macro viruses. Word warns you when you open a document containing macros and gives you a chance to cancel the operation. To keep extra safe, scan each Word file that you receive from an outside source with an antivirus program that detects macro viruses before opening the file.

Bright Idea
Even the best
antivirus program
can't catch every
new virus. To be
really secure, run
multiple scanners
on your system.
You might notice a
slight impact on
performance, but
the extra security
can be worth it.

files as they are accessed. Here are my recommendations of commercial antivirus programs:

- **Dr. Solomon's Anti-Virus:** A very fast antivirus scanner, this program is also specially configured for Internet users, scanning all files downloaded via HTTP, FTP, and email attachments. It even watches for activities that might indicate a previously unidentified virus, a feature that can result in false alarms. Updates are costly when compared to other antivirus programs—$29.95 per year. Windows 3.x/95/98; $29.95 (evaluation available); http://www.drsolomon.com/products/antivirus/index.cfm.

- **Norton AntiVirus:** This program scans the largest number of file types and catches the greatest number of viruses among antivirus programs (see Figure 12.6), but it's one of the slowest scanners and can decrease system performance. If you're looking for accuracy rather than speed and you want something easy to use, this is the antivirus program for you. Norton AntiVirus also features regular updates from a highly regarded research facility. Windows 95/98/NT and Mac OS; $36 (30-day trial available); http://www.symantec.com/nav/index.html.

Figure 12.6
Norton AntiVirus
scans all of your
files for lurking
viruses.

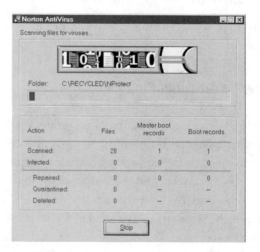

- **VirusScan:** This program is very configurable, offering many ways to set up scans. And unlike many other antivirus programs, VirusScan pops up prominent warnings when you need to update. But it might prove too confusing and cumbersome for the average user, and its performance is slow. DOS and Windows 3.x/95/98/NT; $49.95 (evaluation available); `http://www.nai.com/ products/antivirus/virusscan/default.asp`.

Separating Fact from Fiction

For every legitimately destructive virus floating around in cyberspace, there's an equally virulent hoax. You've already learned how virus hoaxes can spread through email faster than chicken pox in a schoolyard. They also find their way into the news media, on Web pages, and everywhere a gullible person can spread the misinformation. In fact, hoaxes are probably the real reason why the danger of computer viruses has become so exaggerated, and they certainly have detracted from genuine virus alerts.

If you receive a virus alert, check with a reliable source before going into panic mode. If you run an antivirus program and download updates regularly, you should have no problems—the program's associated virus update center keeps track of new viruses for you. These centers also track hoaxes. The following are the Web locations of the virus update centers for the recommended antivirus programs:

- **Dr. Solomon's Anti-Virus:** `http://www.drsolomon.com/ vircen/index.cfm`

- **Norton AntiVirus:** `http://www.symantec.com/avcenter/ index.html`

- **VirusScan:** `http://www.nai.com/vinfo/`

Another good place to regularly visit is the International Computer Security Association Web site at `http://www. icsa.net/`. This organization certifies antivirus programs, monitors the progress of known viruses, publishes alerts about new viruses and virus hoaxes, and provides a wealth of additional information.

Moneysaver
Don't have the money to spend on a commercial antivirus program? Disinfectant is a freeware alternative for Mac OS 7.0 that does a good job of detecting and cleaning up Macintosh system viruses. On Windows 3.x/95/98, get the free ViruSafe Web, which scans every file downloaded by your browser, your FTP client, or via email attachments. Neither program is a complete antivirus solution, though—Disinfectant won't find macro or Windows viruses, and ViruSafe Web won't detect viruses already on your computer. Get either at your favorite software search engine.

Inside Scoop
So, just how bad
is the computer
virus problem?
According to the
International
Computer Security
Association,
almost all medium-
sized and large
organizations in
North America
have had at least
one encounter with
a computer virus.

Bright Idea
The best way to
keep kids safe
while they're
online is to put
the computer in
the family room,
rather than in the
child's room. You
can monitor what
they're doing on
the computer,
making it less
likely that they'll
break the rules or
get into a danger-
ous relationship
without you know-
ing about it. This
also helps make
the Internet a fam-
ily activity rather
than a babysitter.

Keeping Kids Safe

When it comes to the Internet and kids, it's all too easy to get carried away. It seems that a week doesn't go by without another frightening news story about all the pornography freely available on the Web or about how a child was stalked by someone he or she met online.

The first step is to calm down and realize what the dangers really are. Yes, there's the chance that kids might run into offensive Web sites. This includes not only all that pornography you've been hearing about, but also hate pages, pages that promote the use of drugs or violence, or even pages that use excessive advertising—anything that you, as parents, feel is unacceptable until your kids are old enough to make their own value judgments. Only you can decide when and if your children can handle controversial information.

There's also the possibility that your kids might encounter predators who strike up a conversation and eventually form a relationship with them. Obviously, this is the scarier of the two dangers. Generally, these predators hang out in places where you can easily prevent your kids from going, such as the IRC Networks. And if you teach your kids street smarts for cyberspace, they shouldn't get into trouble anywhere else.

There's a much higher percentage of valuable stuff out there than offensive content and predators, including sites that help kids write school reports, find information about favorite hobbies, and meet other kids around the world. For instance, they can visit the White House (http://www. whitehouse.gov/WH/kids/html/home.html), NASA (http:// liftoff.msfc.nasa.gov/kids/), and the Internet Public Library (http://www.ipl.org/youth/). Most valuable of all, they get comfortable with the computer and the Internet, skills that stay with them for life. There are proven ways to keep kids safe no matter where they go online, without preventing them from enjoying all the benefits of the Internet.

Guarding Against Dangerous People

Pedophiles and other online predators prey on new, inexperienced kids. If your kids show cyber-smarts, they won't be appealing targets. Teach kids the rules for staying safe online before you teach them how to use Internet tools, and reinforce the rules often. It's a good idea to write up the house rules for using the Internet and have everyone sign them like a contract. Post the rules by the computer to remind everyone of how to keep safe.

The following rules are essentials for staying safe online, not only for kids but for adults as well:

- **Never give out personal information online.** Obviously, kids should never give out their addresses or phone numbers in any online forum, including Web-page forms, email messages, bulletin boards, and chat areas. Kids should also keep last names, school names, passwords, parents' names, ages, and other private information secret— anything that might help a predator locate them in the real world.

- **Never share your picture.** This falls under the category of personal information, but I feel it warrants a separate rule, because a picture is something that predators often ask for. Forbid your kids from sending any Internet friend a photograph.

- **Never agree to meet someone that you know only from the Internet.** This is a good rule for kids and adults alike. If you must meet someone, arrange the meeting for a crowded, public place and take a friend or two along. Where your kids are concerned, I'd recommend that you forbid any meetings with Internet friends unless you confirm first that the friend is another child and you talk to the friend's parents. And of course, you should accompany your child to the meeting.

- **Make sure a parent is present before filling out a Web-page form.** Many kid-friendly sites require kids to register to keep unauthorized people out of the communication

Bright Idea
PBS Kids
TechKnow teaches
cyber-literacy and
safe surfing
behavior. There's
even a quiz that
kids (and adults)
can take to find
out if they have
the know-how to
use the Internet
wisely. Explore the
site together at
http://www.pbs
.org/kids/
techknow/.

areas. The site's privacy policy should explain exactly how the information requested by the registration form is used.

- **Get a parent's permission before downloading any pictures or software.** This helps protect your computer from viruses and corrupt files, as well as shield kids from inappropriate downloads, such as pornographic pictures.

- **If something makes you feel uncomfortable, stop what you're doing and tell a parent.** This is the most important rule. Make absolutely sure that your kids feel comfortable coming to you whenever something bothers them, including mean or offensive behavior. They should also know to tell you if someone asks for personal information, if someone tries to arrange a meeting, or if someone asks to keep a conversation secret from parents.

In addition, keep kids out of dangerous areas, such as IRC and Usenet. These networks are too unruly and too unregulated to be used safely by kids. Many dangerous people hang out on IRC, trying to strike up conversations with children and teens. And on Usenet, it's very likely that kids will see language and pictures that you don't want them to see.

Email isn't nearly as dangerous, and it's fun for kids to get mail. However, with young kids, you should monitor their mail to screen out spam and anything else that you don't want them to see. I recommend setting up your email client so that your younger kids share your inbox; that way, you can see their messages when they come in. (Turn back to Chapter 5, "Email Magic," for more information on managing multiple email accounts in one email program.)

Guarding Against Offensive Web Sites

Several content-filtering software programs have cropped up to help do the job of blocking offensive content. I'm suspicious of this solution to the problem, however. For one thing, no piece of software knows what you, as a parent, consider appropriate. Some of them block too many valuable sites, such as those containing breast cancer or AIDS information. Others don't block the right kind of content, such as sites that promote hate or violence—kids don't have the radar that adults have developed to help us judge the messages we receive. And what some programs might consider offensive—such as homosexuality—you might not.

I think the best way to keep kids from wandering into Web sites they shouldn't see is to make Web surfing a family affair. Even if you can't be with them all the time, if you surf with them often enough, they won't even think to look for forbidden sites.

Content Filtering in Your Browser

Content-filtering features are built right into both Navigator and Internet Explorer. But I don't recommend that you rely on either of these systems to block offensive content. These systems are based on the Web-site rating system currently being developed by the Internet community—the Platform for Internet Content Selection (PICS). Although a good first step for self-regulating Web sites, PICS is still fairly new. For it to work, Web sites must voluntarily rate themselves, and 95% of them just don't. You can choose to block all sites that don't carry a rating, but that filters out most of the Web.

To see if a site carries a PICS rating, view the Web page's source: Select View, Page Source in Navigator or View, Source in Internet Explorer. At the top of the page, you should see a META tag called PICS-Label, which carries the page's rating. If you don't find this tag, the page isn't rated. All of the following valuable sites don't carry a rating at all: National Public Radio (http://www.npr.org/); the Franklin Institute Science Museum (http://sln.fi.edu/); the Smithsonian Institute (http://www.si.edu/); and National Geographic for Kids (http://www.nationalgeographic.com/kids/index.html). And this is just a small sampling of what your kids could be missing.

If you do want to add an extra layer of security by turning on your browser's content-filtering features, understanding that this only blocks a small fraction of Web sites, you should

Moneysaver
An alternative to purchasing a content-filtering program is to find an ISP that provides ways for parents to set restrictions on their children's use of the Internet. While shopping around for an ISP, ask if any parental controls are provided with your Internet access account.

Watch Out!
Navigator's built-in content-filtering feature is called NetWatch (select Help, NetWatch). At the time of this writing, a serious bug prevented Navigator from recognizing NetWatch passwords, so you can't change settings, access blocked sites, or turn it off. But I was able to erase all of my NetWatch settings by editing the preferences file directly—it took me about two minutes to find the correct file and trash the settings. If I can do it, I'm sure your kids can, too. So, even when the bug is fixed, NetWatch won't be a secure way to keep kids out of offensive sites.

use Internet Explorer. Because Navigator's content-filtering system is buggy and insecure, I don't recommend it. Not only are your kids easily able to get past the ratings you set, but a bug might prevent you from changing settings or turning off content filtering.

Here's how to turn on Internet Explorer's Content Advisor feature:

1. Open Tools, Internet Options.

2. Click the Content tab.

3. Under Content Advisor, click the Settings button.

4. In the Password box, enter a password that's easy for you to remember but difficult for your kids to guess; if you forget your password, you won't be able to turn Content Advisor on or off, change settings, or access blocked sites.

5. Click OK; the Content Advisor dialog box opens (see Figure 12.7).

6. The RSACi Rating System that Internet Explorer uses is a standard PICS rating system. It enables you to set the acceptable level for four categories of Web-page content on a scale of 0 (greatest protection) to 4 (least protection). Select each category in the Category window—Language, Nudity, Sex, and Violence—and slide the Rating bar to the level that you want to set.

7. Click the General tab.

8. Make sure that the Supervisor Can Type a Password to Allow Users to View Restricted Content check box is selected; this enables you to access blocked sites when Content Advisor is turned on. Notice that you can also change the password on this tab.

9. Notice that the Users Can See Sites That Have No Rating check box is deselected by default. You should select this option if you want to allow unrated sites to be loaded—the majority of the Web.

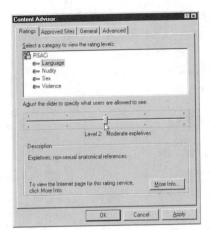

Figure 12.7
Setting up Content
Advisor's ratings in
Internet Explorer.

10. If you decide to block unrated sites, you can still specify that some unrated sites that you deem appropriate are allowed. To set this up, click the Approved Sites tab and type the URL of the site in the Allow This Web Site box. Then, click the Always button. Note that this tab also enables you to specify sites that can never be viewed, regardless of the site's rating.

11. Click OK.

12. On the Content tab, click the Enable button under Content Advisor.

13. Type the password that you set for Content Advisor and click OK. This turns on Content Advisor.

14. Click OK again to close the Internet Options dialog box.

Getting a Kid-Friendly Browser

If you have younger kids, get them a kid-friendly Web browser instead of letting them use the full Navigator or Internet Explorer browser or relying on a content-filtering program. These browsers are intended to be kid-friendly and put them in the driver's seat, with larger, easier-to-use buttons and a hotlist of sites with kid appeal. They also eliminate features that could lead to offensive sites, such as the Address box. Try one of the following:

Timesaver
Internet Explorer supports all rating systems that conform to the PICS standard, not just the default RSACi Rating System. SafeSurf (http://www.safesurf.com/) has a competing rating system that enables you to set ratings in ten categories on a scale of 1–9. To use this system, download a .RAT file from SafeSurf and then tell Internet Explorer to recognize it: select Tools, Internet Options; click the Content tab; click the Settings button under Content Advisor and enter the password; click the General tab; click Rating Systems; click Add; and locate the downloaded .RAT file that you'd like to use.

- **Kidnet Explorer:** An ActiveX control for Internet Explorer. The Address window is turned off and URL blocking shuts off hyperlink access to offensive sites. The interface is kid-friendly and there's a list of safe sites to get started. Windows 95/98; requires Internet Explorer 3.x or later; shareware; `http://members.tripod.com/~rescom/kidnetex.htm`.

- **Kids Web:** The first browser designed solely for kids. The interface is meant to be fun and easy-to-use, while cutting down on mistakes that might damage your computer (see Figure 12.8). Several preset sites with kid appeal start them off. Windows 95/98; requires Internet Explorer 4.x or later; free; `http://www.cripton.com/products.html`.

Figure 12.8
Kids Web gives young Internet users their own Web-browsing tool.

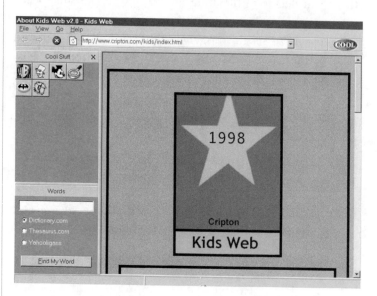

Choosing a Content-Filtering Program

For some parents, the content-filtering capabilities of Internet Explorer or a kid-friendly Web browser might not be enough. Standalone content-filtering programs provide additional features that you might like. Many of these programs don't rely on ratings to filter out Web sites, although all support the PICS standard. They can also block out individual words and phrases in Web sites, chat rooms, newsgroups, email messages, and the like. Some create logs of what your kids do online, and some set limits on how long kids can stay on the Net.

I want to stress, though, that these programs are no substitute for spending time with your kids while they explore online and for teaching them Internet safety. No program can claim to catch everything that might be offensive, although they are effective for getting rid of the worst offenders. Also realize that these products cater to the lowest common denominator, filtering out practically anything that could be considered offensive. For instance, a news story that mentions a sexually related word (such as breast), even in a non-sexual context, could be blocked. Your standards are probably not as strict, and once you turn these programs on, you might discover that your kids are missing out on valuable information.

The following are the best of the content-filtering programs. You might have to try a few to find one you like, so I've only listed programs that offer trial versions. When testing, prepare a short list of sites that you think are inappropriate and a list that you think are valuable but might be blocked. If the program you're testing allows through any of the inappropriate sites or keeps out any of the valuable ones, it's not the right one for your family.

- **Cyber Patrol:** A complete package for filtering Internet access. It also manages time spent on the computer (very useful for limiting game-playing time). It might take some time to get Cyber Patrol up and running, but its versatility and the ability to tailor the program to your family's values are worth the high learning curve. The downside is that Cyber Patrol levies a hefty charge—$29.95 per year—to keep accessing updated restricted site lists. Windows 3.x/95/98/NT and Mac OS; $29.95 (7-day demo available); http://www.cyberpatrol.com/.

- **CYBERsitter:** The easiest program to set up, it filters everything—Web sites, newsgroups, FTP access, IRC, email messages, even advertising. On the downside, it's not very customizable at all, which means that you can't

Bright Idea
Create a home page just for your kids. If you use Navigator, you can set up a kids' user profile that opens this start page automatically—open Utilities, User Profile Manager in the Communicator folder. Put together a bookmarks list of approved links, save the bookmarks file as a local HTML file (select File, Save As in the Bookmarks window), and configure this HTML file as the kids' start page (select Edit, Preferences, Navigator). Teach the kids not to venture beyond the domains of approved links, and make finding new links a family activity.

Timesaver
If you're concerned about how much time your kids spend online, here's a quick way to control their Internet access. Most ISPs require a username and password to connect, which you should keep secret, so your kids have to ask you to get them connected. You can also use time-management software to limit the amount of time kids spend on the computer, such as WatchDog (`http://www.sarna.net/watchdog/`).

tailor the program to what you feel is appropriate. It also has the bad habit of blocking potentially valuable sites, such as sites about sexual harassment. Windows 95/98/NT 4.0; $39.95 (free trial available); `http://www.solidoak.com/cysitter.htm`.

- **Net Nanny:** Very customizable, enabling you to add more off-limits sites, newsgroups, chat rooms, and words to the hit lists (see Figure 12.9). But it's very difficult to set up, and you have to do a lot of work—its restricted lists aren't as complete as the other programs. It logs activity on your computer and can restrict activity based on the logs. It can even prevent access to certain software programs on your PC. A very handy feature is the ability to block the transmission of personal information. Windows 3.x/95/98; $26.95 (30-day trial available); `http://www.netnanny.com/netnanny/`.

- **WebChaperone:** A unique approach—it quickly scans every Web page for offensive words, avoiding reliance on ratings or incomplete lists. Its customization features mean that you can tailor settings for each family member, and you can even edit the ratings to suit your family's values. Unfortunately, the demo was difficult to use and unstable. Windows 95/98/NT 4.0; $49.95 (30-day trial available); `http://www.webchaperone.com/`.

Safe Kid Sites

Many Web sites have been established as all-around Internet services for kids. These online kids' clubs offer monitored chat rooms and bulletin boards, free email that keeps identities safe, penpal services, places where kids can publish stories and artwork, and hotlists of more kid-safe Web destinations (see Figure 12.10). All of them have published privacy policies that explain how kids are protected on the site and how any requested personal information is used (often these sites require kids to register to keep out unauthorized adults). Some of them do carry advertising, but all ads are clearly labeled. Table 12.1 describes the best of these sites.

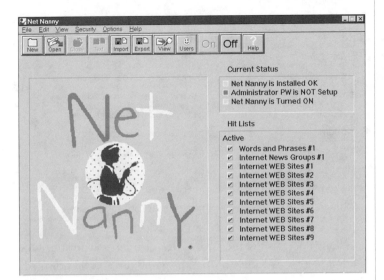

Figure 12.9
Net Nanny gives parents more control over what offensive Web content is blocked.

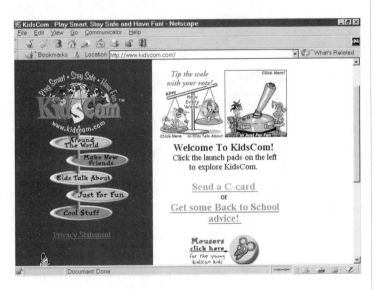

Figure 12.10
KidsCom is a fun, safe Web site geared toward kids.

Bright Idea
With your kids, fear of getting busted might be a more effective weapon than content filtering, and Cyber Snoop can help. It monitors your kids' activities online and keeps a record of everything they do in an encrypted area that they can't access. If they know that mom is checking behind them, the kids might not be so eager to seek out forbidden sites. At the same time, they learn how to use the Internet responsibly. And you can keep an eye on what your kids are doing without preventing them from visiting valuable places on the Web. Get Cyber Snoop for Windows 95/98/ NT at http:// www.pearlsw.com/ csnoop3/snoop .htm; it costs $49.95, but a full trial is available.

TABLE 12.1: KID-SAFE WEB SITES

Site	URL
Bonus.Com	http://www.bonus.com/
Cyberkids Home	http://www.cyberkids.com/
Family.Com	http://family.go.com/
Headbone Zone	http://www.headbone.com/
KidsCom	http://www.kidscom.com/
Kid's Domain	http://www.kidsdomain.com/
Kids' Space	http://www.kids-space.org/
Nickelodeon!	http://www.nick.com/
PBS Kids	http://www.pbs.org/kids/

Some porn sites use nasty tricks to get you inside. One common ruse is to use a domain name for a well-known site but with a different suffix, such as http://www.whitehouse.com/ instead of http://www.whitehouse.gov/. To avoid this, always type the full URL—shortcuts might take you to an offensive place. (The major Web browsers have gone a long way toward fixing this problem by guessing that you want to go to the well-known site.)

Just the Facts

- Don't panic! The Web isn't as dangerous as the news stories make it out to be; if you learn where the risks lie, take care who you give personal information to, and use your browser's security settings, you should be safe.

- Whenever you download software over the Internet, you risk exposure to a computer virus; a commercial, frequently updated antivirus program is your best defense.

- We all know there's some stuff online that we'd rather not have our kids see, but by making Web surfing a family affair and using content-filtering programs customized to match your values, you can effectively protect your kids without denying them the Internet altogether.

GET THE SCOOP ON...
Free stuff on the Internet and how to get it ▪ Web sites
that you can actually use every day ▪ Web-based
services and information worth paying for

Secret Sites

T HERE ARE NOW MORE THAN 60 million Web sites, and that number increases every day. So it's really not all that easy to find resources that you can use. This chapter saves you a lot of time by pointing you to the most useful resources on the Web. I've already done all the legwork—all you have to do is follow my lead.

The Web is full of free services, software, and other stuff that more than makes up for your monthly Internet access fees. You'll also discover truly useful Web resources—places that you will return to again and again. Finally, you'll learn about some sites that are worth paying for, because of the expert advice or professionally written content they offer.

Fabulous Freebies

The Internet is the ultimate grab bag. Nearly every Web site is free to access, and more than a few of them offer really valuable information that you'd have to pay for offline (in book or CD-ROM form, for instance). Beyond that, an amazing culture of giving away software has arisen on the Internet, meaning that you can satisfy a lot of your software needs without paying a dime. And of course, online businesses practice the tried-and-true method of offering freebies to entice you to their Web sites, where you might end up paying for something. But you can still take advantage of the free offers, if you know where to find them.

Chapter 13

Timesaver
There's a lot more free stuff on the Internet than I can list in this chapter, and you certainly don't have time to go searching for it. So to save time, visit one of these comprehensive clearinghouses— Free Stuff Central at `http://www.freestuffcentral.com/` and Totally Free Stuff at `http://www.TotallyFreeStuff.com/`.

This section guides you to the best freebies online. From software to services to actual stuff, you can get something for nothing on the Internet.

Free Software

I've described free and almost-free software programs throughout this book, and many of these freeware and shareware programs are as good (or better) than those programs that you have to pay the big bucks for. However, all the software programs that you've read about so far have been Internet-related. If you're looking for software to fulfill other needs, you can probably find it online, as well—for free! In this section, I'll tell you about the best of these programs for the home office, for taking care of household chores, and for having a little fun.

The Cheapskate's Home Office

If you don't have hundreds of dollars to pay for those expensive suites of productivity programs, such as Microsoft Office or the Corel WordPerfect suite, you can get fairly good equivalents from the Internet, all of them free. Of course, these freeware programs don't do everything that the major commercial suites can and they don't come with technical support, but they get the job done (see Figure 13.1).

Figure 13.1
NoteTab Light is a free, fully functional word processor for Windows.

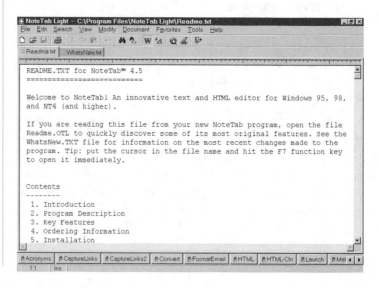

So, if you're in the market for a word processor, database, accounting program, personal information manager, or contacts manager, you might want to try one of these alternatives to the super-expensive commercial programs:

- **Word processor:** Get NoteTab Light for Windows 95/98/NT 4.0 (http://www.notetab.ch/snt.htm) or BBEdit Lite for Mac OS (http://web.barebones.com/free/free.html—scroll down until you see BBEdit Lite).

- **Database:** Get Reach-Out Super Lite for Windows 95/98 (http://www.reach-out.net/download.html).

- **Accounting:** Get 3S Accounting for Windows 95/98/NT (http://www.clarisys.ca/free.html).

- **Scheduler:** Get Calendar+ for Windows 95/98/NT (http://www.jsoftconsulting.com/cal95.htm) or Mac's Cal for Mac OS 7.5 (http://www.sutlief.com/Products/MacsCal.html).

- **Daily planner:** Get BeSmart Daily Planner for Windows 95/98/NT (check your favorite software search engine).

- **Personal information manager:** Get InfoMagic for Windows 95/98/NT (check your favorite software search engine).

- **Contacts manager:** Get Blackbook for Windows 95/98/NT or People Book for Mac OS 7.1 (check your favorite software search engine for both).

Household Helpers

You can also find free software to fulfill many specialized purposes. Freeware can even help you out around the house (see Figure 13.2).

Bright Idea
Microsoft is constantly giving away useful add-ons and utilities, but they're often kept secret. One such secret is Power Toys Tweak UI for Windows 95/NT. Download this package and you get more than a dozen fun utilities and tweaks for the operating system —a must-have. Find the package on your favorite software search engine.

Watch Out!
Even though you can't beat the price, you do have to make some sacrifices when using freeware. Free programs often aren't as usable as their commercial counterparts, they don't offer much in the way of help or technical support, and they might be stripped-down or lacking features. In the long run, you might find the software suite to be a better investment.

Figure 13.2
Keep track of your
valuables with
Home Inventory
Manager, just one
of the many useful
freeware programs
available from the
Net.

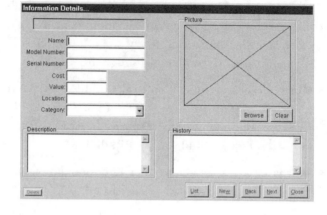

Figure 13.2
Keep track of your valuables with Home Inventory Manager, just one of the many useful freeware programs available from the Net.

Timesaver
Freeware doesn't
only mean
software—it can
also encompass
screensavers,
themes, fonts,
icons, multimedia,
MP3s, and help
files. One such
truly useful free
help file is The
Hardware Book,
which provides
documentation on
connectors,
cables, adapters,
and more. Get it
for either Windows
3.x or Windows
95/98/NT from
your favorite soft-
ware search
engine—it saves
you lots of time
whenever you're
reconfiguring or
adding new hard-
ware. Your favorite
software archive
should help you
find all sorts of
free goodies like
this.

This section describes software that you didn't know you needed, until now. And because all of these programs are free, nothing should stop you from getting them. Just find the tasks that you need a little help for and download the programs listed—they all should be available from your favorite software search engine. (Remember that no software search engine is comprehensive, so you might have to check more than one to find a specific program—I recommend http://www.hotfiles. com/ or http://download.com/ as the most complete.)

The following are my favorite free programs for taking care of household chores. These suggestions should give you ideas for other kinds of programs to search for:

- **Taking inventory?** Everyone should keep track of their possessions, in case of a fire, burglary, or other loss. To help you do this, get Home Inventory (Mac OS 8).

- **Paying the bills?** Keep track of all your monthly payments, payment history, account information, and bank balances with Bill CheckList (Windows 95/98/NT), or set up an annual budget with Wivan Account Organizer (Windows 95/98).

- **Tracing your roots?** If you're a genealogy buff or just try-ing to learn more about your family, Generations is a great help with building the family tree (Windows 95/98/NT).

- **Organizing your recipes?** Meal-Master enables you to search recipes by ingredient, title, or category, create shopping lists, and even exchange recipes over the Internet (Windows 3.x/95/98).

- **On a diet?** Get DietWatch Diary to track your progress and count calories (Windows 95/98/NT; requires Navigator 3.x or Internet Explorer 3.x, or later versions).

- **Taking care of the kids?** Sean's Magic Slate (Windows 3.x/95/98) and Al's Coloring Book (Mac OS 7.0) are fun coloring programs. Get KKGames to give your kids something educational to do (Mac OS 7.1). Or get your toddler using the computer with Time for Toddlers (Windows 95/98; requires 16MB RAM).

- **Studying the stars?** Use Adastra to explore the night sky from any location or date (Windows 95/98/NT). Keep track of sky events with Sky Calendar (Windows 95/98/NT; requires 32MB RAM and 10MB disk space); or download Distant Suns to put an observatory on your computer (Windows 3.x/95/98).

- **Learning the guitar?** Use your computer to tune your guitar while learning chords with Nice Licks (Mac OS 7.1). Even accompany yourself with Virtual Drummer (Mac OS 8.1; requires QuickTime 3.0).

- **Having bad dreams?** Find out what they really mean with Dreams Interpreter (Windows 3.x/95/98).

Bright Idea
Want to dress up your computer? Try a new screensaver, desktop theme, or font. For screensavers, go to http://www. bonanzas.com/ ssavers/, where you'll discover over 800 arranged by platform and category—free screensavers are clearly marked. If it's themes you want, there are over 3,700 at http://www. themeworld.com/, all of them neatly categorized and rated. Head on over to http:// www.chank.com/ freefonts.html for a selection of free fonts.

Time-Wasters

Of course, the real reason we bought these expensive computers was so we could play games, and now that we spent all our money on hardware, we can only afford freeware games. Whenever there are reruns on TV, or you're trying to avoid work, or you're waiting for a particularly long download, you'll appreciate these free time-wasters and amusements (see Figure 13.3).

Figure 13.3
Solitaire is the
ultimate time-
waster; greatly
expand your reper-
toire with Free
Solitaire.

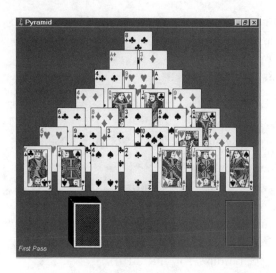

Again, you can get all of these free games from your
favorite software search engine:

- **Arkanoid:** Who knew that bouncing a ball could be so
  much fun? (Windows 95/98; requires DirectX Drivers 6.0
  and a Pentium-100 processor).

- **Bomberman:** Blow stuff up (Windows 95/98; requires the
  DirectX Drivers).

- **Casino Regal:** Play more than 20 gambling games
  (Windows 95/98; requires 8MB RAM and SVGA).

- **Chess-It:** A free chess game (Windows 95/98/NT).

- **Expert Backgammon:** Play Backgammon against the computer (Windows 3.x/95/98/NT).

- **Free Solitaire:** Suite of one-player card games (Windows
  95/98/NT).

- **Grand Slam:** Electronic baseball (Windows 95/98).

- **Igowin:** Play Go against the computer (Windows
  95/98/NT).

- **Pac the Man:** Relive the days when Pac-Man was the ultimate video game (Mac OS 7).

- **Prize Golf:** Compete in cyberspace-based golf tournaments (Windows 95/98; requires 20MB hard disk space).

- **Sigma Chess Lite:** Free master-strength chess program (Mac OS 7).

- **SK-111 Star Killer:** Outer space shoot 'em up (Windows 95/98/NT).

- **Sumo:** Yes, it's marble sumo-wrestling! (Mac OS 7).

- **Tetris Pro:** Tetris with a twist (Windows 3.x/95/98).

- **You Don't Know Jack:** Wacky multiplayer triva game that you play over the Net (Mac OS; requires a PowerPC and 16MB RAM).

Free Services

Free software is great, but it's by no means the extent of what you can get for free on the Net. You can access many valuable free services using nothing but your Web browser. For everything from expert advice to technical support, someone on the Internet is willing to help you.

Computer-Related Services

Need computer-related advice or services? Check out the following:

- **Free technical support:** Having trouble with your Macintosh, Windows computer, UNIX box, or the Web? Don't purchase that costly tech-support option or wait on hold forever. No Wonder provides free technical support on most hardware and software problems. Just fill out the handy form and you get a personal answer in about 24 hours (see Figure 13.4). Go to `http://www.nowonder.com/` and look under Free Technical Support Services.

Moneysaver
The only real cost of going online is the monthly access fee (and the computer, of course). But you can get all the software you need without paying a dime, as described throughout this book. Return to Chapter 2, "Choosing the Right Tools," for free email programs (Eudora Light, Pegasus Mail), newsreaders (NewsWatcher, Free Agent, News Xpress), FTP clients (WS_FTP Light), and browser suites (Internet Explorer, Communicator). In Chapter 7, "Getting Personal with Real-Time Chat," find a wide selection of free chat clients, conferencing tools, and Internet pagers. Throughout the book, look for free accessories, such as plug-ins, bookmark managers, browser add-ons, utilities, and all sorts of useful tools.

Figure 13.4
Free technical support is just a click away at No Wonder.

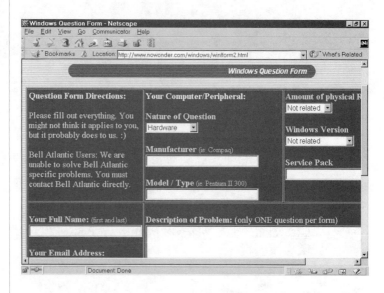

Bright Idea
What do you do when you forget your boss's birthday or your six-month anniversary and you don't have the time or money to find a nice card? Send a personalized electronic postcard. It's high-tech, it's impressive, and best of all, it's usually free. The widest selection can be found at CardCentral.Net (`http://www.cardcentral.net/`).

- **Free scanning:** If you have a photo or two that you want to convert to digital form, don't invest in a scanner—go to Digital Shoebox. They scan up to two photos for you, free. You have to send a SASE to get your pictures back (scans are delivered to your email inbox). Go to `http://members.xoom.com/shoebox/index.html` and click Free Stuff.

Expert Advice

Why pay exorbitant hourly fees when some people are giving their expert services away on the Web? Try these sites to get free advice:

- **Professional advice:** Do you need legal, financial, business, medical, career, or computer advice? MyService Experts Avenue at `http://www.myservice.com/MyService/index.html` gives you free, 24-hour consulting in all of these fields and more. Just browse to the kind of advice you need and enter your question in the form.

- **Investment help:** Get the annual report for almost any company in technological, financial, and other burgeoning industries from the most expert source—*The Wall Street Journal.* At `http://www.icbinc.com/cgi-bin/wsj/`, select the companies that you're interested in, and the reports are mailed to you the next business day.

- **Headhunters:** There are lots of employment services on the Web that enable you to post résumés and search jobs for free (see Figure 13.5). Hit a few during your job search. Your first stops should be HeadHunter.Net (http://www.headhunter.net/) and Monster.Com (http://www.monster.com/).

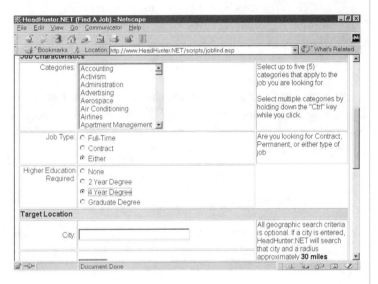

Figure 13.5
Search through all kinds of jobs at HeadHunter.Net —free.

Saving Money

Some free services are just a means to saving even more money on down the road. If you're a bargain hunter, check out these online services:

- **Clip coupons.** Don't waste time hunting through newspapers and mailers for coupons when you can print them out from the Web. All you have to do is tell these sites your zip code, and they'll give you free coupons for local businesses. CoolSavings (http://coolsavings.com/) concentrates on the big department stores, restaurants, and other well-known businesses, while Hot Coupons (http://www.hotcoupons.com/) provides more generic product and service coupons.

Moneysaver
Online airlines offer many free services on their Web sites, including booking and fare comparisons. They're also extending special fares and bonus frequent-flier miles to those who buy tickets online. Check out your favorite airline for such sweet deals. Find a comprehensive, searchable index at http://AIRonline.com/AIRwelcome.shtml.

- **Place an ad.** Need to sell something? Don't pay to put your ad in the newspaper—put it online for free. Yahoo! Classifieds at `http://classifieds.yahoo.com/` makes it easy to place an ad, with forms tailored to whatever you might be selling, whether it's a used car or a collectible Beanie Baby or a purebred dog (see Figure 13.6). Also browse the ads, look for jobs, place personals, offer services, or make announcements. Be sure to take advantage of the free notification service that informs you when ads matching your criteria come online.

Figure 13.6
Yahoo! Classifieds makes it easy to put free classified ads on the Web.

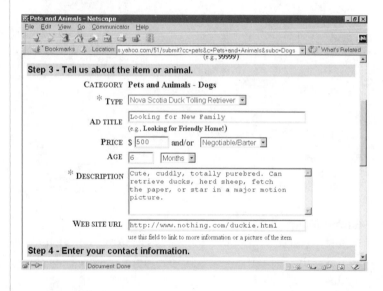

Moneysaver
Cut exorbitant legal bills! Find free fill-in-the-blank contracts, generic legal documents that you can adapt to your own purposes, and other useful legal resources on the Web. Here are a few sources: `http://www.courttv.com/legalhelp/business/forms/` (for small businesses) and `http://www.consumer-publications.com/` (for individuals).

- **Search for financial aid.** If you're college-bound, just create a personal profile, and FastWeb searches for financial aid and scholarship activities, funneling all matches into your emailbox on the site. You can even apply for some scholarships online. Check out this great timesaving service at `http://www.fastweb.com/`.

- **Find the best fares.** At `http://www.etn.nl/inforeq.htm`, fill out a form with information about a flight or cruise you'd like to take. The form is sent to five independent travel agents, and their best fares land in your email inbox. You can also get hotel, car rental, and tour prices. Another fare search service is Priceline.Com (`http://www.priceline.com/`), where you name your price for the airline tickets that you want, and the service attempts to find seats for you at that price.

Miscellaneous Free Stuff

I know what you're wondering: What about the stuff? We all want free stuff, and there's a lot of it to be had on the Internet. Most of it, such as the free software that you've already downloaded, is stuff that you can't actually hold in your hands, but it helps you pass the time. Other sites can get you free things, if that's what you need. So if you're looking for something for nothing, check these sites:

- **Books:** Find lots of books online, free for the downloading. Many of them are in the public domain—the classics—but who among us can't use a little refinement? Find a lot of recent nonfiction, too. For the best selection, go to the Online Books Page at `http://www.cs.cmu.edu/books.html`, a comprehensive index to all electronic publications. Or try Macmillan USA at `http://www.mcp.com/personal/` to find a library of over 200 great computer books that you can check out free for 90 days.

- **Newspapers:** We all know that the big papers, such as the *New York Times* (`http://www.nytimes.com/`) and the *Washington Post* (`http://www.washingtonpost.com/`) are online, but maybe your hometown newspaper is, too. Search for it at `http://www.newspapers.com/`—if you find it, you can save the subscription fee.

- **Screenplays and scripts:** Why spend the money for a night at the movies, when you can read the movie instead? Script-O-Rama (`http://www.script-o-rama.com/`) is a comprehensive index to all the movie and TV scripts online— your imagination supplies the pictures.

- **Movies:** You can watch movies online, as well. At XOOM's Classic Movies Community (`http://xoom.com/cobrand/classicmovies/classicmovies/`), download full-length classics and watch them with the RealPlayer (see Figure 13.7).

You'll also find a huge selection of clips, trailers, and cartoons from more recent releases at Jurassic Punk (http://www.jurassicpunk.com/).

Figure 13.7
No need to go to the video store—you can watch classics like *The Battleship Potemkin* on your computer.

Watch Out!
Help yourself to the freebies, but keep in mind that you still might have to pay a price. Most sites want you to register or provide information about yourself in exchange for what they're giving away, to help them market their paying products to you. You might end up receiving email ads or snail mail catalogs. You decide whether the free offer is worth it.

- **TV show tickets:** You probably know that tickets to tapings of sitcoms, talk shows, and game shows are usually free, but you might not know where to get them. Now, you can order them on the Web. If you're planning a trip to Hollywood, check http://www.tvtix.com/ or http://www.audiencesunlimited.com/ for free entertainment ideas (each site represents different shows).

- **Recipes:** There are so many recipes on the Web that you should never have to buy a cookbook again. Some of my favorite sources are SOAR (http://soar.Berkeley.EDU/recipes/), the Epicurious Recipe File (http://food.epicurious.com/e_eating/e02_recipes/recipes.html), and Veg-Source (http://www.vegsource.org/recipe/). Each of these sites contains thousands of recipes, all searchable.

- **Genealogy materials:** Researching the family tree is becoming a popular hobby. Go to http://www.genrecords.com/freebies.htm, where you can view and print free charts and forms to help with your family research efforts (you need the Adobe Acrobat Reader to view the files).

- **Business plans:** So, you're thinking of starting your own business. You won't get far without a plan. At `http://bplans.com/start.cfm`, find a large selection of sample plans for small and medium-sized businesses to get you started, plus other help for entrepreneurs.

- **Catalogs:** Some of us just can't get enough catalogs. Now your search is over—at the Catalog Site (`http://www.catalogsite.com/`), you can sign up to receive hundreds of free catalogs. This is also a great resource if you're searching for specialty catalogs. Be sure to check the sale page.

- **T-shirts:** Do you need to extend your wardrobe? Go to `http://www.idealist.com/free-shirt/` to find 101 ways to get a free T-shirt on the Web. You might have to sign a guestbook, give feedback to a site, or enter a contest, but each of these easy actions puts a new shirt on your back.

Sites Worth Bookmarking

The Web is full of sites that help you waste time—those are easy to find. Web sites that save you time are a lot rarer. In this section, I list a ton of secret sites that helps you do everyday things quickly and without a lot of hassle. Just decide what you want to do and visit the appropriate sites. And be sure to put these URLs in your bookmarks or favorites—you will return to them frequently.

All-Purpose Sites

The following sites are just generally useful—visit them to learn something new, answer a question that's been bugging you, or consult a virtual reference book:

- **Learn how to do it.** Go to `http://www.learn2.com/` to learn how to do almost anything—package fragile items, be a best man, eat sushi, catch a mouse, fix a zipper, and whatever else you need to know.

- **Go to the library.** At `http://www.websonar.com/websonar/sonar.html`, search over 120,000 archived documents—a great resource for answering literature, religion, geography, and other reference questions.

Moneysaver
You can save lots of money by faxing over the Web— eliminate long-distance charges, the cost of a fax machine, and the cost of a second fax line. With Internet faxing, your encrypted document travels over the Internet to the fax service, where it's routed over the phone lines to the fax machine at its destination. Online fax services can also deliver faxes to your email inbox. Often, the fax software is free, and you pay a small fee for a limited number of fax minutes per month (around $4.95); some services even offer trial accounts. Check .comfax (`http://www.comfax.com/comfax.htm`) to learn more.

- **Look it up.** At http://www.itools.com/research-it/, use a handy form to quickly look up answers in all sorts of references—dictionaries, foreign language dictionaries, thesauruses, the Bible, Bartlett's Quotations, atlases, and telephone books (see Figure 13.8). You can also convert currencies, get stock quotes, find zip codes, and track packages.

Figure 13.8
Search several kinds of dictionaries from one handy form at Research-It!.

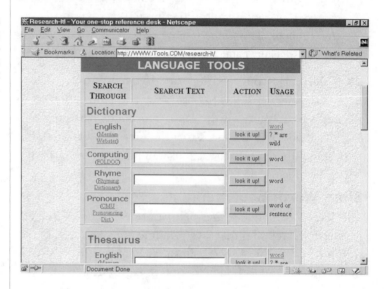

- **Answer unanswerable questions.** At http://www.last-word. com/, you get the last word on all those nagging questions, such as why onions make your eyes water and what causes quicksand—perfect if you have a curious toddler.

- **Write your congressperson.** At http://www.visi.com/ juan/congress/, find complete, searchable contact information for all U.S. Senators and Representatives, along with non-partisan biographies.

- **Translate a phrase.** At http://babelfish.altavista.digtal. com/, type a phrase, select the language it's in and the language you want to translate it to, and click Translate to get the real meaning—perfect for deciphering foreign phrases that crop up in books, menus, and other places.

Bright Idea
If you're not looking for anything useful, there's a site for you as well—the Useless Pages at http:// www.go2net.com/ internet/ useless/. Check out the Useless Hall of Fame, the Useless Site of the Week, and categories like cows, Elvis, and wackos.

Money Matters

When it comes to saving, spending, managing, and making money, the Internet is a bonanza of useful information. The following sites are among the best places to get the answers to money-related questions:

- **Manage your money.** At `http://www.financenter.com/`, find over 100 online calculators to help you figure how much to borrow, set a budget, plan for retirement, and answer other financial questions.

- **Find out what your car is worth.** At `http://www.kbb.com/`, use the famous Kelley Blue Book to learn the value of your car or what you should be paying for that used car you've had your eye on. Another good resource for car-buying advice and car reviews is `http://www.edmund.com/`.

- **Get tax forms.** At `http://www.irs.ustreas.gov/prod/forms_pubs/index.html`, download and print any IRS tax form or publication (Adobe Acrobat Reader required).

- **Win the lottery.** At `http://www.lotteryamerica.com/list.htm`, get the results for every lottery drawing in the United States.

At Work

Whatever you might need to do in the business world, there's a Web site that can make the job easier. The following sites are among the best of these work-related resources:

- **Plan a career.** At `http://www.adm.uwaterloo.ca/infocecs/CRC/manual-home.html`, go through the step-by-step process of assessing your strengths and interests, deciding on a career, and finding the perfect job—you can't fail!

- **Get a job.** Even tougher than putting together a resume is writing the cover letter. At `http://www.careerlab.com/letters/default.htm`, find over 200 sample letters tailored to different situations to help you land the perfect job.

Moneysaver
Looking for a deal? At BargainWatch (`http://lycos.internetshopper.com/bargains/`), discover a new Internet-based bargain every day. Look here for great deals on hardware, books, videos, CDs, clothing—everything. Be sure to click the Freebies button.

Bright Idea
Contests and sweepstakes are a great way to get something for nothing, and if you enter a bunch of them, your odds for winning go way up. To make your job easier, there are many central clearinghouses of contest and sweepstakes information on the Web. Try out `http://www.contestguide.com/` and `http://www.sweepstakesonline.com/index.shtml` to find the most complete listings.

- **Find out how much you should be making.** At `http://jobsmart.org/tools/salary/sal-surv.htm`, get general and profession-specific salary surveys, so you know how much to ask for at the interview.

- **Start a business.** At `http://www.sbaonline.sba.gov/`, find all the information you could possibly need, with emphasis on how to start and finance a new business and the government help that you can get.

- **Ship a package.** At `http://www.intershipper.net/`, just enter the package's weight, origin, and destination, and find out what all the major shippers charge to mail it. Also look up zip codes.

At Home

There are all sorts of decisions we must make in our everyday lives, both big and small. Whether you're making a move, getting married, or just doing some jobs around the house, the following sites are a big help:

- **Get married.** At `http://www.theknot.com/default.htm`, find everything you need to plan a wedding, from gowns to honeymoons. Particularly useful features include a budgeter, the ultimate checklist, and an online gift registry.

- **Plan a move.** At `http://www.homefair.com/home/`, play with several calculators to help you decide where to live, organize your move, get the best mortgage, and more. My favorite is the Salary Calculator, which tells you how much you need to make at your destination to maintain your current standard of living.

- **Rent an apartment.** At `http://www.rent.net/`, search a database of apartments and rental properties all over the U.S. and Canada. You can also locate short-term, international, and self-storage rentals.

- **Decide what to have for dinner.** At `http://www.mymenus.com/`, you not only find thousands of recipes, but also complete meal plans and nutritional information for different needs.

- **Get healthy.** At `http://www.phys.com/`, get lots of no-nonsense information on eating right and keeping fit. Calculators help you figure out your nutritional needs and ideal weight, while forums help you find support.

- **Do some chores around the house.** At `http://www.bhglive.com/homeimp/docs/index.htm`, learn how to take care of household maintenance, perform repairs, and do special projects, with step-by-step instructions (see Figure 13.9).

Figure 13.9
Get step-by-step instructions for building a patio at the Home Improvement Encyclopedia.

Moneysaver
For the price of filling out a survey, you can get a phone card with up to $10 of free phone time—a great deal. To learn where to pick up free phone cards, go to `http://www.dreascape.com/frankvad/free.phone.html`.

- **Take care of the lawn.** At `http://www.yardcare.com/`, pose your questions to the Yard-Care Answer Guy or browse general topics.

- **Plant a garden.** But go to `http://pathfinder.com/vg/` first to find to-do lists for the season and your area of the country, look up a plant, tackle a weekend project, or get gardening questions answered.

- **Get a dog.** Go to `http://www.purina.com/dogs/index.html` and click "Find the Breed That's Right for You." Fill out the personal profile to find out what dog breeds are the right fit for you and your lifestyle.

At School

If you're a student, several Web sites can help you accomplish tasks, such as do your homework, score well on the SAT, and find the right college. The following URLs are the best places to start:

- **Do your homework.** At `http://www.homeworkcentral.com/`, get homework answers on the Web, with a list of research sites organized by subject, experts who answer your questions, and helpful tips for doing online research.

- **Start homeschooling.** At `http://www.geocities.com/Athens/8259/`, homeschoolers find lots of valuable information, including curricula, lesson plans, teacher help, and educational resources.

- **Write a paper.** At `http://www.researchpaper.com/`, get ideas for new papers, help with researching online, and tips for improving your writing.

- **Take the SAT.** At `http://www.collegeboard.org/`, prepare for the SAT with sample questions and test-taking tips. Also register for the test online, search for colleges, learn about AP exams, and get loads of other useful information for college-bound high school students.

- **Go to college.** At `http://www.collegenet.com/`, search for the perfect college based on your personal criteria, take virtual tours of campuses, and apply online.

On the Road

If you're planning a trip, the Web can be a big help. The Web has everything from suggested routes to hotel rooms to language help at the following sites:

- **Take a road trip.** Your first stop should be `http://www.roadsideamerica.com/`, where you can discover the locations of wonderfully weird tourist attractions, find coast-to-coast routes, or use a clickable map to plan your own route.

- **Get directions.** At http://www.mapsonus.com/, plan your driving route or get maps to your destination.

- **Avoid a ticket.** At http://www.speedtrap.com/, find out about the speed traps wherever you might be driving, with maps, times, and detailed descriptions.

- **Find the airport.** At http://www.uni-karlsruhe.de/~un9v/atm/ase.html, just type the three-letter code or city and country of the airport that you're traveling to, and you connect right to its Web site, with information on parking, airlines, terminals, and other useful data.

- **Book a hotel room.** At http://accom.finder.co.uk/, search for the perfect accommodations in hotels around the world. Just select your destination and other criteria, such as price and amenities, to find the best match.

- **Talk like a native.** At http://www.travlang.com/languages/, learn how to get along in practically any foreign language. Find useful phrases and words for travelers, and if you have the RealPlayer, play the phrases to learn the correct pronunciation.

Having Fun

We all need to take time out to have a little fun. The following sites can help you relax, whether your brand of fun is sports, video games, or a night out:

- **Find out what's on the tube.** At http://www.clicktv.com/, sign up to get a local lineup (it's free) or just view the standard listings.

- **Get the scores.** At http://scores-espn.sportszone.com/cgi/scoretracker/about.asp, keep up with game scores and plays in real-time (Java and JavaScript required).

- **Play golf.** At http://www.golfcourse.com/, enter the city, state, or course where you'd like to play and you receive a course profile, complete with greens fees, tee times, and other important information. Perfect for the traveling golfer who needs a fix on the road.

Moneysaver
Many Internet fax services offer trials where you can send a free fax from your computer. If you just need to send a quick fax and you're away from your fax machine—if you're on the road, for instance—this free offer can be a godsend. To get started, check out Faxaway's trial at http://www.faxaway.com/ (send up to 15 free faxes).

Timesaver

If you register at http://www. moviefinder.com/ (it's free), you'll get lots of timesaving services in return. For instance, you can receive alerts when your favorite movies air on TV, find personalized recommendations of what you should watch this weekend, and locate tickets and movie-playing times in your area.

- **Cheat on video games.** If you're stuck on level four, go to `http://www.happypuppy.com/` and search the extensive archive of cheats, hints, and tips. You'll also find game reviews and news.

- **Go out on the town.** At `http://www.pubcrawler.com/Template/`, punch in a zip code, area code, or city and state, and get back a list of local beer bars, pubs, and breweries, complete with reviews.

- **Select a wine.** At `http://www.wine-lovers-page.com/index.shtml`, search among thousands of wine reviews to find the perfect accompaniment for dinner or a party. You also learn how to throw a wine tasting, pronounce wine words so you won't embarrass yourself in a restaurant, build a wine cellar, and match wines with foods.

- **Read your favorite comic strips.** At `http://www.unitedmedia.com/explorer/`, read the latest installments of your favorite United Media strips or catch up with a two-week archive (requires Java).

- **Get help with the crossword.** If you're stuck, go to `http://ull.chemistry.uakron.edu/cbower/jumble.html`— type what you know, and the site gives you possible solutions. It also works for the Jumble.

Going Shopping

While Chapter 14, "Going Shopping," is all about shopping, the sites in this section should get you started by helping you find bargains and search for the best prices:

- **Find the best price.** At `http://www.compare.net/`, compare prices and features on all kinds of big-ticket items, including electronics, cars, computer equipment, and appliances (see Figure 13.10). Go to `http://www.bottomdollar.com/` to compare prices of smaller items, such as books, videos, games, and software.

Figure 13.10
At CompareNet, you can find the best price on a digital camera and other essentials.

- **Find a bargain.** At `http://www.andysgarage.com/`, find closeout deals on whatever you might want, from computers to kids' bikes to jewelry.

- **Buy a car.** At `http://autoconnect.com/`, search for the used car that matches your specifications at dealerships near you; you can also sell your car, find out what make and model is right for you, compare the prices and features of different cars, and calculate monthly payments. If you're in the market for a new car, go to `http://www.carprices.com/`, where you can compare prices, get financing quotes, check your credit, and do a whole lot more.

- **Buy a book.** At `http://www.mxbf.com/`, search across the Internet for new, rare, and out-of-print books, including special editions.

- **Put in a bid.** At `http://www.bidfind.com/`, search auction sites for what you want—collectibles, jewelry, toys—and put in a bid.

Sites Worth Paying For

We've all gotten so used to finding valuable information free on the Internet (as you can tell from the rest of this chapter),

Moneysaver
Merchants often offer their Internet customers exclusive deals not available in stores or catalogs. For instance, at Lands' End, you can get up to 75% off overstocked items (go to `http://www.landsend.com/` and click "Overstocks"). Check the Web sites of your favorite merchants for more deals.

that we balk whenever someone asks us to pay. But often, subscription-based Web sites can offer more expert or recent information than the free sites can, especially when you're looking for business or financial news or when you require professionally written and edited content. Besides insider information, subscriptions often give you access to exclusive online communities where you can chat with others in your field or who share your interests. This section describes the best of these subscription-based sites and how much they cost, so you won't waste your money on the dogs.

Investing and Financial Reports

Most subscription-based sites provide investing news and advice, and often the information on these sites is more recent and provided by industry experts, as opposed to what you find on the free-access sites (after all, you have to spend money to make money). The following are among the best of these investing- and financial-related sites:

- **EDGAR Online** (`http://www.edgar-online.com/`): Get real-time access to SEC filings and related business intelligence, personalized to your interests. Subscriptions start at $9.95 per month, and a free visitor's subscription is available, so you can try the service before spending a dime.

- **InsiderTrader** (`http://www.insidertrader.com/`): Get insider information and investment recommendations that are searchable by ticker and organized to help you find new investments. This is a great source for analyzing trades made by company insiders—company executives and major stockholders. Subscription services start at $49.95 per year, with unlimited, premium access priced at $17.95 per month.

- **InterQuote** (`http://www.interquote.com/main.html`): Active traders can get real-time, tick-by-tick stock quotes continuously delivered to their computer screens. The cost is $69.95 per month, but scaled-down services are also offered.

- **Investment Wizard** (`http://www.ozsoft.com/`): Get access to a database of expert investment analysis and opinion. Find out what stocks and mutual funds insiders are buying and dumping, get recommendations for building your own portfolio, learn where the economy is heading, and get other insider advice. The service is recommended by a number of top investment publications and costs only $5.95 per month.

- **The Wall Street Journal Interactive Edition** (`http://www.wsj.com/`): Gain access to a database of business and investment information from *The Wall Street Journal* for $59 per year ($29 per year if you already have a subscription to the newspaper). You can try all of the subscription services free for two weeks, so there's no risk involved.

Services for Savvy Shoppers

If you want to access information that's written by experts in their fields and professionally edited and presented, you often have to pay for it, even on the Web. The following Web sites are low-cost bargains for the average home user:

- **Britannica Online** (`http://www.eb.com/`): Access the most complete online source of information on all subjects, from the people who produce the Encyclopedia Britannica. You won't find a better place to research, with over 70,000 articles and continuous updates. You pay just $5 per month, or purchase a day pass for $9.95. A 30-day free trial enables you to try it without risk.

- **Consumer Reports** (`http://www.consumerreports.org/`): Find unbiased comparisons and reviews of all kinds of products, including cars, appliances, electronics, computers, and most other big-ticket items, from recent issues of the magazine. Make this site your first stop before any major shopping trip. Subscriptions are $2.95 per month.

Bright Idea
Many professional and trade journals offer subscription-based Web sites that contain all the information of the print publication as well as more frequently updated news and rumors. Plus, you can generally get the information faster and more easily over the Web. Check any journals you read or professional organizations that you belong to for these online services.

Sports and Entertainment Watches

Sure, there is a ton of sports and entertainment information on the Internet that's free for the accessing, ranging from gossip to rumors. But if you want the inside dope, you often have to pay for it. The following subscription-based sites are good choices for entertainment industry insiders and fans:

Moneysaver
At PC Zone/Mac Zone, find a collection of rebate coupons for dozens of hardware and software products—everything from floppy disks to Microsoft software to scanners. You don't even have to buy anything online, just download the coupons and print them out (you need the Adobe Acrobat Reader). PC users, go to `http://www.zones.com/PC_Zone/rebate.htm`; Mac users, go to `http://www.zones.com/Mac_zone/rebate.htm`.

- **Baseline on the Web** (`http://www.pkbaseline.com/`): Professionals in the entertainment business find this an invaluable resource. For a one-time fee of $119, you get access to huge film and television archives, the latest news, earnings, and project listings, and directories of people in the biz.

- **ESPN SportZone** (`http://espnet.sportszone.com/insider/`): While there's a lot of great free sports information on ESPN's site, the real value for die-hard sports fans lies in the insider accounts. Get daily coverage, insider information, and interactive features for all major professional and college sports—before, during, and after each game. Insider accounts cost $39.95 per year or $4.95 per month; a 30-day free trial is available.

- **PrepStars** (`http://online.bballrecruit.com/prepstars//`): If you're a sports fan, you can get the scoop on college and professional recruiting information here, with a daily newsletter, player profiles, insider reports, and a scorecard of the nation's top players, all continuously updated on the Web. All of this comes to you for $60 per year.

Just the Facts

- The Internet is a treasure trove of free stuff—everything from software to expert advice to T-shirts; you've just got to know where to look for it.

- There are quite a few truly useful sites on the Web— they're just not so easy to find; after you do find a site of value, bookmark it so that you never lose it.

- We're so used to getting everything for nothing on the Web that we might balk when asked to pay. However, some subscription-based sites do offer valuable information, news, and advice that you can't get anywhere else—look for a free trial or tour before signing up.

GET THE SCOOP ON...
Shopping online safely ▪ Reducing the risks of Internet
auctions ▪ Figuring out how to pay ▪ Finding good
places to shop

Going Shopping

O NLINE SHOPPING IS PROBABLY the fastest growing
Internet activity. Stores, catalogs, and auction houses
are setting up shop on the Web at a dizzying rate, and
the amount of money being spent online is increasing expo-
nentially. Shopping on the Web offers many benefits, including
convenience, selection, easy comparison shopping, and bargains galore. But it can also be scary for consumers to send
credit card numbers off into cyberspace. In this chapter, learn
how to take advantage of all the benefits of online shopping,
while avoiding the dangers.

Safe Shopping

You've probably already heard the horror stories about the
dangers of online shopping. Like many other so-called risks on
the Internet, though, the risks of being swindled or having
your credit card number hijacked have been largely exaggerated. If you use common sense and take care who you shop
with, you'll find that using your credit card online is no more
risky than giving it to a store clerk.

Keeping Orders Secure

Today's encryption and security technologies have advanced to
the point where it's perfectly safe to transmit your credit card
over the Internet—no one can intercept it while it is traveling
through cyberspace. This security is built right into your
browser, so you don't even have to take any special steps to
ensure that your credit card information is safe. You only must

make certain that the order form containing your credit card number and other personal information is sent to a secure server—that it is encrypted during transit. As you learned in Chapter 12, "Safe Surfing," it's really easy to tell whether you're dealing with a secure server—a locked padlock icon appears on the Navigator or Internet Explorer status bar (it also appears on Navigator's Security toolbar button, as shown in Figure 14.1).

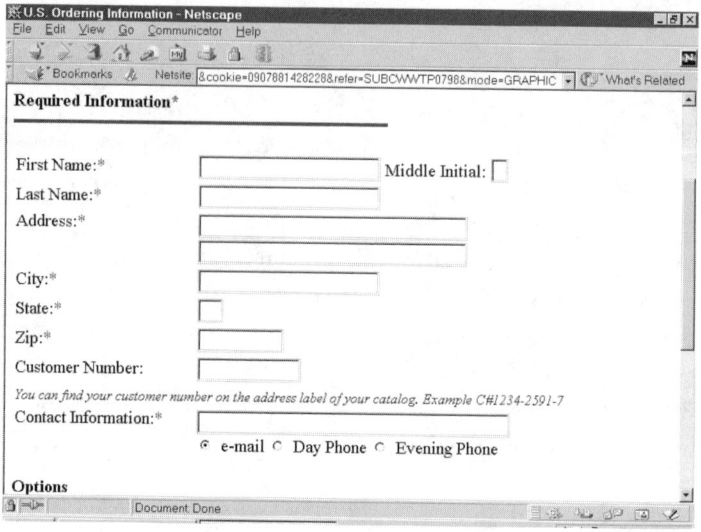

Figure 14.1
This order form is secure—in Navigator, check for the locked padlock icon on the status bar and main toolbar.

Inside Scoop
The credit card industry, along with online merchants and security technology developers, are working on an electronic commerce security standard called Secure Electronic Transactions (SET). SET promises that you can charge purchases without even sending your credit card number to the store that you're shopping with—instead it goes straight to the bank, eliminating the risk of fraud. SET probably won't be implemented for another year or two, but you can keep up with its progress at http://www.setco. org/.

All responsible Web stores use a secure server to process orders—this shows you, the customer, that you can trust the store. Many stores also publish a privacy policy linked to the main page, which states exactly how credit card numbers are collected, what security measures are in place, and what is done with your credit card information after you place the order. If you get ready to buy something and don't notice that locked padlock icon, or if you don't agree with the terms of the privacy policy, go elsewhere. You can probably find the same merchandise at another Web store.

In addition, most responsible stores offer multiple ways for you to pay. It's true that plugging your credit card number into the order form is the easiest and fastest way to pay, but if you're not comfortable with that, you still have a choice. A good store provides an 800 number where you can call in your order and a fax number where you can fax it in. Of all these methods, transmitting your credit card number online via an encrypted connection is the most secure, but do what makes you feel most comfortable.

Protecting Yourself from Fraud

The very real danger of online fraud is a much greater risk than that of your credit card number being stolen by an outside party while it's in transit. I'm talking about Web stores that promise you the goods, but instead disappear with your money. A Web store is not like a store in the "real world" — anyone can set up a Web site in a relatively short time and make it look very professional. Therefore, it can be difficult to determine which Web stores you can trust enough to do business with.

Whenever you go shopping online, take the following precautions to protect yourself from getting ripped off:

- **Try to limit shopping to stores you are already familiar with.** Stores with nationally known brand names, mail-order catalogs that you've previously shopped with, and well-known Internet-only stores like Amazon.Com are the safest bets.

- **If you've never heard of the store before, check it out before buying.** Reputable stores make it easy for you to locate a street address and telephone number on their sites; if you can't easily find these details, or if you only locate a P.O. box and no phone number, shop elsewhere. Use this information to check the store out with an outside organization, such as the Better Business Bureau or consumer agencies. Even a phone call to the store itself can confirm its respectability.

- **Check out refund and return policies before placing an order.** Like the store's privacy policy and physical address, this information should be readily available from the main page of the site. If you don't find it, or if you don't agree with the policies, move on.

Watch Out!
If you're ever asked to email order form information, especially credit card numbers, don't. It's a lot easier to intercept an email message than a Web form transmission, and the message probably won't be encrypted. No reputable online store asks you to email your order.

Moneysaver
Using a credit card to shop online can actually be safer than paying by check or money order. That's because you are only liable for $50 if a credit card purchase turns out to be a swindle; the credit card company will erase any charges beyond that amount if you receive defective goods or don't receive the goods at all. So, it makes sense to use your credit card when shopping online.

Watch Out!
Another clue to a Web store's reliability is its URL. Most stores, especially the well-known ones, have simple URLs, such as `http://www.famousbrandname.com/`. If the store you're visiting has a URL like `http://www.freesitehost.com/~someguysname/famousbrandname.html`, it's probably not a reputable site. To quickly check the domain of the Web page in Navigator, click the Security toolbar button.

Bright Idea
If you're looking for pre-approved places to shop, TRUSTe, BBBOnline, and similar organizations publish a list of stores that have already passed their requirements on their Web sites.

- **Don't supply information that might lead to fraud.** The store should only need your credit card number and its expiration date to process the order, as well as a shipping address and daytime phone number. If the order form asks for your Social Security number, bank account numbers, or mother's maiden name, you're probably being swindled.

- **Print out or save a copy of the order and its confirmation number for your records.** Print the completed order form just before you click the Submit button to save an exact record of your order. Many reputable stores also send you an email confirmation of the order, with an order number. Save this message until you receive the merchandise. You can use the order number to check on the status of your order at the store's Web site or by phone.

- **Avoid deals that seem too good to be true.** They usually are.

The Seal of Approval

Many third-party organizations have been established to help ensure that a business is legitimate and offer a "seal of approval." The most reliable of these watchdog groups are the following:

- **Better Business Bureau Online:** `http://www.bbbonline.org/`

- **Public Eye:** `http://www.thepubliceye.com/`

- **TRUSTe:** `http://www.truste.org/`

- **VeriSign:** `http://www.verisign.com/`

These organizations certify legitimate sites according to strict guidelines, and they take reports of fraudulent sites. BBBOnline, for example, requires that certified organizations have been in operation for at least a year, have a satisfactory complaint-handling record, and agree to binding arbitration for settling disputes. TRUSTe requires that the store develop a privacy policy that meets TRUSTe's standards and that it submit to periodic checks on privacy and security practices.

After a business meets the watchdog organization's standards (and ponies up a membership fee), it can display the watchdog group's graphic on the site (see Figure 14.2). Look for such logos to help determine if a store is reputable and safe to shop with, but be aware that many perfectly legitimate stores don't belong to these organizations or display these logos. A legitimate logo links back to the watchdog organization's site and displays some sort of confirmation message when you click it—watch out for counterfeits.

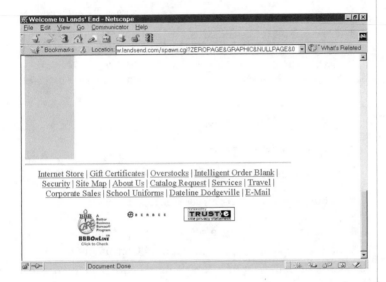

Figure 14.2
These logos on Land's End's main Web page assure customers that the online store is reputable and safe.

Safe Bidding

Internet auctions are one of the fastest-growing areas of Internet commerce. At online auctions, you can buy everything from secondhand computers to collectibles to musical instruments (see Figure 14.3). Just like a real auction, Internet auctions can be lots of fun, as you hunt for one-of-a-kind items and special deals, and then competitively bid on your finds.

It seems like every other Web site has opened an Internet auction recently, but the following are the best and largest of the auction sites:

- **Amazon.Com Auctions:** `http://auctions.amazon.com/`

- **AuctionAddict.Com:** `http://www.auctionaddict.com/`

Figure 14.3
You can buy
almost anything
at an Internet
auction.

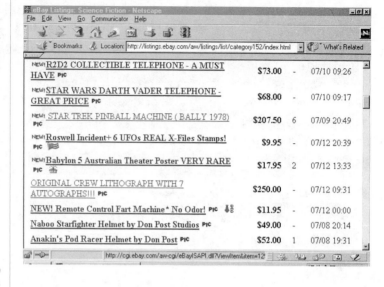

Inside Scoop
Fraud always has
to involve human
intervention at
some point—
computers aren't
interested in steal-
ing your credit card
number. So, it's
actually a lot more
risky to hand your
credit card to a
waiter who then
disappears with it
for several minutes
or to give out your
credit card number
to total strangers
over the phone, yet
we do both these
things regularly.
Comparatively,
transmitting a
credit card number
via an encrypted
form is a lot less
dangerous. We
should start
demanding more
safeguards wher-
ever we use our
credit cards, not
just on the
Internet.

- **eBay:** http://www.ebay.com/

- **eBid.Com:** http://www.ebid.com/

- **Utrade Online Auctions:** http://www.utrade.com/

- **Yahoo! Auctions:** http://auctions.yahoo.com/

Internet auctions are also the most prevalent source of online fraud, according to the National Consumers League in a statement delivered to a U.S. Senate hearing in 1998. Most instances of fraud concern a seller who puts items up for bid, takes the money, and never delivers the merchandise. Other common problems include misrepresented items, particularly collectibles, and defective or damaged goods.

Because you're dealing with individuals rather than busi-nesses, it's difficult to know who to trust at an Internet auction site. The laws governing transactions at auctions and between individuals are different than those governing transactions with retailers, and they don't give the buyer as much protec-tion. For instance, you can't back out of the transaction once you make a deal with the seller, and the goods don't have to be free of fault; they do have to live up to the description given at the auction site, though. In addition, most individuals don't have the means to accept credit card payments, so if you get swindled, you don't have any reliable way to recoup your losses.

You can protect yourself by taking advantage of the auction site's built-in protections and by following these tips:

- Read the auction site's rules and regulations, and understand exactly how the auction works. Many auction Web sites don't verify if the merchandise offered by their users actually exists or if descriptions of merchandise are accurate.

- Know with whom you are dealing. Many auction sites provide ways for former customers to rate the people they bought from, giving you a good idea of who is a legitimate seller and who is not.

- Don't hesitate to email or even call sellers for more information about the product. Don't do business with sellers who won't provide a street address and telephone number.

- If a bidder has the same email address as the seller, or if you see too many bids from different email accounts at the same ISP, there may be a shill in the audience. Don't let yourself get goaded into a bidding war. Report suspicious activity to the auction site for investigation.

- Research the product before bidding, and set a limit on what you will pay based on the product's value (don't forget to count shipping and handling charges).

- Read the fine print in the item's description (if there is any). Be especially wary of items described as "refurbished," "close-out," "discontinued" and "off-brand."

- If you're buying electronics or appliances, find out if there's a warranty and how to get service before bidding.

- Be suspicious of claims about collectibles—you have no way of determining if they're valid until after you buy the item. To protect yourself, insist on getting a written, signed statement describing the item and its value before you pay.

Timesaver
At the time of this writing, over 1,700 auctions had opened shop online. Some, such as eBay, sell everything but the kitchen sink. Others serve a narrow niche, such as antiques or computer equipment. At the Internet Auction List, you can locate specific categories of auctions or search for keywords, saving you a lot of time when searching for just the right auction to fit your needs. You'll also find a lot of auction information at this site. Go to http://www.internetauctionlist.com/.

- Insist that the seller insure the shipment, and get a definite delivery time.

- Check on return policies. Sellers should allow you to return the item for a full refund if it doesn't reasonably match the description given at the auction.

- If you can, pay by credit card, which offers you better recourse in a dispute than paying by money order or check. Or consider using a third-party escrow service, such as i-Escrow (http://www.iescrow.com/) or Trade-direct (http://www.trade-direct.com/), which only passes along payment to the seller after the buyer verifies that the item is satisfactory. Never pay with cash.

- Let common sense be your guide. Is the offer too good to be true? Is the offer really a bargain, or can you buy the item more safely at a retail store for the same price?

- If you do have a problem, report it to the auction company so that it can investigate the problem. Many auction sites now offer free insurance (up to a certain amount).

Paying for Your Purchases

The large majority of online stores—if not all of them—let you pay by credit card, and for many, credit cards are the only way you can pay. Using a credit card is the safest payment method, by far, because credit card transactions are protected by federal regulations. The Mail/Telephone Order Rule requires the merchant to deliver your goods within 30 days or give you a chance to cancel the order and payment. The Fair Credit Billing Act gives you the right to withhold payment in the event of billing errors or disputes, including when you return items or when items aren't delivered as agreed.

Credit cards have two distinct disadvantages, however:

- Many shoppers don't use credit cards to avoid interest payments or building up debt.

- Credit cards don't have the same anonymity as cash.

Timesaver
You can spend way too many hours searching the millions of items offered on Internet auction sites again and again for something specific. Instead, put the iTrack service to work for you. Once or twice a day, iTrack searches an auction site for the items you specify; if it finds anything, it sends an email message directly to your inbox. The service is free; sign up at http://www.itrack .com/.

If you prefer to pay by check or cash, there are alternatives to credit card payments. These include digital money and electronic wallets. Also, check the store's policies—many of them enable you to mail in a check or money order, if you're willing to wait a little longer for your order to be delivered.

Using Digital Money

Digital money is a fairly new technology, and it has a lot of promise if it ever becomes widely adopted. The idea behind digital money is to institute an online form of payment that's equivalent to paying by cash. You simply convert real dollars into electronic dollars, download the electronic dollars into a "wallet" on your computer, and use them to pay for your transactions. The transaction can't be traced back to you, so it's completely anonymous. Digital money is particularly useful for micropayments, which are too small to put on your credit card. In theory, it can also easily be used for private transactions as well as purchases from online stores.

The problem with digital money is that it's not universal like cash. Both you and the other party must have an account with a bank that issues the digital money for it to be any good. Because of this limitation, it hasn't become widespread, so you may find that you can't spend your digital money in very many places.

Currently, the only form of digital money available is eCash, invented by DigiCash (go to `http://www.digicash.com/index_e.html` for more information). If you want to use eCash, you have to set up an account with an issuing bank. Currently, eCash issuers are limited to banks in Europe and Australia. eCash accounts should be available in the United States in late 1999 or early 2000. If you're interested in getting an eCash account, you can sign up for a mailing list that notifies you when accounts become available at `http://www.digicash.com/news/mailinglist/mailinglist.html`.

Using Electronic Wallets

The "electronic wallet" is a more established technology than digital money. Electronic wallets have two primary benefits:

Bright Idea
Do you need to check on the legitimacy of a business, online or in the real world? To locate the phone number or address of the nearest Better Business Bureau, visit the BBB Web site at `http://www.bbb.org/`. Another good resource for reporting and learning about consumer fraud is the Federal Trade Commission's site at `http://www.ftc.gov/`.

Inside Scoop
Micropayments are the only viable means for charging for the sale of intellectual property and one-time services over the Web. For example, you might pay a few pennies to read selected articles in a Web-published magazine, instead of buying the entire magazine on a newsstand, or you might pay a small fee to access pay-per-play games. The micropayment is deducted from your electronic wallet on a "pay as you go" basis. Digital's MilliCent (http://www. millicent. digital.com/) and InterCoin (http://www. intercoin.com/) are early models for micropayment transactions.

- **Added security:** The wallet encrypts your financial information, both on your computer and in transit. This information is accessible only via a password.

- **Convenience:** Wallets can store many different credit cards, so you can choose which one to pay with. They can also store multiple shipping addresses, saving you from having to retype this information. Some allow you to pay by check. And wallets can support micropayments for low-charge purchases.

There are three widely established electronic wallets:

- **BlueMoney:** Instead of giving you a software wallet, this electronic wallet is stored on the Internet; thus, it's more convenient because you can access it from any Internet-connected computer, not just your own, but it's also less secure. It supports credit card payments. To get it, go to http://www.bluemoney.com/.

- **CyberCash:** This is probably the most widely accepted electronic wallet, and it has the most payment options, supporting credit cards, checks, and cash (see Figure 14.4). To get it, go to http://www.cybercash.com/cybercash/consumers/.

- **Microsoft Wallet:** Because it's built into Internet Explorer, this is the most convenient of the electronic wallets if you already use IE (it also works as a plug-in for Navigator 3.x and later). It supports credit card payments, but Microsoft promises that it can be extended to other payment methods, such as eCash. To get it, go to http://www.microsoft.com/wallet/default.asp.

All of these electronic wallets are free, so you can easily use one or all of them. Again, paying with a wallet is limited only to stores that accept it, so you won't be able to use your wallet everywhere you shop.

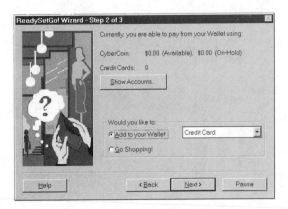

Figure 14.4
The CyberCash electronic wallet offers the most payment options.

Watch Out!
Unlike credit card protection, consumer protections for new payment methods such as digital money are unclear. So, you might not have any legal recourse if you experience problems while using these payment methods.

Timesaver
All the electronic wallet developers provide a list of online stores that support the wallet at their Web sites, so check there first to find places to shop.

Using Microsoft Wallet

This section shows you how to set up Microsoft Wallet for online shopping. If you decide to get the CyberCash or BlueMoney wallets, the setup process is fairly self-explanatory, and each wallet's Web site offers lots of help with using the programs.

Follow these steps to configure billing and credit card information in Microsoft Wallet:

1. In Internet Explorer, select Tools, Internet Options.

2. Click the Content tab.

3. Click the Wallet button; the Wallet window opens, showing the Payments tab.

4. First, set up shipping and billing information; click the Addresses tab.

5. Click the Add button.

6. Fill out the fields for the billing or shipping address that you want to use when shopping online (see Figure 14.5). Be sure to assign an easy-to-remember name to the address in the Display Name field, such as "home" or "office"; use this name to select the address from the wallet. Click OK when you're done.

Figure 14.5
Entering address
information for
Microsoft Wallet.

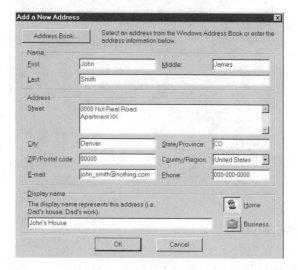

7. Repeat the process to add as many billing or shipping addresses as you think you might use, including the billing addresses for your credit cards (you can always add more later). All the addresses appear in the Addresses window; to edit or remove one, select it in this window and click the Edit or Delete button.

8. Make sure that the Warn Me Before Sending Addresses Over The Internet box is checked, so you are alerted if a Microsoft Wallet–compatible site requests an address from you.

9. To configure credit card information, click the Payments tab.

10. Click the Add button, and select the type of credit card from the drop-down menu.

11. Click Next, and fill out all the fields with your credit card information (see Figure 14.6). Be sure to give the credit card a display name that you can easily remember.

12. Click Next, and select the billing address for that card from the drop-down menu of Addresses (or click New to enter a new billing address).

Timesaver
If your're an
Internet Explorer
5.0 user, you can
quickly install
Microsoft Wallet.
In IE, select Tools,
Internet Options,
click the Content
tab, and click the
wallet button.
Then, click
Download when
prompted, and IE
downloads and
installs the wallet
component.

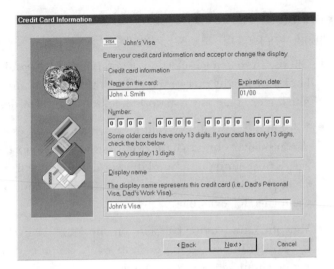

Figure 14.6
Adding credit card
information to
Microsoft Wallet.

13. Click Next, and enter a password for that credit card in the Password box. You're asked for this password before sending credit card information to an online store that requests it.

14. Retype the password in the Confirm Password box.

15. Click Finish; the credit card appears in the Payments window.

16. Add as many credit cards as you'd like to your Wallet, using the same procedure. You can give each one a unique password or the same password.

17. Your receipt information, which shows what you ordered, where you ordered it from, and how much you paid for it, is also protected by a password. To set up the password, click the Receipts tab and enter the password into the boxes. You can use the same password protecting your credit cards to keep things simple.

18. When you're done, click Close to close the Wallet program.

19. Click OK to close the Internet Options dialog box.

Finding the Best Shopping Sites

Online shopping offers many benefits:

- Choose from a huge selection of goods for sale. An online bookstore might carry over 50,000 titles, for instance—much more than any real-world bookstore can provide.

Timesaver
Web stores can save you a lot of time when you're buying gifts that need to be shipped to destinations other than your home. The store often giftwraps your purchase and sends it directly to the recipient, saving you the hassle of having to perform these chores yourself.

- You can not only shop at your favorite national stores, but also at smaller stores that were previously confined to a city across the country or around the world. Buy coffee from a small shop in Seattle and get wine from the vineyard in California, for example.

- You often find more bargains on the Web. Many Web stores offer Internet-only discounts, deals, coupons, or saving on shipping costs, for example.

- Comparison-shopping is easy. In fact, several Web sites have sprung up to help you compare the prices of products at many different online stores at one time. (You'll learn more about these services later in this chapter.)

- Online stores often offer a lot of useful, free information to help you make purchasing decisions, such as reviews, personalized recommendations, and multimedia samples—more than you get in a catalog or even in the store.

- The convenience can't be beat. You don't even have to leave your house or office, avoiding traffic, long lines, and rude salespeople, and making it practical to shop on your lunch hour.

Now that you know how to avoid the security risks of online shopping, there are very few additional disadvantages, but some of them might be off-putting to you. You have to wait for your merchandise to arrive; for me, this isn't such a big deal with some items such as clothes, but with others, such as books and CDs, I want instant gratification. Also, not being able to handle the merchandise is a distinct drawback. The Web is very useful for researching a new car purchase, for instance, but I'd definitely want to drive it before putting my money down. I'm sure that everybody finds things that they'd rather buy out "in the real world," but that shouldn't prevent you from taking advantage of the convenience of online shopping for those items that you don't mind waiting for.

When it comes to shopping on the Web, you've got more choices than you probably know what to do with. You can buy almost anything online these days, from groceries to fine jewelry to cars. So, when you're looking for something, it can often be too much of a chore to figure out which store to give your money to. This section helps you out by providing tips for choosing shopping destinations, pointing you toward some of my favorite stores, and telling you about some Web sites that do the shopping legwork for you.

What to Look for in a Web Store

Whenever I visit a Web-based store for the first time, I do the same thing that I do when I walk into a new "real-world" store—walk around and get to know the place. If I like the décor and the merchandise, and if the salespeople seem friendly, I might stay long enough to buy something. But if anything turns me off, I leave.

First impressions are very important when shopping online. When you enter a store's Web site, check out the design, ease of use, and introductory information. If you don't like the way the store looks, if you find it difficult to browse the merchandise or search for something specific, or if you can't easily find important information, such as privacy and return policies, you're free to go elsewhere before buying something.

Your first impression should be the number-one factor in deciding whether you stay at the site long enough to consider buying something. Also, follow these suggestions to make sure that your shopping experience is a pleasant one:

- **Shop with a name you know.** I've said this before, but I think it bears repeating. If you make your first shopping trips to stores that you're already familiar with, or better yet, that you've previously shopped with by catalog or out in the "real world," you feel more at ease. As you get more comfortable with online shopping, you can branch out to lesser known, specialty stores (but make sure they're safe first).

Watch Out!
Because you can't directly handle items before you buy them on the Web, it's particularly important to locate the store's return and refund policies and make sure that you agree with them *before* you buy. You want to be able to easily get your money back if the item you bought doesn't live up to your expectations.

Bright Idea
Because you have to depend on pictures and descriptions when shopping on the Net, it's a good idea to make your first few purchases items that are the same no matter where you buy them—books, CDs, videos, software, and the like. That way, you know exactly what to expect.

■ **Look for stores that understand their customers.** Stores that manage huge inventories should offer robust search capabilities, while smaller specialty stores should provide a sense of atmosphere and lots of information about their products. Remember that you're always free to leave the site if you're not satisfied with the layout or information about products that you're getting.

■ **Look for stores that offer that something extra.** To woo customers, many Web stores provide freebies, such as personalized recommendation programs, interesting content like reviews, interviews, and articles, or chat forums for customers to meet others who share their interests. Extra free services let you know that the store is serious about wanting you as a repeat customer.

■ **Look for stores that make it easy to buy.** Most stores should provide a "shopping cart." You put items into your cart and then take it to the checkout when you're done. As you're browsing the store, you should be able to easily view your shopping cart at any time, add and remove items, and total up your order (see Figure 14.7). If you can't do these things, abandon your cart and leave; you won't have to pay for the items in your cart if you don't actually submit an order via an order form.

Watch Out!
For shopping carts to work properly, you must have the cookies feature turned on in your Web browser. Otherwise, the program won't remember which products you put in your cart.

Figure 14.7
At Land's End, items appear in your "shopping cart," along with the amount of each purchase; you can easily add and remove items with the click of a button.

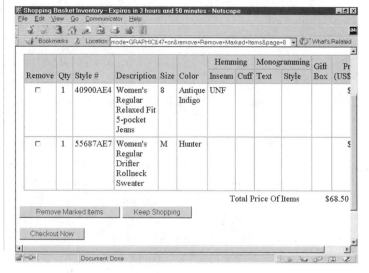

The Best Shopping Destinations

The sites listed in this section are my favorite shopping stops on the Web, and they're all good places to get started with online shopping. As a general rule, these stores are well-designed, easy to browse and search, contain full-featured shopping carts, and provide extra services and deals—and most importantly, they're safe.

Of course, this is just a small sampling of what's out there, so definitely continue exploring on your own. Checking out these sites gives you a good idea of what a reputable online store looks like; as you venture into unknown destinations, put this knowledge to use in deciding where else to spend your money.

Catalogs and Department Stores

If you're looking for clothing, stuff for the house, and other basics, catalog and department store sites are the best places to start. You're already familiar with the name and the products, so you know you can trust the Web store. The best of these include the following:

- **Eddie Bauer:** Features a variety of personalization features, a reminder service, and a wish list—a password-protected area in which you list items that you'd like to be given as gifts. Go to `http://www.eddiebauer.com/`.

- **The Gap:** Features a program that puts together outfits for you, a virtual dressing room, and other interactive toys (requires Shockwave). Go to `http://www.gap.com/`.

- **JCPenney:** Features Internet-only coupons, a gift registry, and a whole lot of stuff to buy. Go to `http://www.jcpenney.com/`.

- **Land's End:** Check the overstocks section for great bargains, or find interactive shopping aids like an outfit selector (see Figure 14.8). Go to `http://www.landsend.com/`.

Moneysaver
Do you need shopping help? Try out an online personal shopper. Just tell the shopper what you'd like to buy, including size, style, and price, and it searches the store for you and sends recommendations via email. Many Web stores offer this service at no charge.

Figure 14.8
Put together an outfit the virtual way at the Land's End Web store.

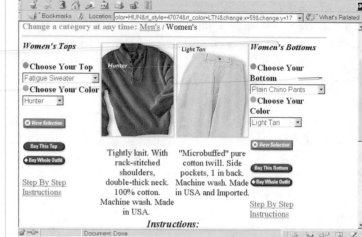

Timesaver
Check your favorite catalogs for the URLs of their Web sites—most of them now have Web stores where you can conveniently place orders online. You can not only visit Eddie Bauer and Land's End on the Web, but also Spiegel (http://www.spiegel.com/spiegel/), L.L. Bean (http://www.llbean.com/), J. Crew (http://www.jcrew.com/), Lillian Vernon (http://www.lillianvernon.com/), and Hammacher Schlemmer (http://www.hammacher.com/), for instance.

- **Macy's:** Features personal make-up consultations, a bridal registry, and online-only sale prices. Go to http://www.macys.com/.

- **Patagonia:** features beautiful photos, environmental resources, and an outdoor information service, along with great outdoor clothing and gear. Go to http://www.patagonia.com/.

Books, Music, and Movies

The Web is a great place to buy entertainment items, if you don't mind waiting for them to be shipped to you. You'll find a huge selection online, including hard-to-find items. You can often get personalized recommendations based on your likes, and you can easily comparison shop. Often, prices for these items are significantly cheaper on the Web. Here are some of my favorites:

- **Amazon.Com (books, CDs, and videos):** Features a huge inventory, personalized recommendations, a robust search, discount prices, and reviews and links to similar products on every page. Go to http://www.amazon.com/.

- **Bargain Book Warehouse (books):** Features discount prices on overstocked, remainder, and out-of-print books—find a lot of real bargains here. Go to `http://www.bargainbookwarehouse.com/`.

- **Barnes and Noble (books):** Features reviews, synopses, and excerpts of many books, personalized recommendations, and a book-related community with chat forums, live author interviews, and literary events. Go to `http://www.barnesandnoble.com/`.

- **CD Now (CDs):** Features reviews from popular magazines, a robust search, personalized recommendations, and RealAudio samples from the collection of over 215,000 CDs. Go to `http://www.cdnow.com/`.

- **DVD Flix (DVDs, videos, and laser discs):** Features a wish list that notifies you by email when your favorite movies are released, plus pre-ordering and shipping discounts. Go to `http://www.dvdflix.com/`.

- **MusicHQ (CDs):** All CDs are linked directly to reviews from the All-Music Guide, a constantly updated music info resource; you can even design your own customized CDs. Go to `http://www.musichq.com/`.

- **Reel (videos):** Features over 85,000 new, used, and rare movies, video trailers of new releases, discount prices, and ratings based on violence, sex, humor, and art-house appeal; a bargain bin sells previously viewed tapes for $5 each, and you can even rent movies. Go to `http://www.reel.com/`.

Computer Stuff

The Web is an obvious choice for shopping for computer items. You have lots of choices when it comes to computer-related shopping outlets, but here are a few that I like:

- **Computer Discount Warehouse:** Features discount prices for bargain hunters, a powerful search, on-site price comparisons, weekly specials, and manufacturer's coupons;

Watch Out!
Be sure to calculate the costs of shipping with your order, so the surcharges won't take you by surprise. But remember that most purchases won't require sales tax if you shop with out-of-state businesses. Therefore, sales tax savings often offset shipping charges.

Timesaver
Generally, the Web isn't the best place for idle browsing—there's such a large selection that it can be overwhelming. Amazon.Com, CD Now, and Reel all carry tens of thousands of books, CDs, and videos, for instance. To save time, have specific products in mind when you visit Web stores. Save idle browsing for the "real-world" stores.

Bright Idea
If you try a shopping site and have a good experience, bookmark it—you definitely want to return. I suggest creating a "shopping" folder containing only bookmarks to those stores that you have tried and liked.

Timesaver
If you want to buy a new computer system or piece of hardware, you can save time and money by buying direct from the manufacturer over the Internet. Gateway (http://www.gw2k.com/home/) and Dell (http://www.dell.com/) both let you put together a customized computer system at their Web sites, for instance.

even sign up for a newsletter that alerts you to deals. Go to http://www.cdw.com/.

- **CompUSA:** Features a massive inventory, powerful search, online help with computing questions, a kid's section, and some fun and games. Go to http://www.compusa.com/.

- **Egghead:** Features an auction on surplus items, a discount software superstore, and many other deals. Go to http://www.egghead.com/.

Food and Drink

You might wonder why anyone would buy food from the Web. Actually, you can find many gourmet and specialty items at online stores that you might not be able to get locally. So, the following stores are well worth your browsing time:

- **GreatFood.Com (specialty and gourmet foods):** Features a huge selection that you can browse by category, review, and meal occasion, as well as weekly bargains, recipes, and a gift finder. Go to http://www.greatfood.com/home.html.

- **NetGrocer (groceries):** Features a very easy-to-use navigational system that takes you through a huge inventory of products (see Figure 14.9), as well as discounts on grocery store prices, reusable shopping lists, and recurring orders. Go to http://www.netgrocer.com/.

- **Only Gourmet (specialty and gourmet foods):** Features lots of free information, including recipes, cooking tips, restaurant and cookbook reviews, and food news. Go to http://www.onlygourmet.com/.

- **Virtual Vineyards (wine):** Features a powerful search that enables you to look for a wine by various criteria, as well as "instant picks," a wine glossary, party menus, seasoned advice in choosing a wine, and more useful (and free) content. Go to http://www.virtualvin.com/.

Figure 14.9
After browsing NetGrocer's attractive site, you might not want to return to the local grocery store.

Inside Scoop
Despite media-propelled fears, online shopping is quickly becoming a very popular activity. According to Cyber Dialog, 3.3 billion dollars was spent online in 1997, and Activmedia predicts that that figure will soar to 75 billion dollars for 1998.

- **Wilderness Coffee House (coffee):** Features an abundant selection, a coffee glossary, and a rundown on the history and origins of each coffee you consider, and your order is roasted just before it's sent out for the best flavor. Go to `http://www.wilderness-coffee.com/`.

Specialty and Gift Stores

The stores listed in this section defy classification, but they might be the perfect places to find that one-of-a-kind gift or novelty item. Check out the following:

- **1-800-Flowers:** Features a large selection of floral arrangements and gift baskets, as well as extras, such as flower-arranging tips, a calendar of flower-giving occasions, a reminder service, and suggestions on what to put on the card. Go to `http://www.1800flowers.com/`.

- **American Greetings:** Offers a huge number of personal services for greeting card buyers; for instance, you can customize cards with a message, signature, and photo. Other features include a mailing service, an online address book, a reminder service, and electronic postcards. Go to `http://www.americangreetings.com/`.

Timesaver
Even if you don't intend to buy anything online, you can use Web-based stores to help you decide what to buy. Instead of spending hours driving from store to store, go window-shopping on the Web—you learn what's available and how much it costs before ever heading out to the mall.

- **Archie McPhee:** Features a huge selection of novelty items, everything from rubber chickens to voodoo dolls. Go to `http://www.mcphee.com/`.

- **De La Concha Tobacconist:** Features a rated selection of fine cigars and pipe tobacco, and lots of additional information about cigars and cigar-smoking. Go to `http://www.delaconcha.com/`.

- **eToys:** Not only is this a huge toy store, but it also sells software and video games; the site features recommendations and a way to search for appropriate toys by category, age, and price range (see Figure 14.10). Go to `http://www1.etoys.com/html/et_home.shtml`.

Figure 14.10
Find just the right gift for a kid you know using eToys' extensive search features.

Watch Out!
If a Web store asks you to create an account with a username and password, don't use the same password that you've given to other accounts, especially email or Internet access accounts. It's a good idea to come up with a unique, easy-to-remember but difficult-to-guess password that you use at all online stores, so that you don't have to remember 20 different passwords.

- **The Ferret Store:** If you have a pet ferret, this place is a must-visit; it also features chat and bulletin boards for ferret owners and lovers. Go to `http://www.ferretstore.com/`.

- **Fortunoff:** Purchase fine jewelry from a retailer with over 77 years' worth of experience; find high-resolution photos of each piece, along with important details such as clarity and color ratings of diamonds, or search for items within a certain price range. Go to `http://www.fortunoff.com/`.

- **OfficeMax:** Choose from a huge selection of office supplies, and create template order forms for regularly purchased items. Go to `http://www.officemax.com/`.

- **Online Sports:** Features a huge inventory of sporting goods and collector's items, plus a powerful search, many ways to browse, and the ability to compare products from several different suppliers. Go to `http://www.onlinesports.com/`.

- **PetMed Express:** Features deep discounts on prescription pet medicines, specialty pet items, and other pet-related items—a great bargain for pet owners! Go to `http://www.petmedexpress.com/`.

Comparison-Shopping with Bots

If you don't have the time to shop online or off, let a robot (or bot) do the dirty work for you. These shopping agents scour the Web for the best prices on whatever you're looking for and return a consolidated price list with links to places where you can buy (see Figure 14.11). Although the technology hasn't yet been perfected, particularly in regard to how many stores these bots search, shopping agents can still save you both time and money. I suggest that you try several to find the one that works best for you.

Timesaver
If you're looking for a very specific product but you don't know where to start, go to Shopfind at `http://st2.yahoo.com/shopfind/`. Using this specialized search engine, you can search a wide range of shopping sites or limit your search to a specific category of stores.

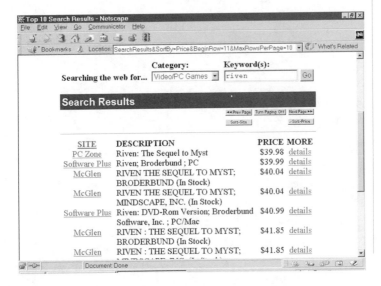

Figure 14.11
Use a shopping agent, such as the Top10Guide, to find the best prices on video games and other items.

Moneysaver
Comparison-shopping is well worth your time, in case you're wondering. Even on inexpensive items, prices can vary greatly from site to site. For instance, I was recently shopping for videos. I used a shopping agent to determine that the same video cost $12 at one site and $8.50 at another; I saved $3.50 in less than a minute. (By the way, the movie cost $16 at the local video store.)

The following are the best of the shopping bots:

- **Bottom Dollar:** http://www.bottomdollar.com/

- **Excite Product Finder:** http://jango.excite.com/

- **RoboShopper:** http://www.roboshopper.com/

- **Top10Guide:** http://www.top10guide.com/

Just the Facts

- Protecting yourself while shopping online is no mystery—just be sure that the order form is secure and that the store is trustworthy.

- Probably the most risky form of online shopping is bidding at Internet auctions, but you can lessen the risk by thoroughly checking out both the goods and the seller before you put in your bid.

- Even though it's perfectly safe to use a credit card online, you do have choices, such as digital money and electronic wallets, but I don't recommend these until they become more widely established.

- When searching for good shopping sites, look for stores that you feel comfortable in, offer lots of extras, and make it easy to find products, cancel orders, and pay.

Creating a Web site with a purpose ▪ Finding tools for putting together your Web site ▪ Finding a place to host your site

Putting Your Web Site to Work

NOWADAYS, IT SEEMS AS THOUGH everyone and his dog (literally) has a home page. You're probably itching to make one for yourself, if you haven't already. But almost everyone who rushes to put up a home page seems to end up with something no one wants to look at, including the author. And just the process of creating and publishing a set of Web pages can seem so daunting that you may feel tempted to quit before you even begin, what with having to learn HTML, graphic design, page layout, and even programming languages.

You *can* avoid all that. You can create a Web page that you and others will actually use every day, and you can do it without having to learn anything new or complicated—only as much as you want to. In this chapter, I'll begin with some ideas and guidelines for creating a Web site that will go to work for you. You will also find tools and tips for putting together that Web site. You can learn just as much as you want and take shortcuts everywhere else. You'll then discover how to get that site on the Web. And you'll do it all in very little time.

Chapter 15

Timesaver
If you want to create a new start page in a hurry—one that sits on your local disk instead of out on the Web—then you should get StartPage. This freeware utility creates a home page with links to search engines, news services, and more in less than a minute. You don't have to learn HTML or fiddle with Web page design techniques. If you do want to edit your start page later, just open the HTML file that StartPage created in an HTML editor. Get it for Windows 3.x/95/98 from your favorite software search engine.

Creating a Useful Web Site

Why do you want a personal home page? To share photos of your cat? To tell the world about your passion for Alyssa Milano? Because everybody else has one? Your answer should be none of the above. The best reason to have a personal home page is so you can put it to work for you.

After all, you're competing with millions of other personal home pages (not to mention all those commercial and ad-supported sites). Unless you have something truly compelling to say, few Web surfers are going to click your way. (If you do have something compelling to say, though, you should publish it on the Web; I guarantee that somebody—maybe even a lot of somebodies—will be interested.)

In this section, I'm going to discuss two ways to put your Web site to work: as a personal portal for your own use, and as an informational site for acquaintances. I'll give you many tips and guidelines, but I encourage you to become creative and discover other ways that your Web site space can fulfill your individual needs. Think of this chapter as a jumping-off point to get your creative juices flowing.

Putting Together a Personal Portal

Back in Chapter 9, "Cutting Through the Hype," I said that the best portal site is one you create yourself. After all, who knows your likes and needs better than you? Putting together a personal portal site is not that difficult. You can use an actual portal site as a template and replace the links, forms, and other elements with substitutions that are meaningful for you. For an example, look at my personal portal page, shown in Figure 15.1.

Here are some ideas for what you can put on your personal portal page:

- **Search engine forms:** It's OK to copy the form from a search engine's site to yours, as I have done with Yahoo!'s search form. This enables you to search your favorite search engines directly from your home page. To copy a search form, save the page containing the form as a local file, open it in an HTML editor, and cut and paste the entire form to your home page.

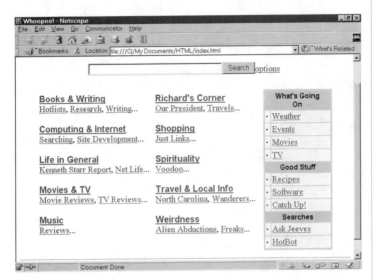

Figure 15.1
My personal portal
page.

- **Links to local information:** You'll often want to quickly
find out what's going on where you live—on TV, at the
movies, in concert, or whatever is important to you—as
well as check on local news, weather, classified ads, and
sports scores. If you're having trouble finding these links,
try the Web site of a local newspaper or look up your city
in Yahoo!'s Get Local directory (go to http://www.
yahoo.com/ and enter your zip code in the box at the bottom of the page).

- **Links you visit every day:** News, daily cartoons, jokes of the
day, recipe archives, software downloads, search engines,
or anything else that you visit almost every day should go
on your main portal page.

- **Links you visit frequently, but not every day:** These links
should go on secondary pages—I've divided mine into categories that reflect my interests, each category on a separate page. For example, I've put together a list of sites
where I like to shop and collected several links that I use
to research my books. Short descriptions remind me
what's at the end of each link, and the asterisks highlight
my favorites (see Figure 15.2). I'm always tinkering with
these lists—removing links that no longer interest me and
adding new pages as I find them.

Bright Idea
Another good use
of your home page
space is as a fam-
ily portal. Every
member of the
family gets a dif-
ferent area of the
portal for organiz-
ing quick links to
favorite, kid-safe
Web sites. Make
the portal your
browser's start
page, and teach
the kids not to
venture beyond
the portal's links,
which you've
already checked
out. Over time,
finding more links
and adding to the
portal will turn into
a fun family pro-
ject.

Figure 15.2
A page of my
favorite links.

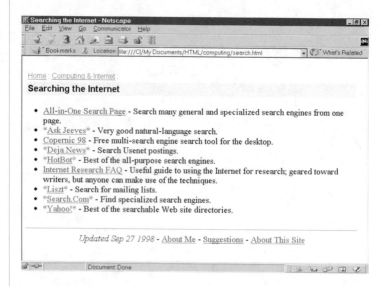

Timesaver
It's very easy to
save a page from
the Web and use it
as a template for
your home page.
Open the Web
page that you want
to base your portal
page on in your
browser, and select
File, Edit Page in
your browser. The
page opens in the
default HTML edi-
tor, so you can edit
it any way you like.

- **Anything you want:** The point is, it's your portal, so you can put anything you want on it. Again, it will probably keep evolving as you discover new resources and abandon old ones.

Most importantly, optimize your page for your use. This is your start page—the one you look at first whenever you start up your browser—so it should fit your needs. Make the page the same size as the size you usually set your browser to, be sure that it looks good on your computer and in your browser, and design it so that it loads quickly.

But don't let your portal page take over your life. I update my home pages once a week or so, spending an hour or two on adding new links and checking the old ones. This keeps my home pages at the level of a fun hobby—they don't become so much of a drag that I abandon them.

So, how do you get started? The easiest way is to use another page on the Web as a template. Adapting someone else's design is perfectly fine as long as you're not making a commercial or ad-supported site and the home page will be for your own personal use. I obviously copied Yahoo!'s design (as did every other portal site) because I find it easy to use and fast-loading. The design is also so simple that it's easy to cut out

Yahoo!'s stuff and put in my own. But notice that I only adapted the most basic design—I didn't copy copyrighted images or content, I changed the color scheme, and I otherwise altered the design to fit my needs.

If you need a template to get started, you can copy the design of my page. Just go to `http://www.arcana.com/shannon/index.html` and select File, Save As in your browser to save a copy of the page to your drive. Then, open this file in an HTML editor (which you'll learn about later in this chapter), and make whatever changes you like.

Creating an Informational Resource

Another practical use of a home page is making it a central repository for information on the Web that you need to share frequently with others. Then, you can just direct whomever needs the information to your URL, making it convenient for them to get the information and saving you some trouble in the bargain. You could do any (or all) of the following:

- **Network:** Publish your credentials and information about your work for potential employers, colleagues, and teammates to access. For instance, I've created a list of my publications so that publishers and editors can quickly find my qualifications (see Figure 15.3).

Watch Out!
When I say that it's all right to copy another Web site's design, I don't mean that you should make your site look exactly like another. Unless you're parodying the site, this is plagiarism. To be safe, use the basic site design as a template, but make the details your own. Also, never copy anyone else's content or graphics, unless you have made absolutely sure that you're copying copyright-free clip art or text that's in the public domain.

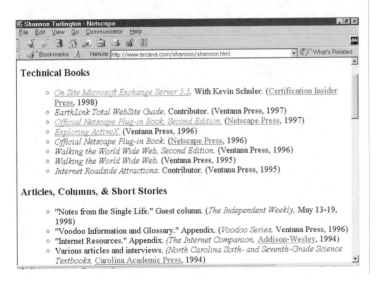

Figure 15.3
My publications page for professional contacts.

- **Promote yourself:** Create Web pages that help promote whatever you may do. For example, I put together an informational page about each of my books, with a description, excerpts, and a link to where readers can buy the book online (see Figure 15.4).

Figure 15.4
A self-promotion page for one of my books.

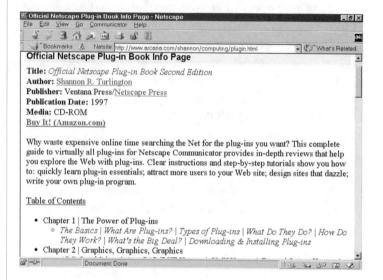

- **Share your work:** If you're a hobbyist or semi-professional writer, artist, photographer, musician, filmmaker, or software programmer (or a creator of anything that can be put on the Web), then share samples of your work. For instance, I've published sample essays and stories on my home page. At best, you may attract the attention of someone who wants to pay you for your work; at the least, you'll probably receive valuable feedback.

- **Share your interests:** If you've amassed a large amount of information on anything—from raising tropical fish to refinishing antique furniture—publish it on the Web. A lot of people will probably be interested in what you have to say about the subject, and if you attract enough attention, you may be able sell advertising space and make a little extra money or even turn your hobby into a full-time business. It's happening all the time.

- **Create a community:** Use your home pages to bring together a group. Friends or family who are scattered all over the place can use your pages as a central gathering place to find news about everyone else in the group, announcements of upcoming get-togethers or chat sessions, and photographs. For example, my brother is on an extended road trip; I publish his letters on my home page so that other family members can easily find out what he's been up to.

I'm sure that you can come up with a lot more ideas to fit your needs and interests. No matter what you use your home pages for, make sure that the URL gets into the hands (or email inboxes) of the people who need it. If you've created a professional resource, for instance, put your URL on your business cards and in your signature file so that interested parties can easily learn more about you.

A Web Page Style Guide

No matter what you use your Web site for, you need to have a basic understanding of Web-page design rules. Even if you're the only person who looks at your home page, you'll be glad that you made it fast-loading and easy-to-use. If you publish your home pages on the Web, though, it's essential that they are well-designed. You'll make a better impression on professional contacts, attract more visitors, and help your Web site grow into a useful resource.

The basics of good Web-page style are simple and easy to remember. In fact, if you've done any Web browsing at all, you already know what a bad Web page looks like. The most fundamental rule is to create pages that you like to look at and that work well for you; if you don't find them cumbersome, distracting, slow, or illegible, others probably won't either.

Timesaver
Once you learn a little HTML, you'll discover that one of the most frustrating aspects of Web page design is figuring out the six-digit codes for adding color to backgrounds, text, and links. Let a software program do the work for you. ColorHexer lets you choose colors from the Windows palette and converts your choices to the proper hexadecimal code, which you can then cut and paste into your HTML file (Windows 95/98/NT). Get this shareware program from your favorite software search engine.

Bright Idea
In HTML, tables serve an additional purpose beyond just serving as tables. They also control the layout and placement of elements on your page. Usually, text automatically wraps to the width of the browser window as the user has set it. Therefore, the page's layout can differ greatly from browser to browser. But tables constrain text to a particular width. No matter what size the user's browser is, text and other elements remain in the same place. So, it's worth your while to learn how to design tables with your HTML editor.

You should also follow these guidelines:

- **Make a plan.** Determine the purpose of your site. Is it a professional resource, a family gathering place, or a personal portal? Plan your site to fit that goal. If you're designing a set of pages, planning is especially important for mapping out the navigational system and making it easy to get around your site.

- **Mark up HTML files to reflect what the information is, rather than how it's displayed.** HTML is a logical language. A paragraph style may look different from browser to browser, but it still presents the same information consistently. For example, a heading is a heading in every browser, although in some browsers it may be bold and in some it may be underlined. Designing your pages with this principle in mind, rather than by how the formatting looks in *your* browser, results in better-looking pages that retain their meanings across all browsers.

- **Present text in short, clearly separated chunks.** Separating page sections with divider bars and headings keeps Web pages concise and makes them more comprehensible. If a page is too long—if you have to scroll through several screens to see everything—consider dividing it into multiple pages.

- **Make text easy to read.** Don't overuse bold, italic, uppercase, exclamation points, and other emphatic elements. They're distracting and make blocks of text hard to read. In addition, be conservative when using text colors. Black on white is easiest to read, particularly with large blocks of text.

- **Make linked text meaningful.** Don't just link the words, "Click Here"—that doesn't tell the reader anything about where the link goes. Instead, describe what the link is in the linked text. This also helps users who bookmark the link, since the linked text becomes the title of the bookmark.

- **Sign and date all your pages.** A Web page signature includes your name, an email address, a link back to the main page in your Web site, and the date the page was last updated. It might also include the date the page was first published, your credentials, a copyright notice, and other relevant information. The signature adds authenticity to the page and helps readers find you if they want to know more.

- **Be consistent.** Use the same basic design and layout for all your pages, so that your site has one unified look. Also, use the same navigational scheme on each page, so that readers can easily find their way around. It's a good idea to create a master or template HTML file, which becomes the basis for all your pages.

- **Use multimedia, Java applets, and the like only when necessary.** While these elements certainly add interest to your site, they also lengthen downloading time and strain the patience of your audience. Try to keep them to a minimum, and use them only when they truly add to the content. Remember that the fewer multimedia files you use, the more impact each one will have.

- **Provide an alternative version if you use frames, multimedia, Java, and so on.** Not all Web surfers have the latest version of their browsers, so they may not be able to view your site properly if it contains a lot of high-tech elements. Other users may not want to wait around for lengthy multimedia and Java files to download. Always provide an alternative, low-resolution version for these users at the entrance point to your site.

Getting Web Site Creation Tools

Back in the early days of the Web, we had to type the HTML code for Web pages into text editors like Notepad and hope that we hadn't forgotten a tag or miscoded something. That's not the case anymore. Now, you have almost too many choices when it comes to Web site design tools—many of them too

Watch Out!
Earlier in this book, I told you how to cruise the Web faster by turning off graphics, Java, and so on. If you make a Web page, keep in mind that others also follow those tips. To help them out, assign all your graphics alternative text so that visitors can decide whether to load them. (Alternative text is inserted into the IMG tag using the ALT attribute; your HTML editor should support this feature.) Also, don't rely too heavily on Java or multimedia, and always provide a low-bandwidth alternative. I avoided the whole problem in my Web site—I didn't use any graphics, applets, or multimedia at all. Instead, I used text and background colors to gussy up my pages while keeping them fast-loading.

powerful and expensive to use just for designing personal home pages.

At the very least, you need an HTML editor; actually, you don't really need one if you learn HTML and type the code into a text editor yourself, but an HTML editor sure makes the job go faster. If you plan to put original graphics in your Web pages, then you need an image editor, and you can also find a variety of little programs designed to create graphical effects and optimize images for the Web. Beyond that, you may want tools to write Java applets, multimedia files, and other special effects. Or you can bypass the development and design work and snag free graphics, applets, and scripts for your pages from all over the Web. (I've included download URLs for all tools where available; if you don't see one, look for the tool on your favorite software search engine.)

Choosing an HTML Editor

There are two kinds of HTML editors: WYSIWYG editors and code-based editors. WYSIWYG (or What You See Is What You Get) editors function like word processors, enabling you to design pages using friendly toolbar buttons and dialog boxes. WYSIWYG editors are all you need to create a small Web site; they're easy to learn, they're cheap, and for the most part, you won't even have to know HTML. The features of WYSIWYG editors are often limited to the basic elements of HTML, however. If you plan to use a lot of scripts and other fancy coding, a code-based editor gives you more precision and power. I wouldn't recommend one, though, unless you need to create a large, feature-rich Web site or you really like the technical stuff.

In this section, and in the rest of this chapter, I focus on cheap, easy-to-use tools best-suited for building the personal Web sites that I described earlier in the chapter. Remember that the choices I offer here are only a small sampling of what's available, although they will suit most of your needs. Web site design tools are probably the fastest-growing section of the Internet software market. So, don't worry if you outgrow these tools—you can always move up to the next level later.

Bright Idea
Web pages can look quite different when viewed at various screen resolutions. What looks great on your computer at 1024x768 resolution may look horrible on a screen set to 640x480. A little tool called BrowserSizer enables you to easily preview your pages at various resolutions. It's free; get it for Windows 95/98/NT 4.0 at http://www.vasile.com/racecar/stampware/browsersizer/.

Netscape Composer and Microsoft FrontPage Express

Both of the major browser suites come with a basic HTML editor. Unfortunately, Internet Explorer 5.0 no longer includes FrontPage Express, but if you upgraded from version 4.0, then you probably still have FrontPage Express on your computer; if you don't have FrontPage Express installed, consider getting one of the other HTML editors described in this section.

These tools have several advantages for the personal Web site designer:

- They're free.

- They're very easy to use.

- They integrate well with your browser, helping you design pages that look good in the browser you use most often.

- You've probably already got one on your computer. If you use Internet Explorer, launch FrontPage Express from the Internet Explorer program folder. If you use Navigator, click on the Composer button in the browser's component bar to open Composer.

These HTML editors should suit your basic needs just fine. In fact, I use Composer to create and maintain my home pages with no problems. Both are very similar to a word processor and to each other (see Figure 15.5). They both support all of these essential features: text and paragraph formatting via toolbar buttons and menus, image placement, hyperlinking of text and images, table design, formatting of page properties, and publishing to an FTP site or Web server.

However, FrontPage Express and Composer are limited in the features they support. For instance, you can't create frames, scripts, or forms inside Composer; instead, you must open a text editor and code this complicated HTML yourself. FrontPage Express is a little more powerful—you can create forms using toolbar buttons, and you can insert applets, videos, sounds, and scripts directly into the page layout, but you still can't create frames.

Watch Out!
Although your page may look fine in your browser, it may not look so good to other users. Different browsers and even different versions of the same browser interpret HTML slightly differently. Colors, graphics, and fonts may also appear differently on other computer setups. If it's a primary concern that your page look as good as possible to every user—if you're designing a business Web site, for example—test the site on as many computer systems and in as many browsers as you can before publishing it.

Figure 15.5
Both Composer
and FrontPage
Express have word
processor-like tool-
bars and support
WYSIWYG format-
ting of all basic
HTML elements.

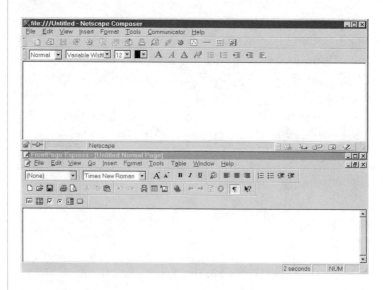

Figure 15.5
Both Composer and FrontPage Express have word processor-like toolbars and support WYSIWYG formatting of all basic HTML elements.

Timesaver
Both Composer
and FrontPage
Express include a
wizard that walks
you through the
steps of creating a
basic home page,
if you don't have
the time to put
together your own
home page design.
In Composer, click
the New toolbar
button and click
the From Page
Wizard button—
this takes you to
the wizard on the
Web (you must be
connected to the
Internet to use this
feature). In
FrontPage Express,
select File, New,
choose Personal
Home Page Wizard,
and click OK.

If you're a beginning Web site designer, I recommend one of these tools. Use it to learn basic Web page design. Once you're comfortable with one of these editors, you may want to move up to something more powerful, but not until you've pushed the boundaries of what these editors can do.

Arachnophilia

If you're not satisfied with the capabilities of Composer or FrontPage Express, Arachnophilia is a good alternative. This free editor is also a better choice once you gain more experience with HTML. Eight toolbars and several wizards enable you to create most HTML elements in a code-based environment (see Figure 15.6). Arachnophilia also has some additional features that you'll find useful for putting together a more powerful Web site: multiple document searching, support of JavaScript and other scripts, drag-and-drop conversion of Rich Text Format (RTF) files to HTML, frame support, and previews of your pages in up to six browsers. Using Arachnophilia to its fullest requires a thorough understanding of HTML, however.

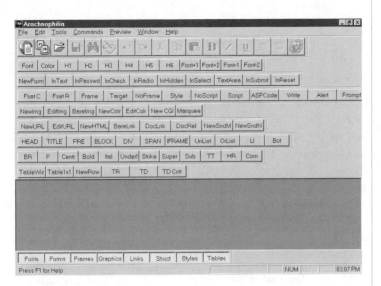

Figure 15.6
With eight toolbars, Arachnophilia adds more tools to the basic HTML editor.

- **System Requirements:** Windows 95/98/NT

- **Price:** free

- **Download:** http://www.arachnoid.com/

PageSpinner

This HTML editor combines WYSIWYG features with a code-based environment, so it's powerful enough to support more complex coding than can FrontPage Express or Composer. It supports the advanced elements required for a more complex site, including Java, JavaScript, Cascading Style Sheets, and forms. It can also connect to a database, convert text to HTML, and preview your pages in up to six Web browsers. You need to know some HTML to take advantage of the more advanced features, though.

- **System Requirements:** Mac OS 7.0.1

- **Price:** $25 (30-day trial version available)

- **Download:** http://www.sportsurf.net/PROVING/hi/htmlmac/
  pagespinner.html

Commercial HTML Editors

If you outgrow freeware and shareware HTML editors, or if you find yourself faced with the task of creating a more complex, larger Web site than a set of personal home pages, you do have alternatives. However, bear in mind that these tools carry a hefty price tag along with a powerful feature set. Table 15.1 describes the best of these commercial HTML editors and points you to the Web sites where you can learn more about them.

TABLE 15.1: A SELECTION OF COMMERCIAL HTML EDITORS

HTML Editor	Features	Price	System Requirements	URL
BBEdit	HTML and text editing in one package; powerful and fast	$119 (free demo available)	Mac OS 7.0	http://web.barebones.com/products/bbedit/bbedit.html
HomeSite	Powerful, code-based editing; suited for fast creation of complicated pages	$99 ($10 rebate if you purchase the downloadable version)	Windows 95/98/NT 4.0	http://www.allaire.com/products/homesite/
HoTMetaL Pro	Combines code-based and WYSIWYG editing; supports the latest Web technologies; the best tool for hardcore HTML programmers	$129 (evaluation version available)	Windows 95/98/NT 4.0	http://www.softquad.com/products/hotmetal/
Microsoft FrontPage	Best suited for creating and managing large Web sites that share a consistent design; includes a full-featured WYSIWYG editor	$149 ($40 rebate for Office users)	Windows 95/98/NT 4.0	http://www.microsoft.com/frontpage/

Learning HTML

No matter what HTML editor you choose, even if it's the most basic WYSIWYG editor that you can find, you must learn some HTML. You might need to add coding for features that aren't supported by your editor. You might have to tweak the code created by your editor or quickly insert new elements without even firing up the editor. Or your might need to check your pages for errors. No matter what, a basic knowledge of HTML will come in handy.

You don't need an HTML editor to write or edit the source HTML code of your pages—you can do that in any text editor. Most WYSIWYG HTML editors enable you to easily open the source code in the default text editor so you can edit the raw code (the default text editor is usually Notepad on Windows). In Composer, for instance, select Edit, HTML Source; if you haven't assigned a text editor for editing the HTML code, you're prompted to pick one. In FrontPage Express, select View, HTML; this opens an editor that makes your job easier by highlighting the HTML code in different colors (see Figure 15.7).

HTML is not that difficult to learn, but teaching you HTML is beyond the scope of this chapter. However, you can turn to the Web for tutorials. Table 15.2 lists the best places online to learn the basic and more advanced techniques of HTML coding and Web site design.

Watch Out!
On the Web, things change quickly—new HTML techniques are introduced one day and then denounced as clichés the next. Avoid these overused techniques in your own pages, because they'll just signal to your visitors that you're behind the times. These clichés include blinking text, scrolling messages in the status bar, pop-up windows, "splash screens," rainbow-hued graphics, black backgrounds, "under construction" signs, multicolored text, and pictures of your pets. Of course, be on the lookout for a whole new crop of clichés to appear tomorrow.

Figure 15.7
FrontPage Express
displays the HTML
source code in a
text editor, making
it easy to directly
edit the code.

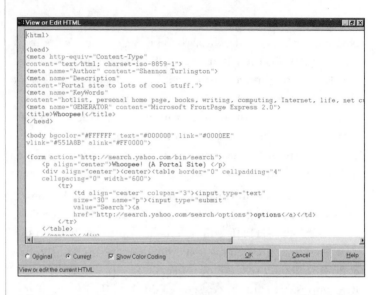

Figure 15.7
FrontPage Express displays the HTML source code in a text editor, making it easy to directly edit the code.

TABLE 15.2: WEB SITES FOR LEARNING WEB PAGE DESIGN

Site	URL	What You'll Learn
Beginner's Guide to HTML	`http://www.ncsa.` `uiuc.edu/General/` `Internet/WWW/` `HTMLPrimer.html`	Introductory tutorial to HTML; covers the basics but doesn't get into advanced design
HTML: An Interactive Tutorial	`http://www.` `davesite.com/` `webstation/html/`	Also aimed at beginners, this tutorial goes beyond the basics and provides interactive exercises for learning all aspects of HTML
How Do They Do That With HTML?	`http://www.` `nashville.net/` `~carl/htmlguide/` `index.html`	Nifty tips and tricks
Project Cool Developer Zone	`http://www.` `projectcool.com/` `developer/`	Goes way beyond the basics; a good resource for learning about JavaScript, XML, and Cascading Style Sheets
Java Tutorial	`http://java.sun.` `com/docs/books/` `tutorial/index.html`	Learn Java

Site	URL	What You'll Learn
HTML Helpdesk	http://web.canlink.com/helpdesk/	Come here if you're having trouble with any aspect of Web page design—you'll probably find the answer to your question
Bare Bones Guide to HTML	http://werbach.com/barebones/	Complete reference to every HTML tag; use it to check coding or look up a tag

Creating Web Page Graphics

Graphics are the easiest way to dress up Web pages. Use them for navigational buttons and maps, backgrounds, divider bars, logos, and ads. But to create graphics, you need an image editor. You might require additional tools to make your images Internet-ready and to add special effects, as well.

Choosing an Image Editor

You may already have a perfectly good image editor that you can also use to design Web page graphics, such as Adobe PhotoShop, Adobe Illustrator, CorelDRAW, or Macromedia FreeHand. If you don't have a commercial image editor, I don't recommend buying one just to create the images for your personal home pages—good graphics programs are way too expensive. Instead, try one of the following low-cost tools:

- **NetSketch:** Adapted from a high-end drawing program specifically for creating Web graphics, this program enables you to make your own images or edit existing ones. Windows 95/98/NT; $69 (try before you buy); http://www.vegasfx.com/netsktch.html.

- **Painting:** This basic image editor is most useful for creating icons and simple graphics. Mac OS 7.5; shareware; download from your favorite software search engine.

Watch Out!
When creating a Web page, it's very important to strictly follow HTML standards. This may seem like a lot of extra work, but it ensures that all browsers display your pages properly and efficiently. For instance, if you specify the height and width of your graphics in the <IMG> tag, Navigator and Internet Explorer will insert sized placeholders for all images, loading your pages faster.

- **WebPaint:** This image editor was designed specifically for creating Web page graphics (see Figure 15.8). It includes a built-in GIF animator, and it can import images in many formats for conversion to Web-compatible formats. Windows 95/98; shareware; download from your favorite software search engine.

Figure 15.8
WebPaint is a low-cost alternative to commercial image editors.

Bright Idea
Although PhotoShop is a powerful image editor, it wasn't expressly designed for creating graphics for the Web. Fortunately, you can add additional tools via PhotoShop's plug-in support. I recommend SPG WEB Tools—you get a GIF animator, a Web file format batch-converter, a background renderer, a banner builder, and lots more cool tools. SPG WEB Tools does carry a hefty price tag—$99— but if you've already invested in PhotoShop, it may be worth it. It's available for Windows 95/98/NT 4.0 at `http://www.spg-net.com/product1.html`.

Creating Graphical Effects

After you get beyond the simple business of attaching a single hyperlink to an inline image or tiling a background graphic (both of which any HTML editor can do), you may need some specialized tools. Fortunately, these freeware or shareware utilities are readily available for download over the Internet. The functionality supported by many of these tools may also be included with your commercial HTML or image editor. (If a download URL isn't listed, get the program from one of the major software search engines.)

The following are ways you can greatly enhance the performance of your graphics:

- **Image maps:** You've run into these many times—different areas of the image link to different pages, creating a map. Some commercial HTML editors make it easy to create image maps, but if your editor doesn't have that capability, the following image map editors can help: Mapper (Mac OS 7.0; shareware), or LiveImage (Windows 95/98/NT 4.0, $29.95, http://www.mediatec.com/).

- **Animated GIFs:** Although many Web users find these simple cartoons distracting, one or two may spice up a Web page, and no plug-ins are required to play them. (An animated GIF is basically just a series of GIFs played in sequence in the Web page.) Use one of these tools to make them: GifBuilder (Mac OS; free; http://iawww.epfl.ch/Staff/Yves.Piguet/clip2gif-home/GifBuilder.html), or Animagic GIF Animator (Windows 95/98/NT 4.0; $29; http://www.rtlsoft.com/animagic/index.html).

- **Backgrounds:** All image editors can be used to create a graphic for tiling on the background of a Web page, but it can be tricky to come up with a graphic that really works as a background. You may want to get some help from a tool designed just for making backgrounds, such as TextureMill (Mac OS 7; shareware), or EmptyPic (Windows 3.x/95/98; shareware).

- **Interlacing and transparent backgrounds:** Interlacing makes a cool "fade-in" effect that's most effective on large images, and transparent image backgrounds make the page's background color shine through. Many image editors support these effects, as do some HTML editors.

Timesaver
All Web page graphics must be in GIF or JPEG format—the image formats supported by all browsers. JPEG is the better choice for detailed graphics and photographs, while the smaller, faster-loading GIF format works well with icons, cartoons, and other simple graphics. The Windows version of Netscape Composer automatically converts bitmaps to JPEG format when you insert them in an HTML file, so you can create Web page graphics with Paint, which you already have on your system. (On the Mac, Composer automatically coverts PICT files to JPEG format when you insert them in an HTML file.)

Watch Out!
Any GIF file can be made into a tiling background image, but very few of them make effective backgrounds. The best backgrounds contain neutral colors, such as gray, beige, white, or pastels, so that text and images show up well against them. Good backgrounds also have simple patterns that don't distract from the page's content and small file sizes that don't add too much waiting time during downloading.

Getting Graphics Ready for the Web

Be careful how you use graphics. It's all too easy to overload your Web pages with them, and anything that significantly slows Web page downloading is going to turn visitors away. A few small, well-designed graphics can be very effective—take a look at Yahoo!'s Web site for a good example. Each graphic that you choose should serve a specific purpose: better convey information, help users navigate, or advertise something.

Once you put all the graphics and other media on your home page, test the page's usability by downloading it from the Web server with a slow modem connection. If it takes more than 30 seconds or so to display the entire page, consider cutting down the number of graphics that you're using.

There are a number of techniques that you can use to make your image creations more Internet-friendly:

- **Palette optimization:** The lower the color depth, the smaller the images are, and the better they look on all computers. Many commercial image editors include palette optimization tools. For example, Xara Webster—a complete Web graphics package—adapts a 256-color or smaller palette to your existing images (Windows 95/98/NT 4.0; $49; http://www.xara.com/webster/).

- **Anti-aliasing:** Scaling down an image can make it more Web-friendly, but it can also seriously degrade the image's quality, particularly if it contains text. Anti-aliasing functions are built into most commercial image editors, but if you don't have one, Smoothie will help you compensate (Mac OS; $24.95; http://www.peircesw.com/Smoothie.html).

- **Thumbnails:** Sometimes, you do have to put that large image on the Web. Make it easier on your audience by linking the full image to a smaller version, called a thumbnail. Users can then preview the image and decide whether to take the time to load the full version. Most image editors give you the capability to create a small thumbnail version of an image.

- **Low-resolution images:** Create a smaller version of complicated images that the browser loads first, so that the user has something to look at while the main image downloads and displays. Just create a version of the image with a smaller file size by reducing the number of colors in the image. When placing images with an HTML editor, you should be able to assign each image a low-res alternative.

Finding Other Developmental Tools

You might want to add more advanced functions and enhancements to your Web pages than graphical elements support. ActiveX controls, Java applets, and CGI scripts provide interactivity and functionality. Or you can add multimedia, such as audio, video, and VRML.

Again, don't overload your pages with these elements—you'll just drive visitors away. Only use applications and multimedia files when they are truly necessary—when the same effect can't be created with text or graphics but must be there to make your pages work.

The following tools will help you add these extras:

- **CGI scripting:** Use CGI*StarPro to create CGI-scripted forms (Windows 95/98/NT; $99; http://www.webgenie. com/). Note: Your Web server will need to support CGI scripts for them to work on your pages.

- **Streaming Media:** Windows Media Tools create streaming audio and video for playback in Windows Media Player (Windows 95/98/NT 4.0; free; http://www.microsoft.com/ ntserver/nts/downloads/recommended/mediaserv/netshow3. asp). RealEncoder creates streaming audio and video for playback in RealPlayer (Windows 95/98/NT, Mac PowerPC, and Linux 2.0; free; http://www.real.com/ products/tools/index.html and scroll down to the bottom of the page).

- **Java:** To create Java applets, get the Java Development Kit (Windows 95/98/NT 4.0 and UNIX; free; http://java. sun.com/products/jdk/1.1/).

Timesaver
After you build a large collection of Web page graphics (as well as sounds, applets, controls, scripts, and HTML files), it can be difficult to remember what is what just from cryptic filenames. That's where a tool like WebGAL comes in handy. It organizes all your Web page resources into easily viewable galleries, so you can see at a glance what art you've got or preview HTML, applets, controls, and scripts in Internet Explorer. Get WebGAL for Windows 95/98 at http://www. spidersoft.com/; it's free to try, $25 to keep.

- **ActiveX:** ActiveX Control Pad provides a basic control toolkit and a WYSIWYG editor for creating ActiveX-enabled sites (Windows 95/98/NT 4.0; free; `http://msdn.microsoft.com/workshop/misc/cpad/default.asp`).

Finding Free Stuff for Your Site

A lot of us don't want to take the time to design graphics, program applets, or write scripts for our Web pages. That, or we don't have the talent to do it (I know I fit in the latter category). Fortunately, the Internet is a treasure trove of free stuff, and that's especially true when it comes to finding copyright-free goodies for your Web site. Get started with the sites in Table 15.3; they'll lead you to more Web-page enhancements than you can ever use.

TABLE 15.3: FREE STUFF FOR WEB SITES

Free Stuff	Where to Get It
Clip art	`http://webclipart.about.com/`
Backgrounds	`http://www.fishlinkcentral.com/backs.hts`
Animated GIFs	`http://www.animfactory.com/`
CGI scripts	`http://icthus.net/CGI-City/`
JavaScript scripts	`http://www.javascriptsource.com/`
Java applets	`http://javaboutique.internet.com/`

Putting Your Site on the Web

When you've created your home pages, you need to publish them on the Web. For that, you must find a Web server to host your pages. You have two choices: rent Web server space (or find free space) from a hosting service; or maintain your own Web server.

For most personal home pages, it makes more sense to find a third-party Web server that will host them. Although you can easily find low-cost or free Web server software, there are many other considerations and costs in hosting your own server. The server computer must be fairly fast and have a lot of memory, for one. You will also need a dedicated Internet connection so

Watch Out!
Don't succumb to temptation and put MIDI files that start playing automatically on your pages. Imagine that someone is surreptitiously browsing the Web at work when he stumbles across your page—that blaring music will instantly give away the fact that he is goofing off. Or another person might be browsing the Web late at night, while the rest of the family is asleep; your suddenly blaring sound file might give him or her a heart attack. If you must include music, do the polite thing and give visitors a choice of whether to start playing it.

that your Web site is always up and running, and the more traffic you get, the faster that connection must be. Hosting your own server might be more trouble than it's worth.

Finding a Hosting Service

A Web site hosting service provides the equipment to open your site to the entire Web and the expertise to keep it running. Renting server space doesn't have to cost you an arm and a leg. You have several choices when it comes to hosting services, and many of them will cost you very little or nothing at all.

First, check with your ISP, company, or school. Many ISPs include a certain amount of Web server space with an Internet access account, but you're usually limited in how much storage space you get—often just enough to host a small set of Web pages. Generally, ISPs provide additional server space for a fee. An organization that you're affiliated with may also provide free Web server space for publishing personal home pages, but you may be limited in the kind of content you can publish.

If you can't get Web server space for your personal home pages at your ISP, school, or company, a free Web site hosting service may be the answer. Read the terms of service carefully, though—you may be limited in how much server space you get, the design tools that you can use, and even the kind of content that you can publish. You'll also have to put ads for the hosting service on your pages, and you won't be able to accept paid advertising from any other sources (see Figure 15.9). Finally, these services host so many pages that visitors may find that visiting your site is way too slow. Free hosting services are a good alternative if you want to publish a small, personal site, such as a community for your friends and family.

Watch Out!
Once you find a clip-art graphic that you want to use, open your browser's pop-up menu over the image and choose Save Image As (Navigator) or Save Picture As (Internet Explorer) to snag a copy of it. Since it's so easy to save graphics from the Web, you must be careful only to get images that you're sure are copyright-free. Clip-art sites usually post a notice about how their images can be used and what kind of credit you should give; follow these instructions to the letter. If you're unsure of an image's copyright, don't use it. Also, avoid using clip art from the Web on business sites, as it's usually not licensed for commercial use.

Figure 15.9
GeoCities, a free
Web hosting ser-
vice, hosts more
than 2.5 million
(and growing) Web
sites; each page
must carry
GeoCities' adver-
tising, like the ads
on the main page.

Bright Idea
You don't have to
publish your home
pages to a Web
server in order to
make good use of
them. Just use a
free HTML editor,
such as Composer
or FrontPage
Express, to design
a personal portal
that you access
from your local
hard drive. A start
page that you
make yourself
loads faster and is
better customized
to your likes than
any portal site
that you can
access on the
Web.

If you decide to go with a free hosting service, check Table
15.4 for some places to start. This is just a small selection of the
more popular free hosts; more than 100 places offered free
Web site space at my last count. For a more complete list, go to
`http://www.freeindex.com/webspace/index.html`; this list also
describes how much server space you get, restrictions, and supported Web site design tools to help you narrow your choices.
Be sure to visit the home page of each service that you're considering, look at the kinds of sites each hosts, and read the
terms of service before signing up with any free service.

TABLE 15.4: FREE WEB SITE HOSTING SERVICES

Free Web Site Host	URL
Angelfire Communications	`http://www.angelfire.com/`
Crosswinds	`http://www.crosswinds.net/`
GeoCities	`http://www.geocities.com/`
The Globe	`http://www.theglobe.com/`
Homestead	`http://www.homestead.com/`
Xoom	`http://xoom.com/home/`

The next step is to rent Web server space from a commercial Web hosting service. This is a good choice if you plan to
publish a large set of pages or pages that require a lot of storage space, or if your Web site is in any way commercial. Web

site hosts also provide valuable services that an ISP or free hosting service may not, such as technical support, security features, your own domain name, support for Java and CGI scripts, and 24-hour monitoring. Generally, prices run from $15–$50 per month, with a setup fee of $25–$50, but these rates may vary considerably depending on how much server space you require and how much traffic your site will get. The best place to start searching for a commercial hosting service is the Ultimate Web Host List at `http://www.webhostlist.com/`.

Hosting the Site Yourself

Often, only businesses running very large, high-traffic Web sites need their own Web servers. But for the kind of Web site you may be dreaming of, a hosting service may be too limiting. For instance, the Web site host may not support programming tools like Java or CGI. Your site may be so large that the cost of renting Web server space is prohibitive, or you may want your site to interact with a large database. Or a Web site host may not give you the amount of control over your own site that you'd like.

If you don't mind a little extra work, you can easily find low-cost or free server software that you can host on your own computer. Check out the following programs:

- **NetPresenz:** This simple program can function as an FTP, Gopher, or Web server. It features security protection for the nonpublic areas of your computer, and it has full CGI scripting support. Mac OS 7.0; shareware ($10); `http://www.stairways.com/netpresenz/`.

- **Personal Web Server:** Provided by Microsoft, this Web server is designed for hosting small, personal sites. It supports the HTTP and FTP protocols, as well as CGI scripts. Windows 95/98/NT; free; `http://www.microsoft.com/Windows/ie/pws/default.htm`.

Watch Out!
Free home pages have acquired a reputation for amateurishness and a lack of useful content. GeoCities was recently referred to as "the trailer park of the Internet," for instance. I wouldn't let this reputation stop me from visiting a page on GeoCities or on any other free Web site host—there are bad sites and good sites all over—but some people might. If the reputation of your host is important to you—particularly if you're putting a business online—consider renting Web server space from a commercial host instead.

Timesaver
Always keep a copy of your Web pages on your local disk, even if you publish them to a Web server. Not only does this make it easier to edit your pages, but it also ensures that you have a backup in case the server crashes.

Bright Idea
Millions of people surf the Web, including those with disabilities. Make sure that your pages are accessible to everyone by visiting Bobby at `http://www.cast. org/bobby/`. This free service analyzes your pages and suggests how to make them more accessible to those with disabilities; it also checks download times and compatibility with different browsers. If none of the pages on your site contains accessibility errors, you can display the Bobby-Approved graphic.

- **TinyWeb Server:** A simple but functional Web server, this one can handle HTTP requests, execute CGI scripts, and keep logs, and it requires only a small portion of your computer's resources. For security, you can also get TinySSL, a free Secure Sockets Layer server, from the same source. Windows 95/98/NT; free; `http://www.ritlabs.com/ tinyweb/`.

Note that these servers are designed for hosting small to mid-sized Web sites, anything from a set of personal home pages to a small business site to an advertising-supported site with a limited number of pages and other elements. If you're planning to implement a large Web site, such as a site for a large business or store, or one that receives a heavy amount of Internet traffic, you'll probably need to invest in a commercial Web server, such as WebSTAR or Netscape FastTrack Server. A good place to start shopping is ServerWatch (`http://serverwatch.internet. com/home.html`), which rates servers on reliability, performance, and other factors and provides details on price, market share, and system requirements.

Before setting up a personal Web server, you should be aware of the hidden costs. In addition to the server software, you need a dedicated connection to the Internet, so that your site is accessible to Web surfers 24 hours a day. This means that your monthly ISP bill will be higher, and you will have to install a second phone line if you don't already have one.

You don't have to register a domain name for your server, but if you don't, you're stuck with whatever name your ISP gives you, usually something like `yourname.ispname.net`. Registering a domain name, which gives you an address like `www.yourname.com`, will cost you $35 per year (for more information about domain name registration, go to `http://www. networksolutions.com/`). You'll also have to pay your ISP an additional fee to maintain the Domain Name Service (DNS) for you.

Maintaining Your Site

After your site is up and running, your job isn't over. The best sites are constantly evolving, which means that you must update your site regularly. You don't have to spend a lot of time on it, but a little regular maintenance keeps your site fresh and keeps visitors coming back.

One important part of site maintenance is keeping everything organized. Grouping related pages and their graphics into subdirectories helps you keep track of where things are and makes it easier to find pages that need updating. You should also maintain the integrity of your site—check for "orphan" pages that are no longer linked to anything, for instance.

But the most important job is staying on top of those links. You already know how quickly things change on the Web, with Web sites moving around or going off the air all the time. Updating the links in your Web pages to reflect these changes keeps your site fresh and usable.

This sounds like a lot of work, but fortunately many low-cost link-checking and search-and-replace tools can help automate the job. Full-featured site-management tools that validate HTML code, check for orphan files, maintain site maps, and otherwise help you keep up with the organization and integrity of your site can cost $100 or more. These tools are best suited to large, complex sites, though—not a small set of personal home pages.

Link Checkers

Checking for dead or changed hyperlinks is the most important—and most time-consuming—aspect of site maintenance. If your home pages have more than a handful of links, you definitely need to get a bot to help you with the job. A link-checker bot crawls along all the links in your site, checking outside links, links among local pages, and links to images. When it's finished, the link checker displays a report describing which links are down and which have relocated to a new address (see Figure 15.10). Then, you can quickly go through your site and fix the bad links.

Figure 15.10

A link checker like Linkbot Express checks all the links in your Web site and returns a report of the results.

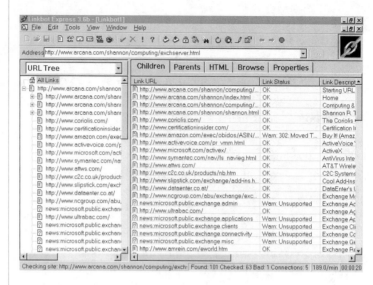

See Table 15.5 for a list of the best link checkers.

TABLE 15.5: RECOMMENDED LINK CHECKERS

Link Checker	System Requirements	Cost	Download URL
Big Brother	Mac OS 7.5	Free	`http://pauillac.inria.fr/~fpottier/brother.html.en`
LinkCop	Windows 95/98/NT 4.0	$29.95 (30-day demo available)	`http://linkcop.com/`

Watch Out!

Avoid changing your pages' file-names or moving them among directories or Web servers. As others start to visit your pages, they'll add them to their bookmarks or link to them from their own sites. If you frequently move or rename your pages, loyal visitors will be unable to find them the next time they follow the bookmark or click on the link. If you absolutely must move your pages—if you're switching Web site hosts, for instance—include a notice at the old location with a link to the new URL, so that visitors can update bookmarks and links.

Search-and-Replace Tools

Often, you must change one thing on several of your Web pages. You may need to adjust a navigational link, background image, text color, or page signature, for instance. Instead of editing each page individually (and perhaps introducing mistakes), get a search-and-replace tool that will globally search for and replace whatever you tell it to. Check out the following search-and-replace tools:

- **HTML Grinder:** An overall site-management tool that enables you to create indexes, navigational maps, labels, date stamps, and other stuff for your Web pages. The full version costs $89, but if you download the demo version, you get to keep the Global Find and Replace tool, no strings attached. Mac OS 7; free; `http://www.matterform.com/grinder/`.

- **Search and Replace:** Not only can search and replace within your Web pages, but also inside any files on your computer, making it a handy overall utility. Windows 3.x/95/98/NT; shareware ($25); `http://www.funduc.com/search_replace.htm`.

Just the Facts

- Your personal Web site can actually be useful—it can serve as a customized portal to the Web, provide information about you to colleagues and employers, or act as a gathering place for friends and family.

- You don't have to spend a lot of money on the tools needed to create a Web site; HTML editors, graphic utilities, developmental tools, clip art, and sample scripts can often be found on the Internet for a small fee or free.

- You have several choices when it comes to getting your site on the Web: take advantage of a free hosting service or Web server space offered by your ISP; rent space from a commercial hosting service; or run your Web server.

Timesaver
When you finish your Web site, check all the HTML code to be sure that it's accurate. This is a time-consuming task to perform manually, so have an HTML validator do the job for you in a fraction of the time. My favorite is Dr. Watson at `http://watson.addy.com/`, which not only checks the HTML code, but also verifies links, spell-checks, checks compatibility with search engines, estimates download times, and finds out how many pages have linked to yours. Best of all, it's free! Enter your page's URL into the form and select what you want to check (your page must be on a Web server).

GET THE SCOOP ON...
Announcing a new site ▪ Getting listed on search
engines ▪ Targeting site promotion to an interested
audience

Promoting Your Site

Chapter 16

O NCE YOU'VE PUT TOGETHER a Web site, whether it's a personal home page, a commercial site, or a publication of ad-supported content, you've got the get the word out. Even if your site is packed with outstanding content and cutting-edge design, no one will come if they don't know it's there.

Of course, you don't have to promote your Web site. If you've created a personal portal or a family- or work-oriented resource, promotion isn't really necessary, other than giving the URL to those who need it. But if you want to attract an audience, promotion is key.

Promoting a Web site can be a confusing process, though. How do you get your URL listed in search engines? What are banner-exchange programs? What's the most effective way to announce a new site? This chapter answers all those questions and more, taking away the mysteries behind Web site promotion. The techniques described in this chapter are tailored to personal home pages and content-driven sites; owners of Web stores and other business sites may have to put quite a lot more effort (and money) behind their promotion campaigns.

Watch Out!
Be wary of any company that charges to promote your site. You may end up paying too much or even getting scammed. For instance, some companies charge thousands of dollars to register your domain name when you can do it yourself for 70 bucks. Others charge hundreds of dollars to submit your site to search engines without guaranteeing the results. Unless you're running a commercial site, it's probably not worthwhile to pay for site promotion. If you do decide to go with one of these services, check it out carefully with customers, the Better Business Bureau, and other outside sources before signing up.

Announcing a New Site

Several announcement services exist to tell the Internet community about new sites. Most of these are email newsletters and Usenet newsgroups that post the new site announcements they receive. When you first open your site to the world, you should announce it in these venues. First, though, follow these tips to ensure that your announcement gets the best response:

- **Be sure that your site is ready to be opened to the public.** It does no good to announce a new site when you don't have anything online for visitors to see—they won't come back a second time. Be sure that your entire site is on the Web and has been checked over before sending out announcements.

- **Write a brief description of your site.** Have an interesting, snappy description ready that you can reuse at all the announcement services. The description should be brief—less than 25 words. Don't throw it away when you're done with this step; you can reuse it when submitting your site to search engines and other places.

- **Include a subject line that concisely describes your site.** Since most announcement services are newsgroups and email newsletters, readers use the subject of the announcement to determine whether they're interested in the site. A short but descriptive subject line communicates what your site is all about and brings in more visitors.

- **Don't forget the URL.** Many people forget to list the all-important site address in their announcements.

- **Read the announcement service's guidelines carefully before sending in your announcement.** Some services don't allow commercial sites; others focus on a narrow audience, such as educators or academics. Exactly follow whatever guidelines are given, or your site won't be announced.

Table 16.1 lists some places where you should definitely announce a new site. The URL leads to the announcement service's Web site where the guidelines are located; often, you can post your announcement using an online form at the Web site. Any restrictions are also noted.

TABLE 16.1: IMPORTANT WEB SITE ANNOUNCEMENT SERVICES

Announcement Service	URL	Restrictions
comp.infosystems. www.announce (newsgroup)	http://boutell.com/ ~grant/charter.html	No commercial sites
Net-Happenings (newsletter and newsgroup)	http://scout.cs.wisc. edu/caservices/ net-hap/index.html	Announces sites of interest to the K–12 community
Netsurfer Digest (newsletter)	http://www.netsurf. com/nsd/index.html	Announces selected sites only
Scout Report (newsletter)	http://scout.cs.wisc. edu/report/sr/current/ index.html	Announces sites of interest to researchers and educators; selected sites only
Starting Point (Web page)	http://www.stpt. com/general/ newsite.html	None
What's New (Web page)	http://www. whatsnu.com/	None
What's New at Netscape (Web page)	http://home. netscape.com/ netcenter/new.html	Announces selected sites only
What's New Too (Web page)	http://newtoo. manifest.com/	None

Timesaver
Once your site is up and running, you need to know how many people are visiting, where they come from, and which pages they're viewing. This information will be helpful when coming up with new promotion ideas, redesigning your site, or accepting advertisements. Your Web site host should provide server logs that give you this information, but they can be difficult to decipher. Log-analysis tools simplify the task. I suggest getting either Analog for Mac OS 7.0 or NetIntellect Lite for Windows 95/98/NT; both are free and available from your favorite software search engine.

Listing Your Site on Search Sites

As you already know, many Web surfers make a search engine their first stop when looking for something specific on the Web. Consequently, you should ensure that your site is included in the search engine's database of sites so that it will turn up when others are looking for sites like yours.

Bright Idea
If your site is hosted by a free service or your ISP, you may have a long, hard-to-remember URL. A shorter URL will probably bring in more traffic—especially when announcing the site in news-groups, mailing lists, and offline—because there's not so much to retype. Several free services will give you a shorter URL, such as `http://come.to/yourpage/`, which is a lot easier to remember. You also get a free list-ing in the redirec-tion service's directory. Try one of the following: `http://webalias.com/;` `http://click-on.to/home.html;` or `http://come.to/.` (You may be required to display ads for the redi-rection service on your site.)

How to Get Listed

All search engines use a bot to create their indices of Web sites. The bot crawls through the Web along hyperlinks, indexing every page it finds for its database. Eventually, the bot will probably index your pages as well, but you can't count on it. Therefore, you need to tell the search engine to send the bot to your URL and index your pages. This is a pretty simple process, and you should be able to submit your URL to the major search engines for indexing in a few minutes.

Web site directories work a little differently. Some of them, such as Galaxy, add every submitted site to the directory. Others, such as Yahoo!, review submitted sites and only add a selected few. The submission process differs from directory to directory, but generally it's a matter of going to the site and fill-ing out a long submission form.

Search Engines

Submitting your site's URL to search engines ensures that your site will be indexed for the search engine's database the next time the bot comes around. Usually, all you have to do is tell the search engine the URL for the main page of your site. Take HotBot as an example:

1. Open `http://www.hotbot.com/addurl.asp` (the submission page). Most search engines have an Add URL or Add Site link on their main pages that takes you to the submission page (see Figure 16.1).

2. Type the main URL for your site in the URL to Add box.

3. Type your email address in the Your Email Address box.

4. Click the Add My URL button.

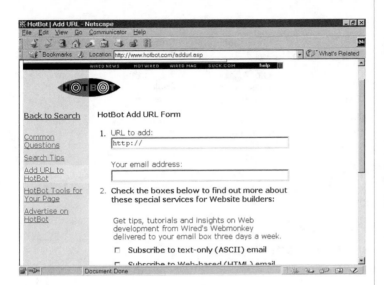

Figure 16.1
Submitting a URL
to HotBot.

Timesaver
When submitting
to search engines,
you only have to
enter the main
URL of your site—
the one that con-
nects to all your
other pages. The
bots for most
search engines,
such as HotBot,
will crawl through
all the links on
your main page
and index every
page in your site.
However, some
search engines,
like AltaVista, only
index the first two
or three levels of
your site. If impor-
tant pages are
located deeper
inside, you should
submit those URLs
separately.

Table 16.2 lists the submission pages for each of the major search engines. The table also tells you approximately how long it takes to get your site indexed and how frequently the database is refreshed, or when changes to your site are updated in the search engine's database.

TABLE 16.2: SEARCH ENGINE URL SUBMISSION PAGES

Search Engine	Submission Page	Turnaround Time	Database Refresh
AltaVista	http:// altavista. digital.com/av/ content/addurl .htm	One to three days	Monthly or longer
Excite	http://www. excite.com/ info/add_url/	Two to four weeks	One to three weeks
HotBot	http://www. hotbot.com/ addurl.asp	Two to four weeks	Weekly
Infoseek	http://www. infoseek.com/; click the Add URL link at the bottom of the page	One to three days	Every three weeks

continues

Watch Out!
Two weeks after submitting your URL, run a search for it in all the major search engines. If you don't find it, keep submitting your URL and checking back until it shows up. After that, you only need to resubmit your URL to all the major search engines whenever there is a major change to your site, such as a URL change or an extensive content change. You also should submit changed URLs, descriptions, or categories to any Web site directories where you have a listing.

TABLE 16.2: CONTINUED

Search Engine	Submission Page	Turnaround Time	Database Refresh
Lycos	http://www.lycos.com/addasite.html	One to three weeks	One to two weeks
Northern Light	http://www.northernlight.com/docs/register.htm	Two to three weeks	Every two weeks
WebCrawler	http://www.webcrawler.com/info/add_url/	Three to four weeks	Weekly

Yahoo! and Other Web Site Directories

Yahoo! is probably one of the most popular places on the Web for finding new sites. It's also one of the most difficult places to get your site listed. Yahoo! editors visit every submitted site personally and ensure that the site is appropriate for the directory to placed in the correct categories. Definitely submit your site to Yahoo!—if you do get listed, the listing will quite possibly generate more traffic for your site than all the search engines combined.

The submission process for Yahoo! is a bit more difficult than for the search engines. Follow these steps:

1. Connect to Yahoo! at http://www.yahoo.com/ and locate at least one category that your site fits into (if you have sub-sites, submit them separately). The best way to do this is to search for the categories that match your site's content. There are three rules that you must follow when choosing categories:

   • Business and commercial sites must go somewhere in the Business and Economy: Companies hierarchy.

   • Local or regionally specific sites must go in the Regional hierarchy.

   • Personal home pages must go in the Society and Culture: People: Personal Home Pages category.

2. Choose the most appropriate, most specific category, and open that category's page (note any other categories that your site also belongs in).

3. At the bottom of the page, find the Suggest a Site link and click it.

4. Click the Proceed to Step One button.

5. Fill out the fields under Site Information (see Figure 16.2); you must provide a title, a URL, and a brief description of your site (use the same description you wrote for the announcement services). Be sure that you follow all the rules when entering the description, or your site won't be listed.

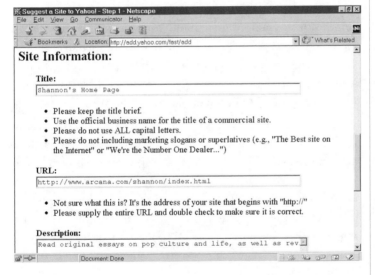

Figure 16.2
Submitting a Web site to Yahoo!.

Timesaver
It seems to be much easier to get your site listed in Yahoo! if it belongs in the Personal Home Pages category. Also, if your site has any local or regional interest whatsoever, fill out the Geographical Information section of the submission form; Yahoo! is much more likely to list sites in a local directory than in the main directory.

6. Click the Proceed to Step Two button.

7. In the first text box, enter the name of any other matching categories you found. You can also suggest new categories in the second text box (be sure that your suggestion is a subcategory of an existing hierarchy).

8. Click the Proceed to Step Three button.

9. Fill out your contact information accurately.

10. If your site is of local or regional interest, fill out the Geographical Information section; this may get your site listed in the Get Local area of Yahoo!.

11. Click the Proceed to Step Four button.

12. If your site will only be online for a brief time, enter the appropriate information. You also get the chance to provide any final comments at this point.

13. Click the Submit button to submit your site for consideration.

Bright Idea
The best source of site redesign and promotion ideas is visitors to your site. Include a feedback form on your main page that asks visitors what they like and dislike about your site, offering specific choices like content, graphics, and navigation. Respond personally to everyone who writes, and use the good suggestions that you get. It's also helpful to turn email questions and their answers into a FAQ for your site.

Because a person actually visits each submission, it may take from six to eight weeks for your site to appear in Yahoo!'s directory (or it may not appear at all). If you can't find your site in Yahoo! eight weeks after submitting it, try submitting again with the same information. You can submit your site to Yahoo! as many times as you like without penalty, so you should keep trying until you get in. Once you're in, Yahoo! won't ever remove you unless you inform the directory's maintainers that your site has been taken off the Web.

The submission process for most other Web-site directories is similar to that for Yahoo!, although the submission form usually isn't nearly so long. The most important step is to determine which categories of the directory your site belongs in before submitting. Table 16.3 lists the submission pages and criteria for other Web-site directories where you should try listing your site. As you surf the Web, look for other directories and submit your site wherever you can; you can't have too many links to your site.

TABLE 16.3: SUBMISSION PAGES FOR MAJOR WEB-SITE DIRECTORIES

Directory	Submission Page	Submission Criteria
About.Com	`http://www.about.com/`; find the guide that your site best fits in and email an announcement to the guide's editor.	Adds editor-selected only

Galaxy	http://galaxy. einet.net/galaxy .html; find the best category and click the Add Your Site link.	Adds all submissions
LookSmart	http://www. looksmart.com/; find the category that best fits your site and click the Submit button.	No pornographic or offensive sites
Magellan	http://www. mckinley.com/ magellan/Info/ addsite.html	Adds all submissions to the database; editors choose reviewed sites
Snap	http://www.snap. com/; choose the best category and click the Submit link at the bottom of the page.	Adds editor-selected sites only
WWW Virtual Library	http://vlib.org/ Overview.html; find the category that your site best fits in and email an announcement to the category's editor.	Adds editor-selected sites only

Moneysaver
You're probably wondering how you can make extra cash with your site. Two popular methods for smaller sites are to join an affiliate program or sell click-based banner advertising. In an affiliate program, you set up links to products at an online store, such as Amazon.Com, and get a commission for each sale made through your site. With click-based advertising, you receive a commission every time a visitor clicks a banner ad at your site. Unless your site gets a lot of traffic, you may not see much of a return. You might do better if you put a lot of effort into promoting and developing your site. These programs also work best if you target a niche audience.

Automating the Job

It's not much of a chore to submit your URL to the major search engines—it shouldn't take you more than a few minutes. To prevent errors, you should manually submit your site to every search engine where you want to ensure a listing—all the major ones, in other words. You must also manually submit your site to Yahoo! and the other Web-site directories to ensure that your site is placed in the best categories and has an appropriate description.

After you've hit the major search engines and Web-site directories, though, how do you get your site listed in the hundreds of smaller and specialized search engines? You probably don't want to add your URL to all of those manually; it could literally take you forever. That's where submission tools come in. These software programs automatically submit your site's URL to hundreds of search engines and Web-site directories (see Figure 16.3).

Figure 16.3
AddWeb automatically submits your site to more than 1,500 search engines.

Watch Out!
I don't recommend the Web-based search engine submission services like Submit It! (http://www. submit-it.com/) and Add Me! (http://www.addme. com/). These services tend to be a lot more expensive than the software programs, and you can submit only once for the price. They do offer free submission to the 20 or so most popular search engines, but they ask for way too much personal information, such as phone numbers, fax numbers, and mailing addresses; some of these services have earned a reputation for spamming. You could just as easily submit to these 20 places yourself.

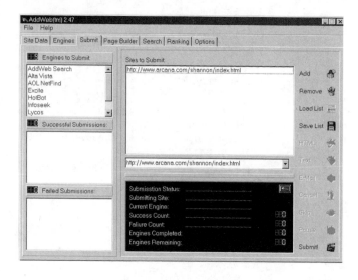

Some search engine submission tools can cost as much as $100. I recommend that you don't pay too much for these tools—get a free trial or a low-cost shareware version. The high price is not really worth it for promoting personal home pages, especially when you consider that these tools can't ensure good results. A free alternative, if you've got a lot of time on your hands, is to go to http://www.mmgco.com/wsrev195.html and individually register at all of the top 100 sites listed.

The following are the better freeware and shareware automated submission agents:

- **AddWeb:** This is the highest rated of the search engine submission agents. It supports over 1,500 search engines, and you get one year of free updates to that list. AddWeb can also generate META tags and check your Web site's ranking in different search engines. Windows 95/98/NT 4.0; $59 (trial version submits your site to 9 major search engines); http://www.cyberspacehq.com/addweb/home.htm.

- **SoftSpider WebPromotion Tool:** The full version submits your site to more than 1,100 sites. Free updates are delivered automatically every two weeks. Windows 95/98/NT; $49.95 (the free version submits your site to 5 randomly selected search engines); http://www.designmaker.com/tools/.

- **Submission Wizard:** The registered version submits your site to more than 900 search engines. You get monthly search engine updates and a report on which search engines accepted your submission. Windows 3.x/95/98/NT; pricing starts at $30 per month (free version limits submissions to 20 search engines); http://www.submissions.com/.

Improving Your Position in Search Results

Just submitting your URL to search engines doesn't guarantee that thousands of people will beat a path to your site. You must also ensure that your site appears attractive in the search results, so that others will click that all-important link to you. Different search engines use various parts of your page's HTML code to determine where to place your site in the search results and the site description that is displayed. Understanding how search engines do this can help you design a Web page that communicates to users what the page is about and invites them in.

Search engine bots check two important areas of your page for indexing keywords and displaying descriptions of Web sites: the title and opening text of the page; and the META tags. Learning how to manipulate these areas of your page for search-engine compatibility ensures that your page ranks higher in search results and that a coherent description of your page displays in those search results, so that Web surfers can tell at a glance what your page is about. Put all these techniques to work in your pages to be sure that you cover all your bases. Some search engines rely more heavily upon META tags than others, and some don't check META tags at all, for example.

Bright Idea
Are you curious about your site's ranking in the search results of various search engines? Go to http://www.rankthis.com/. In the left frame, enter the important keywords and the URL of your site; then, click the search engine that you want to check. Rank This! tells you whether your site is in the top 200 and which sites beat you for the coveted top spots. You can also find tips for improving your ranking.

Using META Tags

META tags appear in the header of your page. They're invisible to anyone looking at the page itself, but they are very visible to search engines. Search engine bots look at two important META tags:

- The keywords tag specifies the keywords that search robots give precedence to when indexing your page.

- The description tag provides a short summary of your page that appears in search results; this description can be more focused than an excerpt from the page itself. The 25-word description that you created at the beginning of this chapter would fit perfectly here.

Look at the META tags for my Voodoo Information Pages, for instance:

```
<HEAD>
<META NAME="description" CONTENT="Information resource
about the religion of vodun, or voodoo.">
<META NAME="keywords" CONTENT="voodoo, vodun, religion,
mythology, loa, houngan, mambo, magic, black magic,
rituals, possession, death, ceremonies, zombies">
<TITLE>Vodoo Information Pages</TITLE>
</HEAD>
```

If someone searched for one or more words listed in the keywords tag, my Voodoo Information Pages would most likely turn up in the search results. Instead of seeing the first few words from the page, which are navigational and don't say much about the page's content, they'd see the short, accurate summary listed in the description tag. As you can see, META tags play a huge role in determining how search engines present your site.

The most important part of writing META tags is coming up with good keywords—words others might search for when looking for a site like yours. Follow these tips to come up with effective keywords:

- Include both general and specific words and short phrases related to your site.

Timesaver
Just so you know, the following search engines use META tags to index and describe sites: AltaVista, HotBot, Infoseek, Northern Light, and WebCrawler.

- Use from three to fifteen keywords, no more; when you specify fewer keywords, each one has more importance, so your site will appear closer to the top of the search results for those keywords.

- Never use irrelevant keywords; you'll just tick off people who come to your site expecting to find something that's not there.

- Use each keyword only once; some search engines ban sites that repeat keywords, considering this to be spam.

- Use plurals when appropriate; many people search for the plural form of noun keywords. Your site still appears when someone searches for the singular form of the word.

- Put related keywords next to each other; some search engines index both the individual words and the words together as a phrase.

- Customize the keywords and description tags for each page on your site; this enables users to find more specific information deeper in your site.

If you use Composer or FrontPage Express as your HTML editor, it's a simple matter to code META tags for your page. In Composer, follow these steps:

1. Select Format, Page Colors and Properties; the Page Properties dialog box opens on the General tab (see Figure 16.4).

2. In the Title field, enter a descriptive title for your page.

3. In the Author field, enter your name.

4. Enter a short description of your site in the Description field.

5. Enter search keywords in the Keywords field; separate each keyword with a comma.

6. Click OK.

Bright Idea
Once you create your META tags, go to Meta Medic at http://www. northernwebs. com/set/ setsimjr.html to test them. This free service checks the effectiveness of your META tags and suggests ways to improve descriptions and keywords. To start, enter the URL in the form (you have to scroll down to the very bottom of the page), and click Process URL.

Figure 16.4
Adding description
and keyword META
tags in Composer.

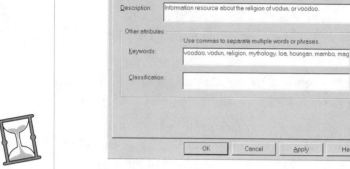

Figure 16.4
Adding description
and keyword META
tags in Composer.

Timesaver
You can also use
the robots META
tag to tell search
engine bots and
other bots visiting
your site how to
behave. If you
don't want the
robot to index a
personal or test
page, for instance,
use this tag: `<META
NAME="robots"
CONTENT=
"noindex">`. You
can even ask bots
to come back after
a certain period of
time, saving you
from having to
resubmit your URL
for indexing when
there are major
content changes.
To do this, insert
the following tags:
`<META
NAME="robots"
CONTENT="all">
<META NAME=
"revisit-after"
CONTENT="14
days">`.

The process is not quite as intuitive in FrontPage Express. Follow these steps:

1. Select File, Page Properties; the Page Properties dialog box opens.

2. Enter a descriptive title for the page in the Title field.

3. Click the Custom tab.

4. Under User Variables, click the Add button.

5. Type **description** in the Name field (see Figure 16.5).

6. Enter a description of your page in the Value field.

7. Click OK; the description META tag appears in the User Variables window.

8. Click the Add button again.

9. In the Name field, type **keywords**.

10. In the Value field, enter the keywords for your Web page, separating each with a comma.

11. Click OK; the keywords META tag appears in the User Variable window (see Figure 16.6).

12. Click OK.

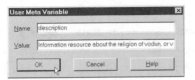

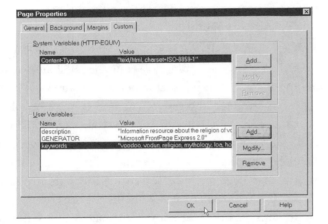

Figure 16.5
Adding the
description META
tag in FrontPage
Express.

Figure 16.6
The User Variables
window displays the
META tags that
you've created.

Making Your Pages Search Engine–Friendly

You need to pay careful attention to two other important areas of your Web page: the title and the opening paragraph. Even if you've already carefully crafted your META tags, you must optimize these areas as well. Some search engines disregard META tags altogether. Instead, they use the title and opening paragraph to gather all the important information about your page.

The title of the page is the most important part. The TITLE tag goes in the page header, and the specified title displays at the very top of the Web browser when the page is open. The page title builds name recognition, gives visitors their first clue as to what the site is about, and draws them in. Page titles are displayed at the beginning of each search result. If your page's title is obscure, cryptic, or missing, no one will click through to the page itself—I guarantee it.

The opening paragraph and title should contain all the important keywords for your page—the same ones that you used in the keywords META tag. Many search engines don't

Bright Idea
If your Web site reflects a mixture of interests, you could create multiple versions of your main page, with the title, opening paragraph, and META tags of each version slanted at a different audience. Suppose your site is a place for job seekers to post résumés and look for job openings. One version could target people looking for jobs, and another could target employers with openings to fill.

Watch Out!
The desire for high search engine rankings has spawned a new form of spam. Search-engine spamming can take many forms: stuffing META tags with keywords that don't relate to the site's content; copying the META tags of other sites that receive high rankings; and repeating keywords by putting them in comment tags, printing them in the same color as the page's background, or inserting a text block at the very bottom of the page. Don't attempt these tricks—they'll backfire. Many search engines, most notably Infoseek and HotBot, avoid indexing or penalize the rankings of pages that repeat keywords too many times or use keywords that don't relate to the page's content.

index the page beyond the first 200 characters. Putting important keywords in the first few sentences, or in the title of the page itself ensures that those keywords are associated with your page. Don't just make your title a list of keywords—this turns a lot of Internet users off. Instead, put the two or three most important keywords in the title, and scatter the rest throughout the opening paragraph.

Search engines that don't recognize META tags display the first 200 characters as a summary of your page. If a well-written paragraph is the first thing that appears on your page, it will also show up in the search results, prompting more people to visit because they know beforehand what your page is about. If instead you put a list of links or some pictures at the very top of the page, this displays as the summary. To see what I mean, go to any search engine and search for a common phrase. Check the first few results. I'll bet that the majority of them are incomprehensible nonsense because the page's author did not put a text paragraph about the page at the top of the page. If you do see something with a coherent summary, aren't you much more likely to click that link?

Also give your pages descriptive URLs. Some search engines place importance on keywords found in the URL, so name your HTML files accordingly. If your page is about *Star Wars*, for example, call it starwars.html, not index.html or page1.html.

Targeting Site Promotion

Now that I've devoted all that space to search engines, I have to say that they aren't the most effective places to promote your site. They're important, which is why you should go ahead and submit to them first. But you're going to draw in a lot more traffic if you obey the first principle of marketing—target your promotion efforts to those who'd be most interested.

You can do two free, simple things to target your site to an interested audience: announce your site to related mailing lists and newsgroups, and exchange links with related sites. This part of Web-site promotion is a never-ending process. Always be on the lookout for related venues that might mention your site, so you can continue getting the word out to an interested audience.

Targeting Mailing Lists and Newsgroups

As you know, there are thousands of Usenet newsgroups and email discussion lists covering every topic imaginable. Each of these groups has an audience of subscribers who might be interested in visiting your site, as long as your site relates to the group's topic of discussion.

Since newsgroup and mailing list readers have the most animosity toward spam or anything that seems like spam, you must take care not to offend members of the group when you tell them about your site. The following steps will help get the word out while not offending anyone:

1. Search for mailing lists and newsgroups related to your site.

2. Subscribe to the mailing lists and newsgroups you find, and monitor them for a while. Find out what the group's interests are and how they feel about Web-site announcements; read the FAQ as well.

3. When an appropriate subject comes up, post your URL in a way that doesn't seem like an advertisement. For instance, you have a site about rose gardening. On a rose-gardening newsgroup, someone asks a question that you know the answer to. In your reply, add a note that says something like this: "For more information on this, go to my Web site at..." This gets your URL out there and makes a valuable contribution to the group at the same time.

Bright Idea
You can promote your site every time you post a message to a mailing list or newsgroup *and* every time you send an email message. Just put your site's URL in your signature, along with a brief, one-sentence description that hooks the reader into visiting.

Trading Links

Exchanging links with related Web sites and getting your site listed on related hotlists is a very effective way to promote your site. The more links to your site there are on the Web, the more people will find you and come to check out your site. There are four general methods for exchanging links:

Watch Out!
At all costs, avoid
making a Web site
announcement
posted to a news-
group or mailing
list look like spam.
This will not only
prevent others
from visiting, but it
may earn your Web
site a bad reputa-
tion, which can be
poison on the
Internet. Anything
that is posted to
an inappropriate
forum—one that
isn't interested in
your site's topic—
or that overtly
resembles an ad
will be considered
spam by many.
Also, if you cross-
post to too many
newsgroups, your
message will look
like spam.

- Trade links directly with the owners of related sites.

- Get on webrings.

- Join banner exchange programs.

- Win awards.

Direct Link Exchanges

A direct exchange of links with sites that cover similar subjects as yours is the most effective way to promote your site, bar none. You'll accomplish two important goals: reach a targeted audience, and get links to your site out on the Web.

I know what you're thinking—those other sites are competing with me, so why should I link to them? The trick is to link to sites that you don't directly compete with. Point your site visitors to places where they can get more information in addition to what you provide. For instance, I maintain a set of pages about voodoo. In the links section, I connect to stores that sell voodoo-related stuff, Haitian art galleries, and information about other Caribbean and African religions—all sites that cover different aspects of the subject matter than I do. And many of those sites link back to mine. It's a win-win situation.

Here's what you should do to start exchanging links:

1. Set up a "related links" page on your site (if you haven't already). Organize the links and describe each one briefly, so that you have more than just a jumbled list of links.

2. Make a list of sites that are related to, but not in direct competition with, yours. Choose sites that seem to be similar in size, quality, and number of visitors.

3. Compose a short, personalized email message to the owner of each related site. Describe your site briefly, mention the URL so that the other site owner can check you out, and request a link exchange.

4. Honor your promises. Put up a link to the other site as soon as you get the go-ahead.

5. Check out the other site to ensure that there's a link back to your site. If the link hasn't appeared within a month, send a polite follow-up letter.

You can even find directories of sites that are looking for other sites to trade links with. Search these directories for likely link-trading partners or add your own site to the list. Start by visiting `http://www.exposepromotions.com/resources/reciprocaldirectory/`.

Webrings

Webrings are a new concept in site linking. A webring is a ring of sites on one subject—one site connects to the next, which connects to the next, and so on until you circle back to the beginning. Besides giving you a way to go back to the last site or forward to the next one, each site in the webring provides links to an index of the entire ring, a random site, and a list of the next five sites.

Webrings are most effective when you join one with an extremely narrow topic. If your site is about *Star Wars*, for instance, it's better to join a *Star Wars*–specific webring, rather than one about movies in general. Of course, you could join both. But be aware that you'll have to display the webring's graphics and links on your main page, which can take up quite a lot of space (see Figure 16.7). You must also meet the webring's specific requirements before joining, so be sure to read the guidelines.

Timesaver
You should keep tabs on sites that link to your site, because some-times links get lost when a site is redesigned. A quick way to do this is to use AltaVista, Infoseek, or HotBot to search for sites that contain links to your pages (return to Chapter 11, "Searching Savvy," to review how to set up this filter).

Figure 16.7
The navigational box for a webring.

Bright Idea
A very effective way to get and keep loyal site visitors is to make them site members. You can do this in many ways: Mail out an email newsletter that tells subscribers about site happenings and provides useful information; set up an interactive bulletin board or chat room; or hold contests, such as for the best poem or photo. Try to come up with your own ideas. Once you create a community based around your site, you've got a loyal audience.

If you want to join a webring, the following are some central directories where you can start finding the best rings for your site:

- **Looplink:** `http://www.looplink.com/`

- **RingSurf:** `http://www.ringsurf.com/`

- **The Rail:** `http://www.therail.com/cgi-bin/station/`

- **Webring:** `http://www.webring.org/` (the original webring site)

Banner Exchanges

You can't be on the Web long without noticing those banner ads everywhere. Some people find them unbearably annoying; others obviously think they're an effective way to advertise a Web site. If you're one of the former, you probably should skip this section altogether.

Most banner ads that appear on the smaller and mid-sized sites are not actually paid advertising. Rather, they're participants in a banner exchange. The principle behind a banner exchange is fairly simple—you display a randomly selected banner on your site, and your site's banner displays randomly on other sites all over the Web. You earn credits based on how many times a banner on your site is viewed. Each credit earns your banner a viewing on some other site. Banner exchanges also provide free tools for designing banners and traffic reports for your Web site.

Although banner exchanges have become quite popular, they do have some serious drawbacks you should consider before joining:

- The banners must appear at the top of your site's main page, inviting visitors to leave before they've even had a chance to look around your site.

- You can't control what the banner looks like; its colors may clash with your site's design, and if it's animated, it may annoy your visitors.

- You can't control what the banner is advertising; for instance, ads for adult sites may display on your Web page without your knowing.

- Since the banners load from another server, they really slow down your site.

- Banner ads may not be very effective advertising. It's not unusual for a banner ad to be displayed more than 100 times and receive just one click; I suspect that as Web surfers become more accustomed to (and annoyed by) banner ads, they'll click the ads even less often.

- You can't control where your banner appears, so it's not targeted advertising; more likely than not, your banner won't show up on sites whose audiences would be interested in your site. (Some banner exchange services do allow you to target a category of sites, though.)

If you do decide to participate in a banner exchange, I recommend one of the following:

- **EIS Banner Swap** (`http://einets.com/stats/gsa/`): This exchange service displays your banner once each time a banner on your site is viewed; this is the highest ratio offered by any banner-exchange service.

- **LinkBuddies** (`http://www.linkbuddies.com/`): This service uses bigger banners than other exchanges. It displays your banner three times for every four banners viewed on your page and gives you 500 credits just for joining. It also doesn't accept adult advertising.

- **LinkExchange** (`http://adnetwork.linkexchange.com/`): The most popular banner-exchange service, LinkExchange displays your banner once for every two banners viewed on your site. It also allows targeted advertising.

Watch Out!
Designing an effective banner ad is not easy. Here are some tips:
- Keep your message short.
- Use attention-getting words.
- Put "click here" on the banner.
- Keep the banner's size under 15KB.
- Change or rotate banners periodically to keep them fresh.

Timesaver
If you want to make a banner ad in a hurry, but you don't know how to begin, get CoolBE Light. This free program for Windows 3.x/95/98 helps you design catchy ads with animated designs. Download it from `http://www.CoolBE.com/`.

Winning Awards

Receiving an award can be an effective way to increase traffic to your site, and it can give your site a little prestige. Hundreds of award programs are on the Web, and they vary greatly in who they give awards to, what they base awards on, and their popularity. In return for the award, the award giver wants you to display a graphic on your site that links back to the award-giving site (see Figure 16.8). This is just another form of link exchange—you get a link on the award giver's site in exchange for a link back to their site.

Figure 16.8
Awards that my site has won.

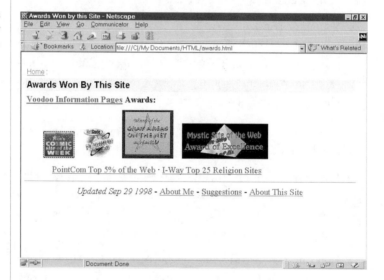

There are more awards programs than you or I could keep up with. Some of them are quite prestigious, which means that a lot of people check out the reviewed sites. You may want to submit your site to these programs for consideration (they are listed in Table 16.4). Don't waste your time submitting your site to every award program out there (unless you have a lot of time on your hands). But if you do receive an award out of the blue—and you will if your site is popular or cool—be grateful. It's free advertising.

TABLE 16.4: PRESTIGIOUS AWARDS PROGRAMS

Award	URL
Cool Site of the Day	`http://cool.infi.net/`
Dr. Webster's Web Site of the Day	`http://www.drwebster.com/`
Lycos Top 5% of the Web	`http://point.lycos.com/ categories/index.html`
Project Cool Sightings	`http://www.projectcool.com/ sightings/`
Too Cool	`http://www.toocool.com/`
Your WebScout	`http://www.webscout.com/`

Before you submit your site for consideration for these bigger awards, make sure you're not wasting your time. Awards are most often given to sites that are rich in content, offer useful information or services, are frequently updated, and are well designed. Award-winning sites have that indefinable quality called "coolness," as well. Pages that are basically lists of links or multimedia-heavy sites need not apply. Many awards programs have their own specialized guidelines, as well, so it helps to look at other sites that have won the award to see if they're similar to yours.

If you do have that free afternoon and want to spend it submitting your site for awards, go to `http://www.focusa.com/ awardsites/menu.htm`. This site rates more than 1,200 awards programs, previews the award graphics, and describes the requirements for winning. There's also a list of specialized awards divided by subject.

Just the Facts

- When your site is ready for publication, post to the popular announcement services; many people watch these lists to find new sites to visit.

- It's important that the major search engines and Web-site directories index your site; descriptive META tags, page titles, and opening paragraphs can greatly improve your site's position in the search results

Watch Out!
You don't have to display those large award graphics on your main page—they may slow page loading and clash with your existing design. I suggest creating a separate awards page where you can put the award badges in one place, out of the way.

- The most effective form of site promotion is targeting interested audiences via related mailing lists and newsgroups and by exchanging links with related sites.

Glossary

A

Active Desktop   Component of Windows 98 and Windows NT 5.0 that integrates the desktop with the Web, replacing the Windows Explorer with Internet Explorer and enabling the desktop to display active content and other Web-like elements; Windows 95 and Windows NT 4.0 users may upgrade to the Active Desktop by installing the Windows Desktop Update.

Active Server Pages (ASP)   Specification developed by Microsoft for dynamically generating Web pages when the browser requests them, so that they can differ depending on the user, situation, or any other variable.

ActiveX   Set of technologies developed by Microsoft for adding interactivity and functionality to Web pages; ActiveX technologies encompass Active Server Pages and ActiveX controls, among other technologies, and are natively supported by Internet Explorer.

ActiveX control   Small program embedded in a Web page that can be downloaded and run automatically by an ActiveX-enabled browser, such as Internet Explorer.

add-on   Software program that works with another program, complementing and adding to the original program's features; many add-ons are available for Navigator and Internet Explorer, for instance.

Address Book   Email program component that stores names and addresses of frequent correspondents, as well as personal distribution lists.

agent   See *bot*.

AIFF   File format for storing sampled sound; AIFF was developed by Apple and is the standard audio format on the Macintosh. (Short for *Audio Interchange File Format*.)

American Standard Code for Information Interchange   See *ASCII*.

animated GIF   A kind of Web page graphic that is animated by combining several GIF graphics in one file and playing them in sequence; although the animations are usually simple, they are widely used on the Web because they download quickly and don't require a special player.

anonymous remailer   Service that strips out the sender's name and email address in an email message and then forwards it to the recipient, making the message anonymous.

anti-aliasing   Technique for diminishing jagged lines in a graphic that often appear when the graphic has been scaled down.

antivirus program   Utility that searches files, folders, and disks for computer viruses and removes any that are found; it can also scan any files downloaded from the Internet for viruses. Antivirus programs must be updated frequently to recognize new viruses as they are discovered.

Archie   Program that searches for files on any FTP server by filename; you can run an Archie program on your computer or search via an Archie gateway on the Web.

ASCII   Code that represents English characters as numbers; most computers use ASCII codes to represent text, making it possible for data to be transferred from one computer to another—in an email message, for example. (Stands for

American Standard Code for Information Interchange; pronounced "ask-ee.")

ASP   See *Active Server Pages.*

attachment   File, generally a binary file or a formatted document, that is attached to an email message so that it can be transferred via email; while email messages cannot carry viruses, executable attachments can.

AU   Sound file format popularly used on the UNIX operating system; also the standard audio format for the Java programming language. (Short for *audio.*)

Audio Interchange File Format   See *AIFF.*

authenticode   Technology natively supported by Internet Explorer that uses personal certificates to identify who created a software program and whether it has been tampered with before downloading and running it.

avatar   Graphical icon that represents a real person in a chat network or virtual world.

AVI   See *Video for Windows.*

B

bandwidth   The amount of data that can be transmitted in a certain amount of time; bandwidth is usually expressed as bits per second (bps).

Basic-Rate Interface (BRI)   ISDN configuration consisting of two channels, each carrying data at the rate of 64Kbps; most home ISDN connections are of the BRI type.

BBS   See *bulletin board system.*

BCC   See *blind carbon copy.*

binary digit   See *bit.*

bit   Smallest unit of information; a bit can hold one of two variables: 0 or 1. A byte is equivalent to eight bits. (Short for *binary digit.*)

blind carbon copy (BCC)   Copy of an email message sent to a recipient without the recipient's email address appearing in the message header, preventing other recipients from seeing who else received the message.

bookmarks   Netscape Navigator's system of marking and organizing URLs for later retrieval; the equivalent feature in Internet Explorer is Favorites, but often it is generically referred to as bookmarks.

Boolean logic   Form of algebra in which all values are returned as either true or false, named after the nineteenth-century mathematician George Boole; this system works well with the binary numbering system of computers. On the Web, Boolean logic is an almost-standardized way to interact with search engines of all types.

bot   Computer program that performs an automatic function on the Internet, such as indexing Web sites for search engines. (Short for *robot*; also called a *spider, worm,* or *agent.*)

bounce   Email message that is returned, or "bounced" back, due to an unknown email address.

Bozo filter   Specific kind of message filter supported by many email clients and newsreaders that enables users to block messages from specific individuals in an attempt to reduce flames and spam; the list of blocked addresses is called a killfile.

BRI   See *Basic-Rate Interface.*

browser   See *Web browser.*

bug   Error in a software program that causes the program to malfunction; bugs are often fixed by a patch or program upgrade.

bulletin board   Electronic message center; users post messages to the "bulletin board" and other users later read them and post replies. Usenet newsgroups are a kind of bulletin board, and bulletin boards are also found on many Web sites.

bulletin board system (BBS)   Computer that you connect to directly with a modem to read messages posted by others and leave replies.

byte   Unit of storage capable of holding a single character and equivalent to eight bits; large amounts of memory are referred to in terms of kilobytes (1KB = 1,024 bytes), megabytes (1MB = 1,048,576 bytes), and gigabytes (1GB = 1,073,741,824 bytes).

C

CA   See *Certificate Authority*.

cable modem   Modem designed to operate over cable TV lines; cable modems provide more bandwidth and faster connection speeds than modems that work over telephone lines.

cache   Web browser component that temporarily stores downloaded Web pages; when the page is reloaded, it displays much faster from the cache than it would if it had to be re-downloaded over the Internet. (Pronounced "cash.")

cache browser   Web browser add-on that pre-loads Web pages into the cache, so that they display immediately when requested, speeding up Web browsing.

Cascading Style Sheets (CSS)   HTML specification that enables Web designers to create a style sheet, or template, to define how Web page elements are formatted throughout a site; Cascading Style Sheets permit site-wide elements to be edited from one document.

certificate   See *personal certificate*.

Certificate Authority (CA)   Trusted third-party organization that issues digital certificates used in S/MIME encryption; VeriSign is a well-known CA.

CGI   See *Common Gateway Interface*.

channel   In IRC, a specific discussion; users join a channel to participate in an ongoing conversation.

chat   Real-time, text-based communication on the Internet. Chat generally involves a group of people who gather in a room or channel hosted by a chat server and who send messages to each other with a chat client; unlike email and Usenet discussions, chat discussions take place in real-time. IRC is a popular chat network, but many other networks and online services also offer chat.

client   Software program that makes requests of a server in order to retrieve information and perform operations; Web browsers, newsreaders, FTP programs, chat programs, and email programs are all clients.

Common Gateway Interface (CGI)   Script that transfers data between a Web server and a program; CGI scripts are the most common method for users to interact with Web pages, generally through Web page forms.

compression   The process of storing data so that it takes up less space than usual; many software programs and multimedia files on the Internet are compressed so that they require less storage space and shorter download times.

computer virus   Program code that, when run, replicates itself and performs other actions against the user's wishes, such as erasing files or displaying messages; even the simplest viruses are capable of consuming all available memory and halting the system. All viruses are manmade and can be contained in any executable code, such as software programs.

Content Advisor   Internet Explorer component that filters Web pages based on their PICS ratings.

content-filtering software   Program that blocks or filters Web pages whose content has been designated offensive or unacceptable; these programs can often block outgoing data as well, such as personal information. Parents and schools generally use content-filtering software to keep children from accessing adult-oriented Web pages.

cookie   Text file given to a Web browser by a Web server and stored on the user's computer; the message is sent back to the server each time the browser requests a page from the server. Cookies are most often used for customizing the appearance of Web pages and keeping track of items in a shopping cart, but because they are stored on the user's computer without his or her knowledge, they have raised security concerns.

CSS   See *Cascading Style Sheets.*

cybercast   Broadcast made over the Internet, such as a live concert, radio program, or television program; generally, cybercasts use streaming video and audio, such as RealMedia.

cybersex   Slang term that refers to sex-related conversations in chat rooms.

cyberspace   The non-physical space created by computer networks such as the Internet where people communicate with each other and exchange information; the term was coined by science-fiction author William Gibson.

D

Data Communications Equipment (DCE) speed   Rate of data transfer between a modem and a remote computer to which the modem is connected. (Also called *line speed.*)

Data Terminal Equipment (DTE) speed   Rate of data transfer between a computer and its modem. (Also called *port speed.*)

DCC   See *Direct Client-to-Client.*

DCE speed   See *Data Communications Equipment speed.*

decryption   Process of decoding an encrypted file using a private key that matches the public key used to encrypt, or code, the file.

Denial of Service (DoS) attack   Attack on a computer or network designed to disable the system by flooding it with useless traffic—an illegal act; mailbombs are one type of Denial of Service attack.

DHTML   See *Dynamic HTML.*

dial-up account   Internet access account that enables a computer to connect to the Internet by dialing into an ISP's computer with a modem; the speed of the connection is limited to the speed of the modem.

digital certificate   See *personal certificate.*

digital money   The electronic equivalent of cash—funds are converted into electronic "dollars" by a bank and can then be used to purchase goods or services over the Internet; like cash, digital money is anonymous and completely transferable. (Also called *electronic cash* or *e-cash.*)

digital signature   Code that is attached to an email message and uniquely identifies the sender to assure the recipient that the message is authentic.

Direct Client-to-Client (DCC) Function of some IRC clients that enables secure, private, one-on-one chat and file exchange; also can be used to transfer harmful scripts.

DNS See *Domain Name Service.*

DNS Lookup Utility that provides a computer's domain name based on its IP address.

domain name Name that corresponds to one or more IP addresses; domain names are used in URLs and email addresses because they are easier to remember than numerical IP addresses. Domain names always take this form: example.com; the second part is the suffix, or top-level domain.

Domain Name Service (DNS) Internet service that translates domain names into their corresponding IP addresses; you must run a Domain Name Service if you own a domain name so that other computers can find the computer(s) corresponding to your domain name.

DoS attack See *Denial of Service attack.*

download To copy data from its source to another computer over a network.

DTE speed See *Data Terminal Equipment speed.*

dynamic fonts Fonts embedded in a Web page that download and display dynamically, similarly to the way inline images display; this enables Web site designers to include unusual fonts in their pages regardless of whether the users have the font installed on their computers. Netscape Navigator natively supports dynamic fonts.

Dynamic HTML (DHTML) Set of HTML extensions that enables a Web page to react to user input without having to send additional requests to the Web server; thus, page content can change dynamically, depending on the user's actions. DHTML has not yet been standardized, and Microsoft and Netscape have implemented it differently in their respective browsers.

dynamic IP address IP address that changes each time the computer reconnects to the Internet; dynamic IP addresses are usually assigned to computers using dial-up connections by their ISPs.

E

e-cash   See *digital money*.

e-commerce   See *electronic commerce*.

electronic cash   See *digital money*.

electronic commerce   Business conducted online, usually the buying and selling of goods. (Often called *e-commerce* for short.)

electronic mail   See *email*.

electronic wallet   Software program that contains encrypted credit card, digital money, and billing information and can be used to purchase goods and services over the Internet.

email   Electronic messages transmitted over any computer network, including online services and the Internet; the messages are stored on mail servers and retrieved by email client programs. (Short for *electronic mail*.)

email address   Unique address that identifies an inbox where electronic messages can be sent; on the Internet, all email addresses have the form, `username@domain_name`.

email client   Program that can connect to a mail server to send and retrieve email messages; many email clients also enable the user to organize, search, and filter messages, as well as compose and send messages. Popular email clients include Eudora, Messenger, Outlook Express, and Pine.

email virus   Not literally a computer virus, but rather an email message that is forwarded to so many people that it becomes an unstoppable, never-ending chain, thus replicating itself like a virus.

emoticon   See *smiley*.

encryption   The process of encoding a file to protect it from being read by unauthorized parties; usually, the file's author uses a public key to encrypt the file, and the file's recipient must have the matching, secret private key to decrypt, or decode, the file. There are several kinds of encryption, including PGP and S/MIME.

executable A file in a format that the computer can execute, such as a software program.

eXtensible Markup Language (XML) Markup language in development that enables designers to create customized Web page tags for providing functionality not supported by HTML; if XML becomes widely supported by the major browsers, it may supplant HTML as the markup language of the Web.

external viewer Program that a Web browser launches automatically to display files not supported by the browser, such as multimedia and formatted documents; unlike plug-ins, external viewers operate outside of the browser. (Also called *helper application.*)

F

FAQ See *Frequently Asked Questions.*

Favorites Internet Explorer's bookmarks feature, which enables users to save and organize URLs for later retrieval.

File Transfer Protocol (FTP) Internet protocol used to transfer files from an FTP server to an FTP client; FTP is primarily a means of storing and transferring software, but it can be used to transfer any type of file.

finger Utility that queries a finger server for information about the owner of an email address; generally, EDU and ORG domains run finger servers, while COM and NET domains do not.

fingerprint In PGP, a unique string of characters attached to a public key; users can check the fingerprint to make sure that the key belongs to the person they think it does.

firewall Hardware or software designed to prevent Internet users from accessing private areas of computer networks that are connected to the Internet; all messages entering or leaving the network pass through the firewall, which blocks those messages that don't meet the security criteria.

flame Searing email message or newsgroup post in which the author attacks someone else in overly harsh, often personal, terms; flames are an inevitable element of unmoderated forums. A *flame war* occurs when two or more people continuously flame each other.

fragmentation   Condition of a hard disk when files are divided into pieces and scattered throughout the disk. Fragmentation occurs naturally when the disk is used frequently, but it can slow data access; defragmenter utilities are used to fix this problem.

frames   Divided areas of the browser display, each area showing a different Web page.

freenet   Network, often community-based, that offers free email and sometimes full Internet access, as well as access to other community-oriented information and services.

freeware   Copyrighted software that is provided free and as-is for anyone's use; the freeware culture originated on the Internet as a way for programmers to collaboratively develop software.

Frequently Asked Questions (FAQ)   Document that provides information about a topic in question-and-answer format; FAQs were first created by the members of Usenet newsgroups to answer common questions so that the questions would no longer be posted to the newsgroup, but now they are prolific all over the Internet. (Pronounced "fak.")

FTP   See *File Transfer Protocol.*

ftpmail server   Server that lists and transfers files on public FTP servers via email in response to commands in email messages.

full duplex   Transmission of data simultaneously in two directions; full-duplex modems enable voice-conferencing programs to behave like telephones.

G

GB   See *gigabyte.*

GIF   Compressed graphics file format that is natively supported by all graphical Web browsers; GIF is the most common graphic file format in use on the Web. (Short for *Graphics Interchange Format;* pronounced "giff.")

gigabyte (GB) Unit of storage capable of holding 1,073,741,824 bytes.

Graphics Interchange Format See *GIF.*

H

hacker Slang term for a non-professional computer programmer; depending on the context, a hacker can be someone who breaks into computer systems without permission or someone who experiments with programming techniques and advances programming knowledge.

half duplex Transmission of data in one direction at a time; half-duplex modems enable voice-conferencing programs to behave like CB radios.

helper application See *external viewer.*

history Web browser log of the last several documents that were opened; the history list enables users to easily revisit Web pages.

home page This term has several meanings: a Web page about a person, company, or individual; the entrance page for a Web site; and the start page of a Web browser.

host Computer that is connected to a TCP/IP network, such as the Internet; each host has a unique IP address. The term can also refer to a computer that stores resources for access by remote computers, such as a Web page host.

hotlist List of links to Web pages and other Internet resources; often refers to a Web page made up entirely of links to other pages.

HTML See *Hypertext Markup Language.*

HTTP See *Hypertext Transfer Protocol.*

hyperlink Part of an HTML file that is clickable and connects to another resource on the Internet; hyperlinks enable Web pages to connect to each other, creating a "web" of cross-referenced documents.

Hypertext Markup Language (HTML) Markup language used to create the documents displayed by Web browsers; HTML is a logical language that formats documents that can be universally understood, regardless of the Web browser that displays them.

Hypertext Transfer Protocol (HTTP)   Protocol used by Web browsers to retrieve Web page files from Web servers.

I

image map   Single graphic in a Web page that contains more than one hyperlinked area, called hot spots.

IMAP   See *Integrated Message Access Protocol.*

inbox   Folder in an email program where new messages are stored until they are moved to another folder or deleted.

inline image   Graphic that is displayed alongside the text inside a Web page.

instant messenger   See *Internet pager.*

Integrated Message Access Protocol (IMAP)   Protocol used to retrieve email messages from a mail server with an email client; IMAP enables messages to be read, stored, and searched on the mail server, instead of downloading them to the local computer.

Integrated Services Digital Network (ISDN)   A kind of direct Internet connection; most telephone companies provide two channels for one ISDN connection—one can be used for voice and one for data, or both lines can be used for data for transfer speeds of up to 128Kbps.

interlacing   Preparing a graphic so that alternating rows display in separate passes, creating a "fade-in" effect—the entire image displays first, and then the details are filled in; this technique is widely used for large Web page graphics to make up for slow transmission speeds.

Internet   Global network of computers that use standard protocols to exchange information.

Internet pager   Program that can instantly send messages to anyone else running the same program over the Internet; generally, the user must know the other person's email address in order to send the message. Popular Internet pagers include AOL Instant Messenger and ICQ. (Also called *instant messenger.*)

Internet Relay Chat (IRC) Internet-based chat system composed of several IRC networks, or nets; anyone connected to an IRC server can participate in the live chats taking place on that server's net.

Internet service provider (ISP) Company that provides access to the Internet via dial-up modem connections and direct connections.

intranet TCP/IP network that behaves like the Internet but belongs to an organization and is accessible only to authorized users, generally the organization's employees, partners, and/or customers; intranets are inexpensive to build and maintain, and any Internet software can be used on intranets, as well.

IP address Numerical identifier for a computer that is connected to a TCP/IP network, such as the Internet; all IP addresses are made up of four numbers from 0–255, each number separated by periods, such as 1.160.10.245.

IRC See *Internet Relay Chat.*

IRC net Network of several IRC servers; anyone connected to a server on one net can chat with anyone else connected to a server on the same net, but users cannot chat with those connected to the servers of separate nets.

ISDN See *Integrated Services Digital Network.*

ISP See *Internet service provider.*

J

Java Programming language developed by Sun Microsystems for creating small applications suitable for running over the Web; Java was conceived as a language for writing applications that can run on any computer, regardless of operating system.

JavaScript Scripting language developed by Netscape to add interactivity and enhanced functionality to Web sites; JavaScript can interact with HTML to create dynamic pages, and it can integrate plug-ins, Java applets, and other JavaScript scripts with each other.

Joint Photographic Experts Group   See *JPEG*.

JPEG   Compressed graphics file format that is natively supported by all graphical Web browsers; although not as common as the GIF format, the JPEG format is often used for photographs and other large graphics embedded in Web pages. (Stands for *Joint Photographic Experts Group*; pronounced "jay-peg.")

Jscript   Microsoft's implementation of the JavaScript scripting language, which is natively supported by Internet Explorer, but isn't entirely compatible with Netscape's version of JavaScript.

K

KB   See *kilobyte*.

Kbps   Measure of data transfer speed; one Kbps equals 1,000 bits per second. Modem speed is measured in Kbps. (Short for *kilobits per second*.)

keyring   Component of the PGP program that stores the user's public key and all the public keys that the user has collected from his or her correspondents.

killfile   List of email addresses blocked by a bozo filter.

kilobits per second   See *Kbps*.

kilobyte (KB)   Unit of storage capable of holding 1,024 bytes.

L

LAN   See *local area network*.

LDAP   See *Lightweight Directory Access Protocol*.

Lightweight Directory Access Protocol (LDAP)   Protocol for accessing information directories, such as company address books; LDAP is implemented in many email clients as a way to search company directories for email addresses.

line speed   See *Data Communications Equipment speed*.

local area network (LAN)   Computer network that spans a relatively small area, such as an office building; LANs enable users to communicate with each other via email and chat and to share devices like printers or a single Internet connection.

lurking Eavesdropping on a chat, mailing list, or newsgroup without posting any messages; lurking is an acceptable method of becoming familiar with the topic and rules of the discussion group before joining in.

M

macro Symbol, name, or key that represents a list of commands, actions, or keystrokes; many programs, such as Microsoft Word, allow users to create macros to carry out frequently performed tasks. Word macros and other macros can carry computer viruses.

mail filter Filter set up in an email client to process incoming messages based on the message's characteristics; a mail filter might move all messages from one sender into a folder, or it might delete all messages with a certain word in the subject line.

mail server Computer that receives email messages, filters them into each user's email account, and passes them on to the email client when it requests them.

mailbomb The process of sending large numbers of email messages or huge attachments to someone in an effort to fill up that person's inbox and shut down his or her email account; mailbombs can even disable an entire mail server.

mailer form A kind of Web page form that sends an email message; mailer forms are often used in place of mailto links on Web pages.

mailing list A discussion group via email. To participate, users must subscribe to the list by sending a subscription command in an email message to a mailing list manager; then, the subscriber receives all messages that are sent to the mailing list's email address.

mailing list manager Program that manages a mailing list by processing subscriptions and other commands and by automating the process of emailing messages to the entire list; popular mailing list managers include Majordomo and Listserv.

mailto link   URL for an email message; mailto URLs look like this: `mailto:shannon@arcana.com`. Clicking on one in a Web page opens the default email program and addresses a message to the referenced address.

MB   See *megabyte.*

Mbps   Measure of data transfer speed; one Mbps equals 1,000,000 bits per second. Network speed is often measured in Mbps. (Short for *megabits per second.*)

megabits per second   See *Mbps.*

megabyte (MB)   Unit of storage capable of holding 1,048,576 bytes.

message header   Top portion of an email message that indicates who sent the message, its subject, when it was sent, and all the computers it passed through on its journey to the recipient's computer.

META tag   HTML tag that provides information about the Web page. META tags can specify the HTML authoring program, the PICS rating of the page, and how robots should behave when they access the page; they also specify keywords and descriptions for access by search engine bots.

micropayment   A very small payment for a one-time service, such as accessing an article or a pay-per-play game; micropayments are the most feasible way of paying for intellectual property over the Internet, but won't be implemented until a standard form of digital money is adopted.

MIDI   Standard for creating electronic music; playing MIDI files requires a player or plug-in that supports the file format. (Short for *Musical Instrument Digital Interface*; pronounced "middy.")

modem   Hardware device that enables a computer to connect to another computer over the telephone lines, so that the two computers can exchange data. In a dial-up Internet connection, your modem connects your computer to your ISP's computer, which in turn is connected to the Internet backbone, so that data can be exchanged among any of the computers along the network. (Short for *modulator-demodulator*).

Moving Picture Experts Group   See *MPEG*.

MP3   An MPEG format used to compress audio files; because MP3 files are very small, the format has become popular for transferring song recordings and even entire albums over the Internet.

MPEG   Standard for digital video compression; also a video file format that generally produces better-quality video than competing standards. (Short for *Moving Picture Experts Group*; pronounced "m-peg.")

multicasting   Transmitting a message to a selected group of recipients; the term generally refers to group voice conferencing and video conferencing, although it also applies to sending an email message to a list of addresses. (Also called *narrowcasting*.)

multimedia   Integrated presentation of text, graphics, video, and audio; the term often refers to non-text files on the Web.

munging   The process of altering an email address to keep the address from being added to a spammer's mailing list; generally, extra text is added to the address that human correspondents can easily remove, such as shannon@NO_SPAMarcana.com.

Musical Instrument Digital Interface   See *MIDI*.

N

narrowcasting   See *multicasting*.

Netizen   A member of the Internet community—an Internet citizen.

netsplit   Occurs when the servers on an IRC net split apart, so that everyone in a chat room appears to leave at once.

newbie   New user of the Internet, or someone who behaves like a new user.

newsgroup   Forum on the Usenet network; users participate in newsgroups by reading and posting messages to the newsgroup address with a newsreader.

newsreader   Client program that enables users to subscribe to Usenet newsgroups and read and post messages to them;

NewsWatcher, Free Agent, Messenger, and Outlook Express are all newsreaders.

nick   A user's handle in IRC, the name by which he or she is known; short for *nickname.*

O

offline   Not connected to the Internet; also refers to any program that performs Internet functions without being connected, such as an offline Web browser or an offline newsreader.

online service   Centrally controlled network that provides customers who dial in with a variety of services, including email, chat, electronic information, and access to the Internet; popular online services include America Online and the Microsoft Network.

P

P3P   See *Platform for Privacy Preferences.*

Packet Internet Groper   See *Ping.*

patch   Temporary fix to a bug in a program—a piece of program code that is inserted into the original program.

PDF   See *Portable Document Format.*

personal certificate   In S/MIME encryption, contains the public key used to encrypt messages sent to the certificate's owner; also used to verify a person or company as the author of a message, software program, or applet and ensure that the file hasn't been tampered with since it was authored. (Also called *certificate* or *digital certificate.*)

personal distribution list   List of email addresses identified by a single name, so that one message addressed to that name is sent to every address in the list; most email clients support the creation of personal distribution lists.

PGP   See *Pretty Good Privacy.*

PICS   See *Platform for Internet Content Selection.*

Ping   Utility that determines whether a specific IP address is accessible by sending a data packet to that computer and waiting for a reply; Ping is primarily used to troubleshoot Internet connections. (Short for *Packet Internet Groper.*)

Platform for Internet Content Selection (PICS) Standardized system for rating Web page content that is currently in development. PICS ratings are inserted into META tags; any content-filtering software that supports the PICS standard can detect these tags and block or display a Web page based on them.

Platform for Privacy Preferences (P3P) Proposed standard that would enable users to create a personal profile and then pass only approved portions of that profile to Web sites that request it; P3P is intended to give Internet users greater control over who has access to their personal information.

plug-in Small program that "plugs into" a larger program to add additional features or functionality; Web browser plug-ins can enable the browser to display multimedia or VRML files, for example.

Point of Presence (PoP) Telephone number that enables a modem to dial up an ISP's computer and connect to the Internet.

Point-to-Point Protocol (PPP) Protocol for connecting a computer to the Internet via a dial-up modem connection.

PoP See *Point of Presence.*

POP3 See *Post Office Protocol.*

port speed See *Data Terminal Equipment speed.*

Portable Document Format (PDF) File format developed by Adobe that captures formatting information from a variety of desktop-publishing programs, enabling formatted documents to appear on other computers exactly as intended. PDF is often used to share formatted documents on the Web; the Adobe Acrobat Reader program is required to view the documents.

portal site Web site that offers a broad array of services and information, including free email, chat, Web search, and personalized start pages, and is intended as an entry point into the Web. The first portals were online services like America

Online, but now many search engines (Excite, Infoseek), Web site directories (Yahoo!), and other sites (Netscape, Microsoft) have positioned themselves as portals.

Post Office Protocol (POP3) Protocol used to retrieve email messages from a mail server with an email client; POP3 clients must download and store messages on the local computer before they can be read.

PPP See *Point-to-Point Protocol.*

Pretty Good Privacy (PGP) Encryption system that uses two keys—a public key and a private key—to encode and decode messages; PGP was developed by Philip Zimmerman and is a very popular method of email security because it's effective, easy to use, and free.

PRI See *Primary Rate Interface.*

Primary Rate Interface (PRI) A type of ISDN connection designed for large organizations that is generally transmitted through a T-1 line and contains 23 64Kbps channels.

privacy policy Page linked to the main page of a Web site that explains how personal information is collected at the site and exactly what it's used for.

private key Cryptographic key that can decrypt messages encoded with the corresponding public key; it is virtually impossible to decode an encrypted message if the private key is not known.

profile A collection of personal information, such as hobbies and dislikes, that is available for anyone to read on an online service or chat network; in Internet Explorer, users can set up a profile that is selectively delivered to servers that request it. In Communicator, a user profile is the set of preferences, bookmarks, email messages, and subscribed newsgroups associated with one user of a copy of the program.

protocol Agreed-upon format for exchanging a specific kind of information between two computers; protocols enable different kinds of computers and programs to communicate in a standardized way, a concept that helped make the Internet a global network. FTP, POP3, IMAP, SMTP, LDAP, and HTTP are all Internet protocols.

proxy server   Computer that sits between a client program, like a Web browser, and a real server; it intercepts all requests to the real server, and if it cannot fulfill the requests itself, it passes them on to the real server. Proxy servers can improve performance for groups of users, filter requests, and make the client anonymous.

public key   Cryptographic key that is made public and is used to encrypt messages sent to the key's owner, which can then be decrypted with the corresponding private key. Public-key encryption is both very secure and very easy to use; PGP is an example of public-key encryption.

public key server   Server that stores public keys for easy access by the Internet community.

push technology   Any technology that enables a server to send data to a client program without the client requesting it; the term typically refers to broadcast Web sites, although technically email is also a push technology.

Q

QuickTime   Video and animation format created by Apple Computer. QuickTime is built into Macintosh computers and is used mostly by Mac OS applications; Windows users need QuickTime for Windows and a QuickTime player or plug-in to play files in the QuickTime format.

R

RealMedia   Streaming audio and video file format supported by the RealPlayer application.

return receipt   A feature of some email programs that enables a message's sender to request an automatic notice when the message has been retrieved by the recipient's email program.

revocation   Designation of a personal certificate as invalid or untrusted.

Rich Text Format (RTF)   Standard developed by Microsoft for specifying the formatting of ASCII-text documents.

robot   See *bot*.

root   Designation given to the manager of a computer system; someone with root access can go anywhere in the system and view any file. The term also refers to the top directory of a file system.

RSACi Rating System   Standard system for rating Web page content that fits the PICS specification; RSACi allows users to specify settings based on four categories—language, nudity, violence, and sexual content—and then blocks all Web pages that supercede the settings. Internet Explorer and Navigator natively support the RSACi system.

RTF   See *Rich Text Format.*

S

S/MIME   See *Secure/Multipurpose Internet Mail Extension.*

sandbox   Protected, limited area where applications can run without risking damage to the hosting system; most Java applets run this way.

search engine   Program that searches a database of indexed information for specified keywords and displays the results with the best matches at the top of the list. Popular Web page search engines include HotBot, Excite, AltaVista, and Infoseek; specialized search engines include Deja.Com, which searches archives of Usenet newsgroups, and software search engines, which search archives of software programs.

Secure Electronic Transaction (SET)   Proposed security standard that uses digital signatures to verify the identities of credit card holders; it also protects against merchant fraud by transmitting credit card numbers directly to the credit card issuer for processing a purchase.

secure server   Web server that encrypts all transmissions between the browser and the server; secure servers are generally used to protect personal information in order forms and other Web page forms. A locked padlock icon appears on the Web browser's status bar when a secure server is accessed.

Secure Sockets Layer (SSL)   Protocol developed by Netscape for securely transmitting encrypted information over the

Internet; SSL is primarily used to send the encrypted contents of a Web page form to a secure server.

Secure/Multipurpose Internet Mail Extension (S/MIME)
Public-key encryption system that uses personal certificates to encrypt and decrypt messages.

security hole   Bug in a program's code that could allow access to a hacker; many Internet programs have security holes, but patches are issued to fix them as soon as they are detected.

security zone   In Internet Explorer, a grouping of domains that are collectively given the same security designation, such as "trusted" or "restricted"; this enables the user to run programs from sites in the trusted zone without encountering security warnings, and it automatically refuses any risky transfers from sites in the restricted zone.

server   Computer that receives and fulfills requests made by a client program over a network; for example, a Web server fulfills requests made by a Web browser, and an FTP server fulfills requests made by an FTP client. This client/server architecture works particularly well on the Internet, because the client only has to connect to the server for as long as it takes to fulfill the request; then, the client disconnects, allowing other clients to connect.

SET   See *Secure Electronic Transaction.*

shareware   Copyrighted software that is distributed on the honor system; users can try the software, and if they decide to keep it, they send a fee to the developer. Shareware is a means for independent programmers to distribute their programs directly to customers.

shell account   Internet access account accessed by connecting to a UNIX computer with a Telnet client. Shell accounts provide access to UNIX utilities, like finger and whois, and enable users to perform other Internet activities, such as send email, browse the Web with Lynx, and chat on IRC; with the advent of PPP accounts, they are becoming less common.

Shockwave   Technology developed by Macromedia that enables Web pages to display multimedia files created in

Macromedia Director; to play the files, users need either the Shockwave plug-in for Navigator or the Shockwave ActiveX control for Internet Explorer.

shopping cart   Program that stores items for purchase at a Web store; the shopping cart travels with the user throughout the store, and the user can add or remove items at any time.

signature   Text file that is appended to the end of email messages and newsgroup posts and contains information about the sender, such as email and Web page addresses. (Often called *sig* for short.)

signed applet   Java applet that requests greater access to a computer (outside the sandbox), so it can run more powerful functions; a digital signature attached to the applet identifies its developer and ensures that it hasn't been tampered with to alleviate security risks.

SIMM   Small circuit board that holds a group of memory chips and is easier to install than individual memory chips. (Short for *Single Inline Memory Module.*)

Simple Mail Transport Protocol (SMTP)   Protocol that enables email servers to send email messages to each other over the Internet; also used to transfer messages from an email client to its outgoing mail server.

Single Inline Memory Module   See *SIMM.*

SMIL   See *Synchronized Multimedia Integration Language.*

smiley   Small icon composed of ASCII characters and intended to convey emotion in email messages, newsgroup posts, and chats; :-) is a common smiley. (Also called an *emoticon.*)

SMTP   See *Simple Mail Transport Protocol.*

snail mail   Normal postal mail, as opposed to email (so called because it takes a lot longer to arrive).

spam   Unsolicited email messages or newsgroup postings that are almost always commercial in nature. Spam wastes time and bandwidth, and thus is generally reviled by the Internet community; any business that sends spam is likely to lose its

Internet access accounts and to be blacklisted. Although the origin of the term is in debate, most think that it was taken from a well-known Monty Python skit, which gradually disintegrated into an endless repetition of the word "Spam."

spambot   Type of bot that patrols the Web and Usenet newsgroups, collecting email addresses to add to bulk email lists.

spider   See *bot*.

SSL   See *Secure Sockets Layer.*

start page   The Web page that first appears when the Web browser is started.

streaming   The process of transferring video and audio files over the Internet as a continuous stream; streaming enables long video and audio files to play without waiting for a lengthy download to be completed, and it also enables live broadcasts over the Internet. RealPlayer is a widely used streaming audio and video player.

suffix   See *top-level domain.*

Synchronized Multimedia Integration Language (SMIL) Markup language based on XML and currently in development that would enable multimedia content on the Web to be divided into separate streams, sent individually to a user's computer, and then displayed together as if they were a single stream; this would make the multimedia content smaller, so it would take less time to travel over the Internet.

T

T-1   Dedicated Internet connection that supports a data transfer rate of 1.544Mbps; T-1 connections are primarily used by ISPs and large organizations to connect to the Internet backbone.

tag   In HTML and other markup languages, a command inserted into the file that specifies how portions of the document are formatted; for instance, the <P> tag specifies a new paragraph in HTML.

TCP/IP   See *Transmission Control Protocol/Internet Protocol.*

telephony Refers to computer hardware and software that perform functions traditionally performed by telephone equipment, such as voice-conferencing or voicemail software. Internet telephony refers to using the Internet to place telephone calls, which essentially provides free telephone service, although telephone companies are cracking down on this practice.

Telnet Program that enables a computer to dial into a remote computer over the Internet and then behave like a terminal of the remote computer; Telnet is a common way to access UNIX shell accounts.

temporary Internet files Web pages stored in the cache by Internet Explorer.

terminal adapter Device that connects a computer to an external digital communications line, such as an ISDN line.

thumbnail Small version of a graphic in a Web page that is linked to the full version.

top-level domain Suffix attached to Internet domain names that refers to either the geographical location of the organization hosting the domain (.us, .ca, .jp), or the type of organization (.com, .edu, .org, .mil). Also called the *suffix*.

traceroute Utility that traces a data packet from one computer to another over the Internet, showing how many computers the packet passes through and how long each leg of the journey takes; traceroute is generally used to determine where delays are occurring and to find upstream Internet providers for a domain.

Transmission Control Protocol/Internet Protocol (TCP/IP) Standard suite of protocols used to connect computers on the Internet and on intranets.

U

uniform resource locator (URL) Global address of any resource on the Internet, including HTML files, files on FTP servers, Usenet newsgroups, and email addresses; URLs are universal because any program that understands them, such as a Web browser, can access an Internet resource via its unique

URL. The first part of the URL always specifies the protocol used to access the resource, but the formatting of the second part depends on the kind of resource being addressed. (Pronounced "U-R-L.")

UNIX   Small, flexible operating system that was designed to be used by programmers and therefore isn't very user-friendly; UNIX is widely used on workstations due to its flexibility and the tremendous amount of freeware available for it. (Pronounced "yoo-nix.")

URL   See *uniform resource locator.*

Usenet   Worldwide network of over 14,000 bulletin boards called newsgroups; users talk on a variety of topics by posting and reading messages on these newsgroups.

user profile   See *profile.*

V

video conferencing   Real-time interaction between two or more people over a computer network using audio and video; video conferencing enables users to both see and hear who they're talking to, but it requires a high-end computer, video camera, and video capture device. Popular video conferencing tools include Microsoft NetMeeting and CU-SeeMe.

Video for Windows (AVI)   Standard video file format developed by Microsoft for Windows computers.

Video RAM   See *VRAM.*

virtual memory   Imaginary memory area supported by some operating systems that uses extra space on the hard disk as memory; as data is needed, it is moved from disk memory to real memory in a process called paging. Although virtual memory can increase the total amount of memory of a computer, paging can significantly slow the computer's overall performance.

Virtual Reality Markup Language (VRML)   Markup language for specifying three-dimensional worlds and objects; using a VRML client, users can move through the world and examine objects. (Pronounced "ver-mal.")

virus   See *computer virus.*

Visual Basic   Programming language developed by Microsoft and often used in ActiveX, such as to create Active Server Pages.

Voice conferencing   Real-time interaction between two or more people over a computer network using audio data; voice conferencing enables all participants to talk to each other, but audio quality and speed may suffer due to network traffic. Many voice-conferencing programs also support collaborative applications like a shared whiteboard and Web browser.

VRAM   Special-purpose memory used by video adapters; it yields better graphics performance but is more expensive than normal RAM. (Short for *Video RAM;* pronounced "vee-ram.")

VRML   See *Virtual Reality Markup Language.*

W

WAV   Sound file format developed by Microsoft and IBM; WAV support is natively built into Windows, and WAV files can be played by nearly all Windows applications that support sound.

Web   See *World Wide Web.*

Web browser   Client program that requests Web page files from Web servers and displays the files; Netscape Navigator and Microsoft Internet Explorer are the two most widely used Web browsers.

Web page   The combination of an HTML file and all its multimedia components—graphics, audio, and video—that is displayed in a Web browser.

Web page form   Form that appears on a Web page and enables the user to interact with the Web server, typically via a CGI script; forms are generally used to collect feedback, take orders, and query a search engine or database, although they can fulfill many other functions.

Web server   Computer that stores Web page files and delivers them to Web browsers that request them; any computer can be made into a Web server by installing server software on it and connecting it to the Internet. All Web servers have an IP address, and most can also be addressed by a domain name.

Web site   Collection of Web pages on a single topic; each Web site resides on a single Web server (although one server may host multiple sites) and has a main entrance, or home page, that is typically addressed by the server's domain name alone.

Webcasting   Broadcasting information over the Web using push technologies.

Webmaster   Owner or manager of a Web site.

webring   Collection of Web sites on one topic that link to each other in a ring; travel from one to the next, and eventually you'll return to the beginning.

WebTV   Category of products and technologies that enable users to connect to the Internet and surf the Web via their televisions.

white pages   Web site where users can search for a person's contact information—email address, mailing address, and phone number; white pages are analogous to, and often taken from, the white pages of a telephone book. Yellow pages are the same thing, except they list business contact information.

Whois   Utility used to look up the contact names and addresses of a domain name's owner.

Windows Desktop Update   Component included with Internet Explorer 4.x that installs the Active Desktop.

World Wide Web   Network of HTML files stored on Web servers that are linked to other HTML files via hyperlinks, creating a "web" of interconnected documents. (Often shortened to *Web* or *WWW*.)

worm   See *bot*.

WWW   See *World Wide Web*.

WYSIWYG   Application that displays documents on the screen exactly as they appear when printed; word processors, desktop-publishing programs, and some HTML editors are WYSIWYG programs. (Stands for *What You See Is What You Get*; pronounced "wizzy-wig.")

X

XDSL   Collectively refers to all digital subscriber lines for connecting to the Internet; they operate over telephone lines and support very fast data transfer rates—32Mbps downstream and 1–32Kbps upstream.

XML   See *eXtensible Markup Language.*

Y

yellow pages   See *white pages.*

Z

ZIP   Data compression format that is often used to compress software programs transmitted over the Internet; to decompress the file so that the user can run it requires an unzip utility like WinZip.

Unauthorized Resources

This appendix lists loads of useful online resources for Internet insiders beyond those found in the text of the book. There are four types of resources: bonus Internet-related Web sites in addition to the ones found throughout the book; mailing lists to keep you up to date on Internet news and developments; Usenet newsgroups for thoughtful discussion and good advice; and a rundown of the most useful Web sites mentioned elsewhere in the book. Enjoy!

Unauthorized Web Sites

Check the Web sites in Table B.1 for Internet-related news, reviews, gossip, software, tips, and tricks—all the insider information you could need.

TABLE B.1: UNAUTHORIZED WEB SITES

Site	URL	Description
News and Gossip		
CNET	http://www.cnet.com/	General computing and Internet news resource.
Feed	http://www.feedmag.com/	Commentary and discussion on the information age.
HotWired	http://www.hotwired.com/	News and opinion on the Internet and cyberculture.
InternetNews. Com	http://www.internetnews. com/	Real-time Internet news source.
News.Com	http://www.news.com/	Internet-related news and rumors.
ZDNet	http://www.zdnet.com/	Huge Internet and computing information center.
Internet Issues		
Blacklist of Internet Advertisers	http://math-www. unipaderborn.de/ ~axel/BL/	List of spammers and spam-fighting information.
Coalition Against Unsolicited Email	http://www.cauce.org/	Major anti-spam site.
COAST	http://www.cs.purdue. edu/coast/hotlist/	Complete index to computer security, virus, and privacy information.
Computer Virus Myths	http://www.kumite.com/ myths/	Complete resource about virus myths and hoaxes.
Consumer World	http://www. consumerworld.org/	Information for Internet shoppers.
CyberAngels	http://www.cyberangels. org/	Information about child safety on the Internet.
Electronic Frontier Foundation	http://www.eff.com/	Leader in the campaign to protect civil liberties online.

Site	URL	Description
Internet Issues		
Electronic Privacy Information Center	http://epic.org/	Focuses on emerging civil liberties issues related to the Internet.
Junkbusters	http://www.junkbusters.com/	Spam and junk-mail information resource.
Peacefire	http://www.peacefire.org/	Anti-Internet censorship site, with a focus on content-filtering software.
Privacy Page	http://www.privacy.org/	Information and news about computer-related privacy issues.
Reign Your Domain	http://www.ReignYourDomain.org/	Covers legal issues and frauds related to domain names.
Webgrrls International	http://www.webgrrls.com/	For women on the Internet.
Insider Information		
2600	http://www.2600.com/	Definitive hacker's magazine.
Chatter's Jargon Dictionary	http://www.stevegrossman.com/jargpge.htm	Learn the language of chat.
IRC Central	http://www.connectedmedia.com/IRC/	Complete IRC information resource.
MUD Resource Collection	http://www.godlike.com/muds/	Learn all about and join in the first virtual worlds.
Netiquette Home Page	http://www.albion.com/netiquette/index.html	Learn how to act like a Netizen.
Net Legends FAQ	http://www.ews.uiuc.edu/%7Etskirvin/faqs/legends.html	About those few who have earned a place in Internet history.
Online Insider	http://www.onlineinsider.com/	Insider Internet information, with a focus on business issues.
Usenet FAQ Archive	http://www.faqs.org/faqs/	Searchable archive of all Usenet FAQs.
The Well	http://www.well.com/	One of the oldest online communities.
Wiretap	http://wiretap.area.com/	Huge archive of electronic documents.

continues

TABLE B.1: CONTINUED

Site	URL	Description
Software and Tools		
ActiveWindows	`http://www.activewin.com/frames/frmhome.shtml`	Complete information source for Internet Explorer/Active Desktop users.
ActiveX	`http://www.download.com/PC/Activex/`	Library of download-able ActiveX controls.
BotSpot	`http://www.botspot.com/main.html`	Clearinghouse for bot information.
Browsers	`http://www.download.com/Browsers/`	News, reviews, and downloads of Web browsers, add-ons, and plug-ins.
Cool Tool of the Day	`http://www.cooltool.com/`	Find a new cool soft-ware download every day.
Email Today	`http://www.emailtoday.com/`	Email-related news, information, and soft-ware.
Internet Help Desk	`http://w3.one.net/~alward/`	Troubleshooting, FAQs, guides, and other help with Internet software and Web-based tools.
Plug-in Plaza	`http://browserwatch.internet.com/plug-in.html`	Complete index of Netscape plug-ins.
Search Engine Watch	`http://www.searchenginewatch.com/`	News, information, and tips about search engines.
Unofficial Netscape Resources	`http://people.netscape.com/olcen/`	Complete information and software source for Navigator/Communicator users.
Development and Technologies		
Developer.Com	`http://www.developer.com/`	Complete guide to developmental tech-nologies.
Internet Engineering Task Force	`http://www.ietf.org/`	Concerned with Internet standards and development.
SiteOwner.Com	`http://siteowner.linkexchange.com/`	Collection of Web site promotion and man-agement tools.

Site	URL	Description
Development and Technologies		
Web Building	`http://builder.cnet.com/`	Information on all aspects of Web site development.
Web Developer's Virtual Library	`http://www.stars.com/`	Encyclopedia of Web technologies.
Webmaster Resources	`http://www.webmasterresources.com/`	Free stuff and information for Webmasters.
World Wide Web Consortium	`http://www.w3.org/`	Group that determines HTML and Web standards.
Web Site Guides		
CoolShopping. Com	`http://www.coolshopping.com/`	Guide to the coolest online stores.
Cool Site of the Day	`http://cool.infi.net/`	A daily dose of cool.
Full Coverage	`http://headlines.yahoo.com/Full_Coverage/`	Web sites related to the important news stories of the day.
Uroulette	`http://www.uroulette.com/`	Go to a random site.
Web 100	`http://www.web100.com/`	Top 100 user-rated sites; changes hourly.
Worst of the Web	`http://www.worstoftheweb.com/`	A daily dose of bad sites.
WWW Virtual Library	`http://www.vlib.org/`	One of the oldest Web site directories.
Yahoo! Internet Life	`http://www.zdnet.com/yil/`	Web site reviews and Internet-related opinion.
Only on the Internet		
Center for the Easily Amused	`http://www.amused.com/`	Complete resource for wasting time online.
Dance-O-Rama	`http://www.laughs.cc/dance/`	Watch those Web pages dance!
Dialectizer	`http://www.rinkworks.com/dialect/`	Convert Web pages to the dialect of your choice.
Diary Registry	`http://www.diarist.net/registry/`	Index to journals, diaries, and true confessions on the Web.

continues

TABLE B.1: CONTINUED

Site	URL	Description
Only on the Internet		
Episodic	http://www.cultureland.com/episodic/	Reviews and links to episodic soap opera–like Web sites.
International Home of Internet Romance	http://www.soft.net.uk/ashford/iromance/index.htm	All about meeting and falling in love online.
Mr. Edible Starchy Tuber Head	http://winnie.acsu.buffalo.edu/potatoe/	Web-based Mr. Potato Head.
WebCam Central	http://www.camcentral.com/	Index of live cameras connected to the Web.
Yecch!!!	http://www.yeeeoww.com/yecch/yecchhome.html	Yahoo! parody.
Zarf's List of Interactive Games on the Web	http://www.leftfoot.com/games.html	Play Web-based games all night long.

Unauthorized Mailing Lists

The newsletters and email zines listed in Table B.2 deliver valuable, Internet-related information and advice straight to your inbox. Go to the subscription URL to subscribe to the newsletter and learn more about it.

TABLE B.2: UNOFFICIAL MAILING LISTS

Mailing List Name	Subscription URL	Description
Community Memory	http://memex.org/community-memory.html	Moderated discussion of the history of cyberspace.
Computer Underground Digest	http://sun.soci.niu.edu/~cudigest/	Weekly newsletter of news and discussion about computer culture.
Cybermind	http://www.lm.com/~tellis/cyber/cm.html	Discussion of cyberspace-related philosophical and social issues.
CyberWire Digest	http://cyberwerks.com/cyberwire/howto.html	News service focusing on cyberspace issues.

Mailing List Name	Subscription URL	Description
DreamWave Mailing List	`http://www.cybercom.net/~wmcguire/dreamwave.html`	Discusses, speculates, and shares information about new Internet technologies and trends.
Internet Scambusters	`http://www.scambusters.com/scambusters.html`	Newsletter about online scams and hoaxes.
Internet Tourbus	`http://www.tourbus.com/`	Twice-weekly tour of nifty Web sites.
Neat Net Tricks	`http://www.neatnettricks.com/`	Bimonthly newsletter of useful Internet and computer tips and tricks.
Net-Happenings	`http://scout18.cs.wisc.edu/cgi-bin/lwgate/NET-HAPPENINGS/`	Announcements of new sites, events, and other Internet news.
Netsurfer Digest	`http://157.22.1.70/nsd/`	Announcements of new and interesting Web sites.
Scout Report	`http://scout.cs.wisc.edu/report/sr/current/index.html`	Announcements of valuable education- and research-related Internet resources.
SPAM-L	`http://oasis.ot.com/~dmuth/spam-l/`	Discussion and tips for spam prevention.

Unauthorized Newsgroups

Check the newsgroups in Table B.3 for information, lively discussion, and expert advice on Internet-related subjects. Remember to read the FAQ first!

TABLE B.3: UNAUTHORIZED NEWSGROUPS

Newsgroup	Description
`alt.best.of.internet`	Collects the best postings from all newsgroups in one place.
`alt.comp.shareware`	Shareware discussion and announcements of new programs.
`alt.culture.internet`	Cyberculture discussion.
`alt.folklore.internet`	Internet myths and legends.
`alt.internet.services`	Services available via the Internet.
`alt.internet.mediacoverage`	Discussion of the press's coverage of the Internet.

continues

TABLE B.3: CONTINUED

Newsgroup	Description
alt.privacy	Discussion of privacy issues in cyber-space.
comp.infosystems.www.announce	Announcements of new, non-commercial Web sites.
comp.infosystems.www.authoring.misc	Discussion of miscellaneous Web site authoring issues.
comp.infosystems.www.misc	General discussion of Web-related topics.
comp.os.ms-windows.misc	General discussion of Windows-related topics.
comp.sources.mac	Macintosh software announcements.
comp.virus	Moderated discussion of computer viruses and security.
misc.kids.computers	Discussion of software and computer equipment for kids.
news.answers	FAQs for all newsgroups.
news.groups.reviews	Reviews of newsgroups and mailing lists.
news.newusers.questions	For newcomers to Usenet.
news.software.readers	Information about newsreaders.
rec.humor.oracle	Dubious advice from the Usenet Oracle.

Useful Resources

Table B.4 is an index to the most useful Web sites mentioned elsewhere in the book. Use the index as a quick reference guide to the Web sites that you'll be visiting most frequently. Visit these Web sites to search for services and resources on the Internet.

TABLE B.4: A SELECTION OF USEFUL WEB SITES

Site	URL
Business Search	
AnyWho	http://www.anywho.com/tf.html
GTE SuperPages	http://superpages.gte.net/
WorldPages	http://www.worldpages.com/global/wpglobal.whtml

Site	URL
Chat Search	
Liszt's IRC Chat Directory	http://www.liszt.com/chat/
Ultimate Chat List	http://www.chatlist.com/
Yahoo! Net Events	http://events.yahoo.com/
FTP Search	
Archie Gateway	http://archie.rutgers.edu/archie.html
Hosting Service Search	
Free Home Page Guide	http://www.freeindex.com/webspace/index.html
Ultimate Web Host List	http://www.webhostlist.com/
ISP Search	
ISP Finder	http://www.pcworld.com/interactive/isps/isps.html
The List	http://thelist.internet.com/
Kids' Sites Search	
Yahooligans	http://www.yahooligans.com/
Mailing List Search	
CataList	http://www.lsoft.com/lists/listref.html
List of Lists	http://catalog.com/vivian/interest-group-search.html
Liszt	http://www.liszt.com/
Publicly Accessible Mailing Lists	http://www.neosoft.com/internet/paml/
Reference.Com	http://www.reference.com/
Tile.Net Lists	http://tile.net/lists/
People Search	
Bigfoot	http://www.bigfoot.com/
InfoSpace	http://www.infospace.com/
MESA	http://mesa.rrzn.uni-hannover.de/
Switchboard	http://www.switchboard.com/
WhoWhere	http://www.whowhere.lycos.com/
Yahoo! People Search	http://people.yahoo.com/
Shopping Site Search	
Shopfind	http://st2.yahoo.com/shopfind/

continues

TABLE B.4: CONTINUED

Site	URL
Software Search	
Download.Com	http://www.download.com/
Filez	http://www.filez.com/
Freehound	http://www.freehound.com/
MacUpdate	http://www.macupdate.com/
Shareware.Com	http://www.shareware.com/
WinFiles	http://www.winfiles.com/
ZDNet Software Library	http://www.hotfiles.com/
Usenet Search	
Deja.Com	http://www.deja.com/
Utility Gateways	
DNS Lookup	http://www.osilab.ch/services/dns_e.htm
Finger	http://www.cs.indiana.edu:800/finger/gateway/
Traceroute	http://net.yahoo.com/cgi-bin/trace.sh
Whois	http://www.allwhois.com/
Web Search	
About.Com	http://www.about.com/
All-in-One Search Page	http://www.allonesearch.com/
AltaVista	http://altavista.digital.com/
Ask Jeeves	http://www.askjeeves.com/
DogPile	http://www.dogpile.com/
Excite	http://www.excite.com/
HotBot	http://www.hotbot.com/
Infoseek	http://www.infoseek.com/
Internet Sleuth	http://www.isleuth.com/
Magellan	http://www.mckinley.com/
MetaCrawler	http://www.go2net.com/search.html
SavvySearch	http://www.savvysearch.com/
Search.Com	http://www.search.com/
Yahoo!	http://www.yahoo.com/

Symbols

473

G

Z